Rinse, Reflect, Repeat

An action-driven guide to reading the Bible
alphabetically in a year. It includes a daily devotion and
challenge, making The Word applicable for today -
yes, even Leviticus.

Anita Cordell

Disclaimer: The memories mentioned throughout this book are my memories, from my perspective, and I have tried to represent events as faithfully as possible. Some sample scenarios in this book are fictitious. Any similarity to actual persons, living or dead, is coincidental.

To request permission, contact:

Anita Cordell
anitacordell@gmail.com
anitacordell.com

ISBN: 979-8-9910868-0-6 (hardcover)
ISBN: 979-8-9910868-1-3 (paperback)
ISBN: 979-8-9910868-2-0 (ebook)

Edited by Kimberly Richardson
Cover design by Raney Day Creative LLC
Cover image generated by Midjourney AI
Back cover photo by Chris Myer
Interior photo by zhang kaiyv

Printed in the United States of America.

ACKNOWLEDGEMENTS

Shy of a few years where I was a little off course in my devotions, I have been studying the Bible since high school in my morning quiet times. At one point, I started taking notes of the nuggets I learned, verse by verse, and capturing them in a three-ring binder, alphabetized by the books of the Bible. Through the years, that binder expanded into four full three-ring binders (including topics I've spoken on at women's events). Each time I reread a book, I change the color of the pen when I make notes, making note of the month and year corresponding to that color of ink. This helps me keep track of notes based on that season in my life. My pages are full of colored notes, making it fun to go back and reread the golden nuggets of years gone by.

One year, I decided to start reading the Bible in alphabetical order, going through all four notebooks, starting with Acts. I posted a picture on social media of my open Bible on top of one of my binders, with a caption about what I was doing. Michael Engberg immediately commented,"There's a book to be written. IT'S ALL THERE!!!! Now share it with us." With his encouragement, I began a six-year journey of capturing some of the golden nuggets from my binders. Who would have thought that my colored notes would be the foundation for a devotional? God did. And so did my friend, Michael. I would never have even begun this journey if it had not been for Michael believing my notes were something more than just references and reminders to myself. Thank you, Michael, for believing in me.

Next, I want to thank my tribe. This tribe consists of three beautiful friends, Stacey Hershberger, Kari Fabian and Dawn Long. Stacey and I met in 2016, in San Antonio at the Christian Worldview Film Festival. She is the first of our tribe that I met, and one that I have enjoyed getting to know as a woman full of joy, adventure, and creativity. Her faith encourages me, and her entire essence is magnetic, attracting both believers and nonbelievers. I met both Kari and Dawn in person in 2018, when we stayed together in a short-term rental with about 10 other people, while attending the Christian Worldview Film Festival. Kari is a woman who holds no bounds on what women can do. If I were lost in a jungle, she is one I would want by my side. Kari is gifted beyond comprehension, including the fact that she thinks the best of people when it may be hard for me to do so. She encourages and brings the Word of God to life in ways I never thought of. And then there is Dawn. Several of the devotions in this book will reference a close friend. Dawn is that friend. Thank you, Dawn, for your unconditional love, your influence on my life, and our friendship that has bonded us like sisters. Our tribe would not be the same without you. All four of us were in that rental house, along with other women, but the four of us have stayed connected in a friendship that has found us to have nearly daily conversations. We call ourselves The Tribe.

I also want to thank my friend Cherie Alison. I have known Cherie since the 1980s. We have watched each other grow up, were roommates as young adults, and she was even in my wedding. Through the years of change, growing and maturing, Cherie has been yet another friend who has encouraged me to capture my spiritual growth in books. So thank you Cherie, for the constant friendship, believing in me, and always being a phone call away.

And now there is one last friend who I MUST mention. She is an extension of the Tribe group I mentioned, and her name is Jeannie Garcia. I met Jeannie back in 2016 at the first film festival I ever went to, The International Christian Film and Music Festival. This woman is a woman who relates to my heart in so many ways. She challenges me when I need my crown straightened, lifts me up when I am struggling, cries with me, laughs with me, and believes in me beyond what I often believe about myself. She is a friend who knows how to pray, and she prays deep for me. Thank you, Jeannie. I love you.

I am also grateful to my family. My growth comes from many examples of doing life with my favorite people, and I am honored to be a wife, mother, grandmother, sister, daughter-in-law, niece, sister-in-law, and pretty much any other label I'm not listing here. LOL My family is not just forced relationships due to birth or marriage, they are friends. My parents, Pastor David and Susan Hintz, have done an amazing job, and I'm forever grateful for their legacy of faith. I'm surrounded by this legacy and am honored God would use me to help pass it on. I joke and say, I'm a PK, PGK, a PN and PS. I'm a Pastor's Kid, and Pastor's Grandkid, a Pastor's Niece and a Pastor's Sister. And I can't think of a better way to live. So thank you all for living life with me and being such a big part of my faith walk.

I am always grateful to God for His unconditional love for me, His inspiring Words that bring me hope every day, and for blessing me with stories and insights to fill these pages. Having a belief in God and a relationship with Him gives me a daily purpose to strive to continue living my life for Him.

And lastly, I thank YOU for embarking on this journey to study God's Word with me in such a creative fashion as this alphabetical devotional. I pray you are challenged and inspired daily, and ultimately stay on the course until the very end. This devotional is one that can be read repeatedly, capturing your continued thoughts of not only the short devotions, but capturing your growth through the years.

INTRODUCTION AND INSTRUCTIONS

Have you ever wanted to read the Bible through in a year, but a month into your adventure you get discouraged and stop? Maybe you stop because you get off track and your whole year is now off schedule, so you never start back up again. Maybe you stop because you come to a book that just does not appear to be relevant, and you get unmotivated. Or maybe you stop due to a life situation that changes your morning routine, making it difficult to begin again.

This book is designed to help you not only stay on course, but provide ways to help you see the relevancies, even in the chapters where only genealogies are listed. And it will give a different twist to reading the Bible. AND, if you get off the schedule and get behind, you can easily start fresh at a new month or book. If it takes a few years, then at least you are reading, so keep going and keep growing.

You will not start in Genesis or Matthew, the traditional ways. Instead, you will read the Bible alphabetically, giving most months a mix of both the Old and the New Testament. PLUS, this devotional is divided in a fashion to let you take just a month at a time, if you want. The New American Standard version is the translation used for the Featured Verses in this devotional.

SO – Here goes…

Each day you will have a Morning Rinse, Featured Verse or Verses, a short Devotion highlighting my thoughts about the Featured Verse or Verses, a Daily Challenge, and then an Evening Reflection. They are described below.

Morning Rinse:
These are your daily chapters to read to get through the Bible in a year. Sometimes you will only have one or two chapters. Other days it may be four or five.

Featured Verse or Verses:
Pulled from the Morning Rinse, I will feature a verse or verses.

Devotion:
Each day you will be given a short devotion based on the Featured Verse or Verses.

Today's Challenge To Dig Deeper:
Each day will have a challenge to dig deeper and personalize the devotion. This challenge is derived from the devotion, and will give you relevant, and sometimes tangible things to do to help you dig deeper in your walk with Christ.

Evening Reflection:
In the evening, when you are ending your day, you will be asked to write down something about that day's challenge, what you learned throughout the day, or nuggets that God gave you.

I hope this devotional helps you not only cultivate the habit of reading The Word daily, but making The Word come to life, and capturing your growth for years to come. Enjoy, and happy repeating.

Want to go deeper as you reflect and connect with God?

As my way of saying, "Thank you," for reading the *Rinse, Reflect, Repeat* devotional, I'd like to gift you a complimentary downloadable copy of the *Rinse, Reflect, Repeat Companion Journal* to help guide you. Scan the code to get it sent to your inbox.

Alternatively, if you prefer handwriting things out, you can order a printed copy sent directly to your doorstep by scanning this code:

TABLE OF CONTENTS

January Rinsing

DEVOTED TO PRAYER
January 1

Morning Rinse: Acts 1-3
Featured Verses: Acts 1:14-15 *These all with one mind were continually devoting themselves to prayer, along with the women, and Mary the mother of Jesus, and with His brothers. At this time Peter stood up in the midst of the brethren (a gathering of about one hundred and twenty persons was there together).*

Today begins a new day, a new year, and a new journey. So what better way to lay this exciting new beginning, than with it bathed in prayer? Those who gathered right after Jesus' ascension were great examples of this. They were about to embark on a new journey themselves, full of growth, depth, and passion, and they chose to begin it devoted in prayer. We, too, can join in on a similar journey. I have often read today's Featured Verses and asked myself more than once, "As I am going about my day and living my life, am I devoted to prayer?" The answer is different for everyone, I am assuming. But the fact is, for 7 days, the disciples and those with them congregated in an upper room of a building, unified and committed to prayer. It honestly surprises me, speaking from a pastor's kid's point of view, that the general church body does not really practice this, despite Jesus calling the church to be a house of prayer. In fact, I think I can count on one hand the number of churches I know of that make it a regular calendar event for devoted prayer, like what the people in Acts did. Why is this? One large reason is we let excuses of busyness govern our conversations and transform behaviors, making life priorities higher than the priority of prayer. And unfortunately, the convenience of our couches and remote controls can supersede the false perception and inconvenience of regular prayer meetings. If the culture of the church is to change in this area, we must do our part individually, and commit to living a life of devoted prayer. Are you willing?

Today's Challenge To Dig Deeper:
Put a reminder on your phone to say a devoted prayer at least one time a day, so that prayer becomes a lifestyle habit of conversation with God. You will eventually find yourself praying more often. It will become natural as you are in your home, driving your car, or sitting at your desk. Commit to having an attitude of prayer every day, and be intentional about praying in all you do. It begins now.

Evening Reflection:
Write down what changes you made today to help become focused and devoted to prayer.

EVERY TASK IS IMPORTANT
January 2

Morning Rinse: Acts 4-6
Featured Verses: Acts 6:2-3 *So the twelve summoned the congregation of the disciples and said, "It is not desirable for us to neglect the Word of God in order to serve tables. Therefore, brethren, select from among you seven men of good reputation, full of the Spirit and of wisdom, whom we may put in charge of this task."*

In yesterday's Morning Rinse, we learned that seeking God through devoted prayer is important to lay a strong foundation for growth. The leaders in the book of Acts show us a wonderful example of not only living a life of devoted prayer, but also showing us everything we do for the kingdom of God is important, and there are no tasks too small in value. In fact, the disciples and those around them saw value in even the administration of meal planning and preparation. They treated this responsibility very seriously, and even pulled the leaders of this ministry aside to pray over and commission them. I like to think of these seven men as the first chefs of the Bible. Pretty cool! Meal planning was viewed as vitally important and was covered in prayer, as should every ministry and serving opportunity be. Unfortunately, there may be times we are asked to serve, but the tasks are not taken seriously by man. When this happens, we must remember that God's point of view is different. People in society can condition us to perceive the large accomplishments as more valuable than the small, yet this is simply not true in God's eyes. Never underestimate the importance of your work for God's kingdom. Every task is important on this side of heaven, even preparing a meal.

Today's Challenge To Dig Deeper:
Ask God to help you see value in all you do for Him, even the little things. Also, pray over a friend today. Ask God to bless whatever they put their hands to, and ask a friend to pray for you as well.

Evening Reflection:
Write down what God revealed to you through this story. Do you now view your ministry just as important as the ministry of others?

STANDING OVATIONS
January 3

Morning Rinse: Acts 7-9
Featured Verses: Acts 7:55-56 *But being full of the Holy Spirit, he gazed intently into heaven and saw the glory of God, and Jesus standing at the right hand of God; and he said, "Behold, I see the heavens opened up and the Son of Man standing at the right hand of God."*

This story always excites me. This moment had to have been immensely intense. Usually in scripture, Jesus is noted as seated on the throne at the right hand of God. But here, Stephen can see into heaven, and Jesus is standing. What makes Jesus stand in this noteworthy moment? Right before this scene, Stephen was preaching the gospel to a crowd. However, the crowd did not want to hear what he had to say, and in fact, became so angry they made him a martyr. They cover their ears, storm at him all at once, drive him out of the city, and proceed to stone him to death. It is at this time Stephen gazes up into heaven and sees Jesus standing. I am sure Jesus' heart was grieved as He watched His son going through this torture. I can imagine Him slowly rising to His feet to look deep into Stephen's eyes. His loving eyes were giving Stephen strength to endure the large rocks flung at his body, killing him with each impact. Jesus stood. And in standing, He was also waiting in anticipation for Stephen to walk through the pearly gates and exchange a long-awaited embrace. As an actress and performer, the idea of receiving a standing ovation from a crowd gives a sense of inward confidence and thrill. Watching a crowd respond with this kind of accolade shows there was a high sense of accomplishment. The thought of Jesus though, giving a standing ovation, tops it all. I believe He wants to stand for all of us as we live for Him.

Today's Challenge To Dig Deeper:
Find someone today to say a loving thing to, and help them feel special. Ask God who you can give a 'standing ovation' to today, and act on it. This can be a phone call of praise or an encouraging text message. Actions such as these make the stories in the Bible applicable in our own life. Let us be doers.

Evening Reflection:
Write down the response of those you praised. Did you enjoy giving a 'standing ovation' of your own?

LEADERS LEARN
January 4

Morning Rinse: Acts 10-12
Featured Verses: Acts 10:33, 48 *"So I sent for you immediately, and you have been kind enough to come. Now then, we are all here present before God to hear all that you have been commanded by the Lord." … and he ordered them to be baptized in the name of Jesus Christ. Then they asked him to stay on for a few days.*

Cornelius was a wealthy centurion overseeing multiple people including servants and soldiers. He was a man who feared God and even helped the Jews out in times of need, but he had not heard the gospel of Jesus Christ yet. One night, during his prayer time, an angel told him to find Peter. I am sure that Cornelius was very careful who he listened to and who he took advise from. But he knew when God spoke to him. Can you imagine how excited he was, knowing he would hear something from the Lord through Peter? He even gathered his relatives and close friends together so they could all hear what Peter had to say. He was hungry to hear. I am guessing that probably right about the same time Cornelius received this vision from God, Peter was receiving one as well, preparing him for this meeting. Before God would have them meet, He had to first work on Peter's heart. God had to show Peter through this vision, that the gospel was not only for the Jews, but it was also for the Gentiles. Once Peter understood this and had a change of heart, the spread of the gospel to the entire world began. It started with two leaders open to learning. Ultimately, Cornelius got saved, and shortly thereafter was baptized. It does not matter how long a person has been studying The Word, or how many years one has taught the Bible, there is always room for us to learn. Both men were hungry to know God in a deeper way. They were hungry to learn.

Today's Challenge To Dig Deeper:
Be open and excited for what God wants to say to you through those around you. Watch for Him today, and be open to a heart change, if God is directing that. Be ready to learn.

Evening Reflection:
Was there anything that transpired today that caused some teaching moments for you? If so, what were they?

SET APART
January 5

Morning Rinse: Acts 13-15
Featured Verse: Acts 13:2 *While they were ministering to the Lord and fasting, the Holy Spirit said, "Set apart for Me Barnabas and Saul for the work to which I have called them."*

"To set apart" in essence, really means "to dedicate something or someone for a special purpose." We set apart outfits for a special occasion. We set apart time to spend with a loved one. We set apart money for that special gift, and we even set apart a person for our mate. I believe we set apart things for a specific purpose probably every day of our lives. In today's Featured Verse, the Holy Spirit told the prophets and the teachers of the church to set apart Barnabas and Saul. These two men, and all the leaders there, were already busy with ministry. Each of them was already kingdom focused and serving in the church body. My mind's eye can imagine what it may have looked like. Barnabas in one corner of the room, is teaching a group of people about the gospel. Maybe in another corner, Saul is praying over a newlywed couple. Then possibly in the back of the room, a few leaders are singing praises in a time of worship. They were all practicing the act of ministering because they were committed to the life of ministry, their hearts already set apart for serving. While they were serving, God did something greater. He called these two men to a larger responsibility. Did you get that? It was WHILE they were ministering. I think sometimes we want to be called to a place of great influence before we are willing to serve in areas less visible. But not Barnabas and Saul. I doubt that was on their mind. And I believe God knew that their hearts were ready and willing. Therefore, the Holy Spirit set them apart for what He needed from them next.

Today's Challenge To Dig Deeper:
Examine your life through the eyes of Jesus. What does He see? Does He see you in the act of ministry now? Does He catch you serving, fasting, praying for others, or ministering in some way? Are you positioning yourself to be set apart for your next moment?

Evening Reflection:
What did God show you today about the act of serving and being set apart?

ALL THEY DID WAS PRAISE
January 6

Morning Rinse: Acts 16-18
Featured Verses: Acts 16:25-26 *But about midnight Paul and Silas were praying and singing hymns of praise to God, and the prisoners were listening to them; and suddenly there came a great earthquake, so that the foundations of the prison house were shaken, and immediately all the doors were opened, and everyone's chains were unfastened.*

Why can it be so difficult to praise amid our trials? Probably because we forget the power of praise, thus defaulting to compliance. But we must remember that our response to life's challenges will not only free us, but could free others as well. Let us be honest. Paul and Silas were not having the best day in this situation. They had just been mobbed by a crowd, their clothes were ripped from their backs, and they were beaten and thrown into prison. They were not just put into an entry level jail cell either. They were put into the 'inner prison' (16:24), which was probably very similar to our modern day 'maximum security' cells reserved for the most dangerous prisoners. Their feet were shackled into stocks, which were basically two boards attached together with iron clamps. The guards would use these stocks to secure a prisoner by putting their ankles through the clamps. Not only was this very uncomfortable, but I am sure they were in extreme amounts of pain from being beaten. All they could do, was sit in their shackles. All they could do, was use their voices. And that is exactly what they did. But instead of complaining, blaming, and defending themselves to the other prisoners about their predicament, they began praying, and singing hymns of praise. And guess who heard them. All the other prisoners! Miraculously, while Paul and Silas praised, not only did their individual chains fall off, but ALL the prisoners' chains were unfastened, and the prison doors were opened. These prisoners had the hardest of hearts, and had committed the greatest of crimes. And that is who God wanted to make Himself real to. All Paul and Silas did was praise. Our praise unshackles. This type of response to life's challenging situations brings freedom. Not just to ourselves, but to others as well.

Today's Challenge To Dig Deeper:
Are you going through a life challenge where your circumstances might make it easy to complain? Turn the protests into praise. Try it. You will feel the chains of despair come off, and you never know who needs their chains unshackled by your praise as well.

Evening Reflection:
Write down an example of when you turned a protest into praise today.

STATEMENT OF SUCCESS
January 7

Morning Rinse: Acts 19-21
Featured Verses: Acts 20:24, 27 *But I do not consider my life of any account as dear to myself, so that I may finish my course and the ministry which I received from the Lord Jesus, to testify solemnly of the gospel of the grace of God… For I did not shrink from declaring to you the whole purpose of God.*

If you are following this devotional by the dates, then you know it is January, and a new year is here. When one replaces an old calendar with a new one, it is natural to set goals for that new year. Some write these goals down and some even design vision boards that include visual elements representing desired accomplishments. As Christ followers, our goals will usually align with what God has placed in our heart, truly linking to the ministry God has called us to do. Paul always knew what his ministry was, and he was focused on fulfilling that purpose. His purpose was to tell others about Christ (Phil 3:7-13). Today's Featured Verses describe what some may call his end of life 'Statement of Success.' This statement was simply saying he knew he was a success in giving his all to his purpose. He was able to say, in good conscience, that he never held back. In the context of our actions, shrinking back does not necessarily mean giving up. It can refer to being reluctant, unwilling, or to even simply slowing down in the journey of reaching our full potential. Why do we shrink back at times? Do we think we are unworthy to walk out great things? Are we afraid, or do we get lazy? Could it be a combination of all these reasons? Paul was a powerhouse and did some amazing things for God's kingdom. In today's Morning Rinse, we read that he raised a boy to life. He also laid his hands on people, and they began speaking in tongues and prophesying. And we read how he touched handkerchiefs or aprons and sent them to the sick, and they were healed. He lived his purpose out to the fullest measure. We all can do the same. If we do not shrink back, we will see that purpose come to life. You are chosen. You are worthy. And God wants your actions to be driven towards your purpose so you, too, are able to declare your own 'statement of success.'

Today's Challenge To Dig Deeper:
To live out a 'statement of success,' we have to have action steps that align with God's plan. Ask Him to help you make 3 actions today that align with your purpose. Do not hold back. Give 100% like Paul.

Evening Reflection:
What were your 3 action items today? Did you get them completed?

A PERFECT CONSCIENCE
January 8

Morning Rinse: Acts 22-24
Featured Verse: Acts 23:1 *Paul, looking intently at the Council, said, "Brethren, I have lived my life with a perfectly good conscience before God up to this day."*

Paul was not perfect by any means, and yet he was able to say he lived his life with a perfectly good conscience before God. As we look at our own lives, do we question the ability to also state this? Sometimes it is easier to focus on the act of sin, rather than the One who gifts us forgiveness and wipes away those sins, never to hold them against us again. So to be able to state this, staying repentant is key. While we all are sinners, we can have a perfectly good conscience before God by staying humble and repentant of wrong thoughts, actions, and intents of our heart. So yes, we do have the freedom to declare this as well. But we must believe and receive that freedom. We must accept that we are fully redeemed, no matter what we have done. Fighting our own guilt and shame is half the battle. Fighting the condemnation of others and the enemy is the other half. After Paul said the statement in today's Featured Verse, he was smacked in the mouth (23:2). There will always be people in our lives who do not feel we are worthy of the freedom of a perfect conscience, even after we have repented. The smacks, the negative perceptions of others, and the dislikes from those who know our past may always be present. We may always be misunderstood. But if we stay humble and repentant, living a life fully for God, He will continually create in us a clean heart, and our conscience will stay perfect.

Today's Challenge To Dig Deeper:
Do you have a perfectly good conscience before God in every area of your life? If there is any area needing to be addressed, or anything you need to repent about, respond today and renew your perfect conscience.

Evening Reflection:
What did God talk to you about today regarding sustaining a perfect conscience before Him?

STAND UP
January 9

Morning Rinse: Acts 25-28
Featured Verses: Acts 26:28-29 *Agrippa replied to Paul, "In a short time you will persuade me to become a Christian." And Paul said, "I would wish to God, that whether in a short time or long time, not only you, but also all who hear me this day, might become such as I am, except for these chains."*

In today's Morning Rinse, Paul shares his testimony with King Agrippa. Paul certainly did not come with a clean past. But wait! Did he not claim, as we read in yesterday's Morning Rinse, that he had a perfect conscience? How can this be? Was he not an enemy of the Jews? In his testimony, he shared this past of imprisoning saints and voting to put many to death. He shared how he punished them in synagogues and tried to force them to blaspheme God. He even admitted to being *"furiously enraged at them"* (26:11), and pursuing to kill them. He also shared, though, while on a pursuit of them to Damascus, Jesus appeared to him and changed his heart. He was transformed from a destroyer to a rescuer, and from a hater to a lover. He was a man who was blinded, but made into one whose eyes were opened to the gospel. He became a forgiven man, now commissioned to preach his testimony. When Jesus called him, he said, *"But get up and stand on your feet."* (26:16) And that is what he did. Paul got up and took his mission, preaching the gospel, seriously. He became a man wishing ALL men would believe. This came from just one encounter with Jesus. That one encounter was all he needed to stand up. Are we like Paul? Do we have this type of passion for others?

Today's Challenge To Dig Deeper:
Has God asked you to get up and begin sharing with others about the love of Christ? We all have a mission. "A Heavenly Call." All our missions are linked to reaching people for Christ. Ask God today to help you stand up. What is it that He wants from you?

Evening Reflection:
What is it that God wants you to stand up and do?

A SHEPHERD TURNED PROPHET
January 10

Morning Rinse: Amos 1-4
Featured Verse: Amos 3:7 *Surely the Lord God does nothing unless He reveals His secret counsel to his servants the prophets.*

I once heard a joke centered around the word *adolescent.* A person I was listening to defined his own funny description of this word. He illustrated a kid getting close to his teen years. Suddenly, as if overnight, the kid forgot most of the childhood instructions from his parents. The parents then had to *add-a-lesson*, or repeat a lesson all over again. "No, I said do not run out into the street." I chuckle because someone should come up with a portrayal like this for adults. I can speak from experience, that God must repeat things to me. Subjects like trusting in God, remaining hopeful, having more faith, and then of course, the repeat message to not fear. I know God wants to be present every day to help us walk out this life. But I wonder if He ever gets a bit frustrated, just like the parent of that adolescent, when His children need repeat correction. Especially on subjects that we should already know about. In the book of Amos, correction was what God needed to repeat to His children. And sometimes His correction will come through people like Amos. Interestingly, God will often use people who are not evangelists, preachers, or priests. He will use people like you and me. Amos was not a full-time pastor, nor was he even from a line of prophets and priests. He herded sheep and tended to sycamore-fig trees as his full-time job. But God turned Him into one. He was a shepherd (1:1) turned prophet. He was a man of God, living a life fully devoted to Him, and that is what God wants from all of us to further His kingdom. We do not have to be born into a preacher's family, or be a famous evangelist, missionary, or youth pastor to be used, even if it is to convey those repeated corrections. But there is one catch. We must be like Amos and obey. Whatever God wants to turn you into, be ready. He may not turn you into a prophet, but he may turn you into someone who is bold, courageous, and willing to deliver a message for Him.

Today's Challenge To Dig Deeper:
I remember several specific times when God wanted me to correct someone, but I disobeyed and remained silent. It is not always easy to convey a message like this. However, we must be willing, especially if it will set someone free. If there is a message of correction in your heart, ask God to help you convey it in love.

Evening Reflection:
Did you have a message of correction for someone? Did you deliver it? How did it go?

MEASURING UP TO GOD'S PLUMB LINE
January 11

Morning Rinse: Amos 5-7
Featured Verses: Amos 7:7-8 *Thus He showed me, and behold, the Lord was standing by a vertical wall with a plumb line in His hand. The Lord said to me, "What do you see, Amos?" And I said, "A plumb line." Then the Lord said, "Behold I am about to put a plumb line in the midst of My people Israel, I will spare them no longer."*

A *plumb line* is simply a cord with a weight attached to one end. In Bible times, carpenters and builders used this device to help ensure a foundation or structure was straight. They would hold it in the air and let the weight fall. If the cord was an exact vertical line, the wall was straight. If it was not, then the foundation was crooked and could eventually collapse.[1] The gravity pulling the plumb line would not change its course when the carpenter moved his body, and its standard did not adjust to even the opinion of the builder on his personal work. The standard was trustworthy, and its purpose was truthful. Every handiwork of the carpenter had to line up with the plumb line, or they risked the structure being curved. God's plumb line is the same. It is His measuring stick and standard. "I will make justice the measuring line and righteousness the plumb line." (Isaiah 29:18 NASV) God does not want any crookedness, or sin, in His kingdom. So He gives us His *plumb line* to keep us on the straight path. When He said He was setting a plumb line among His people, He was calling them out on their crooked ways, and was about to measure their sin according to His standard. His ways are nonnegotiable, and they do not change with the times, seasons, or trends. His moral law determines right from wrong, and helps us know when sin is in our lives. Just like a carpenter's plumb line is not measured by the opinion of the builder, God's moral standards are not subject to the opinions of man, and they will not change based on what an individual wants to believe. It may be difficult to change our opinion to line up with God's standards versus satisfying our own agenda. But it is a must to keep growing in His ways.

Today's Challenge To Dig Deeper:
How do you measure up to God's plumb line? Ask Him to show you, so you can live according to His standard.

Evening Reflection:
What did God say to you as He measured your life against His plumb line? Thank Him for showing you. And be happy and proud of yourself for allowing Him to do that.

---

[1] https://www.gotquestions.org/plumb-line-Bible.html

SPREADING THE MESSAGE OF HOPE

January 12

Morning Rinse: Amos 8-9
Featured Verse: Amos 9:14 *Also I will restore the captivity of My people Israel, and they will rebuild the ruined cities and live in them; They will also plant vineyards and drink their wine, and make gardens and eat their fruit.*

Congratulations on finishing the book of Amos. It is not an easy book to understand, nor is it usually a book often found on a top list of reading materials. The minor prophetic books in the Old Testament can sometimes be a little confusing, and take some theologians years to understand. This book started with a simple shepherd named Amos who ended up preaching to the nations, including Israel. Amos was used by God to point out the many sins of the people, and at one point, Amaziah the priest even tried to stop his preaching because the messages were hard to hear (7:10-13). It is safe to state that not many people really enjoy being corrected regarding their bad behavior. Whether it is becoming complacent, worshiping idols, or being selfish and ignoring the needs of others, we can be assured, though, that our wrong behaviors will always get addressed by our Heavenly Father. While the book of Amos is harsh, and the judgements are heavy, we can still apply it to our own lives by simply asking God to renew our hearts in any area needing addressed. Even though the judgements found in this book are many, it ends with a message of hope and restoration. This message is one we can also claim for our own lives. Despite how Israel and the other nations disobeyed in their actions, we know God is a redeeming God. He is a God of restoration and rebuilding, even if there is an appearance of something completely ruined. At some point in our lives, we all need to hear a message of hope, even those who are locked in a maximum-security prison. Do you need this message of hope? Or do you know someone who does?

Today's Challenge To Dig Deeper:
If you know someone who needs this message, call them today. After having a loving conversation with them, schedule a follow-up with them over lunch or coffee. Make sure it is on your calendar and stay on top of this appointment. This devotional is all about making the messages in the Bible applicable to today. It is all about 'action.'

Evening Reflection:
Did you reach out to someone today? Who was it? Write down the story.

EVERY PERSON BEHIND A NAME IS VALUABLE
January 13

Morning Rinse: 1 Chronicles 1-2
Featured Verses: 1 Chronicles 2:30-31 *The sons of Nadab were Seled and Appaim, and Seled died without sons. The son of Appaim was Ishi. And the son of Ishi was Sheshan. And the son of Sheshan was Ahlai.*

Have you ever come to the end of a movie, and once the credits start to role, you either get up and leave the theatre, turn the power off on your device, or barely take note of the names as they scroll across the screen? I will admit, there have been times through the years that I have come to a passage like today's Morning Rinse, and either skip or skim over the chapters in a very similar fashion. It is not that I do not want to read these passages with integrity. But scriptures like this contain multiple chapters of names that are hard to pronounce or people I do not know about. And since some never appear again in the Bible, I am guilty of skipping over them. I am sure I am not the only one guilty of this, right? Have you ever wondered why these names are listed? While I cannot answer that question about everyone, I am confident in one thing. God sees value in each of these individuals, and He knows them each by their name. It does not matter to Him what they did as a profession, how big or small their homes were, or even how wealthy they became. God sees everyone as valuable. And He also sees each of us as valuable, too. I had to ask myself these questions, "If any of my friends' names were written in the Bible, would I read these chapters differently?" And, "If my friends' names were in the credits, would I leave the movie, or find them on the list?" Yes. Yes, I would. I bet God reads our names, and the names in these chapters in the Bible with excitement, because every person behind those names is important to Him. May we also have this excitement towards people.

Today's Challenge To Dig Deeper:
As uncomfortable as it may be, tell someone how valuable they are in God's eyes. You just might change a life. Also, ask God to give you a new excitement, when reading chapters that are filled with unrecognizable names. Ask Him to help you remember the value in each one of the people behind the names.

Evening Reflection:
Who did you reach out to today? How did you tell them they are valuable? How did the interchange go? Finish your reflection by writing how it made you feel.

JABEZ INFLUENCE
January 14

Morning Rinse: 1 Chronicles 3-6
Featured Verses: 1 Chronicles 4:9-10 *Jabez was more honorable than his brothers, and his mother named him Jabez saying, "Because I bore him with pain." Now Jabez called on the God of Israel, saying, "Oh that You would bless me indeed and enlarge my border, and that Your hand might be with me, and that You would keep me from harm that it may not pain me!" And God granted him what he requested.*

As the list of names continues in our Morning Rinse, we read names from the family of David as well as the genealogy of the tribes of Israel. Right in the middle of reciting the line of Hur, Ezra, the believed author of the Chronicles pauses. Out of nowhere, he shifts from just listing the names in the genealogy, to spotlighting a man named Jabez. It is almost like a commercial break, or an intermission in a play. It is the kind of interruption to stick around for versus getting popcorn. I can envision Ezra slowly lifting his eyes to the crowd, and loudly emphasizing his name, Jabez. It was as if Ezra would want everyone's attention before stating what was special and noteworthy about him. Once he got the crowd's attention, he would give insight into who this amazing man was. I can almost hear Ezra when he states Jabez was known for being more honorable than all his brothers, and for calling on God with a powerful prayer, captured in today's Featured Verses. Wow! What wonderful character traits to be known for, and a perfect reason to cause ears to perk up! He was an example and an influencer. Not much else is written in the Bible about Jabez. We do not even know for sure if he is an ancestor of the kings of Judah. In his short prayer, he asked for four things; for God to bless him, enlarge his borders, keep His hand upon him, and keep him from harm, or some translations say *evil*. Despite being birthed in pain, Jabez did not want to cause pain. So he prayed a prayer of blessing and increase, asking for God to give him greater influence. What a way to want to live, and what a wonderful legacy to desire. I believe Jabez was already in a position of influence, especially since he was known for his honorable character. And I believe he knew this. But even if I am in error and he had no influence at all, God answered his prayer. He was not afraid of being in the spotlight.

Today's Challenge To Dig Deeper:
Memorize the prayer of Jabez. Write it on an index card and put it on a mirror or wall for you to see daily. Now pray the Jabez prayer over you and your loved ones.

Evening Reflection:
What are some thoughts you had today regarding this verse?

GOING AGAINST THE ODDS
January 15

Morning Rinse: 1 Chronicles 7-10
Featured Verse: 1 Chronicles 7:24 *His daughter was Sheerah, who built lower and upper Beth-horon, also Uzzen-sheerah.*

Sometimes when I come to passages like these last few chapters, it is easy to skim over them and not take notice of all the people listed. As mentioned in the devotion for January 13, we know people are truly important. But what stuck out to me in today's Morning Rinse was that God chose to mention a daughter along with the Chief of men in the genealogy. What made her stand out? What caused her name to be placed in this great lineup despite the standard for men to hold that spot? Listing mainly men in a genealogy is not bad or unequal, but rather cultural. I liken it to when a couple get married. Usually the woman will take the man's name. It's a form of respect and honor, and how families are named. But this lady, Sheerah, caused a comma in the list of descendants of Ephraim. Her actions instigated the writer to insert her name, like how he did with Jabez from yesterday's devotion. She was viewed as an equal among other great leaders. What did she do that made such an impact for her to be remembered? We can gain a lot of information about her from just one verse. She was named the builder of not one, not two, but three cities; Lower and Upper Beth-horon, and Uzzen-sheerah. I have been on building committees before. Each member is on the team for a specific purpose, and brings a high level of expertise so the job gets completed. This is who Sheerah was. She was a business leader and head of probably multiple departments. She made a difference for the people, meeting needs for more homes, more buildings, and more marketplace spaces. She pursued her giftings despite the challenges of a male dominated culture and industry. She was not afraid to go against the odds. And she had to have been successful at her skills, because after the first city was built, she was asked to come back to build two more. You may feel like you are up against the odds, but keep working. Keep rising. Keep making a difference.

Today's Challenge To Dig Deeper:
No matter your age or gender, write down one thing that is in your heart, that you desire to do, even if you feel the odds are stacked against you. Now, list four things that you need to do to begin moving towards this vision. Keep this 'to do list' on your planner everyday moving forward.

Evening Reflection:
What was the one thing you did today that went against the odds? Feel good that you are making daily goals to accomplish the big picture.

BE A BOOMERANG FRIEND
January 16

Morning Rinse: 1 Chronicles 11-14
Featured Verse: 1 Chronicles 14:1 *Now Hiram King of Tyre sent messengers to David with cedar trees, mason and carpenters, to build a house for him.*

Hiram was a ruler over a nation that worshiped many idols. Why was this significant to point out? Because despite his spiritual beliefs, he was a friend to both King David and his son King Solomon. This neighboring nation shows how even in biblical times, nations helped nations. As their friend, Hiram helped them carry out several large tasks at hand, including providing resources for the construction of David's house, and then again providing resources in 2 Chronicles 2:3, when Solomon later built the temple. Hiram helped complete their vision, regardless of any spiritual differences they had. Sometimes our greatest resources will come from those who are different from us. Yesterday's challenge was to write down something in your heart that you want to complete, including four small tasks to help you get started. Now look in your group of friends, or those you are associated with. Many times God will put others in your life to help complete your God-given desires. Your answers may be right in front of you. So do not disregard anyone based on what you see. Instead, look through God's eyes. And on the flip side, as you look around, ask yourself if you are being a resource to others as they carry out the desires of their heart. Just as King Hiram was a resource to David and Solomon, I believe they were a resource to him as well. David was friends with him for many years. I am not indicating they were close friends. But their friendship was strong enough that Hiram helped Solomon years later, when he built the temple. What comes around goes around, just like a boomerang. See value in what others bring to your vision, and then remember to give back in return. Be a boomerang friend.

Today's Challenge To Dig Deeper:
Pull out your notebook from yesterday, and start making a list of all the people you know who could potentially help you, and include their skillset. Do not discount anyone. Make two phone calls to people on your list. Tell them your big idea and your needs. Ask them for help. Now keep your ears open today for an opportunity to give back.

Evening Reflection:
Did something amazing occur in your phone calls today? Were you encouraged at how God worked through your conversations? Or did you learn that you need to keep pursuing other help? Write what happened on your journey towards your goal. Include any needs you stepped up to meet for other people. Were you a boomerang friend?

ARE YOU PREPARED?
January 17

Morning Rinse: 1 Chronicles 15-18
Featured Verses: 1 Chronicles 16:41-42 *With them were Heman and Jeduthun, and the rest who were chosen, who were designated by name, to give thanks to the Lord, because His lovingkindness is everlasting. And with them were Heman and Jeduthun with trumpets and cymbals for those who should sound aloud, and with instruments for the songs of God, and the sons of Jeduthun for the gate.*

I must admit, I do not watch television much. I seem to have a hard time sitting still. I have to force myself to be intentional and purposeful at what I want to watch, and sometimes I lack motivation. But one thing I am filled with excitement about, and I love gathering my loved ones to join me, is watching the annual Macy's Day Parade on Thanksgiving morning. I get such a thrill seeing all the floats, the bagpipes, the singers, the clowns, and the marching bands as they pass by the television cameras. I can almost feel the energy through my television screen, and yes, sometimes I even cry tears of joy. Talk about delight. But today's Morning Rinse includes a parade far more electric than the one I like to watch in November. This parade is when King David brings the ark back to Jerusalem. The city streets are filled with people praising God for answering their prayers. They waited a long time for this moment, and their hearts are ready for a party of praise. Some play instruments, some dance, and some were asked to lead in a prayer of thanksgiving. Whatever way each person expressed themselves, there was unity in the articulation. Most had prepared for this moment, just like those who participate in the Macy's Day Parade prepare. The question for today is, am I doing what it takes to prepare for my parade of praise? Our individual preparation comes before the opportunity. This includes preparing not only our craft of worship, but our hearts as well. Heman and Jeduthun were skilled and ready to lead in the praise. They were ready. Are you prepared to be used?

Today's Challenge To Dig Deeper:
You have a skillset and a gift that is needed. However you use your skills will be an act of praise. Are you practicing your craft? Are you preparing your heart? Ask God to make you fit for the position He desires you to play in His kingdom. Ask Him what he'd like you to start doing to prepare you for that position He needs fulfilled.

Evening Reflection:
Write down what you feel God spoke to you about today in your journey of preparation for the position in His kingdom.

CAN SATAN MAKE US DO WRONG?

January 18

Morning Rinse: 1 Chronicles 19-22

Featured Verses: 1 Chronicles 21:1, 8 *Then Satan stood up against Israel and moved David to number Israel... David said to God, "I have sinned greatly, in that I have done this thing. But now, please take away the iniquity of your servant, for I have done very foolishly."*

I honestly do not like when people make the statement, "The devil made me do it." I personally do not believe it is a true statement for a Christ follower. Now, do not get me wrong. Satan knows our weaknesses, and will tempt us to get on a path leading us to fall short, or to cross over into sinful acts. But God gave us all a free will to make choices without being strong-armed by Satan or anyone else. Our free will gives us our own individual choice to make decisions that will ultimately either lead us towards God, or turn us to a path that follows Satan's lead. I once heard a pastor describe this very scenario, when he described God as a gentleman. Gentlemen do not force their will on others. They express their will, and request support in their desired behavior, but they do not force it. In today's Morning Rinse, we learn that David took a census. Taking this census was not against God's Law, but the reason behind taking the census was wrong. David's motive was not pure, and Satan knew this. So Satan tempted David, and targeted his ill motive to show off his mighty army. This revealed his prideful heart. Actions that are motivated by greed or selfishness can lead to sin. When Satan sees this in our heart, he will tempt us in that selfish area, knowing full well it is a personal weakness. Satan knew pride was in David's heart, and he knew exactly how to tempt him to act in an unpleasing way that went against the nature of God. Unfortunately, David fell right into the trap of temptation. For us to stay on the right path, we must always weigh our motives while making life choices. Our sinful nature will always lurk, and forever be ready to creep in if we are not careful. But staying humble will keep us from making choices that could cause us to fall. When David finally realized his wrong motives and choices behind his motives, he took full responsibility and asked for forgiveness, not placing blame on Satan.

Today's Challenge To Dig Deeper:
Search your heart and ask God if you are falling into temptation in an area you know God would want you to make a different choice in. Sometimes it may be an area that is not necessarily sinful, but the motive may be wrong.

Evening Reflection:
Write down what you feel God spoke to you today about your heart and motives.

WE PROPHESY WHEN WE PRAISE
January 19

Morning Rinse: 1 Chronicles 23-26
Featured Verse: 1 Chronicles 25:1 *Moreover, David and the commanders of the army set apart for the service some of the sons of Asaph and of Heman and of Jeduthun, who were to prophesy with lyres, harps and cymbals.*

Have you ever been guilty of complaining about the type of songs the worship team sings in your church? Maybe you do not like the style of the songs, or maybe you feel the songs are not modern enough. Then of course, there is the flip side of that preference. Maybe the songs are too upbeat for your taste. The fact of the matter is, God may not even actually be moved by our opinion, or what we do or do not like. Why? Because when we sing praises to Him, we are prophesying over our lives and over our loved ones. This is what is important to Him. I used to think prophesying occurred when someone was stirred by the Holy Spirit during an anointed moment, and then they would give a prophetic message, or what some may call a *Word of Knowledge* about the future or a person. While this is true to some extent, it does not encompass all the types of prophetic messages, or how and when they are delivered. According to today's Featured Verse, we can prophesy when we praise during singing, and even while playing instruments! The more I think about the songs we sing in church, the more I realize we are speaking over our lives, and giving thanks to our Heavenly Father through prophecy. If we could only grasp how powerful this truly is, I think our perspectives would change.

Today's Challenge To Dig Deeper:
Think of one worship song that you have not been overtly fond of for reasons other than lyrics. Now, look up the lyrics of this song and read them out loud. Ask God to open your eyes to the true 'prophecy' within the song. Now, pray the song over your life, and ask God to give you a new perspective of the song.

Evening Reflection:
Write down the song from today, any thoughts of reflection you had regarding the song, and your new perspective of it.

TRUSTWORTHY POSITIONING

January 20

Morning Rinse: 1 Chronicles 27-29, 2 Chronicles 1
Featured Verse: 2 Chronicles 1:7 *In that night God appeared to Solomon and said to him, "Ask what I shall give you."*

Have you ever heard people ask, "If you won a million dollars, what would you do with it?" Or what about the question, "If money were not an issue, what would you accomplish?" If I were to playfully answer these questions, I would joke about building a castle on a cliff, or buying a ranch on two hundred acres in the mountains, and transforming it into a vacation spot. I might even joke about buying a cruise ship. But if God were to tell me to ask Him for anything, I would quickly change from joking about the answer, to a full-out serious mode. I may even take a moment where I second guess my ears, and see if I truly even heard the request correctly. How long would I need to ponder what I would ask for? How long did it take Solomon to make his request? Did he already have his wish tucked in his heart? How did God know He could tell Solomon to ask Him for anything, and be confident it would come from a heart He could trust? I do not know these answers, but I do know God trusted Solomon and opened the door for him to ask for anything. Anything! So knowing this, I forced myself to ask the hard questions, "Am I trustworthy enough for God to give me the same request? Have I positioned myself to be able to handle this open door from Him?" I know He wants to bless His children. But what was it about Solomon that gave God the confidence to let him ask for anything? Do I have this same trustworthy trait, or do I need to do better at taking care of what He has already given me? I pray we all strive to create trustworthy positioning, so God can tell us all to *"Ask what I shall give you."*

Today's Challenge To Dig Deeper:
If you know any area of your life that needs some attention, whether in your actions, speech, desires of your heart, or how you treat what you already have, ask God to help you get to a place of trustworthy positioning.

Evening Reflection:
Write down what God showed you, and the changes you made today to increase your trustworthy positioning.

SPEAK IT OUT
January 21

Morning Rinse: 2 Chronicles 2-5
Featured Verse: 2 Chronicles 2:5 *The house which I am about to build will be great, for greater is our God than all the gods.*

"God has called you to greatness. God has big plans for you. There are amazing things in store for your life. You will accomplish great things." Has someone ever prayed or spoken things to you like these statements? I can imagine we all have had this happen at some point. I do not know about you, but I must admit, being told these things sometimes makes me uncomfortable. I believe we all want greatness. But what is greatness? My carnal mind often wants to believe my accomplishments will be huge feats for the public eye to see. This is true for Solomon, of course. But really, a better word might be *significant*. What we do for God is significant for His kingdom. Do you believe this for yourself? How do you respond to this truth? Solomon not only believed what he would build for God would be great, but he told people. He made it known and repeated it back to himself as well. Why are we shy about saying things like this? Is it because we are nervous that those who hear it may believe we are arrogant, or they will misunderstand us? Sometimes I shun the statements because I do not want to sound like my plans are bigger and better than other Christ followers. So how should we deal with these words? Solomon did not seem to have an issue with claiming them for his life. In fact, he did three things that can help us learn to be more confident about the great things we will do for God's kingdom.

1. Solomon claimed the mission as his own.
2. Solomon determined in his heart to complete it.
3. Solomon verbally called the mission *great,* before he even started the work.

It is not only powerful when we claim our mission, but when we determine in our hearts to finish it, and state that what we will do for God will be great and wonderful. It helps us to truly understand these statements. We do not have to build a huge monument or a prestigious church building for it to be great, though. If we always do everything for the Lord with excellence, then naturally everything we do for Him will be full of significance. Now, go speak it out.

Today's Challenge To Dig Deeper:
You have something great in your heart that God is pulling at you to complete for Him. What is it? Repeat out loud 10 times what you will do for God will be great and wonderful. Do not be afraid to say it.

Evening Reflection:
Write down what it is you are determined to do for God, and include in your sentence, "it will be great and wonderful."

LIVING ABOVE OUR REPUTATION
January 22

Morning Rinse: 2 Chronicles 6-9
Featured Verses: 2 Chronicles 9:5-6 *Then she said to the king, "It was a true report which I heard in my own land about your words and your wisdom. Nevertheless I did not believe their reports until I came and my eyes had seen it. And behold, the half of the greatness of your wisdom was not told me. You surpass the report that I heard."*

In today's Morning Rinse, we came to the point in King Solomon's story where he had just completed the job of building the temple. For all of you who create vision boards, this accomplishment took him and his dad twenty years to complete. I am sure there were many conversations throughout the land, as the people watched the construction of this grand building year after year. Stories of his fame, wisdom and wealth probably became household conversations. It was no wonder when the Queen of Sheba heard about Solomon's life, she decided she had to meet him for herself. His reputation would make anyone want to be in his presence and glean from him. When she arrived from her journey, witnessed the greatness of Solomon's kingdom, and listened to the wisdom that he spoke, she was blown away! Yes, his material possessions were stunning, but many aspects about his life were notable, including the way he treated others. The queen was astonished by his wisdom, the words he spoke, his luxurious home, and even the stairs going up to the temple captured her eyes. She was also amazed at the magnificent food he served, and even how he and those around him dressed. Every aspect of Solomon's life bewildered her. She knew the stories she had heard about him had truth. But when she saw his magnificent life with her own eyes, and when she heard his words of wisdom with her own ears, she admitted the stories she had heard, his reputation that was so popular, still did not do him justice. What was truly startling to the Queen of Sheba, was that Solomon lived a life ABOVE his reputation. He was far better in real life. May it be so for us all.

Today's Challenge To Dig Deeper:
How do others see and experience you? Do you have a high reputation? Do you keep your word? Can you be trusted to fulfill commitments, or rather are you considered 'wishy-washy'? How do you display your life? Do you count your blessings? Do you honor God in how you dress, talk to others, and how you live? Think of 1 or 2 areas that you can improve today to live ABOVE your reputation. Let God show you.

Evening Reflection:
Write down what you feel God spoke to you today about how you can live ABOVE your reputation.

SETTING OUR HEARTS
January 23

Morning Rinse: 2 Chronicles 10-12
Featured Verse: 2 Chronicles 12:14 *He (Rehoboam) did evil because he did not set his heart to seek the Lord.*

With one hand, a jeweler lifts a diamond with his special tweezers. With his other hand, he gazes through a magnifying glass at this precious gem, analyzing the natural cut. Propped upward on the workspace in front of him is a gold band with an empty prong setting. He smiles, and with careful precision, sets the diamond into its new home. Once the precious gem is placed into the setting, he delicately squeezes the prongs over the diamond, completing his masterpiece. The prongs wrap around the stone, setting it into place for permanence, so it remains secure and long-lasting, positioned to endure the unforeseeable hits and dings in the many years to come. Setting a stone has a distinct parallel to setting our hearts towards seeking the Lord. When we intentionally set our hearts to seek the Lord, we position ourselves to remain steadfast and secure in our faith, despite the many challenges and hurts we will face in our lifetime. And setting our hearts to seek the Lord will help keep us from evil. How do we do this? It is not just a one-time salvation prayer. It is an intentional decision to seek God by reading The Word and making each decision we make encased in what God would have for our lives. Just like the diamond is permanently set in the prongs, it is an intentional decision to set our hearts in the prongs of Jesus. For if we do not set our hearts to seek God, we have already made the decision to set our hearts to seek evil.

Today's Challenge To Dig Deeper:
Listen for the still, small voice of God in making your decisions throughout the day. When you hear it in your heart prompting you, stop what you are doing and answer the prompt. Obeying the little things helps us 'set' our hearts each day to seek Him.

Evening Reflection:
Write down any little prompting you had today that helped you seek God and obey. Each time we obey, we secure our setting in Him. Our roots grow a little deeper and we get a little stronger in Him.

HONORING AN UNBELIEVING PARENT
January 24

Morning Rinse: 2 Chronicles 13-15
Featured Verse: 2 Chronicles 15:16 *He also removed Maacah, the mother of King Asa, from the position of queen mother, because she had made a horrid image as an Asherah, and Asa cut down her horrid image, crushed it and burned it at the brook Kidron.*

Growing up in a family of faith afforded me the opportunity to be around loved ones all my life, who tried to live a godly lifestyle. Granted, we were not perfect by any means. But I never had to go through a conflicting scenario like what Asa had to endure. I am sure he loved his parents and grandparents dearly. But when one is faced with a decision based on a familial status versus on faith, it can make it exponentially difficult, if the outcome may cause a wedge in family relationships. It was mighty brave of Asa to remove Maacah from her position as queen, since she didn't follow God's principles. He did this in front of an entire nation. Following her removal, he then tore down and crushed the idols she had built. Was this dishonoring and disobedient, especially since honoring our parents is part of the Ten Commandments? What exactly does it mean to honor our mother and father? This commandment might be especially challenging for those with unbelieving parents, like Asa. But obeying and being loyal to God must come first. Respecting our parents should never keep us from following God. How do we make this relevant in modern day life? It is learning to show admiration, devotion and respect to our loved ones without compromising faith. It is giving our parents their rightful tribute and reverence in a family line, while obeying Christ in our lifestyle. This may mean setting boundaries, such as asking them to refrain from doing certain things while you and your family are around. Maybe it is requesting they pause from cursing, drinking, watching certain movies around your children, or even saying derogatory comments about your faith. Honoring your parents does not mean you have to allow dishonoring behavior. Honoring is showing love despite the differences. I am sure Asa had to learn this trait as well.

Today's Challenge To Dig Deeper:
Do you have unbelieving parents, or do you know someone who does? First, pray for them, and remember they do not have Christ-like DNA. Once we understand this, it is easier to honor the way God would want us to honor them.

Evening Reflection:
Write down your reflection of this devotion today.

TEAR THE WALL OF FEAR DOWN

January 25

Morning Rinse: 2 Chronicles 16-18
Featured Verses: 2 Chronicles 18:12-13 *Then the messenger who went to summon Micaiah spoke to him saying, "Behold, the words of the prophets are uniformly favorable to the king. So please let your word be like one of them and speak favorably." But Micaiah said, "As the Lord lives, what my God says, that I will speak."*

Imagine this scenario. You have been asked to speak at a convention, but your field of expertise is sometimes controversial. Despite the differing biases, you decide to accept the invitation. Moments before you go on stage, you are pulled into a side room by the organizers of the convention, and a serious conversation unfolds. You are informed the other speakers have communicated a message completely different from what you are known for giving, and they strongly encourage you to change your presentation to line up with the other speakers. Your lecture is based on decades of research, and everyone in the room is aware it will shake the entire industry, causing waves of discord. You leave the room, say a prayer, and enter stage right. The audience is silent as you make your way to the podium. You slowly pull out your notes, and with nervous hands, begin to speak. The audience listens to every word, but they are not privy to what happened just minutes before you left the private meeting. Instead of complying to the request of the organizers, you looked right at them and replied, "Even if I am the only one to release this information, whatever God wants me to say, I will say." While this example is different, Micaiah understood. It takes courage to speak what God wants spoken, regardless of the scenario. I must wonder how many times I have been silent and afraid, when instead I needed to speak to someone who needed to hear what I had to say. Fear can cripple our message and thwart our purpose. It can be the wall that keeps us a prisoner, blocking freedom for not only ourselves, but for others as well. Micaiah tore the wall down by not conforming, and instead spoke out. Thank God for all of the Micaiahs out there who fear (or respect) God more than man. When God puts something on our heart, have boldness to tear the wall down.

Today's Challenge To Dig Deeper:
Are you aware of any walls of fear that need to be torn down? Ask God for courage to speak what He wants you to speak. Ask for boldness, no matter what others try to get you to say, or what they may think of you. Speak it. Tear the walls down.

Evening Reflection:
Did God provide an opportunity to speak a message to someone today? Write down what you said and what happened. Realize that boldness could be the new you.

STUDYING THE ENEMY
January 26

Morning Rinse: 2 Chronicles 19-21
Featured Verse: 2 Chronicles 20:16 *Tomorrow go down against them. Behold, they will come up by the ascent of Ziz, and you will find them at the end of the valley in front of the wilderness of Jeruel.*

At the time of writing this devotional, my daughter is in college playing softball. During the season, her team will watch game footage of their opponents. They observe the athletes in each position, and study their strengths, weaknesses, and game stats. This helps the coaches and players learn what strategies are needed to make themselves wiser in their plays during the upcoming games against them. Studying opponents is a common practice in the sports industry. There is value in this routine. So why is it that many Christ followers remain nervous about studying Satan and his tactics? Why do some not want to learn what it looks like when he comes against us, both in a fighting mode and a temptation mode? Studying our enemy will bring awareness to his tactics. For example, Satan's ways are infiltrated all through society, including through ungodly television shows, suggestive ads or magazines, rated R music, abusive relationships, drugs, and much more. Some of his ways may be easily recognizable, while other ways may be a bit harder to spot. But if we become aware of his tricks, we would become skilled at being on guard against him, not only for ourselves, but for our loved ones as well. Knowing the enemy's ploys will help us understand how to fight back and protect ourselves. We learn about these ploys by reading the Word of God, and becoming familiar with his evil ways. Once we begin to learn about him, his lies, and the schemes he habitually uses, we will also be made aware of ways our actions contribute to his plans. Unfortunately, if we are behaving with un-Christlike actions, such as gossiping or acting judgmental, we may be used to help Satan cause pain in his destructive agenda. That's when we pray for God to show us things. God will, at times, reveal to us the plan of the enemy so we can come against him effectively and be a vessel on the right team.

Today's Challenge To Dig Deeper:
Ask God to show you if you are helping the enemy, even in small ways, with his agenda. It could be as simple as not asking for forgiveness in a matter. Look around you today, and ask God to reveal to you on a broader scope, things the enemy is doing, and ask God how He can use you to be a vessel to thwart the enemy's plan.

Evening Reflection:
Write down what God showed you today about the enemy.

EARTHLY POSITIONING
January 27

Morning Rinse: 2 Chronicles 22-24

Featured Verse: 2 Chronicles 22:11 *But Jehoshabeath the king's daughter took Joash the son of Ahaziah, and stole him from among the king's sons who were being put to death, and placed him and his nurse in the bedroom. So Jehoshabeath, the daughter of King Jehoram, the wife of Jehoiada the priest (for she was the sister of Ahaziah), hid him from Athaliah so that she would not put him to death.*

In today's Morning Rinse, we read about Jehu, who set out to murder the princes of Judah and kill the entire line of Jehoshaphat, including King Ahaziah. Ahaziah's mother was Queen Athaliah who was equally evil. When she found out Ahaziah was dead, she set out a decree to kill off all her royal offspring, with the evil intent to take complete control over the kingdom. Her plan seemed to work when one by one her heirs were killed. However, Ahaziah's sister, Jehoshabeath, discovered her evil plan and hid Ahaziah's one-year-old son named Joash. Jehoshabeath's husband was a priest named Jehoida, and together, they lived inside the church. This story brought back memories of living in the parsonage next to the Texas church my dad pastored during my high school years. While living there, we did not save any offspring from death, but we were eyes and ears to the people around us. Jehoshabeath and Jehoida were able to use their earthly position to protect and hide Joash and his nurse for six years inside the church. Their earthly employment was certainly used for a heavenly purpose. When Joash turned seven years old, Jehoida secretly planned his crowning as the rightful king. Queen Athaliah had no idea this was being organized until it was too late. On the day of the crowning, Joash was brought out of hiding and into the city for all to witness. Jehoida knew the evil queen would kill Joash if she saw him, so he surrounded Joash with men holding swords and spears to protect him. While all could see, Jehoida crowned him king. Unbeknownst to Queen Athaliah, this young boy was the only offspring alive, and the rightful heir to the throne. Talk about a surprise party! Of course, Queen Athaliah was furious when she found out what was transpiring, and was soon killed for her own deception. This husband-and-wife team not only saved a son, and of course a nation from the evil hands of the queen, but they ultimately preserved the line of David. Their courageous and wise act of rescuing Joash was an act of bravery that saved the entire line of David, the lineage that Jesus was born into.

Today's Challenge To Dig Deeper:
Think about the position you hold on this earth, and how you can use it for heavenly matters. No matter what earthly position you hold, there is a heavenly purpose for why you are there. Ask God to make His purpose for you real to you.

Evening Reflection:
Write down what God spoke to you today about the earthly position you hold. How do you feel God wants you to use it for spiritual matters?

GOD COVERS OUR LOSSES
January 28

Morning Rinse: 2 Chronicles 25-27
Featured Verses: 2 Chronicles 25:9-10 *Amaziah said to the man of God, "But what shall we do for the hundred talents which I have given to the troops of Israel?" And the man of God answered, "The Lord has much more to give you than this." Then Amaziah dismissed them, the troops which came to him from Ephraim, to go home; so their anger burned against Judah and they returned home in fierce anger.*

Amaziah was headed off to war and hired one hundred thousand warriors for one hundred talents. Talents are one of several forms of measurement in the Bible. During this time, one talent was equivalent to about three thousand shekels, also a form of biblical measurement. Not only does the weight of a shekel vary from six to ten grams, but the Bible mentions at least three different kinds of shekels, making it impossible to get an exact dollar figure paid to the soldiers.[2] However, using a baseline figure of conversion, one shekel was worth at least $320.00, making three thousand shekels worth at least $960,000.00.[3] If we multiply this figure by one hundred, the base salary paid to this army was roughly $96,000,000.00! Since Amaziah was hiring a military force, we need to assume he paid them out of a national fund. If he had consulted God before he made this arrangement, he would have bypassed a bad decision and the burden of such a financial loss to his nation. However, a man of God came to Amaziah and advised him to send the army home. Fortunately, Amaziah listened. Of course, the soldiers became enraged at Amaziah, which set him up for potential relationship issues. But God redeems us even when we make mistakes, and He honors us when we obey, especially when we break alliances that we should never have had. Just like Amaziah, sometimes our poor decisions can cost us something, including money. But Amaziah realized obedience was worth more than loss. Here is where it gets fun. Despite the large sum of money Amaziah lost with his decision, the man of God told him not to worry and said, *"The Lord has much more to give you than this."* God has limitless funds to cover our losses when we turn from making poor choices.

Today's Challenge To Dig Deeper:
Are there any that you need to break ties with? The freedom you will feel in obedience is worth the sacrifice of any loss.

Evening Reflection:
Write down any relationships or transactions that you are taking steps towards breaking ties with. Write down how you felt after you made this decision. If not you, then did you help someone through this?

---

[2] https://www.jewishvirtuallibrary.org/weights-measures-and-coins-of-the-biblical-and-talmudic-periods

[3] https://findanyanswer.com/how-much-is-a-shekel-in-the-bible

INDIVIDUAL IMPACT OF GOD'S 'SUDDENLY'
January 29

Morning Rinse: 2 Chronicles 28-30
Featured Verse: 2 Chronicles 29:36 *Then Hezekiah and all the people rejoiced over what God had prepared for the people, because the thing came about suddenly.*

Is your church waiting for a *'suddenly'* from God? Maybe it is a financial miracle, or maybe your leaders are longing for a revival in your city. Sometimes it can seem like the wait will never end. But what we do in the waiting can prepare us for His answer. Preparing for what we long for will often include obedience in the little things. Hezekiah's prayer was for reformation of the temple worship. So when he became king, this became his focus. He rallied the priests and Levites to clean the temple and get it back in order (2 Chronicles 29:1-22). He re-established sacrificing (which was an Old Testament approach to restoring a right relationship with God). He also positioned the Levites for praise and worship, by returning musicians to the temple. He assembled singers, brought back the practice of priests consecrating themselves, and restored tithing. Once Hezekiah made the decision to rededicate the temple, the people in the city made this their focus as well, until everything was back to how God intended. Their hearts were changed *suddenly*, due to one man's heart. When we obey, God uses us to establish HIS ways, and people will follow. The people under Hezekiah *suddenly* became unified towards revival, and true temple worship was restored. We, as a church community, should follow this example of unification for God's kingdom under our pastors. We individually play an important role in ushering in God's *'suddenly'* over our church. We can be a part of God's *sudden* blessing and revival if we walk in obedience. Are you doing what you need to, to help usher in the *suddenly* for your church?

Today's Challenge To Dig Deeper:
Ask God for an opportunity to help bring in His *'suddenly'* for your church. Maybe your pastor or a ministry leader has a vision they want to bring to fruition. Consider how much faster your church will be blessed if you jump on board and join with their vision. If God is nudging you to do more for your local church, answer the call today.

Evening Reflection:
Write down your pastor's vision and what you are doing individually so God's *'suddenly'* for your church comes to life faster.

IS TITHING OPTIONAL?
January 30

Morning Rinse: 2 Chronicles 31-33
Featured Verse: 2 Chronicles 31:5 *As soon as the order spread, the sons of Israel provided in abundance the first fruits of grain, new wine, oil, honey and of all the produce of the field, and they brought in abundantly the tithe of it all.*

If one wanted to do an in-depth study about money, the Bible has a lot to say about the subject. We can learn about debt, wealth, how to handle business decisions, tithing, offering, giving to the poor, and so much more. When it comes to tithing, especially during the Old Testament times when a money system had not yet been standardized, people tithed ten percent of whatever increase came into their home. It would include things like crops, fruits, and livestock. When I became a young adult, I started attending a church in inner city Kansas City. The pastor of this church, Dr. George Westlake, would speak of the importance of tithing, and challenge the congregation to test God by this practice. He would often make the statement, "You can't out-give God." I had not been a regular tither, despite being a pastor's kid, until this point. But in 1995, I accepted the challenge and decided to tithe on a regular basis. Once I started, I never quit, and can honestly say that I have been so blessed, just like Azariah witnessed when the people gave (2 Chronicles 31:10). Why are so many Christians afraid to tithe, even though it is clearly expected of us in God's word? Think of how powerful the body of Christ would be, if every Christian had faith and tithed. Yet, statistics show only about twenty percent of Christians practice this, and much less of those give above their tithe. In July of 1997, I started tithing on my gross income instead of my net. WHOA! I have seen God provide in ways I never expected. Then when I got married in 1999, my husband and I made a commitment to God and to each other that NOT tithing would never be an option in our marriage. Yes, tithing is optional. Obedience always is. However, if we want to live a life fully surrendered to God, then obeying Him in every area of our lives, including finances, is not optional.

Today's Challenge To Dig Deeper:
If you are not a faithful tither, ask God to help you begin today. Tithing is not about helping God construct a building or paying a bill. It is about building the hearts IN the building. It is about loving and trusting our Heavenly Father with our finances. If you are already a faithful tither, challenge yourself to increase your free-will offerings.

Evening Reflection:
Did you make a commitment to tithing today? Or did you make a commitment to give above your tithe?

POSITIONING REFORMERS
January 31

Morning Rinse: 2 Chronicles 34-36
Featured Verses: 2 Chronicles 34:1-3 *Josiah was eight years old when he became king, and he reigned thirty-one years in Jerusalem. He did right in the sight of the Lord and walked in the ways of his father David and did not turn aside to the right or to the left. For in the eighth year of his reign while he was still a youth, he began to seek the God of his father David; and in the twelfth year he began to purge Judah and Jerusalem of the high places, the Asherim, the carved images and the molten images.*

My family went through a season where we became foster parents. For nearly three years, we were long term placements to a sibling set of three, doubling our children to six. The youngest was a boy named Brian. We had him during his youthful years, including while he was eight years old. I remember events like teaching him to ride a bike, cooking with him, and watching him get on the bus. I also remember our conversations about God. He was so little back then. And yet, this was the same age as Josiah when he was put into a position as king. Unfortunately, Josiah never got the chance to meet Hezekiah, his great-grandfather. But somehow God passed on Hezekiah's godly legacy to him. These two were a lot alike in some ways. Both had a beautiful relationship with God, were passionate reformers, and made brave efforts to bring the nation back to God. It is recorded, however, that Josiah's dad and grandfather did not follow God's ways. Despite this influence, Josiah continued to obey God, becoming a reformer just like his great-grandfather. God can teach us through examples such as Josiah, to trust Him and still live for Him, no matter our surroundings. He will help us through anything, if we seek Him. I do not know where Brian is now, or his two sisters. He was nine when he was adopted, and his older sisters were still in foster care at the time of this writing. I have heard, though, that the new families do not serve God. This does not mean our godly influence did not stick inside their hearts. Somehow, even though we may never see them again, I believe God will allow our influence in their lives to someday surface, so they will be reformers just like Josiah.

Today's Challenge To Dig Deeper:
Ask God to help you position the next generation of reformers who need your godly influence. Then go out and be one.

Evening Reflection:
Who in your life needs you to position them for influence? Stay on the course. You never know what kind of reformer they will be.

February Rinsing

8 TRUTHS IN 1 SIMPLE PRAYER
February 1

Morning Rinse: Colossians 1-2
Featured Verses: Colossians 1:9-12 *For this reason also, since the day we heard of it, we have not ceased to pray for you and to ask that you may be filled with the knowledge of His will in all spiritual wisdom and understanding, so that you will walk in a manner worthy of the Lord, to please HIM in all respects, bearing fruit in every good work and increasing in the knowledge of God; strengthened with all power, according to His glorious might, for the attaining of all steadfastness and patience, joyously giving thanks to the Father, who has qualified us to share in the inheritance of the saints in Light.*

Just like our January Rinses began with a challenge to be devoted to prayer, we are starting another month founded on prayer. Paul, the author of the book of Colossians, wrote this letter to the church at Colosse from prison in Rome. Talk about a humble and hard place to be, and yet he wrote a power-packed prayer that can be applicable to all believers at any point and time in our lives. We all endure challenging situations. Paul was not only dealing with being bound, but he was having to combat false teachers outside the prison walls as well. In today's Featured Verses, he begins his opening greeting in this letter with a powerful, and yet very simple prayer. In this prayer, there are eight golden nuggets, or items to ask God for that will enrich our lives and help us grow closer to Him in our walk. May we all get into the habit of asking God to:

1. (v. 9) Help us to know His will for our lives.
2. (v. 10) Help us to walk worthy to please Him.
3. (v. 10) Help us to have spiritual understanding.
4. (v. 10) Help us to be fruitful in everything we do.
5. (v. 10) Help us to have more knowledge of Him.
6. (v. 11) Help us to have joy.
7. (v. 11) Give us power and strength.
8. (v. 12) Help us to always be thankful.

The richness of a few verses can change the dynamics of how we walk out our daily lives. It is how we respond to life's challenges that will either break us or build us in Christ.

Today's Challenge To Dig Deeper:
Memorize these verses today and pray them over your life and the lives of your loved ones.

Evening Reflection:
Say this prayer one more time before going to bed. As you memorized it today, how did it affect how you felt?

SALTY TALK
February 2

Morning Rinse: Colossians 3-4
Featured Verse: Colossians 4:6 *Let your speech always be with grace, as though seasoned with salt, so that you will know how you should respond to each person.*

While reading today's Featured Verse, I am reminded of my name. I have been told that *Anita* is Hebrew and means *Grace* or *Favor*. I have often laughed at myself because having grace in my day-to-day activities does not always seem to apply. I am not talking about the act of giving someone grace when they mess up or disappoint me. I am talking about the art of being graceful in ways such as the avoidance of tripping over my own feet, falling UP a flight of stairs, or bumping into things seemingly a mile away, which are all things I have been known to do. My gracefulness, or lack thereof at times, allows for starting points in conversations with family and friends, including opportunities to laugh with me. But the lack of being graceful, or lack of being filled with grace, is when grace is needed. We all have made mistakes, or tripped in ways that require God's grace to flood our lives. Today's Featured Verse reminds me of the grace I need daily, not just in receiving it, but also in giving it to others. When our loved ones mess up, we should want to pass grace on to them. How do we do this? We show grace in how we respond with our speech and our actions towards them. When we respond with grace, it is like salt, giving people a thirst for hope. How we respond to others is how we change lives. It is how we allow room at the cross for those needing redemption, and for those needing Christ. Salty speech is true grace talk. You never know who is thirsty, broken and needing your voice in this way.

Today's Challenge To Dig Deeper:
Today is a day of offering grace, favor, and salt to someone. Look for someone who needs grace for mistakes they have made, or someone who needs favor. Ask God to show you who this is, and then speak what God asks you to speak. You never know what your salty talk can do for a heart, for a life, and for a future. Look for a life who is thirsty.

Evening Reflection:
Write down how God used your salty talk today, and the outcome of that conversation. How did it make you feel?

A KINGDOM MINDSET
February 3

Morning Rinse: 1 Corinthians 1-4
Featured Verses: 1 Corinthians 3:7, 4:2, 6b, 12 *So then neither the one who plants nor the one who waters is anything, but God who causes the growth... In this case, moreover, it is required of stewards that one be found trustworthy… so that not one of you will become arrogant on behalf of one against the others… and we toil, working with our own hands, when we are reviled, we bless: when we are persecuted, we endure.*

Today's Featured Verses include seven traits to practice when pursuing a 'kingdom mindset.' I have found that focusing on these traits is key in my continual growth, but I must admit, I cannot claim mastery. I need reminded of them. In 1 Corinthians 3:7, the first of our Featured Verses, we find two of these traits: **BE TEACHABLE** and **TRUST GOD**. Both can be hard at times since most of us do not usually like being wrong. However, to have a kingdom mindset, we must learn to trust our Father and be teachable when He imparts his wisdom to us. When this happens, our behaviors will organically become more kingdom focused, which is the goal of a kingdom mindset. In 1 Corinthians 4:2, the next of our Featured Verses, we find two more traits: **BE A STEWARD** and **BE TRUSTWORTHY**. God calls us to be stewards and serve our church. But it is not just about joining a ministry. It is about being faithful to that ministry. God expects and requires this of us as we grow. If we do not choose to step up, we put an added burden on pastors and ministry leaders, forcing them to find those who will answer the call and be faithful. However, when we are teachable, trust God, serve and become trustworthy, this allows God to use our talents for His kingdom. But be careful. In 1 Corinthians 4:6b, Paul encourages us to have the next trait of a kingdom mindset: **DO NOT BE ARROGANT**. It is a trait, once again, to be reminded of, especially as we grow in influence. And finally, no matter what we go through from the hurts of others, we need to **BLESS** and **HAVE ENDURANCE**. If we do not see fruit right away, keep going. If we are persecuted for serving Him, bless anyway. Keep pursuing a kingdom mindset and God will get the glory through your journey!

Today's Challenge To Dig Deeper:
Write out these golden nuggets on a sheet of paper, post it in a place that you will see every day, and memorize them: BE TEACHABLE, TRUST GOD, BE A STEWARD, BE TRUSTWORTHY, DO NOT BE ARROGANT, BLESS and HAVE ENDURANCE.

Evening Reflection:
What did God talk to you about today that will help you continue to pursue a kingdom mindset?

DYING TO OUR FLESH
February 4

Morning Rinse: 1 Corinthians 5-7
Featured Verse: 1 Corinthians 6:19 *Or do you not know that your body is a temple of the Holy Spirit who is in you, whom you have from God, and that you are not your own?*

When reading today's Morning Rinse, I was reminded of a childhood song titled *O, be careful*.[4] I remember singing the lyrics while joyfully doing the motions with my friends. "O, be careful little eyes what you see. O, be careful little eyes what you see. For the Father up above is looking down in love. O, be careful little eyes what you see." Verse after verse, the lyrics of this song reference areas of our body to be careful with in our actions. Other verses include, "O, be careful little ears what you hear," and "O, be careful little tongue what you say." And still even two more verses, "O, be careful little hands what you do" and "O, be careful little feet where you go." This song may be targeted to young minds, but the message even teaches adults that everything we do is watched by our Heavenly Father, and we must realize that His standards are higher than that of our flesh. If we are careful how we behave, we will continue becoming more Christlike. Jesus gave His body, His life, so we could live. The least we can do is be a sacrifice in return, so we can glorify Him WITH our bodies. Dying to our flesh is ultimately honoring the death of His. It will not always be easy. There will be times we need to say no to behaviors that do not honor God. Whether it is something our eyes should not see, our ears should not hear, our tongue should not say, our hands should not touch, or somewhere our feet should not go, we can all do better at dying to our flesh. Our bodies are not our own because we were bought with a price. The price was the life and sacrifice of Jesus' flesh. So in the grand scheme of things, He is asking us to make a smaller sacrifice than He ultimately did. The least we can do is be careful and obey.

Today's Challenge To Dig Deeper:
Spend a few moments quietly with our Father, and listen to His still, small voice. Ask Him to show you any areas that you are using your body in ways that are not honoring Him. Ask Him to help you say no when temptation comes, and help you die to your flesh by putting up barriers, boundaries, or walls of protection.

Evening Reflection:
Write the things that God showed you today that you may be doing with your body that do not honor God. Write out what changes He wants you to make and what you did to instill them in your daily life.

---

[4] © Copyright 1956 by Zondervan Music Publishers

ANKLE WEIGHTS AND WEIGHTED VESTS
February 5

Morning Rinse: 1 Corinthians 8-10
Featured Verse: 1 Corinthians 9:27 … *but I discipline my body and make it my slave, so that, after I have preached to others, I myself will not be disqualified.*

When my son started the eighth grade, he decided to play with the school soccer team instead of his recreational team. He had played on multiple teams growing up, but he never pushed himself to excel competitively in the sport. So I had dual reasons for wanting him to join the school's team. For starters, I believed it would be a great place to meet some friends. After ten years of homeschooling, this was our first year in a standard school environment. My second reason was to get him on a more disciplined team. Do not get me wrong, his previous coaches were wonderful and helped grow his love for the sport. But up until this point, he had never had a coach who pushed him to his full potential. He could run slower than his full speed, have less than excellent footwork, and even have a playful demeanor on the field versus having a standard higher than playing just for fun. I knew he needed some stronger guidance. Much to my joy, his new coach recognized it too. Within the first few weeks of practice, he asked if he could give my son lessons. I accepted his help, and when my son showed up for the first one, his coach handed him some ankle weights and a weighted vest to wear while training. After practice, my son was drenched in sweat, and it took several weeks for his body to adjust to this new workout regimen. It was not easy for him, nor was it always enjoyable. But it made him stronger and a better soccer player. When we do the things that others do not want to do, it sets us apart. Comparably speaking, working out spiritually can look like my son's training. Just like working out makes us physically stronger, pushing ourselves to make better choices makes us spiritually stronger. It may not be easy to make better choices, but this is the process of dying to the flesh, which is really living in the Spirit. Living in the Spirit is being disciplined in the areas God wants us to be disciplined in. It means putting on our spiritual ankle weights and weighted vest, and working out in the areas we need to focus on. Spiritual disciple will teach us how to control our bodies instead of our bodies controlling us.

Today's Challenge To Dig Deeper:
Are there areas in your life that need more discipline? Do you need to wake up earlier? Maybe you need to change the music you listen to. Do you need to join a life group in your church for more accountability? Ask God where you need to raise your standards, and choose to put on your spiritual ankle weights and weighted vest.

Evening Reflection:
Write down the changes you made today towards more discipline.

LOVE DOES NOT CLANG
February 6

Morning Rinse: 1 Corinthians 11-13
Featured Verse: 1 Corinthians 13:1 *If I speak with the tongues of men and of angels, but do not have love, I have become a noisy gong or a clanging cymbal.*

As a child, one of the gifts I received from my mother was the clarinet she played when she was growing up. It seemed fitting to play what she played, since my older brother got my dad's saxophone. I began learning to play it in the fourth grade, and continued in band all through my senior year in high school. When I first started learning to play it, I practiced in my bedroom almost every day. I would sit on my bed, put my music stand in front of me, lick the reed, and then pucker up and blow into the mouthpiece. Initially, the sound that came out of the barrel was a horrendous squeak. It took years to perfect it, but as I increased in skill, I eventually earned the spot of first chair in the lineup of clarinet players. My love for band grew, and soon became a favorite class for me. Each time I would enter the practice room, I would excitedly grab my clarinet case and warm up with the other students. The band room would become one large blast of constant noise. It could, at times, get deafening when instrumentalists with tubas, flutes, trumpets, drums, saxophones, baritones, and cymbals all blew at the same time with no direction. But when our instructor stood on his stand and held his arms in the air, the blaring would stop, and the class would begin. He would raise his baton to conduct us in playing music written for beauty. Today's Morning Rinse includes 1 Corinthians 13, known as The Love Chapter. Surprisingly, this chapter does not begin by describing what love IS, but rather what it is NOT. Love does not sound like my band room before the conductor stepped onto his platform. Love does not sound like students squeaking and playing unsynchronized notes. Love does not sound like a noisy gong or a clanging cymbal. Love is the exact opposite. So we must be careful of the things we say so our words are pleasant instead of hurtful. Love is NOT a clanging noise.

Today's Challenge To Dig Deeper:
Have you said anything, even if it was in the wrong tone, or done anything that could have been hurtful to someone? You may have very well needed to say what you said, but if it was not done in love, your message was like clanging cymbals. If this has happened, go to the person, offer an apology, and begin fresh.

Evening Reflection:
Write down how your conversation went today, what you learned, and how you felt after your apology.

INFANCY SINS
February 7

Morning Rinse: 1 Corinthians 14-16
Featured Verse: 1 Corinthians 14:20 *Brethren, do not be children in your thinking; yet in evil be infants, but in your thinking be mature.*

When our oldest child reached her teen years, I found myself in some situations that led me to begin praying a specific prayer. This prayer was not the popular prayer for a child to walk in the will of God for her life. It was not the prayer of protection and security. These prayers were already ones I prayed over her. This one went something like, "God, when my child begins to do something wrong, walks down a path not meant for her, or is tempted to sin, quickly catch her in the act." Asking this from God was not meant to embarrass her, but instead it was meant to stop any seeds of sin from taking root in her heart and growing. When I saw this prayer getting answered, I started praying it over my other children as well. In fact, I also prayed it over myself, ultimately wishing I had started praying it earlier in not just my kids' lives, but my life as well. If we are caught quickly in wrongful acts, and we obey, stopping what we are doing, these acts will remain at an infancy stage, never to grow into maturity. Right thinking and godly thoughts are what we want to grow into maturity, instead of the infancy sins ready to trip us up.

Today's Challenge To Dig Deeper:
Pray the prayer mentioned in the devotion over your life and your loved ones' lives. Look for it to be answered. When it is, offer grace to the individual, and then thank God for the answered prayer. If you have an opportunity, ask the individual caught if they know Jesus as their personal Savior. If they do not, lead them in the sinner's prayer.

Evening Reflection:
Write down how God answered your prayer today. If there was no answer today, be expecting one, and be ready to shine God's love and grace.

IMPERFECT LOVE
February 8

Morning Rinse: 2 Corinthians 1-3
Featured Verses: 2 Corinthians 1:3-4 *Blessed be the God and Father of our Lord Jesus Christ, the Father of mercies and God of all comfort, who comforts us in all our affliction so that we will be able to comfort those who are in any affliction with the comfort with which we ourselves are comforted by God.*

I once bought a ball cap and have it displayed on the bookshelf in my office. It has the word *Champion* on the front. I keep it, not because I love the brand, but to remind me of the champion inside of me. I have taken it several times to speaking engagements, when I want to inspire on this topic, and have also given away a few to people in my audiences, to encourage others to strive for a champion-like mindset. As I write this, though, I do not feel like a champion. You see, I recently hurt someone very close to me. I was hoping that I could write today's devotion about encouraging those who are needing comforted, especially if you have been hurt by others. However, I find myself on the other side of the offense, as the offender. I hate having the perspective of the one seeking mercy instead of the one seeking comfort. I hate being the one who caused the affliction and pain. For me, when I make decisions that cause setbacks in a relationship, it is hard to feel like a champion. It can be easy to believe the person I have hurt will most likely not see me as one, and so therefore, I have a hard time feeling worthy to claim the title. Also, it can be extremely hard to see myself as a champion because embarrassment and shame can easily set in. My husband and I were both part of the actions that I am speaking of, and it unfortunately affected one of our children. Our intentions were one hundred percent right. However, our execution was only eighty percent good, leaving twenty percent causing pain. We threw a punch towards others who were in error towards our family, but when we threw the punch, our kid got knocked down in the swing. So today as I write, my kid has bruises and scars because of our imperfect execution. We did not mean to cause the pain. But it happened. We swung with good intentions to protect what was ours, but we swung imperfectly. We loved imperfectly. Unlike Jesus who loves perfectly, we can make imperfect, loving choices, causing the need for someone else to be comforted. It takes a lifetime to learn to love perfectly. But we cannot stop loving for fear that our swings will be imperfect.

Today's Challenge To Dig Deeper:
Have you recently loved imperfectly? Ask for forgiveness. Now, pray God comforts and helps make the imperfections right, and grab your imaginary champion hat and put it on.

Evening Reflection:
Write down your thoughts or examples of imperfect love.

LIVING A LIFE OF LOVE
February 9

Morning Rinse: 2 Corinthians 4-6
Featured Verse: 2 Corinthians 6:3 ... *giving no cause for offense in anything, so that the ministry will not be discredited.*

During the years we were raising our kids, they would often hear me repeat one of my original quotes, "Live a life so that if anyone talks about you, no one believes it." I have had many teachable moments centered around this quote through the years, so you will see it inserted several places in this devotional. These teachable moments include both learning from other people, as well as unfortunately, moments of pointing to our own personal actions in our family. One thing I have learned is, if we intentionally live a life where we ponder what our actions communicate about Jesus' love, we will make better choices. When we make better choices, we will oftentimes eliminate causing offense, especially if we seek out how to love like Jesus loved. The opposite is true, though. Just as loving behaviors can eliminate offense, unloving choices can cause a whole ministry to be discredited. Paul tried to consider his actions, especially due to his public platform, and the same should go for us. Whether we have opportunities to be on stage ministering to thousands, or we are having a one-on-one conversation with just one person, our actions should never give someone an excuse to think poorly of a ministry, or worse yet, to reject Christ altogether. Instead, our actions should be impacting the world and pointing to Him in a positive light. Causing offense is one of the hardest things to recover from, even if the offense is unintentional. The closer we get to living a life like Jesus would have us live, the less we will cause offense and be offended. Taking daily actions of love like this devotional challenges us to do, is a way to help us live a life so if anyone talks about us, no one believes it. May we commit to individually growing closer to living a life of love like Jesus lived.

Today's Challenge To Dig Deeper:
We all have messed up at one point or another. Whether we've gossiped, gotten angry, or been offended ourselves and held bitterness against someone, all of these types of actions in our heart can cause a negative ripple effect. Repent for your part in these behaviors, and ask God what needs to be done to bring healing.

Evening Reflection:
Write down the actions God asked you to do to begin healing of any offense you have caused. Write out what happened. Let God know how thankful you are for giving you the strength to carry out the action. Now, carry on with more of Jesus' love.

REST STOPS
February 10

Morning Rinse: 2 Corinthians 7-9
Featured Verse: 2 Corinthians 9:8 *And God is able to make all grace abound to you, so that always having all sufficiency in everything, you may have an abundance for every good deed.*

You may be looking at this verse and asking yourself, how does this verse have anything to do with a rest stop? Before I go into it, let us look at the word *grace*. The grace God gives us is help, power, and favor to do what He asks us to do. We receive this grace, not because we deserve it, but because He freely gives it. But we must want it. I love today's Featured Verse because it illustrates the fact that we cannot out-give God. His grace for us is overflowing, and He is able to make that grace pour out on us so we have ALL we need to perform EVERY good deed. This includes our need for emotional grace for others and ourselves, financial grace, energy grace, and ALL grace in EVERY good deed we do... AND every good deed that we want to do in the future. How does this relate to a rest stop? Well, what if you encounter a need, and God has given you the grace, or abundance, to be the answer to meet that need, but you take a rest from doing good deeds. What if you decide on your own accord that the next person in your row at church should meet the need, instead of you tapping into your abundance to meet the need? Or, what if you decide that even though you have been called to pray for people, or have a word of encouragement for someone, you decide to keep your mouth closed? These are perfect examples of taking a rest stop. If God has given us an abundance of grace to do good deeds, imagine what the world would be like if we used that grace to perform good deeds in abundance. What if we became so ministry-minded that we consistently looked for ways to help others? I understand Jesus rested and took breaks to recoup and be alone. But it was after He ministered. Even on vacations with family, and during our play time, we can still perform good deeds.

Today's Challenge To Dig Deeper:
Look today for a way to do a good deed. Search outside the box. While the normal things like paying for the person's coffee behind you in the Starbucks line may be great, look for new ways to do a good deed. Have spirit eyes today. Don't take a rest from doing good deeds today. If you look for a need, you might just be surprised at other needs that pop up that you never noticed before.

Evening Reflection:
Write down the good deed you did today. Write down how it made you feel to answer God's still, small voice when He showed you the need. Now, purpose in your mind to stay open to His voice every day, to do that good deed He has given you the grace to do.

HEAVEN
February 11

Morning Rinse: 2 Corinthians 10-13
Featured Verse: 2 Corinthians 12:4 ... *was caught up into Paradise and heard inexpressible words, which a man is not permitted to speak.*

One of the most fulfilling moments of my wedding day, besides turning around and being introduced as Mr. and Mrs. Nathan Cordell, was witnessing my big idea come to life. This idea was to have an actual theme for our ceremony where everything we did had one central focus. Our theme was *Heaven*. Our desire was to give a picture, or tell a story, to remind those in attendance of who we all are, the bride of Christ. So with the help of some amazing friends, we transformed the church sanctuary into a representation of heaven and our Savior, Jesus Christ. We began by digging through the church's storage rooms for props that were used from past church plays. First, we used a life-size model of the Ark of the Covenant, putting that in center stage to stand in front of. Behind the ark, we hung a floor-to-ceiling representation of the veil of the temple, with two angels painted on this massive piece of material. We also placed two trees of life, one on each side of the ark, full of hanging fruit. The flowers we used for décor were flowers mentioned in the Bible, such as lilies and roses, and we printed the ceremony program on scroll-like paper, rolled them up, and tied them with a gold cord. I also researched the gemstones in the foundation of heaven found in Revelation 19:19-20. I selected five of these colors and used them as colors in our ceremony by first having each of our five attendants wear one of the colors. And then I had a seamstress glue little gems of the five colors all throughout my wedding dress and headpiece. During the ceremony, Nathan washed my feet, showing a picture of Jesus as a servant. (Read the devotion on June 28th for more insight into this part of our ceremony.) Despite our wedding being in 1999, I still receive comments from people reminiscing about it. And even though it was a grandeur ceremony, and I must admit, we went above and beyond what most would choose to do, it still was not as amazing as what Paul saw in his vision of paradise. Why was Paul not able to share what he saw? Some believe he was not morally able, due to customs of that time. Others believe he was not actually able to describe it with words that would give the description justice. Regardless of why he could not share, we know heaven will be a place of wonder as we enter those pearly gates.

Today's Challenge To Dig Deeper:
Is there anyone you know who needs to hear about heaven? Spend today looking for an opportunity to ask someone if they know Jesus as their personal Savior.

Evening Reflection:
Who did you ask about their commitment to Jesus? How did the conversation go?

PRAYER OVER PANIC

February 12

Morning Rinse: Daniel 1-3
Featured Verses: Daniel 2:17-18 *Then Daniel went to his house and informed his friends, Hananiah, Mishael and Azariah about the matter, so that they might request compassion from the God of heaven concerning this mystery, so that Daniel and his friends would not be destroyed with the rest of the wise men of Babylon.*

Have you ever been in a life-threatening situation, or an emergency that could cause panic to the natural eye? Daniel was in this type of scenario. King Nebuchadnezzar had a very troubling dream, so he called in the magicians, Chaldeans, and sorcerers for an interpretation. The kicker was he refused to tell them the dream, but instead commanded those he called in to not only tell the interpretation, but also state the dream. To add to this pressure, he declared that if they were incorrect, they would be killed. When he received criticism from the Chaldeans, the king became furious and gave an order to destroy all the wise men of Babylon. Daniel courageously asked the king for some time before the decree was enforced. When the king granted his request, Daniel went to inform his friends what was going on. I wonder how fast Daniel made it to his house to tell them. Did he run? Was he panicked? Or was he calm and collected, and full of faith? I must admit, I would not be calm and collected knowing that death lurked at my heels for both myself, my friends, and many people around me. It is apparent that these friends were his accountability partners. They did life together, including praying for each other. These men mentioned are Shadrach, Meshach and Abednego, the same men mentioned in today's Featured Verses. In Daniel 1:7, the king changed their names, and they are also the same friends that later get thrown into the fiery furnace together. These men faced death multiple times together and were close friends and prayer partners. To the naked eye, life-threatening situations can destroy us. Logically, it does not make sense to remain calm. However, having prayer partners will help us stay focused on God, help elevate our faith, and keep us calm. I doubt that any of these men were overly thrilled about facing death. But I am sure, since they had been in prayer with each other, the panic did not override their faith.

Today's Challenge To Dig Deeper:
It is so important to have friends who will walk through life challenges with us. Ask God who He wants your prayer partners to be. Prayerfully consider having at least 3. Once the Lord reveals who they are, call them and ask them if they will accept this position.

Evening Reflection:
Write down who your accountability and prayer partners are.

BEING EXTRAORDINARY
February 13

Morning Rinse: Daniel 4-6
Featured Verses: Daniel 5:14, 6:3 *Now I have heard about you that a spirit of the gods is in you, and that illumination, insight and extraordinary wisdom have been found in you... Then this Daniel began distinguishing himself among the commissioners and satraps because he possessed an extraordinary spirit, and the king planned to appoint him over the entire kingdom.*

The Merriam-Webster Online Dictionary defines extraordinary as '*going beyond what is usual, regular or customary.*'[5] When I hear this word, it immediately sets the expectation for someone to be amazing, remarkable, or exceptional in what they do or what they stand for. I believe we all fit this description with those in our inner circle and sphere of influence because we are close to those of commonality. But Daniel was known for his extraordinary wisdom and spirit across an entire kingdom. However, having a reputation for being extraordinary does not mean we will find favor among all men. Daniel still had opposition from those who did not like his decisions and what he stood for. In fact, they tried to find fault in him, but could not. Having opposition can often cause the spotlight to become brighter on our extraordinary characteristics. Daniel's life had a spotlight on it when he faced the lion's den. We can be extraordinary with any belief system of life. But as Christ followers, are we extraordinary in our walk of faith like Daniel was? Many Christ followers fall short in living out an extraordinary, influential life. Why? Fear of man is one reason. We can also let our passion for faith get squelched, especially when the spotlight gets brighter, or the opposition gets louder. Daniel understood this scenario. But he did not sway in being extraordinary when facing the lion's den, or when his friends were put into the fiery furnace. And he did not remain silent when he stood before a king to interpret dreams or writings on a wall. He stayed steadfast, keeping his faith and reputation intact. He let the 'extraordinary' shine, especially during the hard times he faced. How do we become extraordinary? It is living a life with passion in our faith during even the little, daily decisions. It is also taking a stand when others will not, and living a life so no one can find fault in our actions.

Today's Challenge To Dig Deeper:
Will you accept the commission to let your extraordinary characteristics shine? Expect the little, daily challenges that come up in your life. Watch for them. When they come, choose to be extraordinary.

Evening Reflection:
Write down the opportunities that came your way today to be extraordinary. Write how you responded and the growth that you experienced.

---

[5] https://www.merriam-webster.com/dictionary/extraordinary

HEAVY LIFTING
February 14

Morning Rinse: Daniel 7-9
Featured Verse: Daniel 8:27 *Then I, Daniel, was exhausted and sick for days. Then I got up again and carried on the king's business, but I was astounded at the vision, and there was none to explain it.*

Today's Morning Rinse consists of one of Daniel's personal visions. Not only has his anointing to interpret visions been a topic of sermons and teachings amongst pastors and commentators for centuries, but so have his own personal visions. The vision from today's reading was so deep and detailed, the angel Gabriel himself came and appeared to Daniel to explain it (Daniel 8:16-17). I wonder how Daniel felt in this moment. He was the head over the magicians and satraps. He was the 'master interpreter' across the land, and was often called upon to give insight into the dreams of those in high authority, including being the one called upon to interpret the writing on the wall. But this dream was different. It was a dream that foretold the destruction of the land and his people. It was a heavy message to bear, and Daniel was overcome and prostrate at the impact it had on him. God had allowed him to see into the future of what was to come, and it was shocking and upsetting, affecting him to the point of physical illness. It is not known how long he was sick from what God showed him, but commentators believe it was for a considerable period. I wonder what emotions he felt. Could it have included grief, confusion, and concern? Of course, probably also a passion to pray. As he lay sick, still not entirely confident of its entire meaning, I wonder if he pondered whether he could change the outcome. Some prophecies and words from the Lord are encouraging. Others are grave warnings, with the chance for those on the receiving end to change their ways. Was there anything he could do? God used Daniel to deliver or carry multiple heavy messages. He trusted him. God also may need us to carry heavy information at times. And just like Daniel had to get up and go about the 'king's business,' there may be times we will have to go about our day-to-day activities as well. These are moments of heavy lifting. But God trusts us with the weights, even if we think they are too heavy and could cause physical ailment. And remember, God is with us, helping us carry the heavy weights.

Today's Challenge To Dig Deeper:
Are you or a loved one carrying the weight of heavy information or insight from the Lord regarding a serious matter? Know that God trusts you or your friend with what He has revealed. Ask Him to help you know what to do with it, and how to have the strength to go about your day-to-day life activities. He is your Valentine and will not leave you.

Evening Reflection:
Write down how the Lord is helping you with the information He has revealed to you or your loved one.

PURGED, PURIFIED, REFINED
February 15

Morning Rinse: Daniel 10-12
Featured Verse: Daniel 12:10 *Many will be purged, purified and refined, but the wicked will act wickedly; and none of the wicked will understand, but those who have insight will understand.*

The book of Daniel ends with a string of visions that Daniel had. Some of these visions were in the last two devotions, with the rest being in today's. Not only have these dreams been analyzed and studied for years, but Bible scholars have created college courses and curriculum around the books of Daniel and Revelation to help us understand some of the meanings more clearly. What makes Daniel's dreams so hard to understand is, the descriptions and symbols he shared are not images we are used to seeing or hearing. But God used Daniel to describe His plan for the world, all the way to the end of the age. While there is destruction in what is to come, we know who wins. God does. And that means we win, too! It may be easy to get overwhelmed and confused at some of the descriptions Daniel wrote about, but God does not require us to have every detail understood with perfection. What He asks of us is to keep trying to understand, keep steady in our walk, and remain faithful to the end no matter what we go through. Commit to God's purging, purifying, and refining, especially when going through trials, just like Daniel did. This process does not always feel good, but we know God works out our faith, if we let Him use these times. We, as Christ followers, understand these times. And if we surrender to the Holy Spirit during these seasons, people will be encouraged through our growth and refining. Just like salt is refined and brings out the flavor of food, we bring out Christ for others to see, when we are refined.

Today's Challenge To Dig Deeper:
Are you going through a refining season right now? How are you responding? Ask God to help you pass the test. Commit to remaining faithful, knowing that trials test our faith. Stand firm and look to the prize. Remember, God wins in the end, and so do you.

Evening Reflection:
Write down your refinement process. What growth did you have today? Did you pass the test on your way to being totally refined?

ON YOUR MARK, GET SET, GO!
February 16

Morning Rinse: Deuteronomy 1-3
Featured Verses: Deuteronomy 1:7a, 11 *Turn and set your journey and go... May the Lord, the God of your fathers, increase you a thousand-fold more than you are and bless you, just as He has promised you!*

The book of Deuteronomy begins at the conclusion of the Israelite's forty-year journey in the wilderness, right before they entered the Promised Land. Moses gave them a motivational speech that spurred them to make the final lap, and cross the finish line into this land. In this speech, Moses speaks over them a thousand-fold increase coupled with God's blessing. The people had been camped on the mountain, on the brink of being participants of one of the most exciting stories in the Old Testament, the Jericho walls crashing down. Before this event could happen, though, they had to get positioned for the final lap, and their increase. Moses instructs them to get on their mark, get set, and GO! They had to get focused. They had to prepare to get out of their comfort zone, get off the mountain, redefine their position, and see the end mark. God gives us purposes, missions, and direction, and He is ready to bless us abundantly for obeying. But we must get off the mountain. As Moses was encouraging the people for what lay ahead, he told them of God's promise. They had to choose to follow God's leading and obey Him. God desires to increase us too, but we have a part to play in the increase. During Moses' speech to the people, he shared five golden nuggets that helped position them for the Promised Land. We, too, can adopt these nuggets as we position ourselves for a thousand-fold increase.

1. Choose wise and discerning friends (Deuteronomy 1:13).
2. Do not fear, but go up and possess (Deuteronomy 1:20-21, 30).
3. Create a plan with wise counsel (Deuteronomy 1:22).
4. Do not focus on the negative parts of the journey (Deuteronomy 1:27).
5. Remember attitude is everything (Deuteronomy 1:34-36).

If we want God's best for our lives, we must not allow our attitudes to thwart our blessings. Instead, may we get on our marks, get set for our thousand-fold blessing, and go towards our promised land, letting God lead us every step of the way. On your mark, get set, go!

Today's Challenge To Dig Deeper:
Review the five nuggets and ask God to reveal if any of the steps need to be adjusted in your life. Pray for God to help you position yourself for the promises and blessings He has for you.

Evening Reflection:
Write down what God showed you and any adjustments you made in your heart today. Is there anything you will do differently to position yourself for your promised land?

KEEP OUR END OF THE BARGAIN
February 17

Morning Rinse: Deuteronomy 4-7
Featured Verse: Deuteronomy 7:12 *Then it shall come about, because you listen to these judgements and keep and do them, that the Lord your God will keep with you His covenant and His lovingkindness which He swore to your forefathers.*

Today's Morning Rinse is full of warnings about when someone chooses to not obey God. Granted, some of the rules we read must be taken into context, based on the culture and timeframe when these passages were written. But regardless of timing and culture, God still has one standard for everyone. That standard is to love and obey Him, and to love others. I grew up in a strict household, and there were times I did not like the rules my parents set in place. Admittedly, there were times when I misunderstood the rules. But for the most part, I complied, understanding the context of why my parents set the standard they did. In our personal journey of faith, we can often clearly see the big picture. But speaking from experience, there are also times our flesh ignores God's viewpoint. Regardless of our personal desires or our depth of understanding God's standards for our lives, our obedience is in direct relation with our responses to them. The responses to His laws listed in today's chapters really boil down to loving Him with our whole heart and soul. He loves us, and He is a jealous God who is very serious about how we display that love to others. When we look at the rules and commandments in these chapters, it can be easy to focus on the seemingly bigger sins like murder, lying, and stealing. But what about the ones that are not so offensive, or what we view as 'little' sins? Ones like secretly coveting (5:21), or keeping ungodly things in our home (7:26). We cannot expect God to continuously be the God of blessings, if we do not obey Him. I am reminded of what my husband tells our kids. Every decision, whether good or bad, has a consequence. We choose the type of consequence we receive. We cannot expect God to hand us a silver platter with all the 'goods' in life when we refuse to surrender our whole heart to Him.

Today's Challenge To Dig Deeper:
Are there any areas you are not totally surrendering to God? Search deep. Surrender and pray during the day today, that God would strengthen you in these areas. You are an overcomer. Speak death over any sin, even the small ones.

Evening Reflection:
Write down the changes you made today to start anew, to rinse your soul, to redefine your walk and to 'keep your end of the bargain.'

WE HAVE WHAT IT TAKES
February 18

Morning Rinse: Deuteronomy 8-11
Featured Verses: Deuteronomy 8:16-18 *In the wilderness He fed you manna which your fathers did not know, that He might humble you and that He might test you, to do good for you in the end. Otherwise, you may say in your heart, "My power and the strength of my hand made me this wealth." But you shall remember the Lord your God, for it is He who is giving you power to make wealth, that He may confirm His covenant which He swore to your fathers, as it is this day.*

In the devotion from two days ago titled *On Your Mark, Get Set, Go!,* we read the beginning of a speech from Moses to the Israelites. In this speech, Moses blessed them and spoke over them a thousand-fold increase. In today's Morning Rinse, Moses is still speaking, and he circles back around to the subject of this increase. He reminded them it would come. But He warned them to not take credit for it when it begins to flow. This same warning applies to us. If we let our flesh take over when increase comes in our lives, pride will begin to take root in our hearts. When this happens, it is easy to take credit for the knowledge and skillset that has brought our increase and blessings. Moses warned the people of this danger, and reminded them that it is God who gives the power to make wealth. Humility is a subject throughout the Bible, and is a 'kingdom key' for increase. It not only unlocks what God has given us, but positions us to continue managing what He gives us, so we will be trusted for even greater growth. God has given us an extreme amount of potential, with endless capabilities. If we would all truly tap into this potential while remaining humble, we would be power packed offerings to the world, creating not just an increase in our own personal lives, but contributing to the increase in the lives of those around us. God has given us what we need to create wealth. May we remember where it comes from, and stay humble as we go out and create it. God's mission for our lives is not about us. It is about what He wants done through us for His kingdom! Let us not take the glory for this increase, but go claim the promised land inside our hearts.

Today's Challenge To Dig Deeper:
What purpose is birthing inside your heart that will create increase and wealth for you and your loved ones? God has given you the solutions to accomplish it. Write a list today of what you need to do to begin the journey towards this increase and blessings. You have what it takes. Now go do it!

Evening Reflection:
Write down what God spoke to you today regarding the gifts He has given you to create wealth and increase.

BLESSING WITH OUR BLESSINGS!
February 19

Morning Rinse: Deuteronomy 12-15
Featured Verses: Deuteronomy 15:10-11 *You shall generously give to him, and your heart shall not be grieved when you give to him, because for this thing the Lord your God will bless you in all your work and in all your undertakings. For the poor will never cease to be in the land; therefore I command you, saying, "You shall freely open your hand to your brother, to your needy and poor in your land."*

I love all the chapters in the book of Deuteronomy that lead up to the Israelites taking over the Promised Land. These chapters are full of instructions from Moses as he prepares them for the life ahead. While the people heard his teachings of faith and trust in the wilderness for forty years, and while they received the Ten Commandments and were corrected on many behaviors, Moses' sermon on the mountain, before the actual takeover, was a crescendo. Can you imagine the stirring in their hearts as Moses delivered these key messages to them? His words prepared them for the final positioning to claim the Promised Land. You can almost feel the anticipation leap off of the pages of the Bible. Along with the reminders to not fear, to behave with godly conduct, and to remember that God will do the fighting as they go forward, they are commanded to help the poor with their increase. They were already told that the blessing available to them, and to us, is a thousand-fold increase. (See February 16.) But God wanted to reiterate that He does not give an increase for selfish gain. Do not get me wrong. God loves to bless His children, and He enjoys us having nice things. But we are also expected to give freely to those in need. In this sermon, Moses states a commandment saying for us to use some of our blessings to help the poor and needy. God gives us more than we ask for or even think about, and from what we receive, He expects us to be good stewards of the gift, including blessing the poor from our blessings.

Today's Challenge To Dig Deeper:
Think about all the blessings you have. Ask God if there are adjustments you need to make financially so those in need can be blessed from your blessings. These blessings, of course, are above and beyond your tithe.

Evening Reflection:
Write down the adjustments you made, in your plan to bless others from your increase. How do you feel about helping others? Did you bless someone today?

DO YOU KNOW WHAT HE WANTS?
February 20

Morning Rinse: Deuteronomy 16-19
Featured Verses: Deuteronomy 17:19-20 *It shall be with him and he shall read it all the days of his life, that he may learn to fear the Lord his God, by carefully observing all the words of this law and these statutes, that his heart may not be lifted up above his countrymen and that he may not turn aside from the commandment, to the right or the left, so that he and his sons may continue long in his kingdom in the midst of Israel.*

Have you ever read a history book and wondered how it can apply to your life today? Sometimes the Bible may appear like that history book, like a book with laws, or even scenarios, that are hard to relate to. Today's Morning Rinse, though, is not just about the laws set in place when a king was to be chosen, nor is it just a list of dos and don'ts for the Israelites. If you reread today's Featured Verses, you will notice that they focus on the foundation of our entire faith walk. Just like the king in this passage needed to be a man abiding by God's laws, we too need to abide by God's laws and commandments set throughout scripture. The king was told to 'read it all the days of his life.' It is simple. We need to be reading The Word and applying God's truth and standards every day, as we live it out. Just like the Israelites had a culture with laws to please God, we should too. How are we to continue our faith walk, if we do not view The Word as living and breathing, relevant for our lives today? How are we to expect to grow in our love for God, if we do not commit to getting to know Him, and how are we to know what God wants for our lives, if we do not open His manual and study it? With technology so easily accessible, finding a way to absorb The Word is not as hard as we want to believe. Commit to being sharpened every day by God's Word, just like this king in the Old Testament.

Today's Challenge To Dig Deeper:
If you are reading this devotional, you are probably already well underway in the habit of reading the Bible through. However, if you got off track, start again. Find a time in the morning that is just for you and God, and commit to get to know Him. Then search for ways to obey Him in your walk today.

Evening Reflection:
Write down a commitment to God today, that all the days of your life, you will be a lover of His Word, including obeying what you read.

WHY WERE THERE SO MANY LAWS?
February 21

Morning Rinse: Deuteronomy 20-23
Featured Verse: Deuteronomy 22:5 *A woman shall not wear man's clothing, or shall a man put on a woman's clothing; for whoever does these things is an abomination to the Lord your God.*

WHAT? Did you respond the way I did when reading our Morning Rinse and all the laws listed throughout these chapters? I thought to myself, "Why were there so many rules for the Israelites, what did they all mean, and how do they relate to me?" I also wondered if we take these laws literally. I chose today's Featured Verse as one example of many in these chapters, because it is one that hits home. I grew up with a dad who, for a season in his life, believed that this verse was literal, and no lady should wear pants. It is part of my story, as well as part of his. I do not belittle him, but merely am sharing a part of where our family came from regarding some of these Old Testament scriptures. When reading the Bible, we must always remember there is context before the pretext, meaning we must know the context of what is written to fully understand the application for our lives today. I singled out today's Featured Verse as an example to encourage you to look for the reason, or the 'why' behind the laws of that time. My father does not have a problem with women wearing pants anymore. When we are trying to understand scripture, reading thoughts and commentaries helps, and there are multiple around this verse. Some believe it has to do with cross-dressing. Others believe it is about men wanting to become women, and women wanting to become men. The process of truly studying context is part of the journey of understanding scripture. God's laws, or principles to live by, are not just about the dos and don'ts, restrictions, and things we cannot do. If you look deeply, it is about basic things to help us live an easier life, if we follow those principles.

Today's Challenge To Dig Deeper:
While you were reading today's Morning Rinse, was there a 'law' or rule that stuck out to you as odd or out of the ordinary? Do a little research on the customs of that time, probing deeper into the 'why' of the law or rule. You may be surprised at what you find.

Evening Reflection:
Write down your discovery about one of the 'laws' you researched. What did you learn? Did your perception change about anything?

TITHING OR GIVING? WHICH IS IT?
February 22

Morning Rinse: Deuteronomy 24-27
Featured Verses: Deuteronomy 26:10-12 *"Now behold, I have brought the first of the produce of the ground which You, O LORD have given me." And you shall set it down before the Lord your God, and worship before the Lord your God: and you and the Levite and the alien who is among you shall rejoice in all the good which the Lord your God has given you and your household. When you have finished paying all the tithe of your increase in the third year, the year of tithing, then you shall give it to the Levite, to the stranger, to the orphan and to the widow, that they may eat in your towns and be satisfied.*

There are two parts to giving back to God through our finances, tithing and offering. The question I often hear asked regarding this subject is, "Should I tithe, or should I give?" The answer is simply "Yes." First, we are to tithe the first fruits of our increase to the church we attend, or wherever God has you tithing. When my husband and I were engaged, we made a promise to each other that we would always tithe. We believe it is nonnegotiable and is ten percent of our gross income. I have heard others state it is fifteen, but typically, ten percent is the standard tithe, and what most believe to be true. Whatever amount you believe that percentage is, be faithful no matter what you are going through. It is God's money anyway, and should be returned to Him. You will notice in today's Featured Verse, the passage uses the word 'worship' for when you bring your tithe to God. We worship by having an attitude of praise and thanksgiving as we obey through our faithfulness. When we tithe with the right heart, we will authentically rejoice with a heart of worship. Any amount above our tithe is an offering. There is no set amount in the Bible, unlike the tithe, but it is an amount between you and God to give as you see needs arise, and as your heart is stirred. There are multiple avenues to freely give an offering. Look around and watch for needs. Just remember, giving an offering is after giving your tithe. So yes, it is about tithing, and it is about giving.

Today's Challenge To Dig Deeper:
Make a commitment to God to begin tithing at least ten percent of your income. Start today by tithing to your church. You can write a check or go online to their website. Do not worry about back tithing. Just begin today with your commitment. Next, ask God to begin showing you community needs that you can give an offering to. Commit to saving a little back each paycheck, so you are prepared to give when you see the needs around you.

Evening Reflection:
Write down what God did today in your heart regarding tithing and giving.

CHOOSE OBEDIENCE. CHOOSE LIFE.
FEBRUARY 23

Morning Rinse: Deuteronomy 28-31
Featured Verses: Deuteronomy 28:1-2 *Now it shall be, if you diligently obey the Lord your God, being careful to do all His commandments which I command you today, the Lord your God will set you high above all the nations of the earth. All these blessings will come upon you and overtake you, if you obey the Lord your God.*

When I was writing this devotional and came to today's Morning Rinse, I was worried that no one would read all four chapters. Admittedly, I even thought to myself, "This is going to be a long day of reading." But once I opened the pages of my Bible, my heart was stirred. It was even difficult for me to pick the Featured Verses, because these four chapters are so rich. Throughout these chapters, Moses encourages the Israelites to live a life of obedience to God, so they would have a blessed life. We, too, can apply these challenges, so we can experience God's blessings and an abundant life. But it is a choice. How do we choose this? By loving God, by obeying His voice, and by keeping His commandments and standards close to our heart. I love today's chapters because it gives a picture of what God will do for us when we are obedient to His voice. He is willing and ready to shower us with blessings that overtake us when we obey. But just like obedience is a path of choice, there is always another path we can choose, and that is the path of disobedience. Disobedience can creep into our heart at any time in our lives, even after we have been obedient and receive a blessing. We see this occur when the Israelites became prideful after God prospered them. Even after all God did for them, they turned to other gods and began serving them instead of Him. Therefore, it is so important to stay in The Word and continually allow God to work on our hearts, so we remain humble and obedient, before, during, and after the blessings come our way. Let us choose a blessed life until the very end.

Today's Challenge To Dig Deeper:
Has God been nudging you about obeying His voice in a certain matter? Is there something in your heart that needs to be corrected or changed? Maybe you are to start serving in your church, or maybe there is still some hesitancy about tithing you need to let go of and trust Him with. Listen to His voice, and choose to obey. Repent for your disobedience, and ask God to help you. Make the choice to choose a blessed life through obedience.

Evening Reflection:
Write down what God spoke to you about today and how you responded.

CONSEQUENCES TO DISOBEDIENCE
FEBRUARY 24

Morning Rinse: Deuteronomy 32-34
Featured Verse: Deuteronomy 34:4 *Then the Lord said to him, "This is the land which I swore to Abraham, Isaac, and Jacob, saying, 'I will give it to your descendants,' I have let you see it with your eyes, but you shall not go over there."*

We can forget, at times, that God is a just God. Oh yes, He is fair and merciful. But there are times when He is a judge. According to the Bible, Moses was a prophet of faith, one that the Lord knew face to face. He was clearly a man that could be trusted and a leader of lifelong, steady obedience to God's calling. But we also know he was not perfect, and therefore, received a consequence for his actions. God had told Moses to SPEAK to a rock, and water would come forth. Instead, Moses got angry at the Israelites, calling them rebels. Then instead of speaking to the rock as instructed, he struck it. He must have been very angry because he did not strike it just once, but two times, and even insinuated credit for this miracle (Numbers 22:10). Maybe Moses had an anger issue and God had given him multiple warnings to control it. I do not know. But we do know that Moses received a large consequence. His consequence was only getting to see the Promised Land from afar, instead of entering it with the Israelites. His call to lead the Israelites to this chosen land was over with that act of disobedience. My guess is the Israelites knew he disobeyed, and therefore, God had to show the people an example of a consequence, even for a leader. But God is still merciful. He still cared for the people and gave them water despite what Moses did, and then He still called Moses a friend. Also, in my opinion, one of the most amazing things in this story is that despite Moses receiving what could have been the most devastating consequence of his life, it is not recorded that he had any bitterness towards God. He accepted the consequences and owned his error.

Today's Challenge To Dig Deeper:
Ask God if you are bitter towards Him for a consequence you have received from something you have done. Repent and then own your disobedience, and own the consequence. Use it to help others grow in their faith. Be humble and share your story with at least 1 person.

Evening Reflection:
Write down what God spoke to you about today. Who did you share it with, and how does it feel to release anger towards God and own your behavior? Was it difficult? Was it freeing?

A WISE MAN WITH FUTILE ACTIONS?
February 25

Morning Rinse: Ecclesiastes 1-2
Featured Verse: Ecclesiastes 2:11 *Thus I considered all my activities which my hands had done and the labor which I had exerted; and behold all was vanity and striving after wind, and there was no profit under the sun.*

Solomon became the wisest man in the world during his time. Many kings and leaders even came to study under him. I think the natural, default perception of Solomon is that he did everything with a godly, eternal purpose. It makes perfect sense to believe this since he had asked God for wisdom instead of riches, and then ended up with wealth known across the land and a kingdom worth seeing with one's own eyes. I must admit, when I see someone who has godly wisdom, whether from the Bible, or in modern times, it is easy for me to view them as someone who makes ALL their choices with an eternal purpose. But Solomon squelched my perception. By the time he wrote this book, he was reflecting on his life and realized that everything apart from God means nothing, including all his wise actions. This book is Solomon's last written message, and for the most part, is written with a negative tone as he recaps his life's choices. It is interesting that instead of writing about all his blessings and being joyful at all he had accomplished and obtained, he sadly admits that some of his actions were full of vanity and gained nothing for God's kingdom. He strongly wrote for us to stay focused on what GOD wants us to do in our lives, not what our flesh wants. He was not trying to squelch our hope for blessings and increase, but to beg us to focus our hope on the one who will give our life true meaning. He was also not against having wisdom, knowledge, riches, and pleasurable things. But he stressed the importance of seeking them in their proper place for our lives. After spending a lifetime making choices and decisions with the wisdom God gave him, his ending message was for all to realize that every action must be done with an eternal purpose.

Today's Challenge To Dig Deeper:
Wisdom and actions are futile without eternal purpose. Ask God to show you where you need to use your wisdom for eternal purposes. Make a different decision today if He asks.

Evening Reflection:
Write down what God spoke to you today. Can you use your knowledge differently in the future, with eternal purpose?

KITCHEN CHAOS
February 26

Morning Rinse: Ecclesiastes 3-5
Featured Verse: Ecclesiastes 5:1 *Guard your steps as you go to the house of God, and draw near to listen rather than to offer the sacrifice of fools; for they do not know they are doing evil.*

Am I the only one guilty of times when my heart and actions make me unprepared for worship? While worship should be a daily matter of the heart, I admit, I have multiple examples of having a bad attitude at church, causing me to not be able to hear the message as effectively and even behaving in ways I know not to behave. This can be caused by various reasons, and is no one's fault but my own selfishness. My first example pertains to my husband. One Sunday morning, I got upset at him for forgetting to fill up the gas tank the night before. We then had to stop and get gas on the way to church, making our family late. It was a small mistake and yet, I allowed my heart to remain bitter, and showed up to church angry, blocking what God had for me that day. Another example was when my daughter forgot to pick out her church clothes. Admittedly, my morning went from peacefully getting ready for service, to an immediate shift of panic a few minutes before heading out the door. I once again allowed strife to enter my heart towards a loved one, and the rest of the morning was handled inappropriately, including my attitude at church. And finally, I have instances when getting frustrated at myself has caused an issue in my heart. One example was when I forgot to plan out our Sunday morning breakfast. Talk about kitchen chaos! Even though I had inward strife at myself, I portrayed an outward irritation towards my family, which continued throughout the worship service. There are many reasons we may not arrive at church with a pure heart. If carrying strife is not an issue for you, what about the opposite? We may be one who habitually arrives at church with a prepared heart. But if we are not careful, pride can set in BECAUSE we know we are ready. Being puffed up is never right. God speaks very strongly about guarding our heart against sin, especially when we enter the house of God. We, as Christ followers, have the Bible as a gauge to measure against. The unsaved do not use this same gauge. We all fall short. Which is why we all need to make a habit of checking our hearts when preparing for worship.

Today's Challenge To Dig Deeper:
Commit to a daily heart check, especially when attending worship services. Repent of any bad attitudes, and ask God to help you guard your heart against these behaviors.

Evening Reflection:
Write down what God spoke to you today. Commit to continually checking your heart, especially before attending church.

HE MADE THE DAY!
February 27

Morning Rinse: Ecclesiastes 6-8
Featured Verse: Ecclesiastes 7:14 *In the day of prosperity be happy. But in the day of adversity consider – God has made the one as well as the other so that man will not discover anything that will be after him.*

The Merriam-Webster Dictionary describes adversity as misfortune, tragedy, and difficulty.[6] Other words that come to mind are sorrow, heartbreak, and even distress. I am convinced that we can all relate to at least one of these words. Sometimes our adversity may last for just a fleeting moment, like getting past the few hours of panic over a child's broken bone. Other times, the 'day of adversity' may cause months, or even years of difficulty and heartbreak. It is certainly easy to recognize and praise God when our bank account has a few extra dollars in it, or when we feel like blessings are overtaking us. It is also easy to praise God when a friend is healed of a disease, or a wayward child returns home. These examples certainly give way for joy and celebration. But do we respond the same way when adversity turns our world upside down? Why do we praise God on the prosperous days, but on the adverse days, we are tempted to blame Him for allowing the trouble? Today's Featured Verse states that no matter what happens, God made the day. He knew it was coming. Yes, He gives each of us a choice with our behaviors. Whether we make good choices or bad ones, they will affect the lives of those around us. It is the same with the choices of others. They can and do affect our lives at times as well. We must remember God told us in His Word we would have adverse days. Why do we have them? I do not have all the answers, but I do know that if we keep our eyes focused on Him, He will see us through. Look for Him in the middle of it all.

Today's Challenge To Dig Deeper:
Are you, or is someone you know, amid some bad news? Ask God to help you stay focused on Him and to see Him in the middle of the hard day. Also, stay sensitive to others around you, to help them have a God perspective amid their adverse day.

Evening Reflection:
Write down about the adverse day you or your loved one is in the midst of. How did God reveal Himself in the middle of the trouble?

---

6 https://www.merriam-webster.com/dictionary/adversity

NO ONE IS EXEMPT
February 28

Morning Rinse: Ecclesiastes 9-12
Featured Verses: Ecclesiastes 12:13-14 *The conclusion, when all has been heard, is: fear God and keep His commandments, because this applies to every person. For God will bring every act to judgement, everything which is hidden, whether is it good or evil.*

The book of Ecclesiastes, while short, is full of instructions from Solomon. He writes about money, wisdom, obedience to God, death, possessions, work, and much more. When reading the Bible, especially books like this one, it can easily be viewed as not applicable to the younger generation. But Solomon has a whole chapter just speaking directly to youth, encouraging them to remember God even as they grow up. No matter what portion of this book speaks to you, or what portions seem confusing, we cannot skip over the last two verses. No matter what we are going through, and what we are seeking to understand in our lives, we must work towards living for God and seeking His will for our lives. Yes, we need to enjoy life to its fullest, but we must be obedient while we are having fun. As we live our lives, remember that our choices are being watched, even those choices we make when we are alone. Therefore, Solomon instructs us that no matter our age, to fear God and keep His commandments. There will always be those around us who will not heed the commandments of the Bible. There will always be someone disobeying authority. But do not let that sway you from how you act. When we stand before God, we will stand alone giving an account for all our actions, whether good or evil. If we fear God, meaning have full respect for Him, this will help guide our choices out of love for Him. Our love for Him will lead us to make better choices in our lives.

Today's Challenge To Dig Deeper:
Ask God to help you fear Him more deeply, and live more obediently, even when no one is around. Have you been living in 'grey' areas regarding His commandments, making justifications for what you are doing so it is okay? If God has been nudging you to change something, ask Him to help you.

Evening Reflection:
Write down what God spoke to you about today.

March Rinsing

VISION BOARDS AND GOD-SIZED DREAMS
March 1

Morning Rinse: Ephesians 1-3
Featured Verse: Ephesians 3:20 *Now to Him who is able to do far more abundantly beyond all that we ask or think, according to the power that works within us.*

'By any stretch of the imagination' is a popular saying, but holds a little bit of sarcasm to it. It basically gives reference to a near impossible task. I speculate that we have all heard it and probably even have used it ourselves in a sentence or two. But when I read today's Featured Verse, I must wonder if it goes against this scripture. It certainly makes me think it does. I mean, one might say something like, "By no stretch of the imagination, will they raise the needed funds." Or "Their kids are not obedient by any stretch of the imagination." Having an imagination, though, is very scriptural. It is what comes from the creative side of our brain, and is where our ideas, dreams and aspirations are birthed from. I believe God puts ideas into our hearts that coincide with His plan for our lives. He wants us to use our imagination and think beyond what we can see in the natural. This is where our faith comes into play, and where He likes to work. He absolutely can provide the needed funds for something, or bring a wayward child back to obedience. These are God-sized dreams. The things that seem near impossible or too big to be true. I like to make a vision board each October or November. It is a simple thing to create, and anyone can do it. I gather various pictures cut from magazines or printed from the internet. Then I post them to a cork board or poster. Each picture represents something I want to accomplish, or a goal I have. I believe God also has a vision board, and the pictures on His include all of us as well as the things He would like to see accomplished for His kingdom through us. Today's Featured Verse reminds me that God is a dreamer, and we are created to be like Him, using the power in us to fulfill what is inside our hearts. God can accomplish more through us than we could ever think or imagine on our own. We just need to activate the power in us with faith, and ask for the big things. I believe the things in our hearts are a small picture of God's vision board for each of us. If we can imagine it, it is possible. And God can even do more than what we are thinking. We just need to choose to use our God-given power, dream about it, and then act on what is in our hearts.

Today's Challenge To Dig Deeper:
Memorize today's Featured Verse, and then write your God-sized dreams. Buy a poster board or cork board. Print a picture representing each of the items on your list and attach them to your board. Ask God to give you steps to start making them come to fruition.

Evening Reflection:
Write about the pictures you used and the first few tasks you feel God is prompting you to do. Did you begin any of those tasks yet?

THE WARRIOR WITHIN
March 2

Morning Rinse: Ephesians 4-6
Featured Verse: Ephesians 6:11 *Put on the full armor of God, so that you will be able to stand firm against the schemes of the devil.*

I once did a photo shoot with multiple outfits to portray various characters. I went from the standard roles like a soccer mom and a business owner, to a few fun characters. One of those characters was a warrior. I remember putting on the outfit, picking up the shield and bow, and feeling taller and stronger just by wearing the clothes I had on. Paul understood this when he wrote to the Ephesian church, encouraging them to put on the full Armor of God. When we put on this armor, we not only feel stronger and more powerful against the enemy of our soul, but we are stronger and more powerful. Even as a child in Children's Church, we hear how putting on the Armor of God is one of the most important things we can do to fight off the enemy's schemes.

1. When we put on the Belt of Truth, we are telling the enemy that we will not listen to his lies that contradict who we are in Christ.
2. When we put on the Breastplate of Righteousness, we are protecting our heart, showing the enemy that we are righteous through Christ. This piece of armor shuts down his accusations about our past.
3. When we put on the Footwear of Peace, we are choosing to trust God and allow the Holy Spirit to lead us in the peace that passes all understanding, no matter what comes our way.
4. When we pick up the Shield of Faith, we thwart the arrows of doubt the enemy shoots at us, and instead stand on The Word.
5. When we put on the Helmet of Salvation, we are protecting our mind from the lies of the enemy, trying to convince us we are not a child of God when we make a mistake.
6. When we pick up the Sword of the Spirit, we are using God's Word to get the enemy behind us.

Putting on the armor is a choice each day, and reflects the spiritual warrior within each of us as a child of God. The armor is an outward manifestation of the inward warrior through His strength and power.

Today's Challenge To Dig Deeper:
Memorize the pieces of the armor and put them on. Ask God to show you any parts of the armor that you have laid down, or pieces that need sharpened.

Evening Reflection:
Write down areas of your life where you need more of God's power or strength to overcome a struggle you are having. What part of the Armor of God do you need to pick back up?

PREPARATION, POSITIONING AND OBEDIENCE
March 3

Morning Rinse: Esther 1-4
Featured Verse: Esther 2:12 *Now when the turn of each young lady came to go in to King Ahasuerus, after the end of her twelve months under the regulations for the women – for the days of their beautification were completed as follow: six months with oil of myrrh and six months with spices and the cosmetics for women.*

We often hear about Mordecai stating the popular words to Esther that she may have received royalty status for 'such a time as this.' While it is powerful to read how God set up the situation of her saving her people, it can be easy to forget the lifelong choices Esther made prior to her 'such a time as this.' Just as Esther prepared, we must also prepare for our personal purpose. Simply put, we prepare by allowing God to create in us a pure heart towards Him, which is the foundation of the positioning and the formula for obedience. Choosing to be obedient and devoted to authority on this earth, as well as to God, is a lifetime of internal work which Esther, in my opinion, had mastered. She was key to her destiny coming to life. Esther's parents had died, leaving her an orphan. Her father was Mordecai's uncle, making them cousins. When this tragedy occurred, Mordecai took her in as his own daughter, and Esther committed to submitting to him. She trusted and listened to him. This heart decision allowed God to position her for what lay ahead. In the positioning, she ultimately found favor with man, bringing yet another facet to her purpose. She not only had favor with Hegai, who oversaw all the maidens preparing themselves to meet the king, but she found favor with all who saw her, including the king when he crowned her queen. This story is such a beautiful example of preparing through obedience, so one can be positioned for purpose. Remember, as well, the preparation can take time. Even when Esther was positioned with the maidens to meet the king, there was yet more time needed in her preparation. Before each maiden even met the king for his consideration, it took a full year of daily dosages of oil and spices, as well as makeup applications. I am guilty of wanting what God has for me before I am ready, forgetting the work that it takes to be positioned for the purpose. God wants us to prepare our hearts for His positioning. He wants us to obey Him. Esther did exactly that, and ultimately saved a nation from death. It is about obeying in the preparation, being faithful in the positioning, and being obedient in the call.

Today's Challenge To Dig Deeper:
Are you willing to go through the preparation, allow yourself to be positioned, and then obey God and your godly authority? Ask God if you need to make changes in any of these 3 areas.

Evening Reflection:
Write down what God showed you regarding your preparation, positioning and obedience.

DON YOUR ROYAL ROBES
March 4

Morning Rinse: Esther 5-7
Featured Verse: Esther 5:1 *Now it came about on the third day that Esther put on her royal robes and stood in the inner court of the king's palace.*

The title of chapter five in my NASV Bible is "Esther Intercedes for the Jews." Nowhere in this chapter does it say that Esther prayed, and yet I have always thought the word "intercede" means "to intensely pray." I must chuckle because this thought process probably came from my Pentecostal background. I decided to look up the definition. Dictionary.com defines it as 'to act or interpose (to step in) on behalf of someone in difficulty or trouble, as by pleading or petitioning.'[7] I noticed there are two parts to interceding, acting and pleading. We know that Esther called a corporate fast with the Jews for three days, due to Haman's plot to kill her people. They pleaded to God through their prayers. But the second part of interceding that we often miss is the action we might need to take. On the third day of the fast, Esther prepared a banquet for the king. Then she prepared herself by putting on her royal robes to go before the king to invite him and Haman to the banquet. She put action to her steps, despite the risk of being killed for inviting herself into the king's presence. She did not just sit in her prayer closet and ask God to change the king's heart, or miraculously open his eyes to Haman's evil scheme. She rose and allowed God to use her to be the one to expose the plot. Through her brave and personal ACTions of interceding, she saved her people. Haman had convinced the king to issue a decree ordering the extermination of all the Jews. This decree was unable to be revoked, and the Jews were just supposed to accept it with no defense. Through Esther's bold acts, she revealed her identity as a Jew to the king, as well as Haman's scheme to kill her people. Haman was ultimately hanged, and Mordechai took his place. Then a new decree was written, allowing the Jews the right to defend themselves on the day of this attack, instead of merely accepting the fate of execution. The attack was not able to be reversed, but the fact that the Jews were able to defend themselves is what saved them. You may not be the one positioned to go before the 'king' in every dire situation, but when your time comes, will you don your Royal Robes?

Today's Challenge To Dig Deeper:
In your world around you, is there a need? Commit to not only praying for the need, but ask God to help you be open to taking action, steps to be part of the solution. Put on your 'royal robes' and go make a difference. You just might save a life... or many.

Evening Reflection:
Write down the actions you took today to intercede for someone.

---

[7] https://www.dictionary.com/browse/intercede

IDENTITY CHANGE
March 5

Morning Rinse: Esther 8-10
Featured Verse: Esther 8:17 *In each and every province and in each and every city, wherever the king's commandment and his decree arrived, there was gladness and joy for the Jews, a feast and a holiday. And many among the peoples of the land became Jews, for the dread of the Jews had fallen on them.*

What made other nationalities want to become a Jew? What made them want to change their identity and change who they were? Sometimes the fear of not becoming something will overshadow remaining the same. Even though they feared the Jews, they also wanted to become something more, so they chose to become something new. They saw the nation of Israel fight for something bigger than themselves, and then they watched God win, ending in a celebration. This celebration of gift-giving, parades, and feasting is now called the feast of Purim (poo-REEM). Some say that Purim, the 14th day of Adar, is one of the most joyous and fun holidays on the entire Jewish calendar. It acknowledges when the Jewish people living in Persia were saved from extermination by being allowed to defend themselves, with the heroes being Esther and her cousin Mordecai. The feast of Purim was never the end goal. The goal of Esther was to do what it took to maintain her identity. When you fall in love with who you are, it defines what you do, ultimately impacting those who watch your life. People will see your identity-based behaviors, and it will impact some to change their identity as well. Esther risked her life to save her identity. As we continue to fall deeper in love with our creator, our decisions each day, even the small ones, will begin to change, because Jesus came to change our identity. Our goal should not be to just get saved so we can make it to heaven. If that were the case, our behavior would be based merely on what we want the outcome to be. But when we allow Jesus to begin to change our identity, our daily choices become based on who we want to be, to become more like Him. The Jews were very proud of who they were, so they were willing to fight to save that identity. This led to others changing their identity and becoming something new. Who are you becoming? Who do you say you are? Once you believe in your identity, you will act in alignment with that belief. You will not do things because you know you should. You will begin to act like who you already are. And when your behavior and identity line up, the behavior change becomes easy because you believe you are that person. The people became Jews, so they started acting like Jews and celebrating with the Jews. They became Jews. Those around you will see your identity-based decisions. This is how we impact the world.

Today's Challenge To Dig Deeper:
What are three changes you can make today that align with your identity? Could it be changing the way you speak? Could it be laying the cigarettes down, saying to yourself you are no longer a smoker? What can you do and say differently that will cause a string of new actions that solidify your identity? Be mindful of those watching your identity-based decisions.

Evening Reflection:
What identity-based decisions did God talk to you about today?

THE COURSE OF THE CALL
March 6

Morning Rinse: Exodus 1-5
Featured Verses: Exodus 5:20-21 *When they (the foremen) left Pharaoh's presence, they met Moses and Aaron as they were waiting for them. They said to them, "May the Lord look upon you and judge you, for you have made us odious in Pharaoh's sight and in the sight of his servants, to put a sword in their hand to kill us."*

The first five chapters of Exodus document the call on Moses' life. He was chosen to go into Egypt and speak on behalf of the Israelites to Pharaoh, with the mission to free the people from the bounds of the Egyptians. He is known for going to Pharaoh and declaring, "Let my people go." The problem with this call is not many understood it. He was making everyone around him angry with this request. Pharaoh became angry and caused the work to increase for the Israelites. The Israelites were upset because they could not keep up with the workload, and the foremen were getting punished for their lack of performance against these newfound standards. Have you ever felt that no matter what you do, it appears wrong with most everyone around you? What if your actions are right in line with God's plan, and you still feel the disapproval from others? We must remember that God's ways are not our ways. God is working on your behalf behind the scenes and in ways we never will see. Do not give in to the pressure of trying to please people, especially when you feel opposition. Give in to the pressure of the call on your life, and stay committed to answering God's voice and not the voices around you that disagree. There will always be those who do not understand, and there may even be times that we ourselves do not understand. But God's purpose is higher. His ways are mightier. And God will complete His work. Keep giving in to HIS pressure, not mans.

Today's Challenge To Dig Deeper:
Do you feel stuck in a situation where you feel the pressure of God's call, and yet those around you are pressuring you to do something different? Are you wondering what God is doing? Commit today to stay on the course of the call. If you need confirmation, ask God. He is not afraid of your questions.

Evening Reflection:
Did you ask God for clarification? Are you on the right path?

BURY YOUR SEEDS OF DOUBT
March 7

Morning Rinse: Exodus 6-9
Featured Verse: Exodus 6:30 *But Moses said before the Lord, "Behold, I am unskilled in speech; how then will Pharaoh listen to me?"*

God has heard it all. From the very beginning with stories like Moses' example, all the way to present-day, He has heard our excuses. He is used to asking His people to do something, and then we begin to list our limitations and reasons why we cannot complete it. Why is this? Do we forget that God created us and knows everything about us already? Do we doubt that He truly calls us to do something for Him? Is it a lack of trust? I can confidently say most Christ followers have done this at one point in our faith walk. Moses, in fact, did it several times. Our Featured Verse was the third recorded time he tells God his limitations. The first was Exodus 4:10 while God was telling Moses He needed him. The second time was in Exodus 6:12. Both the second and third times Moses told God about his limitation, his lack of ability to speak, DURING his mission, AFTER he had already started the process of freeing the Israelites. AFTER he had already moved to Egypt to start his work. He had started his mission and then got cold feet. Sometimes we sow seeds of doubt before we even begin, and then sometimes we sow the seeds of doubt during the process. We have faith to start, but then we face a roadblock and try to quit. Have you ever started something that God has asked you to do, but when it got too hard, you tried to quit? This is what Moses was doing. He was trying to find a way out. He was pointing out things to God that would make his mission too challenging. If God has asked us to do something, why do we lack the faith to trust He will finish the work that has been started? I think sometimes we expect God to give us grace and coddle us in these moments of doubt, but God got angry at Moses the first time he tried to make excuses (Exodus 4:14a). *"Then the anger of the Lord burned against Moses."* We all can have seeds of doubt creep into our hearts. But discerning when they creep in, grabbing those seeds and burying them, is how our faith grows. If all of God's children would learn to bury those seeds in ground that will destroy them, I can only imagine the work that we would accomplish for His kingdom. So bury those seeds deep in the trash, not in the soil of our hearts. We must bury them, and trust God, the creator of the call and the creator of the one being called. That is you. And we must trust God to provide all our needs during the call.

Today's Challenge To Dig Deeper:
What is God asking you to do? Have you continued to doubt your call, and list your limitations? Search your heart, look for the seeds of doubt, and ask God to help you bury them. Declare you will do what God is calling you to do. Put a line in the sand and cross over to the trust side. Bury the seeds of doubt He has revealed in your heart.

Evening Reflection:
What seeds of doubt did you bury today? What is God calling you to do?

BEING A DISTINCTION!
March 8

Morning Rinse: Exodus 10-13
Featured Verse: Exodus 11:7 *But against any of the sons of Israel a dog will not even bark, whether against man or beast, that you may understand how the Lord makes a distinction between Egypt and Israel.*

God made a distinction between Egypt and Israel and wanted everyone to know about it. He clearly gave signs and wonders confirming this through examples such as the plagues. We can parallel this to modern day faith and realize God still wants to make a distinction amongst His people. The question we must ask ourselves is, are we willing to be a distinction? In our Featured Verse, the Israelites believed the distinction was only between Egypt and Israel, and the issues at hand in their time, including slavery versus freedom. However, God sees so much more than this. We are His chosen people. We are His children. How do we become distinct in our day-to-day living for Christ? It is simple and yet not always easy. God wants us to learn, just as He taught the Israelites, HIS ways. He wants us to be distinct in our lifestyle, our values, our obedience to Him, and our Christ-minded decisions. If we focus on His laws and commandments and do life His way, we will organically and naturally become distinct for Him. Could it be that you recklessly forgive those who have hurt you, and when friends and family want to revisit the pain, you show your distinction by laying it down and living in peace about it? Could it be that you cease from conversations that spur gossip? Could it be that you transform the way you respond to others and allow God to help you show love instead of manifesting a judgmental attitude? Being distinct for Christ is a lifestyle. If we are not distinct, there is a high chance we may be confusing those around us about what we truly stand for. Oh, may it never be that we cause someone to view Christ in a skewed way that causes doubt and confusion about who He truly is.

Today's Challenge To Dig Deeper:
Do you need to readjust some values or lifestyle choices, to be more aligned with godly principles and make you more distinct? Ask God to help you make these changes.

Evening Reflection:
What were the changes God spoke to you about today that will cause your life to be more publicly distinct? Write them down, and write down the change you are making from this point forward.

THE BATTLE OF SILENCE
March 9

Morning Rinse: Exodus 14-18
Featured Verse: Exodus 14:14 *The Lord will fight for you while you keep silent.*

Moses' life was full of cliff hangers. Leading hundreds of thousands of people through the wilderness was no small task. Not only was Moses called to rescue the people, but he was called to move them to the Promised Land, lead them through battles, teach them about faith, go to God on their behalf, deal with conflicts within the people, and ultimately complete his mission. During the battles that the Israelites faced, there is a message that is often overlooked. The first battle in today's Morning Rinse was when the Egyptians chased them and were about to overtake them. The Israelites were trapped, with the sea on one side of them and the Egyptian soldiers on the other side. While the Israelites were complaining and fearing death, the angel of God and the pillar of cloud moved and stood in-between the Israelites and the Egyptians so they could walk across the sea. Today's Featured Verse shows Moses' response. The Israelites did not need to do anything except walk in silence on the path God opened for them. In the 11th hour, God parted the sea. All He needed them to do was walk. In silence. Also in our Morning Rinse, is a second battle where they were attacked again. This time, by the army of Amalek. Miraculously, the Israelites prevailed in the battle when Moses' hands were raised in the air. But they began losing when his hands were let down. As Moses sat on the rock, probably praying, his action was to sit there with his hands in the air. Both examples are victories of God. Both are examples of the battle won in quietness of faith, obedience and the peaceful resolve of silence coupled with action. Can you imagine the Israelites' entire camp silently walking across the sea, while the chaos of the Egyptian army tries to get around the pillar of fire and the cloud? And can you imagine Moses sitting in peaceful resolve with his hands in the air, as the Israelites win a battle one more time? If you are battling something and feel chaos all around you, could it be time to sit in silence? Sitting in silence is not easy. In fact, it can be its own battle in and of itself. But the battle of silence with God will win wars.

Today's Challenge To Dig Deeper:
Is there a battle raging in your life? Have you been caught complaining about your situation? Seek God today in this matter. Sit with Him in silence and let your heart hear His voice instead of the chaos around you.

Evening Reflection:
What is it God asked you to be silent about? Did you find it difficult to stop complaining, or did you find peace in the storm? Was it a battle to be silent? How did you feel?

DOORWAY OF DECISION
March 10

Morning Rinse: Exodus 19-23
Featured Verses: Exodus 21:5-6 *But if the slave plainly says, "I love my master, my wife and my children; I will not go out as a free man," then his master shall bring him to God, then he shall bring him to the door or the doorpost. And his master shall pierce his ear with an awl; and he shall serve him permanently.*

To be a 'slave' to God, is a term used frequently in the Bible. We read about writers in the Bible, including Paul in the New Testament, describing themselves as one. The idea, or concept of being a slave, though, is extremely negative, and according to the spirit of the gospel, it is against slavery in every form. So why is this term used? The actual words for a "slave" in Hebrew and Greek mean "servant or bondservant." It was a custom in the early cultures, in Bible times, to have servants.[8] According to commentators in this footnote, becoming a servant may have been caused by several things. Besides war-captives, another reason for enslavement was theft. There were also standards set in place on how the master had to treat the servant. They needed to treat them as actual hired help, and then once the debt was paid off, or he was able to go free for other reasons, the master was to send him away with something of value such as livestock or some other item of worth. But in some instances, a slave wanted to stay with his master for the rest of his life and serve him, instead of choosing to go free. In today's Featured Verses, we read of a ritual performed when this choice is made. This ritual included the master bringing the slave to a door or doorpost and piercing his ear. Piercing in the Bible is a symbol of a permanent mark. Jesus was pierced on the Cross to forever be marked by His love for us. But why did the master pierce the servant's ear at a door? As a metaphor, a door can be used to symbolize a new opportunity or passage. Depending on the version of the Bible, the word "door" is mentioned in over 150 verses throughout the Old and New Testaments.[9] During our Morning Rinse, the Israelites remember when they were set free from slavery by putting blood on the doorpost. It is no accident that the servant is brought to a door to show his commitment to his master. A new opportunity and an exciting adventure lay in wait for this servant, as he freely bonds with his master at his doorway of decision.

Today's Challenge To Dig Deeper:
If you have not made the decision to commit your life to Jesus, ask Him to forgive you of your sins, be the Lord of your life, and help you make changes that align with His will. For all readers, both new to salvation or already saved, ask God to show you one area that you need to surrender to Him. Make a deep commitment at your doorway of decision, to surrender that area.

Evening Reflection:
Did you give your heart to Christ today? If so, how do you feel? And for everyone reading, what area did He speak to you about surrendering?

---

[8] https://www.biblestudytools.com/dictionary/slave/

[9] https://www.answers.com/Q/How_many_times_does_the_word_door_appear_in_the_Bible

HANGING WITH THE KING
March 11

Morning Rinse: Exodus 24-27
Featured Verse: Exodus 24:11 *Yet He did not stretch out His hand against the nobles of the sons of Israel; and they saw God, and they ate and drank.*

One of my favorite memories when we moved into our new home, was when the neighborhood kids began showing up at our front doorstep to just hang out with our two teenage kids. We initially invited them all over to shoot some basketball, eat s'mores and play gaga ball, a very trendy handball game in a makeshift pit. Once these newfound friends became more comfortable with us, they began showing up at our home unexpectedly, just to hang out. For almost the entire summer months that first year, it was almost a nightly event to have at least several extra kids at our home, and sometimes that number was nearly fifteen total kids just hanging out and having a grand time. The memories of that summer included sweaty teens in and out of our kitchen grabbing snacks and water, kids giggling out on our patio, my husband grilling extra hotdogs for dinner, and a lot of joy. I will be forever grateful that our home was a place of comfort and peace for them to just hang out. Did you know that God loves hanging out with us in this same manner? He enjoys our company. He is not this stern and gruff person with a judge's gavel in His hand, waiting to crack it down onto the sound block to pass judgement on us for our latest wrongdoing. He enjoys us! He created us. As I was unpacking in this new home, I found an old painting of my daughter's from when she was little. So to do some décor revisions, I had it framed and hung it up. In general, we enjoy looking at our own creations, whether that be paintings, handmade decorations, or even those delicious cookies we make for our guests. God is no different. He enjoys being around us, His creations. Can you imagine just sitting with Him, laughing, eating, and talking with Him? This is what He wants. In today's Morning Rinse, God brought Moses, Aaron, Nadab and Abihu along with seventy elders up into the mountain to hang with them. Not to judge. But to be with them. After spending time with them, he gave very detailed instructions to Moses for the building of the tabernacle, so He could also dwell among the rest of the people. He WANTS to be with us. The big question for today is, do you want to be with Him?

Today's Challenge To Dig Deeper:
There are many ways to hang with our Heavenly King! Some hang with Him while meditating on scripture. Others hang with Him by conversing as they drive. Others love the peace they feel while attending their church home. However you like hanging with Jesus, make some effort to do that today. Turn off all other noise around you and just hang. Talk to Him. Laugh with Him. Hang with The King.

Evening Reflection:
What did you do today to hang with God?

MAKING YOUR MARK
March 12

Morning Rinse: Exodus 28-31
Featured Verse: Exodus 28:12 *You shall put the two stones on the shoulder pieces of the ephod, as stones of memorial for the sons of Israel, and Aaron shall bear their names before the Lord on his two shoulders for a memorial.*

Oftentimes, when I am out showing homes, I notice the entryway landscape displaying garden rocks engraved with names or handprints. These engravings are a signet of the important people associated with those living in the home. When I read today's Morning Rinse, I realize God also enjoys making signets, or 'marks,' for His people. I love how He is so detailed, and cares about the little things. These details are seen in the instructions for the building of the tabernacle. He also details out the specific oils to use, the clothes to be worn by the priests, the materials to be used in the decor, and so much more. The entire atmosphere was not just about displaying order in His presence. It was truly giving an experience of holiness. Today's Featured Verse references God's instructions regarding a portion of Aaron's priestly garments, which includes onyx stones set on his shoulders. These stones have the names of the tribes engraved on them in their birth order. When I first read this, a slow-motion scene of Aaron began unfolding in my mind's eye. Aaron dons his garments, carefully placing these onyx stones on his shoulders. Once he is fully dressed, he respectfully walks into the presence of God. He pauses and looks up to the heavens, then bows his head and kneels in prayer. God's point of view is then seen in my mind's eye. Even before Aaron brings any needs to the throne, God sees each of the tribe's names listed next to Aaron's bowed head. The tribes' names were always seen by God first, before Aaron even spoke. These engraved onyx stones were part of Aaron's priestly attire, to be worn every day. In today's culture, we do not bear the weight of stones on our shoulders with names engraved on them. But just like garden stones are placed in yards as a reminder, we can create our own personal 'marks' as reminders to lift up the names of others we care about. I decided to create my own 'mark.' I figured if Aaron wore names as a reminder, I can too. So I grabbed a sharpie, and wrote my husband's, my kids,' including my sons-in-love's, and my grandbabies' names on my bra straps. Each morning, when I get dressed, I see those names and it helps me to remember when I pray throughout the day, God sees those names, too. When we lift up the needs of others before ourselves, our perception begins to shift. We begin to see a deeper way of looking at our family. From God's point of view.

Today's Challenge To Dig Deeper:
Create a 'mark' or 'stone' to remind you every day to take your loved ones to the Lord in prayer before your own needs.

Evening Reflection:
What 'mark' did you create today for your prayer reminder?

DAILY DEDICATION
March 13

Morning Rinse: Exodus 32-34
Featured Verse: Exodus 33:13 *Now therefore, I pray You, if I have found favor in Your sight, let me know Your ways that I may know You, so that I may find favor in Your sight. Consider too, that this nation is Your people.*

In one of the early verses in chapter 33, Moses told the people to dedicate themselves to the Lord so He could bless them. One of the definitions of the word "dedication," according to *The Merriam-Webster Dictionary*, means "self-sacrificing devotion and loyalty."[10] Not only can we be dedicated to a person, like a boss, a mentor, or our significant other, but we can be dedicated and loyal to other things, like a career or a business. We can also be dedicated to volunteering in a local ministry, budgeting consistently, keeping our house clean, eating right, or becoming an expert on a certain subject matter. Just like the definition describes, being dedicated can be clearly linked to self-sacrifice. When we are truly dedicated, we will drop what our flesh wants so our loyalty remains intact. An example would be to still exercise despite feeling tired, or serving our boss in tasks that we absolutely despise performing. Moses had a dedication to God that certainly sets the bar high. In fact, when Moses tells the people to dedicate themselves to God, he tells them to dedicate DAILY. In today's Featured Verse, it is interesting to note that Moses is clearly very hungry to know God and His ways, showing his true loyalty and dedication to his relationship with God. Yet, the question can easily be asked, "Has Moses not been communing with God already more than anyone around him?" Or another idea that may come to mind is, "I thought Moses already knew God." His hunger shows that even though he dedicates himself daily to God, the dedication he had, was not ending anytime soon. Moses is even so comfortable in their relationship, he asks for favor upon his life. And in his conversation with God, he is so hungry for this relationship, it would almost appear he is a brand-new Christian trying to learn the ways of Christianity, as if he still did not know despite his long-time relationship with God. Another way I like to describe being dedicated, is to have a full commitment to seeing something to the very end. Are we committed to God enough to dedicate our TODAY to Him in everything we do, keeping the end in mind? Are we dedicated in our relationship enough to fully seek and know Him?

Today's Challenge To Dig Deeper:
When we dedicate our TODAY to God, we are showing Him that He is important in the NOW, versus only needing Him for the future things we are concerned about. Talk to Him throughout your day today, and ask Him to help you dedicate everything to Him daily. He blesses our yearning to walk this life with Him, fully committed to Him.

Evening Reflection:
What was your day like today? What did you dedicate to Him?

---

[10] https://www.merriam-webster.com/dictionary/dedication

CONTRIBUTION, CRAFTSMANSHIP, AND CUBITS
March 14

Morning Rinse: Exodus 35-37
Featured Verses: Exodus 35:5, 31, 37:6 *Take from among you a contribution to the Lord; whoever is of a willing heart, let him bring it as the LORD'S contribution: gold, silver, and bronze… And He has filled him (Bezalel) with the Spirit of God, in wisdom, in understanding and in knowledge and in all craftsmanship… He (Bezalel) made a mercy seat of pure gold, two and a half cubits long and one and a half cubits wide.*

Many chapters in Exodus document the details, instructions, and blueprints of the tabernacle dwelling. This includes not just the building, but what was inside, including the interior design, the measurements of the curtains, and the description of the various pieces used. God wanted these instructions written in the Bible, and I believe His plan was multi-faceted. First, to show us how specific He is when we are open to hearing, and second, to show how much He cares about craftsmanship. You will notice there are three verses highlighted in today's Featured Verses, which capture three different stages of ministry. The first verse describes Moses conveying a commandment from God to the people. This commandment specifically called on the people to *contribute* materials for the building of the tabernacle. God described what was needed for the construction, which included things like gold, silver, linens, dyes, wood, stones and more. God expected the people to bring these materials so the tabernacle could be built. He gives us our resources, and I believe He expects His people, still to this day, to use some of those resources to contribute to kingdom work. But He also wants us to have a willing heart as we give. God does not force us to contribute to His work. But I wonder how much more impactful ministries would be if there were more willing hearts contributing to kingdom work. The second verse lists those whom God had gifted knowledge and wisdom for *craftsmanship*. God needs people to take what is donated and do the work with skill. We can all offer up our gifts and talents. We all have strengths that can be used for His glory. The last verse describes, in detail, what was made with the contributions, even down to the *cubit*. God will give instructions to those willing to hear. These three stages are relevant in even modern-day ministry phases. God needs people to give, people willing to offer their gifts to further the kingdom, and people who will listen to His instructions on how to complete the tasks at hand. Just imagine. What if the Israelites had not been willing to contribute? What if those gifted in craftsmanship were not willing to use their skillset? Or, what if they were not willing to listen to God's instructions down to the cubit? It is simple. The tabernacle would never have been built.

Today's Challenge To Dig Deeper:
Each of us can contribute our resources, use our craftsmanship, and hone our listening skills down to the cubit detail. What part do you feel God is speaking to you about today? If you lack willingness to contribute resources, ask God for it. If you lack confidence in your craftsmanship, ask Him to help you. If you struggle hearing details, ask Him to teach you to hear.

Evening Reflection:
What area did God talk to you about? What action did you take?

DON THOSE HOLY GARMENTS!
March 15

Morning Rinse: Exodus 38-40
Featured Verse: Exodus 39:1 *Moreover, from the blue and purple and scarlet material, they made finely woven garments for ministering in the holy place as well as the holy garments which were for Aaron, just as the Lord had commanded Moses.*

Remember in Exodus 32, when Moses went up into the mountain to receive the Ten Commandments from God, and while he was on the mountain, the people started getting distracted? They went to Aaron and said, "Come, make us a god who will go before us; as for this Moses, the man who brought us up from the land of Egypt, we do not know what has become of him." The peer pressure Aaron must have felt from hundreds of thousands of people may have been too much for him to bear, and the other leaders under Moses may have been too few to counteract the plea of the people. Unfortunately, Aaron caved and built the golden calf. This act of disobedience was a huge mistake, and I can guess that Aaron had to have felt extreme remorse after his actions. I have no doubt he fully repented of his wrongdoing, and made things right with God, and with Moses as his leader. In today's Featured Verse, we excitedly read about the holy garment being made, per the instruction straight from God. And guess who those garments were made for? That is correct. For Aaron. Even after he turned his back on God, God forgave him and continued with His plan for Aaron as a priest. God is a redeeming God, and He longs to have a relationship with us. God called Aaron to the royal priesthood, and He did not change His mind. Just like His view of Aaron, God sees our potential as well, and calls us to our purpose, despite our past, present and future mistakes. His call on our lives does not change. Once Aaron got his heart right again, the task of building the temple continued. WHY? Because God longs to dwell with us, despite our human nature of messing up. God STILL wants to be with us.

Today's Challenge To Dig Deeper:
No one is exempt from making mistakes, except Jesus. So it is time to lay your mistakes down, and accept the holy garments God wants you to wear. Today, accept God's grace and mercy, forgive yourself for your actions, and move on to the next thing God has for you. God has a call on your life, and He wants you to walk it out with Him. Don those holy garments.

Evening Reflection:
Did you accept God's grace today? Write down the experience.

FIGURES, FIRE, AND FLOATING WHEELS
March 16

Morning Rinse: Ezekiel 1-3
Featured Verse: Ezekiel 2:3 *Then He said to me, "Son of man, I am sending you to the sons of Israel, to a rebellious people who have rebelled against Me; they and their fathers have transgressed against Me to this very day."*

The Old Testament is filled with fascinating encounters with God Almighty. Many of the greats, or outstanding leaders of God, experienced these encounters, and we have the honor of reading about their experiences. These are leaders who God used in mind-boggling ways, called them to great feats, and showed visions of glory that are written down in scripture for us to picture in our mind's eye. Ezekiel is one of these greats. In today's Morning Rinse, we read the dynamic vision he had of the four figures. We get to imagine what it was like when God transitions him from the call of a trained priest to a prophet. After this personal encounter with God, Ezekiel was never the same. God wants to have a personal encounter with each of us as well. God may never give us a vision with figures, fire, and floating wheels, but He wants us to be forever changed when we encounter His presence. How? He will do this through His Word and through a relationship with Him. Is a journey with Christ easy? No. Will there be resistance at times from those around us? Yes. As we journey through the life of Ezekiel, we will read where even the greats of the Bible encountered struggles such as this. In fact, the very people Ezekiel was called to prophesy to, did not listen to him. They rebelled against his voice. Just as you journey through your life as a Christ follower and live out the mission God has for you, there will be those who will not listen or respect your path. There will be those who do not accept your call. Unfortunately, there may even be times that those who reject your call and purpose will be your closest friends and family members. How will you respond when this happens? Will you keep obeying God, despite the rejection? Do you anticipate fear creeping into your heart, and worry settling into your mind about what others think of you? Even after Ezekiel had this incredible encounter with God, and even after he documented his vision, God still had to tell him not to fear the people. What makes fear grip us, even when we know God is for us? Each of us is different and have a weak spot or struggle. Ezekiel may have been prone to intimidation. I do not know. But one thing I do know, he did not let fear control his destiny. He kept God's call as his focus. If we keep our eyes on Christ and remember our personal encounters with Him, it will overshadow fear and intimidation. Ezekiel remembered the figures, fire and floating wheels. Is there an encounter you need to remember?

Today's Challenge To Dig Deeper:
As you go about your day today, ask God for some clear direction on what He is asking you to do for Him. Ask Him to remind you of past encounters with Him, or ask Him for a fresh encounter to give you direction and purpose. Ask Him to birth something fresh in your heart. Where and what is He sending you to go and do?

Evening Reflection:
Be brave and write down the mission He has birthed in you.

JESUS FREAK
March 17

Morning Rinse: Ezekiel 4-6
Featured Verse: Ezekiel 4:4 *As for you, lie down on your left side and lay the iniquity of the house of Israel on it; you shall bear their iniquity for the number of days that you lie on it.*

Ezekiel is a book in the Bible where it can be difficult to find the relevance for today, and some may even look at things Ezekiel did and call him a Jesus Freak. When reading this book, there will be times we need to dig deep for messages that might not necessarily jump out at us. This is certainly how we get nuggets from the Lord. Today's Morning Rinse, for instance, has several examples of odd things God asked Ezekiel to do, that we may never be asked to perform in our lifetime. They will be great conversation pieces, and I certainly plan on talking to Ezekiel about them when I get to heaven. For starters, God asks Ezekiel to lay down (maybe at night or during a time of rest during the day) on his left side for three hundred and ninety days, then switch to his right side for another forty. Then there is the subject of food. Some of it had to be cooked over cow dung. ABSOLUTELY GROSS. Another wild thing God asked of Ezekiel, was for him to shave his head and beard. Then he had to divide the hair into three parts and disperse it. The first part Ezekiel put into a fire. The second part he disperses throughout the city, and the last part he scatters in the wind. He also attaches a few of his hairs to the edge of his robes. Each of these acts are symbolizing a message God wanted the Israelites to hear and understand. Coupled with these odd acts, Ezekiel was also told to prophesy and tell the people their fate due to disobedience. I am quite sure most people questioned Ezekiel's sanity. I am also quite sure most of the people probably tried to distance themselves from him, and probably called him names like 'freak.' But they were in a deep state of rebellion, and God was trying to get their attention through radical acts. Sometimes God must get radical to warn us, and he used Ezekiel with those radical messages to do so. God wanted to make it very clear to the people that He is the one true God. He wanted the people to know Him and hear His voice through Ezekiel. Yes, these acts of Ezekiel seem very extreme, weird, or "way out there." I do not deny this. The question for us is, would we do something weird or extreme if God asked us to? Are we willing to be a Jesus Freak?

Today's Challenge To Dig Deeper:
You may never have to cook over cow dung, or cut your hair and spread it across your city. But digging deeper may mean being bold and different. Today, do ONE thing in an area of timidity that requires more boldness. ONE THING. You know what it is. Pray, and ask God to help you.

Evening Reflection:
What was your one thing? Was it hard? How did you feel?

THE LORD DOES SEE
March 18

Morning Rinse: Ezekiel 7-9
Featured Verses: Ezekiel 8:16, 9:9 *Then He brought me into the inner court of the Lord's house. And behold, at the entrance to the temple of the Lord, between the porch and the altar, were about twenty-five men with their backs to the temple of the Lord and their faces toward the east; and they were prostrating themselves eastward toward the sun… Then He said to me, "The iniquity of the house of Israel and Judah is very, very great, and the land is filled with blood and the city is full of perversion; for they say, 'The Lord has forsaken the land, and the LORD does not see!'"*

Have you ever thought to yourself "The Lord does not see," and therefore, you behave in a fashion that would not necessarily be pleasing to God, ultimately leading to sin? This is what the Israelites who were captive in Babylon were doing. According to the spiritual atmosphere of this time with these people, it is obvious God was not in their midst, and corruption was running rampant. This corruption even became present in the lives of those in leadership positions within the temple. These were people to whom Ezekiel was called to prophesy or preach. Why are there times in our lives when we behave with corruption in our hearts, as if God cannot see us? Sin can easily creep into our actions if we do not keep our hearts and minds on the Lord. This is what happened to these Israelites. Since they were not focused on the Lord, their encounters with Him began to cease. Therefore, they began to forget His presence, and ultimately stray away from His will. In today's first Featured Verse, we get a picture of what they were doing. They were indeed worshiping, but they were not worshiping the one true God. They may have been participating in a form of nature worshiping or other idolization. How often does God look down on His people and find us idolizing something or someone with our backs facing the temple? This could even be manifested as we sit right in church, if our hearts are turned from Him. We must remember that God sees us, even when we turn our backs on Him. Listen to the still, small voice in every moment. When we obey in the little things, our face will stay turned to Him. He sees the good, the bad and the ugly of our hearts, and we cannot hide from His eyes. Let us never own the attitude that the Lord does not see. Instead, may we live our lives for Him as our Savior who DOES see, and loves us through our mistakes.

Today's Challenge To Dig Deeper:
When you go about your day, remind yourself that God is sitting, walking, standing, and driving with you. He is right next to you, He is watching all actions and hears all conversations. He does see us. Since He does, what action or conversation will you need to alter today? Is it exiting a gossiping conversation? Is it being more ethical in how you spend your work time? God will show you. Stay open to His voice and guidance.

Evening Reflection:
What was the action or conversation that got altered today as God nudged you closer to purity? In your act of obedience, what did you do differently as you focused on the fact God was watching you? Make this mindset a daily habit, and watch yourself grow in future actions and conversations.

HEART SURGERY
March 19

Morning Rinse: Ezekiel 10-12
Featured Verses: Ezekiel 11:19-20 *And I will give them one heart, and put a new spirit within them. And I will take the heart of stone out of their flesh and give them a heart of flesh, that they may walk in My statutes and keep My ordinances and do them. Then they will be My people, and I shall be their God.*

Unfortunately, my family has a history of heart disease that is not just on my side of the family, but on my husband's as well. On more than one occasion, we have watched loved ones go through heart surgery, and sometimes multiple ones. We have felt the sting of anxiety and worry for them. We have even wondered if this disease will manifest in our lives or our children's lives. While having a physical heart surgery is not a desirable experience, it can mirror a heart surgery of our soul, which is a good thing. The promise of heart surgery that God gave Ezekiel for the Israelites, is also a promise that God has for us today, and something that will ultimately bring us closer to Him. We can all have a new heart, if we allow God to be the surgeon. The 'one heart' in today's Featured Verses is a heart that is not divided or weak, but a heart solely aligned with God and the leaders He has placed above us. We all can have a heart striving to live for God in every aspect of what we say and do. How do we obtain this kind of heart? We must allow God to perform a heavenly heart surgery, taking out our stony heart and replacing it with a heart of flesh. A heart of stone is hard and rebellious, appealing to our sinful nature. But a heart of flesh is moldable, shapeable, vulnerable, and yielding to the Holy Spirit. It lives and breathes with God's heartbeat, tender and totally responsive to His voice. Praying for a heart of flesh is not just encompassing the Salvation Prayer, though. It can be a lifelong prayer. If you have not given your heart to Christ through salvation, then follow the four-part prayer below. It will guide you to a new life with Christ, and includes a great heart surgery prayer for us all.

1. God, please show me the stony areas in my heart, especially towards colleagues, family members, church members, leaders, or even towards You. Please forgive me.
2. Remove my heart of stone and replace it with a heart of flesh that beats with Your heart. I give you permission to do heart surgery on me.
3. God, help my new heart to be fully unified, not just with You, but with the leaders You have placed in my life. Forgive me for those times when my heart has been against Your will, and keep my new heart pure.
4. Lord, help my 'one heart of flesh' to solely align and serve You in all I say and do.

Today's Challenge To Dig Deeper:
Get into a quiet place and pray the prayer above. Yield to God, the heavenly heart surgeon. Do not try to hold on to any stony areas, but let your old heart go. Accept your new one, and forgive yourself. Let Him guide you as you live with your new, unified heart.

Evening Reflection:
How did it feel to release your heart of stone? Did you feel yourself trying to hang on to it, or even pick it back up after you had heart surgery? Did you feel the nudge of the Holy Spirit as He guided you today with a new, tender heart? Write down your thoughts.

GETTING BURNED
March 20

Morning Rinse: Ezekiel 13-15
Featured Verse: Ezekiel 15:5 *Behold, while it is intact, it is not made into anything. How much less, when the fire has consumed it and it is charred, can it still be made into anything!*

Throughout my years of faith and being a preacher's kid and preacher's grandkid, I have heard many sermons on the importance of going through the fire. Rightfully so, many of these sermons have referenced the hard times we will go through. Going through the fire allows God to work in us, and if we yield to the burning process, we will come out as gold. This analogy is very true. However, Ezekiel's message mirrors sin and how the Israelites were useless to God, due to their idol worship and living in their flesh. In today's Morning Rinse, we read in chapter 15 where the useless vine is compared to those in Jerusalem. If we are not careful, our fleshly nature, like the sinful nature of those in Jerusalem, can be compared to this vine. Our sinful nature does no good for God's kingdom. So it must be burned or destroyed to make room for God's purpose and will for our lives. When our flesh gets burned, it is not a fun process. It hurts. But getting these areas burned out of us will fuel our spirit life. For those who have struggled in an area and cannot seem to conquer it, be of good cheer. God is not finished with you yet. Do not give up on Him, or yourself, but commit to the burning process. Sometimes our flesh will go through one fire and need to go through a second or even third fire. It may take multiple burnings, until all that is left are the ashes, with nothing left to burn. Give it all to God again and again. The more flesh we put through God's fire, the brighter the flame of our spirit will be. God takes us through the burning process, so He can make us into something for His kingdom. Yield to getting burned.

Today's Challenge To Dig Deeper:
Throughout the day today, listen to God. Ask Him to show you any part of your flesh that needs to burn, or that does the kingdom no good. If He shows you an area of your heart that needs burned, then allow Him to walk you through the process until it is gone. Commit to getting it done today. Then ask Him to help you fill the empty void with Him.

Evening Reflection:
What part of your flesh was burned today? How are you going to fill the void for the future?

SPIRITUAL RESUSCITATION
March 21

Morning Rinse: Ezekiel 16-18
Featured Verses: Ezekiel 18:30-33 *"Therefore I will judge you, O house of Israel, each according to his conduct," declares the Lord God. "Repent and turn away from all your transgressions, so that iniquity may not become a stumbling block to you. Cast away from you all your transgressions which you have committed, and make yourselves a new heart and a new spirit! For why will you die, O house of Israel? For I have no pleasure in the death of anyone who dies," declares the Lord God. "Therefore, repent and live."*

During soccer practice after school one day, when my son was a junior in high school, one of the team members collapsed. One team member called 911. Another ran up to the school office to notify the staff. Others positioned themselves in the parking lot to guide the ambulance. Others huddled in a circle to pray. And another student, who was trained in CPR, did mouth to mouth resuscitation until the EMT arrived. It was a scary event for the boys. But they worked together, and later the medical team credited the boys with saving this young man's life. Just like CPR is needed when someone has inconsistent breathing or quits breathing altogether, there may be times when we need spiritual resuscitation. Sin causes spiritual death, or a need to be revived. Much of today's Morning Rinse focuses on the iniquity of Judah, and even compares Judah to Sodom and Samaria (16:44-52). In fact, the comparison in the passages states Judah, in her sin, made these horrible cities look righteous. It must have been grievous for God to have to make these claims about His people. I admit the message portrayed in what we read today has a gloomy tone, almost full of despair. And in chapter 18, verse 24, God reminds us when we turn away from our righteousness and begin to live in sin, all our righteous acts will be forgotten. It seems so harsh. But the choices we make in our lives are just that, our choices. God does not force us to live holy and righteous. But He will warn us that trying to live so close to the world will make us become like the world. We must remember the Bible shows God's FULL character. That character includes traits like love, peace and mercy, just to name a few. But a trait we often want to overlook is God's trait as a judge. God wants us set apart. This is exactly why some of the prophets in the Old Testament were so bold with their warnings. But God's desire is for us to spiritually live with an eternal focus, and for all to come to repentance. Sometimes He needs us to join His team, and resuscitate those dying using forceful messages to get their attention. God used Ezekiel's voice to show His desire for each of us to have a changed and repentant life, and He will use your voice too, if you are willing. God has NO pleasure in anyone dying in their sin. None. He wants all to live. Will you help His team save lives?

Today's Challenge To Dig Deeper:
Do you know someone who is unsaved or needs spiritual resuscitation? Think of that person today and pray for them. As you are praying, ask God if there is anything He wants you to say to them to help resuscitate them to a spiritual life. Then go speak.

Evening Reflection:
Who was the person God laid on your heart, and what action did you take today to join God's team in giving them life?

MISSION OF TRUTH
March 22

Morning Rinse: Ezekiel 19-21
Featured Verse: Ezekiel 20:19 *I am the Lord your God; walk in My statures and keep my ordinances and observe them.*

Since the beginning of time, God has set up His standards and 'ordinances' for us to follow. Since the beginning, He has also watched His people go through times of disobedience towards His ways. From Adam and Eve to modern-day times, God has set people in place to speak out truth and be a voice for Him. Since Ezekiel was one of those voices and we are reading his book, we get to read some of his sermons, which include today's Morning Rinse. The book of Ezekiel is a tough book to read because in these sermons is the constant disobedience of the Israelites. It can feel like a gloomy book full of judgement, versus a sense of joy and peace. But the Israelites were not living the way God desired of them. They were constantly making poor choices. For starters, they participated in idol worship. They also grumbled about many things. They not only complained about what Ezekiel was saying to them, but even complained about HOW he said things. They also refused to listen to him, and they lived a life of hypocrisy. It is obvious that the Israelites were a mess. But God gave Ezekiel a mission to keep preaching truth, no matter their response. Part of this mission of truth was letting them know about the consequences of their actions. I am so glad that Ezekiel committed to being part of God's mission of truth, despite how hard it must have been to tell the Israelites their horrible destiny due to disobedience. My husband used to say to our kids when they were growing up, "Every decision gets a consequence. It can either be good or bad. But whatever the consequence is, the result is ultimately up to you." The Israelites were about to receive bad consequences, and unfortunately, Ezekiel was the continual bearer of that news. Yet the people did not appear to care. It is tough reading stories like this. It is certainly more fun reading about miracles, signs and wonders versus judgement. We know from scripture that later they were captured, many were killed, and their cities destroyed. When we obey, though, it sets in motion God blessing us. THAT is the consequence I want. May we listen and adhere to those preaching with a mission of truth.

Today's Challenge To Dig Deeper:
When someone speaks truth, have you ever ignored them? It can be very difficult to hear truth, especially when we do not want to change our ways. Do you need to adhere to what they are saying and adjust some of your actions? Talk to God about what He needs you to adjust, and celebrate your victory of obedience.

Evening Reflection:
What did you adjust today in your walk? Write it down and be proud of your growth.

BE THE ONE!
March 23

Morning Rinse: Ezekiel 22-24
Featured Verse: Ezekiel 22:30 *I searched for a man among them who would build up the wall and stand in the gap before Me for the land so that I would not destroy it; but I found no one.*

We have already established that the book of Ezekiel documents the sins of Israel and some of the sermons Ezekiel spoke. The symbolism is sprinkled throughout the book, including today's Morning Rinse. You may ask, "How am I to rinse and learn as I read books like Ezekiel?" The learning is still to be found. The nuggets are still there. In today's Featured Verse, God stated that during this time of sinful acts of Israel, He continued to look for people who would help build the spiritual wall and shield evil from the people. He continued to look for leaders to guide the people in a life of purity. He never stopped looking for those who would rise above the standards of the world. Have you ever had a desire to find something, and you continued looking for it despite not being able to see it? When we are looking for something, we are hopeful we will find it. I am sure God was hopeful in His search for even one person. The extremely sad part, though, is that He found no one. Not one person He could entrust in the mission of truth to join Ezekiel. I can only imagine the grief that God felt when He admitted this. I can only imagine how hurt, sad, and pained His heart felt knowing He could not find even one more leader. Not one. Can God trust you to live according to HIS standards, instead of the world's around you? Can He trust that you will be a good example in the world? Or will He have to keep looking because no one can be found? If God is looking for just one more person to speak truth, will you be the one?

Today's Challenge To Dig Deeper:
God is looking for someone to do kingdom work. Will you be that one? Today, pray this prayer, "Lord, when you are searching for the one, please find me. Help me to be the one you are looking for to carry out your mission." Now go out into the world and look for an opportunity to be a leader.

Evening Reflection:
How does it feel to be the one? Did God present to you an opportunity to speak into others around you? Write down what happened.

IF ONLY
March 24

Morning Rinse: Ezekiel 25-27
Featured Verse: Ezekiel 25:17 *I will execute great vengeance on them with wrathful rebukes; and they will know that I am the Lord when I lay My vengeance on them.*

The cities that Ezekiel spoke judgement on were many, encompassing the whole nation of Ammon. As I ponder this book, I wonder just how many times Ezekiel used his voice, shouting from rooftops to try and get the attention of the people. Okay. Maybe not literal rooftops. But certainly his voice was heard by the masses. Unfortunately, though, they chose not to heed what he was saying. They chose to disregard God's instructions. God used Ezekiel many times with messages. The need for repentance remained consistent. God also made it known that He would lay His vengeance on the cities if they kept living a sinful life. Here we are in chapter twenty-five reading more of the same messages encompassed in the entire book. The cities God spoke of were in Gentile nations that openly hated the Jews. While they were not a part of God's nation and people of Israel, God still declared His judgement over them. One does not have to be a Christ follower to receive consequences from Him. These people would also feel the results of not serving Him. We oftentimes forget God is a judge, and He must discipline His people. It can be hard to accept this side of Him when we hear the sermons of grace and mercy Sunday after Sunday. But God has not changed. How can we stay close to Him so we do not invite His anger? Stay repentant. It seems so simple, and yet most do not embrace the simplicity of a repentant lifestyle. Why? That is a simple answer, too. Pride and selfishness. If only we would make our lifestyle a daily walk of repentance, staying humble and meek. If only.

Today's Challenge To Dig Deeper:
Have you embraced a daily walk of repentance? Accepting Jesus as your personal Savior is the first step. Then asking Him to forgive your sins is next. Commit to living a life of walking out repentance daily, being carefully mindful of every action, every conversation, and every thought. Make this a forever habit.

Evening Reflection:
What did your conversations look like today? Did God speak to you about any area of repentance needed?

DANGEROUS DUAL IDENTITY
March 25

Morning Rinse: Ezekiel 28-30
Featured Verses: Ezekiel 28:12-13 *Son of man, take up a lamentation over the King of Tyre and say to him, "Thus says the Lord God, 'You had the seal of perfection, Full of wisdom and perfect in beauty. You were in Eden, the garden of God, Every precious stone was your covering: The ruby, the topaz and the diamond; The beryl, the onyx and the jasper; The lapis lazuli, the turquoise and the emerald; And the gold, the workmanship of your settings and the sockets, was in you. On the day that you were created they were prepared.'"*

The criminal makes his way through a narrow alleyway after committing a felony. He pants as he jumps over a fence, sprints through a backyard, and nears his hideout. The destiny of this villain, though, has an about-face, as Spiderman appears on the scene, captures him, and rescues the town from further harm. We, as the viewers of superhero movies, know the identity of these heroes. We cheer for them. We root for their causes. We even see a little of ourselves in their superpower because we all want to reach greatness and save the day in some capacity. But superheroes are not the only characters with a dual identity. While the identity is known of a superhero, the villains are a different story. Oftentimes, their identity is hidden. You may recognize the names Darth Vader, Thanos, or Loki. Having a dual identity is so dangerous when evil begins to prevail. Today's Featured Verses are about the dual identity of Satan, who he truly is, and where he came from. He was created to be in the presence of God. We read in chapter 28 that he was driven from Heaven, the very place he was created for (28:16-17). Ezekiel was condemning Satan himself, who was motivating the King of Tyre to make unwise decisions and live a life of dangerous dual identity. While we will never fully understand everything in the Bible, we can always find relevance if we seek it. Ezekiel courageously voiced the future destruction of evil, and he was not afraid of the person behind the evil deeds. Unlike the superheroes who seek to save the day and destroy evil, Satan comes to destroy the works of God's kingdom. He comes as a thief in the night, while trying to confuse mankind into believing he is the one to follow. This is the most dangerous dual identity known, and we must guard against this. I am still amazed that Satan chose his own way, his own pride, and his own destruction over humility and the presence of God. If we are not careful, we can also fall into the trap of living this lie. Many have a hard time living as their authentic self, while serving Christ because we are afraid to be 'real.' We walk into a church service with a smile on our face and our hands in the air as an act of worship on a Sunday morning, but we are completely different the rest of the week. May God create in us identity through Him, thwarting the dangerous dual identity that Satan tries to deem attractive.

Today's Challenge To Dig Deeper:
Do you ever feel confused or trapped into making choices that could fall into a dangerous dual identity? It is okay to not be perfect. But with God's help, you can be more authentic in making choices for HIM. Save your day. Ask Him to make you into His superhero with HIS identity.

Evening Reflection:
How do you feel about removing any part of a dangerous dual identity from your life? Did you make any changes today?

TURNING POINT
March 26

Morning Rinse: Ezekiel 31-33
Featured Verses: Ezekiel 33:10-11 *Now as for you, son of man, say to the house of Israel, "Thus you have spoken, saying, 'Surely our transgressions and our sins are upon us, and we are rotting away in them; how then can we survive?' Say to them, 'As I live!' declares the Lord God, 'I take no pleasure in the death of the wicked, but rather that the wicked turn from his way and live. Turn back, turn back from your evil ways! Why then will you, die, O house of Israel?'"*

Today's Featured Verses appear to be a turning point in the book of Ezekiel. Up until now, Ezekiel's sermons and prophecies seemed to be hitting deaf ears. The people of Israel had not admitted, much less faced their sins and offenses towards God. But suddenly, one day their eyes were opened, and the heaviness of their sins began to bring the questions of how they could make it right. Ezekiel answered them and reminded them that God is a forgiving God. He assured them that God takes no pleasure in seeing anyone die, even the wicked at heart. Rather, He wants to see a change of heart, a turning point from sinful ways. He sees our potential. Not only does He see our potential and what He longs for us to become, but He also longs for us to see that same potential in those around us. My husband and I used to be foster parents. During part of our journey, we cared for a sibling set of three for about two and a half years. When we were caring for these precious kids, we also mentored their parents. We welcomed them into our home and sat for hours with them, ministering to them in hopes they would rely on God's strength for new beginnings. We tried our best to help them turn their lives around. However, the story of this family did not end like we had hoped and prayed it would. Sometimes our messages of hope will be vital to life change in others, and sometimes our desire to help will remain seeds for later growth in lives. No matter what, though, our messages of hope should continue on, so the opportunities of a turning point will remain present for those who are ready to turn.

Today's Challenge To Dig Deeper:
Is there someone in your world that needs to hear your message of hope today? Could your story be exactly what they need to hear for a turning point in their life? Regardless of how they respond, be courageous and share a message of hope with that person today. Be willing to be a vessel to help them if they are ready for a turning point.

Evening Reflection:
Who heard your message today? How did they respond?

GOD'S FAMILY CREST
March 27

Morning Rinse: Ezekiel 34-36
Featured Verses: Ezekiel 36:22-23 *Therefore say to the house of Israel, "Thus says the Lord God, 'It is not for your sake, O house of Israel, that I am about to act, but for My holy name, which you have profaned among the nations where you went. I will vindicate the holiness of My great name which has been profaned among the nations, which you have profaned in their midst. Then the nations will know that I am the LORD,' declares the Lord God, 'When I prove Myself holy among you in their sight.'"*

When my second child, Micaiah, was young, one of her school assignments was to make a handmade family crest. These meaningful designs are not as common in modern day, but they were very popular in earlier centuries, and are also called a 'coat of arms.' They are made to represent a family's lineage, accomplishments, what the family stands for, and include symbols of the family's legacy. The family crest my daughter made represented her favorite characteristics of each person in our family. It was a symbol of honor, and a powerful representation of who we were in her eyes. I believe that God also has a family crest made up of His children. The name 'coat of arms' can describe how we arm ourselves to protect the integrity of a family. From a Christian standpoint, I believe we have a responsibility to protect the family of God, which is why I do not fully agree with those who will say things like, "God does not need us to accomplish His will." God can certainly accomplish His will, performing miracles by himself like rolling back the red sea, providing a ram for Abraham, or saving Daniel from the lion's den. But I believe He still needs us. He needed the Israelites to have enough faith to walk on dry ground. He needed Abraham's obedience. And He needed Daniel to remain a man of faith, so He could show an entire nation He was the one true God. During the time of Ezekiel, the Israelites were not helping God with their actions. This is one reason Ezekiel was preaching such strong sermons to them. They had turned their hearts away from God and were causing God's name and reputation to be bruised. They were causing God's family crest to lose integrity, since other nations were watching their behavior. When God's people do not follow His ways, it hurts His name. This is a grave concern for our Father because it can lead others to believe they do not need God. He needs us to live a life of faith and holiness to help usher in His wonder working power. We, as Christ followers, have a major part in upholding His name. We are His family crest. If we, as Christ followers, are behaving in ways that cause His name damage, I believe He will take measures to get our attention. He cares about His people. And He also cares about His reputation. If we are part of the family crest of God, we have a responsibility to protect His family. May we all do our part in helping God's name and reputation remain intact to those watching. May we all take great pride and honor in His family crest.

Today's Challenge To Dig Deeper:
How can you take responsibility in upholding God's family crest? Are there behaviors you need to adjust or change? Today, ask God to show you where He needs you to raise the bar.

Evening Reflection:
What did God talk to you about today regarding His family crest?

LIVE, YOU DEAD BONES!
March 28

Morning Rinse: Ezekiel 37-39
Featured Verses: Ezekiel 37:3-4 *He said to me, "Son of man, can these bones live?" And I answered, "O Lord God, You know." Again, He said to me, "Prophesy over these bones and say to them, 'O dry bones, hear the word of the Lord.'"*

I was 34 years old, 6 months pregnant with my son, and attending the International Institute of Mentoring Conference for Women, led by Judy Jacobs, a gospel singer and pastor. This mentoring program was not designed for women who were wanting to be leaders. It was FOR leaders, and I had the honor of being accepted into the first year of the program, along with about two hundred other ladies from across the globe. To say that I was excited to be there is an understatement. Having another leader see leadership qualities in me is such an amazing feeling. But walking out a lifestyle of leadership is not always easy. There have been times when, despite my devotion to God, I have felt dry or even dead inside. While I was at the conference, I had one of those dry spells. I felt like God was a thousand miles away, and I could not figure out why. I had not been struggling with any major sin or concealing a dark secret. In fact, I had remained faithful to my devotions and continued my walk of faith. Yet there was a part of my heart that felt hopeless, as if I were in a valley of despair. I even felt somewhat forgotten, despite the excitement of being invited to this program with such a well-renowned leader. I loved God and desperately wanted to serve Him. But something was wrong. Every moment of the three-day conference was full of power, prayer, and impartation. But there was one moment that will forever be etched into my spirit as a turning point for both me and my son in my womb. I had on black pants and a royal blue maternity blouse, and I stood on the right side of the sanctuary, about 4 rows from the front. When Pastor Jacobs began singing "Days of Elijah," I felt God call me to come to the altar. As I stood at the front weeping, Pastor Jacobs began singing the verse to this song. "These are the days of Ezekiel, the dry bones becoming as flesh."[11] As she sang on the stage, I desperately cried out to God to speak to me. To say anything. I begged Him to breathe life into my dry soul and restore hope back into my heart. In a single second, He answered my heart's cry by injecting life back into me. I cannot fully explain how, but I felt my spirit come alive. Then He whispered something I will never forget, "You are not forgotten." Together, my son and I experienced this God moment. I knew in my heart he felt it too, and I now have a son named Ezekiel. My miracle of life happened that day.

Today's Challenge To Dig Deeper:
Look up the song "Days of Elijah" and listen to it. Let God jumpstart an area of your life that you have felt was dead. Let Him breathe life into you again in that area. May your dry bones live.

Evening Reflection:
Did God breathe life into you or someone else through you today? Write what happened.

---

[11] **"Days of Elijah Lyrics."** *Lyrics.com.* STANDS4 LLC, 2022. Web. 26 May 2022. <https://www.lyrics.com/lyric/7614214/Don+Marsh/Days+of+Elijah>.

HEAR HIM
March 29

Morning Rinse: Ezekiel 40-42
Featured Verse: Ezekiel 40:4 *The man said to me, "Son of man, see with your eyes, hear with your ears, and give attention to all that I am going to show you; for you have been brought here in order to show it to you. Declare to the house of Israel all that you see."*

Today's Morning Rinse documents a vision that Ezekiel had about the building of a temple. In this vision, he follows an angel around as he measures all the rooms inside the temple, as well as the outside of the temple. Details and instructions for the outside were shown to Ezekiel, such as how many steps were to go into the temple, measurements of the gates and porches, and even the measurements of the walls. The inside of the temple was just as detailed and orderly. This vision included rooms like the inner court and the guardrooms, as well as the windows inside. Scholars have debated on what temple Ezekiel's vision was referencing. Some say it is the blueprint of the temple that Zerubbabel should have built, but never completed. Others say it is the temple to be built during the millennial reign of Christ. Some say it is more of a symbolic temple of worship. And then still others say it is a symbolic representation of the temple when God reigns in the new heavens. No matter what the true meaning is, the vision was meant to be shared with the Israelites, to provide them with hope. The people had just witnessed their nation destroyed, and needed to hear a message from God, that there was something to look forward to. While there are multiple interpretations of what this vision could mean, we all can agree on two things. God cares about the details, and God is a God of order. Are we attentive to His details and the plans He has for our lives? Do we see with our eyes, hear with our ears, and give attention to all that He is showing us? His desire is for us to fit perfectly into His plan, with His measurements. Why? Because we are all part of His story, and He wants us to join in His solution for building His kingdom. We might not know exactly what He is telling us at first, or what His messages all mean, just like these chapters describing this temple. It is not always about knowing every single meaning behind what He tells us before we get started. Sometimes it is about being attentive, and opening our eyes and ears to His voice so He can continue to reveal more. Sometimes He is waiting on us so He can show us more of the details as we step out in faith. He is ready to share. Are you ready to hear?

Today's Challenge To Dig Deeper:
God wants to talk to you today. Tell Him you want to see with your eyes, hear with your ears and give attention to what He wants to show you. Listen all day to His voice. Hear Him. And be attentive to what He is telling you.

Evening Reflection: What did God talk to you about today?

TITHE MY HOME?
March 30

Morning Rinse: Ezekiel 43-45
Featured Verse: Ezekiel 45:1 *And when you divide by lot the land for inheritance, you shall offer an allotment to the Lord, a holy portion of the land; the length shall be the length of 25,000 cubits, and the width shall be 20,000. It shall be hold within all its boundary round about.*

No matter where you live, God can fill your home with His glory, just like He filled the house of the Lord in Ezekiel's vision. What does that mean? First, let us look at what it does NOT necessarily mean. Most likely there will not be a physical fire on top of your roof, or a cloud settling throughout your rooms. It is usually not that kind of glory. What it IS, though, is His peace. His presence. His joy. These are still physical traits of God working in and through our lives, so much, our spirit can tangibly recognize Him in the atmosphere. This is also recognized by others when they enter our home. It is God infiltrating our homes and surroundings until the atmosphere feels different. Sometimes people may feel it, but not know how to describe it other than using the word 'different.' When we give our time, dedication, and ourselves more fully to God, His glory will grow stronger in all that we touch. His presence will be felt. Therefore, in simpler terms, it will be recognizable to those around us through our spirit man. And with that, let us talk about tithing. What if we 'tithed,' or gave an offering of ten percent of our home to God as well, and invited His glory into that part of our world? I am not saying to only invite Him into a tenth of our homes. But dedicating our full home as part of an offering to Him. We are so used to talking about tithing our money or income, but tithing a portion of our home is a different concept. Or is it? What if we went back to the basics of simply dedicating everything? Our prayer for this might sound something like, "God, how would you have me use my home for you, and what changes do I need to make so your glory fills my atmosphere?" What if we prayed this each time we moved, whether to a new apartment, or after we purchased a new home? What if we even prayed this prayer when we purchased a new car? Would it not be amazing to hear comments from friends who enter our home or ride in our vehicle, that they could tangibly feel God's presence? We are accustomed to this prayer when our churches buy a building or utilize a new space. Why is our home or car any different? Be ready for God to answer. He may state the changes that are needed to bring in His presence. Sometimes a small shift will bring big breakthroughs. Other times, it will require bigger adjustments.

Today's Challenge To Dig Deeper:
Dedicating or tithing a portion of your home back to God may require changes. Is it setting up an area of prayer? Is it anointing your home with oil? Is it playing soft worship music 24/7? Is it being more hospitable, and inviting people over? Today, ask God how you can dedicate a portion of your home back to Him, and ask Him what changes can be made to invite more of His glory into your home.

Evening Reflection:
What assignment did God give you regarding your home?

ARE YOU A RIVER?
March 31

Morning Rinse: Ezekiel 46-48
Featured Verse: Ezekiel 47:12 *By the river on its bank, on one side and on the other will grow all kinds of trees for food. Their leaves will not wither and their fruit will not fail. They will bear every month because their water flows from the sanctuary, and their fruit will be for food and their leaves for healing.*

One does not need to be near a river to see the majesty of its formation and glory, and to see the life that surrounds its shores. The birds flying over, the trees blanketing the beaches, and the distant ripples of water indicating animals below the surface are chasing each other. Standing at a distance will give one a bird's eye view, and offer the beholder a perception of wonder. That same wonder is captured up close and personal to the shore, where the river begins. This last portion of the book of Ezekiel gives an exciting description of the new temple and city, all capturing God's holiness and the life He gives us when we enter His presence, including the River of God that Ezekiel writes about. God's reach is far and wide, as seen in the bird's eye view. His life-flowing presence does not stop, but keeps flowing. What happens when we enter His river? Just like a natural river provides life-giving principals to the trees and animals surrounding the water, we will naturally be accepting life from Him. Then as we accept this life-giving water and live it out, it will obviously spread to others because we are living it out. How we live directly affects the lives around us. Is the fruit, or 'water,' that comes out of us from The Word? If so, we will naturally be providing life for others to grow. When others begin to grow spiritually, there will be more fruit present in the world. In the big picture of a vast river, there will be life-giving principles manifested to the masses. It just takes one person to begin spreading this water. Will you be the one? Will you allow your life-giving river to be captured through the eyes of others?

Today's Challenge To Dig Deeper:
Google a picture of any river. Look at the picture with intention for several minutes, capturing the details of the river and its surroundings. Notice the life in the photo. Ask God to show you where in your life He wants you to provide life to others. Say a simple prayer, asking God to help you be that river, providing life to others through the Word and your life.

Evening Reflection:
What did God speak to you about through the picture of the river?

April Rinsing

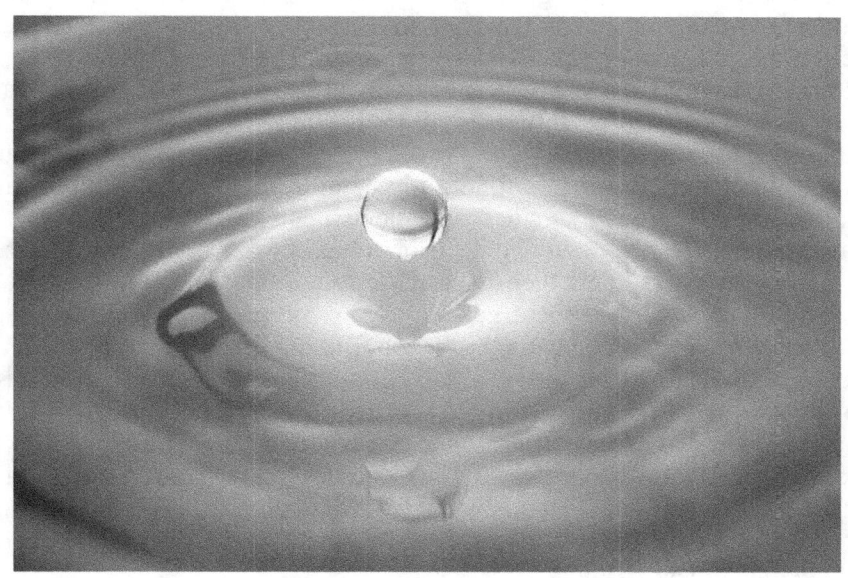

STIRRING THE HEART
April 1

Morning Rinse: Ezra 1-4
Featured Verse: Ezra 1:5 *Then the heads of fathers' households of Judah and Benjamin and the priests and the Levites arose, even everyone whose spirit God had stirred to go up and rebuild the house of the Lord which is in Jerusalem.*

I have many fond childhood memories of my mom standing at the stove, stirring chili in a big silver pot. She nearly always wore a handsewn apron, and most of them matched her also handsewn sunflower curtains that matched the yellow painted kitchen walls. She would stand with her big wooden spoon and slowly stir our dinner. For a young mind, sometimes dinner seemed to take a lifetime. But the stirring of the meal was part of the process. It was almost an art. For dinner to taste its finest, one may need to know when to stir at the perfect time so to not only avoid the food sticking to the bottom of the pot, but also to ensure ingredients were cooked evenly. When it was time for us to indulge, my mom would scoop the meal out and hand us our bowls. I believe God stirs our hearts like this. I like to call our hearts His heavenly pot, where He first drops in the vision for our lives. He then stirs in faith for the journey, people to encourage us, leaders to keep us strong, training in our craft, needed resources, and of course, His Word for guidance. He stirs and stirs with the hope that we will yield to this stirring, or what we also refer to as His calling on our lives. In today's Morning Rinse we begin reading the book of Ezra, one of multiple books that captures the return of some in the exiles to Jerusalem. Ezra documents various pieces to the story, including the work that was entailed with the temple construction. The task of building the temple was no small feat, and required not only many resources, but a unification among thousands of workers. These workers had to decide whether they would answer the stirring in their hearts to help. Despite the tough decision to uproot their families and start over in a new location, these workers knew their mission: to rebuild the temple. Seven months later, roughly the time it took to move and get settled, the people came together to begin this mission. Unified. All with stirred hearts for the job. But did the work really begin at the time of construction? No. The work began when God started stirring their hearts. Just like the soup was ready for us to eat after my mom prepped it. When we obey the stirring of our hearts, we are molded by God's craftiness, and are vessels used in kingdom work. It can be hard answering the stirring of our hearts. It can often require the acceptance of faith and change. And it takes time. But may we all yield to that stirring.

Today's Challenge To Dig Deeper:
The process of 'stirring the heart' is lifelong. God never stops nudging us. While we may never move to a city to build a temple, God needs His kingdom built in other ways. What is He nudging you to do? God has probably already been stirring your heart about something. Talk to Him about it today and work towards making steps to walk out that journey.

Evening Reflection:
Write down what He stirred your heart about today, and one action you took to begin the journey of answering His stirring. Was it writing down what He's talking to you about? Was it making a few phone calls? Whatever step you took, write it down.

FAVOR
April 2

Morning Rinse: Ezra 5-7
Featured Verses: Ezra 7:27-28 *Blessed by the Lord, the God of our fathers, who has put such a thing as this in the king's heart, to adorn the house of the LORD which is in Jerusalem, and has extended lovingkindness to me before the king and his counselors and before all the king's mighty princes. Thus I was strengthened according to the hand of the LORD my God upon me, and I gathered leading men from Israel to go up with me.*

The first six chapters of Ezra capture the return of a group of exiles led by Zerubbabel. Ezra, himself comes on the scene beginning in chapter seven, about eighty years after Zerubbabel. Many teachers and preachers describe Ezra as a hero of faith. Some, in fact, compare him to Moses because he not only studied the Law that God gave Moses, but he was one of the greats in the Bible who lived it out. In today's Morning Rinse we read the story where Ezra went to King Artaxerxes and asked for help in his journey, leading this second group of exiles to Jerusalem. I believe that Ezra was a man of high ranks in the kingdom of King Artaxerxes, and the king witnessed first-hand God working in Ezra's life, which led to the king respecting Ezra. This respect was, in fact so high, he gifted Ezra and the people with gold and silver to use in buying bulls, rams and lambs for their sacrifices. He also gave them extra gold and silver to use in whatever Ezra needed for the journey, and then went above and beyond these extra donations, and told Ezra if he had any other needs, Ezra had permission to take from the royal treasury. Talk about favor. He also wrote a letter for Ezra to carry with him to give to kings along the way. This letter not only documented permission for the exiles to be with Ezra, but it also confirmed that all the gold and silver that they had in their possession was not stolen, but rather gifts directly from King Artaxerxes. In this letter, the king also issued an order for other kings to grant the people passage through their land on their way to Jerusalem. And he also wrote for them to grant to Ezra whatever he needed, and to do it with zeal. It is not recorded in the Bible that King Artaxerxes was a man who practiced God's Law, and yet Ezra found favor with him because of his life of faith. King Artaxerxes knew God was real, and did not want God's anger upon him or his kingdom if he treated Ezra wrong. As we live out our lives of faith, we will find favor with many, even those who are not Christ followers. God can, and will, move many hearts, regardless of their lifestyle, to give us resources that will help us carry out His plan for our lives. This is how God gives us favor. This is how He works. He loves blessing His children and strengthening us this way. Do not be afraid to ask for help from even those who do not live out biblical principles.

Today's Challenge To Dig Deeper:
Is there something that you need in your life today? Do not underestimate the power of living out your faith. The hand of God is on your life, and favor will come. Ask someone to meet a need today, and watch God work through favor.

Evening Reflection:
What favor was given to you today, and who granted it?

UNPLUG IT
April 3

Morning Rinse: Ezra 8-10
Featured Verses: Ezra 9:5-6 *But at the evening offering I arose from my humiliation, even with my garment and my robe torn, and I fell on my knees and stretched out my hands to the Lord my God; and I said, "O my God, I am ashamed and embarrassed to lift up my face to You, my God, for our iniquities have risen above our heads and our guilt has grown even to the heavens."*

In the first week of my daughter's senior year and my son's freshman year, we were all still trying to acclimate to the new routine of the school schedule, after being off for three months. Right before hopping in their car to ride to school together, my daughter hit a round dimmer light switch on the wall to turn a light off. Next to the light switch is our security alarm panel. When she went to hit the dimmer switch, she accidentally hit the security panel instead, and triggered the emergency setting, sending off a screeching noise both inside and outside the house. For 15 minutes, I ran through the house in sheer panic mode, trying everything I knew to turn the annoying noise off so I would not only save my ears, but save the relationship with our neighbors. From calling my husband for help, to punching in the 'normal' code a bazillion times, to nearly pulling out every wire from the alarm box, we discovered the alarm was stuck. My father-in-law, and the builder of our home, stayed on the phone with me ten minutes trying to solve the problem, but to no avail. I sent the tardy kids off to school, and waited for my father-in-law to show up at my doorstep, followed by the police. Later, we were told that our alarm system, once tripped this way, could only be turned off with a secret code, of which we obviously had no knowledge. Extremely stressed, I decided to take one last look at the alarm box mounted in our hall closet. As I opened the door for what seemed the thousandth time, my eyes saw the most embarrassing thing. The system was simply plugged into the wall. All I had to do was reach down and unplug it, and the annoying noise immediately ceased. I could not believe my eyes, or ears for that matter. I laugh about it now. But I learned a lesson that day. Sometimes we simply must unplug the source of our annoyances, or sin. In today's Morning Rinse, Ezra preached this same message to the Jews regarding the men marrying pagan women who brought idols into their marriages. In fact, Ezra took the time to not only teach this lesson, but to repent for the sins of the people. In his own way, he was trying to unplug the sin.

Today's Challenge To Dig Deeper:
Is God trying to get your attention by setting off an alarm in your life? Is sin or behaviors that are not God-honoring in your life, that need to be unplugged? Start today with repenting. Then ask God to help you unplug it.

Evening Reflection:
Describe your 'unplugging' process.

THE BEST NEWS EVER!
April 4

Morning Rinse: Galatians 1-3
Featured Verses: Galatians 1:15-16 *But when God, who had set me apart even from my mother's womb and called me through His grace, was pleased to reveal His Son in me so that I might preach Him among the Gentiles. I did not immediately consult with flesh and blood.*

A couple's long journey of infertility is now over with their first pregnancy... an aspiring actress gets nominated for an award... a young lady in love gets asked to be a bride... a little boy is given a puppy for Christmas. All these scenarios set the recipient up to receive some GREAT and AMAZING NEWS!!! I think it is safe to say that we all have extraordinary days that are etched in our memories, allowing us an opportunity to celebrate. With hope and excitement, we savor these exciting moments from that special day. While these moments create the best days of our lives, there is even better news than this. Today's Featured Verses tell us about this news. Galatians is a book about freedom in Christ through grace. This grace grants us the freedom of salvation, giving us the hope of eternal life through Christ. And it gives us unmerited, or undeserved favor with our Heavenly Father. Being able to receive this grace is the best news we can ever receive! Along with the fact that we all can have this freedom through Christ, Paul also writes in this book about the fact that we are all called by God, even in our mother's womb, for a purpose. The second part of this good news is the realization that not only do we have access to God's grace, but we are all called for kingdom purpose. This kingdom purpose is to help spread the amazing news of God's grace through salvation. This makes the best news ever a doubly good message. The gospel is for everyone. Jesus came that we all might have life through forgiveness in Him, no matter what we have done. So be confident that you were called for kingdom purposes before you were even born. You have an amazing purpose. And that purpose is to help spread the amazing news of grace and hope. Both are THE BEST NEWS EVER!!!

Today's Challenge To Dig Deeper:
Try and find a picture of your mother when she was pregnant with you. Focus on it. Meditate on the fact that God had already called you for a purpose while you were even in her womb. Relish in the fact He knew you even then. Also, pray today for those unsaved. Be confident that God has called them as well.

Evening Reflection:
Did God speak to your heart today about how important you are to Him? Did He embed more confidence into you regarding your calling and purpose? Write about how you feel from this message from Galatians.

BE POLLINATED AND A POLLINATOR
April 5

Morning Rinse: Galatians 4-6
Featured Verses: Galatians 5:22-23, 6:1 *But the fruit of the Spirit is love, joy, peace, patience, kindness, goodness, faithfulness, gentleness, self-control, against such things there is no law... Brethren, even if anyone is caught in any trespass, you who are spiritual, restore such a one in a spirit of gentleness, each one looking to yourself, so that you too will not be tempted.*

My lack of a 'green thumb' is often the topic of household jokes. I have killed more plants than I've kept alive, and yet I keep trying to grow them. I have visions of blueberry bushes, grapevines and fruit trees lining my property, along with multiple flowering Crape Myrtles towering our driveway. Almost every spring I plant something new to fill the spots where plants have died, or where color is lacking in my yard. Since most of the fruit trees I have planted need a partner tree to pollinate, I will often plant multiple bushes or trees to help ensure pollination will be successful. I usually gravitate towards plants that are tough to kill, like my strawberry patch. But even amidst my planning and research, most of what I plant does not survive, due to my lack of watering or feeding properly, or my failure to treat them against the horrible fruit fungus that kills off new growth. Having the Fruit of the Spirit is no different. It takes cultivation by regularly reading the Bible, and it also takes the intentional pursuit to keep sin, or our 'carnal fungus,' at bay. Another way of perfecting the Fruit of the Spirit is by being part of a community of believers who push us to grow in the fruit. The Word of God along with other believers, is pollination. They will both hold us accountable if we let them. As Christ followers, we are never excused from being pollinated and becoming more like Christ. And we are also never excused from being pollinators for others as we make disciples. Here are 6 steps to being both pollinated as well as pollinators, so the Fruit of the Spirit thrives in us all:

1. Have the desire to be pollinated through reading The Word.
2. Obey when God corrects behaviors that do not line up with His fruit.
3. Learn discernment between our flesh versus the Fruit of the Spirit.
4. Do not give up, when growing the Fruit of the Spirit.
5. Be willing to be a pollinator and help others grow their Fruit of the Spirit.
6. Remain open to accountability.

Today's Challenge To Dig Deeper:
Memorize Galatians 5:22-23. Ask God to produce in you more fruit, and remain open to be the pollen for others to grow fruit as well. Watch for daily opportunities to be both pollinated and to be a pollinator.

Evening Reflection:
Did God put an opportunity in your path today to start growing the fruit that you asked him to grow? Did He give you an opportunity to pollinate fruit in someone else's life?

TWO TREES
April 6

Morning Rinse: Genesis 1-4
Featured Verses: Genesis 2:17, 3:22-23 *"but from the tree of the knowledge of good and evil you shall not eat, for in the day that you eat from it you will surely die"... Then the Lord God said, "Behold, the man has become like one of Us, knowing good and evil and now, he might stretch out his hand, and take also from the tree of life and eat, and live forever" - therefore the Lord God sent him out from the garden of Eden, to cultivate the ground from which he was taken.*

AWE. *The Creation Story*! The beginning of our beginning. The alpha of God's design. While many people may not even read the Bible, the creation story is probably one of the most recognizable passages from the Bible. Most are familiar with God taking six days to create, followed by a day of rest. Most know the story when God formed Eve from one of Adam's ribs. And of course, we all know about the Garden of Eden. This perfect haven was home to Adam and Eve, the animals, and to plant life. What often gets missed in the storytelling, though, is the fact that there was not just one tree set apart in the garden, there were two, the tree of life and the tree of knowledge of good and evil. The latter is the tree we hear most about. It is the tree that teachers talk about in Sunday School or children's pastors preach about it in Children's Church. It is the tree that God told Adam and Eve to stay away from. But what about this second tree, the tree of life? This one was different. We know that once someone ate from this tree, their soul was sealed for eternity, whatever state it was in. Once someone ate from the knowledge of good and evil, their eyes were opened to this tree. Both trees reeked of temptation. I believe God's perfect plan from the beginning was to allow Adam and Eve, as well as their descendants, to stay in the Garden of Eden. Along with that plan, and due to His loving heart, He had to give them a choice, just like He gives us a choice in how we live our lives. When they disobeyed and ate from the tree of knowledge of good and evil, their eyes were opened to the sin nature, and they had to suffer the consequences of their disobedience. Since Jesus was not yet born, there was no chance of being saved if they ate from the tree of life. God had to remove them from the temptation. So yes, He kicked them out of their home. God is not one to remove us from fun, loving environments just to be mean. He specializes in trying to save us from something that could harm or even kill us. Of course, I would imagine they were not happy about being moved from their perfect haven, to where they now had to cultivate their own food, versus enjoying a pre-made garden. I am sure they were also not pleased having to suffer pain, such as birthing pains, natural death, and more. But God's love for them, and for us, includes not just giving us consequences to help us learn to obey Him, but protection from future destruction and death, which now faced them every day with the tree of life.

Today's Challenge To Dig Deeper:
Are you living out some consequences right now due to some past choices? Despite the consequences, do you believe God is in your story? Pause and reflect today, and ask God to show you where He is in your story, and ask Him to give you a different perspective of His love.

Evening Reflection:
Did you get a different perspective today, thinking about your life and where you're at?

PITCHING OUR LIVES
April 7

Morning Rinse: Genesis 5-8
Featured Verse: Genesis 6:14 *Make for yourself an ark of gopher wood; you shall make the ark with rooms and shall cover it inside and out with pitch.*

Yesterday, we read one of the most popular stories in the Bible. Today, our Morning Rinse includes yet another one, the story of Noah and the ark. From church nurseries all the way to adulthood, we are taught about the flood waters that destroyed the earth, and how God saved Noah, his family, and the animals, by directing Noah to build the ark. Not only did God give detailed instructions to Noah on the type of wood to use and the measurements in how to build it, but we also get some insight into how he sealed the ark with a protectant called pitch. Today's Featured Verse shows us that Noah covered the ark with this pitch, both on the outside and the inside, giving it a double barrier. Pitch was very similar to a tar-like substance used to keep the ark watertight, and some scholars believe the pitch had a second purpose, to make it impact resistant as well.[12] The extreme, forceful blows from the waves and debris hitting the ark could have caused extreme amounts of damage. This second layer of protection from the pitch provided a covering, or shield, from these types of impacts, making the ark ultimately 'blast-proof.' When I realized how much God had Noah protecting this temporary home for him and his loved ones, I asked myself, "Have I fully 'pitched' my home?" To spiritually pitch our hearts and homes is to make decisions that lead to a 'world-tight' and 'blast-proof' home, protecting from the darts of the enemy. God wants us to protect ourselves and our families from the enemy and his schemes, especially since we know the enemy is out to destroy us. We safeguard by making daily decisions that not only help keep temptations at bay that could lead to destruction, but help keep us close to God. A friend of mine named Russ Tuttle often quotes this statement in his seminars, "We need good men to be better." That is you and that is me. The process of continually safeguarding the inside and the outside of our homes, spiritually pitching, just helps keep harmful things at bay. It is a lifelong, daily process. But once we begin, it makes it harder for Satan to damage the hearts of those we love.

Today's Challenge To Dig Deeper:
Ask God what you need to do to pitch your home. Do you need to change the music or movies you expose your family to? Do you need to change the entertainment choices you make on the weekends? Whatever God is talking to you about, listen to His still, small voice. Yield to His prompting and obey, going the direction He is leading you.

Evening Reflection:
What changes did you implement to pitch your home for your family? How did your family respond?

---

[12] https://creation.com/noahs-ark-pitch

RAINBOWS AND UNICORNS
April 8

Morning Rinse: Genesis 9-12
Featured Verses: Genesis 9:14-15 *It shall come about, when I bring a cloud over the earth, that the bow will be seen in the cloud, and I will remember My covenant, which is between Me and you and every living creature of all flesh; and never again shall the water become a flood to destroy all flesh.*

My middle daughter, Micaiah, began playing softball at the young age of six years old. She not only enjoys the game and being around her friends, but she also loves learning the technical aspects of the sport. Even at the young age of six, she had an eye on the mound, and told us she wanted to learn to pitch. Finally at eleven years old, we realized her desire was not going anywhere, so we began paying for private lessons. Since we waited until she was a little older to start these lessons, she was slightly behind her peers regarding training. She knew this and would oftentimes pitch with less confidence when a storm of insecurity would brew inside her. One day, in a fun conversation, she expressed her love for rainbows and unicorns, and told us how they made her heart happy. We jokingly told her coach about these favorite things of hers, and from that conversation, a small movement of the rainbow message of hope among teammates and parents was birthed. When someone noticed this storm of insecurity manifesting in her by her stressed demeanor, they would suddenly yell out to her, "RAINBOWS AND UNICORNS!" Notoriously, each time she heard it, her face would light up with a smile, and the demeanor of her whole body would change. We all knew the effects this message had on her, and sometimes multiple people would yell in sync, making a ruckus in the stands and dugouts to help her refocus and claim this hope. Her change in mentality would oftentimes ultimately help her lead the team to win more games because she would pitch better. The rainbow message we yelled to her would come at just the right moment in time for her to take a pause on the mound, smile, wind up, and then nail a strike on her next pitch. As I write this, she is now one of the starting pitchers in college, and she also gives private lessons to young girls, teaching them the art of fast pitch and passing on the rainbow message of hope to the next generation of softball players who want to learn to pitch. Maya Angelou once quoted, "If God put the rainbows right in the clouds themselves, each one of us in the direst and dullest and most dreaded and dreary moments can see a possibility of hope. Each one of us has the chance to be a rainbow in somebody's cloud."[13] We live life better with hope.

Today's Challenge To Dig Deeper:
Do you or someone you know need a rainbow message of hope today? God is the God of rainbows. First, print out a picture of a rainbow and put it somewhere to remind you of this hope. Then look for those who may need you to be their rainbow in a storm today.

Evening Reflection:
Write about any interactions you had today that helped spread the rainbow message of hope. Where did you put your rainbow picture?

---

[13] https://www.azquotes.com/quote/799253

TURN BACK
April 9

Morning Rinse: Genesis 13-16
Featured Verse: Genesis 16:5 *And Sarai said to Abram, "May the wrong done me be upon you. I gave my maid into your arms, but when she saw that she had conceived, I was despised in her sight. May the LORD judge between you and me."*

God gave a well-known promise to Abram that his descendants would be like the stars, too many to count. This promise was given to Abram at a time when both he and Sarai, later known as Abraham and Sarah, were not only childless, but they were getting to an age when bearing any children at all seemed hopeless. So Sarai decided to take matters into her own hands and give Hagar, her maid, to Abram as his wife, in the hopes that Hagar would bear him a child and be the conduit to fulfill this promise. Her plan seemed to work when Hagar conceived. However, when this happened, the relationship between Sarai and Hagar became more complicated than probably either of these ladies bargained for. It seems Hagar became a bit prideful, and Sarai became a bit bitter, causing the perfect storm for major conflicts between the two. Sarai even began blaming Abram for the issues in the relationship. How many times do we make choices that involve others, whether it be God's perfect plan or not, and when the fruit of those efforts come to fruition, we have a change of heart and treat those involved poorly? All the intertwining details between the triangular relationship between Abram, Sarai and Hagar are not recorded, but we do know that Hagar had her breaking point and ran away. We later read that God met her where she was, comforted her and allowed her to vent her frustration. After Hagar finished venting, though, God told her to turn back and submit to Sarai's authority. Also in that conversation, God gave her an incredible promise, that He would multiply her descendants as well. I do not know about you, but I am sure that this promise was motivation enough for her to turn back, despite any fear of future harsh treatments from Sarai or consequences of her part in the bruised relationship. While we see in this story that Sarai took matters into her own hands trying to fulfill God's promise her way, God still used the situation for His glory. No matter what situation you are in, even if God did not ordain it, the trial can be an opportunity for God to show up and turn it around, if you trust Him. But He may need you to turn back. Hagar had a change of heart and obeyed, quit running, and trusted God with her future. She turned back. I am fully convinced that God dealt with Sarai as well, making the return of Hagar an example of reconciliation.

Today's Challenge To Dig Deeper:
Are you in a relationship that has become complicated, due to choices either of you have made? If God is nudging you to turn back and re-enter that relationship in obedience, then ask Him what steps He wants you to take. Obey Him so that He can work it out for His glory.

Evening Reflection:
Write down the situation you prayed about today, and what decision you made in turning back.

WILL OUR WALK STIR OTHERS TO MOVE?

April 10

Morning Rinse: Genesis 17-20
Featured Verse: Genesis 19:14 *Lot went out and spoke to his sons-in-law, who were to marry his daughters, and said, "Up, get out of this place, for the Lord will destroy the city." But he appeared to his sons-in-law to be jesting.*

Our Morning Rinse today includes the story of how God warned about, and then followed through with the destruction of two very evil cities, Sodom and Gomorrah. When Abraham found out that God was going to destroy these two cities, he asked God to change His mind. His tactic of negotiating was to plead with God to cease the destruction if there were a certain number of righteous men found there. God initially agreed to fifty (18:23-33). Abraham must have known that finding fifty righteous men would be difficult in such a corrupt area. So he proceeded to continue negotiating with God all the way down to just ten. But unfortunately, Abraham's efforts to save the people did not work. God was willing to spare destruction, but He could not even find ten righteous men. Therefore, the destruction of Sodom and Gomorrah commenced. When the angels told Lot about the destruction, they directed him to gather all his family members and leave. For reasons we can only assume, the men to whom Lot's daughters were engaged, did not believe Lot, and in fact, thought he was joking about the destruction. Why would this be the case? If we are not careful, our environment will affect our lifestyle and could compromise our faith and influence. Was Lot's witness potentially so weak that even his daughters' fiancés would not believe him? One would think Lot pleaded in desperation to save their lives, and yet, these two men were not influenced by Lot's imploration. Because they thought their future father-in-law was joking with them, they would not even take him seriously. We must remember how we live our lives will affect others. While we know that Lot's family was saved, some preachers believe that Lot lived a compromised life, tainted by his surroundings. This may have caused his voice and godly appeal in this moment to be ignored instead of followed by those he would have eventually lead as the frontrunner of his family. Instead of his voice being used to spur others to move, these men stayed behind and were destroyed. We often do not want to face the truth that our choices can affect others. Our lifestyle can make others move, whether towards God or away from Him.

Today's Challenge To Dig Deeper:
Pray this prayer, "God, please forgive all my poor choices and lack of passion towards you that may have caused others to suffer or move away from you. Help my choices and lifestyle always cause others to move towards you. Help me to live my life so that when I speak of you, people believe and move in the right direction."

Evening Reflection:
Pray the prayer again. Write down anything God speaks to you.

THE ALTAR WALK
April 11

Morning Rinse: Genesis 21-24
Featured Verses: Genesis 21:2, 24:58 *Sarah conceived and bore a son to Abraham in his old age, at the appointed time of which God had spoken to him... Then they called Rebekah and said to her, "Will you go with the man?" And she said, "I will go."*

As a preacher's kid, I have been in numerous services and camp meetings. I have heard many people through the years, verbally surrender themselves to God's will and plan for their lives. I have also seen countless alter calls where people have come forward for prayer as they dedicate their lives to God's purpose. Most of these people have made that public declaration by getting out of their seat and walking to the altar when a pastor gives an invitation to come forward. I, too, have been one of those people to make the 'altar walk' towards that commitment. In today's Morning Rinse, we read of two women, Sarah and Rebekah, who made similar declarations. We celebrate their stories and are encouraged to read about the miracles in their lives. Blessings and miracles are easy for us to desire. But let us be reminded about the sacrifices they made when they laid their lives down with a commitment to get those blessings and miracles. Sarah was 90 or 91 years old when she gave birth to Isaac. I wonder if she had to endure judgement from people who lacked faith. And what about the sacrifices to her body? Did she have added aches and pains from being pregnant at this age? And let us not forget how her body responded when she physically gave birth. I wonder how long it took for her to recover, and how weak her body felt. Next, there is Rebekah. She was living a comfortable and secure life with her family. But in ONE SINGLE DAY, the course of her entire future changed. She had to have been spiritually ready for that moment, because when her ONE DAY came, she was willing to step into the plan. Her heart was indeed willing to follow God's direction, and her actions proved it by her public declaration and commitment to follow Abraham's servant. She sacrificed being with her brothers, her parents, and her extended family. She left all that she knew in exchange for trusting God, and walking into the unknown. Both ladies were willing to be noticed by God and used in His plan. Both knew what they were sacrificing in exchange for a blessed life. Both were willing to make the journey of the 'altar walk' in their hearts, followed by their public actions. Are you ready for the walk?

Today's Challenge To Dig Deeper:
Search your heart today. Be willing to let God show you where you are hanging on to the comforts of this life, and ask Him to help you surrender. Then ask Him to help you make the 'altar walk.'

Evening Reflection:
What did God show you today? How do you feel, and did you surrender to the 'altar walk?' Are you ready for change, even if it could be hard and uncomfortable?

HUNDREDFOLD BLESSINGS
April 12

Morning Rinse: Genesis 25-28
Featured Verses: Genesis 26:12-14 *Now Isaac sowed in that land and reaped in the same year a hundredfold. And the Lord blessed him, and the man became rich, and continued to grow richer until he became very wealthy; for he had possessions of flocks and herds and a great household, so that the Philistines envied him.*

Have you ever felt a twinge of guilt for desiring a hundredfold blessing for yourself and your family? I will raise my hand and admit I have. Why is that? Why do we feel guilty for not only having this desire, but for when God's blessings begin to pour on our lives? Are not planting, seedtime, and harvest foundational principles of God's kingdom? Expecting these principles should be a way of life for a Christ follower. Jesus often teaches about this kingdom principle in His parables, so why can it be difficult to receive? Speaking for myself, I have found it difficult at times to celebrate the blessings due to feeling undeserving. I have also found it difficult because of a fear of the jealousy or resentment from the 'Philistines' in my life. Maybe I have been afraid of what they will think of me. Maybe it is a fear of being misunderstood. Regardless of the reasons, we must get past these fears. If God wants to bless us, He can do that. Jealousy is real and can be intimidating, especially if someone accuses us of being prideful or having a bragging spirit. However, God is not afraid of that judgement, and if He chooses to bless His children in any way, it is HIS to give. When we receive blessings, He wants us to be at peace and enjoy His gifts. In fact, when Isaac dug the wells and the disputes arose, Isaac would just pick up and move to another location. He did not even stay around. God just kept blessing him, though, despite having to start over in search of another well. Are you ready for your hundredfold blessings despite feeling undeserving or being afraid of the 'Philistines' in your life? Obedience commands a blessing, and as we continue walking out God's will and obeying Him, blessings will come. And when they come, God wants us to celebrate them. These blessings are from Him. He is a good Father who gives good gifts to His children. And in the right timing and situation, it is okay for others to see these gifts. May we get into the habit of expecting blessings, then thanking Him for the things He has given us. Let God handle the 'Philistines,' or jealous people in your life. Obey and let God bless you how He wants to. Claim the hundredfold and then thank Him when you receive it.

Today's Challenge To Dig Deeper:
Open a Word Document or grab a notebook, and begin writing down one hundred blessings in your life. They can be possessions, monetary gifts, people, health, or anything you claim as a blessing. If you do not finish today, add more in the days to come until you reach one hundred. Put this list in a place you will remember to read every so often. Thank God for each entry.

Evening Reflection:
Reflect on how you felt while capturing your list of one hundred blessings.

MOVING DESPITE FEAR
April 13

Morning Rinse: Genesis 29-32
Featured Verses: Genesis 32:11-12 *Deliver me, I pray, from the hand of my brother from the hand of Esau; for I fear him, that he will come and attack me and the mothers with the children. For You said, "I will surely prosper you and make your descendants as the sand of the sea, which is too great to be numbered."*

How would you feel if you were about to face the person that you deceived and stole from? Jacob was in this exact situation. He was about to face Esau, the brother whom he not only took his birthright from (25:33), but also his blessing (27:27-40). Twenty years had gone by since Jacob fled from Esau. But God told Jacob to return to his father's land and He would prosper him. This land is where Esau lived. Jacob was faced with the decision to trust God and face these fears, despite possible death from his potentially still angry brother. Overwhelmed with fear upon hearing that Esau was on his way to meet him with four hundred men, Jacob separated his flocks and possessions into two parts so that if Esau attacked one part, the other half could escape. He did not know what the outcome of this encounter would be, but believed Esau was setting out to kill him. During Jacob's extreme fear, though, he reminded God of the promises God made to him. Speaking God's promises will bring faith and hope as you face fears. This is what Jacob did. He faced his fears and while facing them, kept moving in the direction God told him to move, hanging on to the hope of God's promise. Despite his fear, he remained determined to obey God. Despite his fear, he did not turn back to the comforts he knew, but instead moved toward the promise. In fact, turning around was never even an option. So he kept walking forward, reminding God of the promise He had given. Even though he was worried about the possibility of losing all his possessions or even being killed during this encounter with his brother, he feared God and the consequences of disobedience even more. He somehow knew that if he would have stayed behind, he may have lived physically, but would have died spiritually because of his disobedience. Keep obeying despite the circumstances around you. Keep moving forward despite any fear you may have. Keep claiming God's promises despite the circumstances around you.

Today's Challenge To Dig Deeper:
What has God promised to you? Is there an act of obedience that may seem counter intuitive, but you believe God is telling you to obey? Are you afraid? Ask God to help you begin moving, despite any fear of His promise never coming to fruition. Ask Him to give you one action item for today and then begin obeying despite any fear.

Evening Reflection:
What is the action He spoke to you about and did you begin moving despite fear?

WHO ARE YOU?
April 14

Morning Rinse: Genesis 33-36
Featured Verse: Genesis 35:10 *God said to him, "Your name is Jacob; You shall no longer be called Jacob, But Israel shall be your name."*

Back in 2001, I went through a personal growth journey called Grace Adventure.[14] This three-month experience still exists as of the writing of this devotion. Any type of person can attend. Pastors, business professionals, college students, or even stay at home moms. It is a journey where people face issues of the heart and try to discover God's perspective of these issues, obstacles, or hard times. The leaders are trained to help guide the participants through their pain, helping them face fears and issues all with grace, and come out on the other side gleaning to victory. If each individual works hard, it can be a powerful adventure of grace. During this time, God reminds each person who He truly made them to be, and He gives character attributes to each person, affirming who they really are. So many times, we take on our pain as part of who we are. We begin calling ourselves words like broken, scared, or imprisoned, and we forget about the freedom we have in Christ. But when we accept God's view of who we are, it is almost like an emotional name change. There are several people in the Bible who received a literal name-change. Jacob was changed to Israel. Abram was changed to Abraham. Sarai was changed to Sarah, and Saul to Paul. These new names were tangible representations, or symbols, of how God's handiwork changed their lives. I even have a friend who was recently given a new name by God and literally changed his name to Christian. Maybe your name has not physically changed from Jennifer to Sally, or from Chris to Mark. But God wants us all to remember our change of heart when we surrender to Him. I believe God created us with certain attributes, and we may need to be reminded of those attributes so we can live them out in confidence through Him. These character attributes will become fresh and new again if we accept them, and they can be just as powerful as a literal name change. Through Grace Adventure, God spoke to me, having me declare my attributes. I learned what to speak to myself. The message that gave me an emotional name change is, "By the grace of God, I am a free, passionate, playful and courageous women who has a voice and who God views as trustworthy." This is who I am. Who are you?

Today's Challenge To Dig Deeper:
God is here to remind you of who you are in Him. Write down every word that you feel God is speaking over you, that describes who you are. Even if you do not believe it or feel it yet, write it down. God sees you for more than you see yourself. You are who God made you to be, and He is here to remind you of that. He loves you. With His help, write your list.

Evening Reflection:
Who does God say you are? Read your list of attributes one more time. Put your list somewhere in your home to see and read every day.

---

[14] http://graceadventure.org/

DON YOUR GODLY RUNNING SHOES!
April 15

Morning Rinse: Genesis 37-40
Featured Verse: Genesis 39:12 *She caught him by his garment, saying, "Lie with me!" And he left his garment in her hand and fled and went outside.*

I think we all know the story. Joseph, a man of integrity, gets tempted and instead of running towards the temptation, he runs away from it. Every day, Potiphar's wife would tempt him to have sex with her. But his godly integrity was stronger than the temptation, and his loyalty to his master was deeper than a sexual desire. So each day he would refuse her pleas. Each day he would decline sin. I am personally convinced that he did what he could, taking whatever action he could take, to avoid scenarios that put him in awkward situations with her. But he was an employee to the king and could not always avoid her presence. Avoiding temptation may not always be enough to keep it at bay. Sometimes temptation faces us so strong there is no way to avoid it. So instead of remaining in the scenario we are faced with, we must figure out a way to get out of the situation. The best way to get away from it is to run in the opposite direction. Grab your running shoes and get out. When Joseph could no longer just avoid Potiphar's wife, do you know what he did? He got extreme. He RAN! When we run away from temptation or sin, we in essence run towards something else. We run TO God and His principles. Despite Potiphar trying to rename Joseph as a rapist, and despite Potiphar believing his wife's accusations, Joseph remained faithful and pure. He knew he did the right thing. He knew he ran in the right direction. Our righteousness will always win. So what are you running away from, and what are you running towards? Is it godliness? Is it righteousness? May I encourage you to don your godly running shoes like Joseph, and sprint away from anything that keeps you from living a righteous life?

Today's Challenge To Dig Deeper:
Are there any temptations you need to run from? If so, focus today on praying for strength. Ask God to help you run from anything that is not His will. Keep this prayer strong in your life every day from this point forward.

Evening Reflection:
Did you put your godly running shoes on today? What temptations are you committed to running from?

GET UP
April 16

Morning Rinse: Genesis 41-44
Featured Verses: Genesis 42:1-2 *Now Jacob saw that there was grain in Egypt, and Jacob said to his sons, "Why are you staring at one another?" He said, "Behold, I have heard that there is grain in Egypt; go down there and buy some for us from that place, so that we may live and not die."*

"Get up and write, Anita." This was, in essence, what a friend said to me. I must admit, writing this devotional has taken years. At times, I have gone through months of it sitting on my desk with no words added. Whether that be from lack of inspiration, fatigue, writers block, or even thinking that it may never be possible to finish. But there is one friend who keeps on me. He is the force behind my push to get this completed. In fact, I have pondered for about a week on how to complete the devotion for today. And just this morning, I get a message from him. He basically told me to get up. "Good morning... I wonder what today's message... in a certain DEVOTIONAL... is about? You know, that DEVOTIONAL by Anita Cordell?... I sure wish it was preaching to me... instead, I am having to use someone else's DEVOTIONAL... I'm sure it's a great message... Somebody should get that thing published." So I write again. I push again. I get up. Thank you, Michael Engberg, for never giving up on me with this vision. We all need someone in our lives to give us a boost. And sometimes, we need to be the boost in the lives of our loved ones so they get up. Jacob was that boost in the lives of his sons. "Why are you just sitting there? Do something!" This question was, in essence, what Jacob asked his sons when he asked, "Why are you staring at one another?" Jacob had the respect of all his adult sons, and when he spoke, they listened and acted upon his direction. So when Jacob heard that there was grain in Egypt, his question was directed to his sons, basically stating, "Okay, what are you waiting for? Go get some grain!" All his sons obeyed his leadership to take care of what he asked them to do. In the stillness of our heart, has there been times where we are presented with the answer to a problem, and yet we sit and stare at those around us as if shell shocked? When we sit and stare, even with God's provision staring back at us, we may still have to take action to receive it. Stop sitting and staring. Get up and move.

Today's Challenge To Dig Deeper:
Are you sitting and blankly staring at God's provision without acting and moving towards it? Ask God to show you where you need to move and start heading towards that provision. And if today you need to be the boost in someone's life, encourage them to get up as well.

Evening Reflection:
What did God reveal to you today about His provision? How did you take action to move towards it?

RULE OUR SOUL AND GIVE LIFE!

April 17

Morning Rinse: Genesis 45-47
Featured Verses: Genesis 45:7-8, 27 *God sent me before you to preserve for you a remnant in the earth, and to keep you alive by a great deliverance. Now, therefore, it was not you who sent me here, but God; and He has made me a father to Pharaoh and lord of all Egypt; come down to me, do not delay… When they told him all the words of Joseph that he had spoken to them, and when he saw the wagons that Joseph had sent to carry him, the spirit of their father Jacob revived.*

In yesterday's Morning Rinse, we read that Joseph begged his brothers to not sell him to the Egyptians, but they did not listen to his heart's cry, and instead sold him anyway. It can be so easy to focus on the wrongdoings of others. In fact, we may have someone in our own personal lives that has treated us wrong or caused deep pain to our heart. But sometimes, these actions could very well be what God needs to occur for Him to fulfill a purpose. I do not believe it is always God's plan for hardship to come our way, or for others to treat us wrong. But according to today's Morning Rinse, it was not the brothers who sent Joseph to Egypt, it was God. Could it have been God who sent the caravan that journeyed right where they were holding Joseph? Could it have been God who planted the seed in the hearts of Joseph's brothers to sell Joseph? It appears it was God's way of orchestrating Joseph being hand delivered to Potiphar, one of the rulers of Egypt. Why? So Joseph could save the lives of his family and many in his nation. God needed a heart like Joseph's to fulfill this mission. While it may look like Joseph had no control over his life, he in essence truly did. He had control over his heart and soul, both before and after this event occurred. He could have remained bitter. But he did not. Instead, he realized the big picture in God's handiwork and came to a place of forgiveness and realization of his role in the plan. He realized that God had sent him there to save not just his family, but a nation. I believe Joseph fully realized God's plan the moment he saw his brothers. It was a moment of healing. That moment when he had his ugly cry, and all those in the house heard him, could have been the moment when he completely forgave his brothers and came to a full understanding. We may not save a nation through ruling or being in a high-ranking position. But if we rule our soul, stay positioned for God's purpose, and keep forgiving those who have done us wrong, we will be used to possibly save even one person who God needs us to save. When Joseph's brothers went back to tell Jacob of all that had happened, and that Joseph was indeed alive, Jacob's spirit revived with hope and life, giving him new energy that was needed in that moment to move his family.

Today's Challenge To Dig Deeper:
Are you going through something right now or are others treating you wrong? There could be a purpose in it. If nothing else, God could be using it to make you stronger so your heart will be positioned to provide life to others. What is God speaking to you about your hardships? Is there anyone you need to forgive so God can complete His work through you?

Evening Reflection:
Write down God's perspective of something hard you are going through right now. Did God reveal it? Now believe it.

PAYBACKS
April 18

Morning Rinse: Genesis 48-50
Featured Verses: Genesis 50:15, 20-21 *When Joseph's brothers saw that their father was dead, they said, "What if Joseph bears a grudge against us and pays us back in full for all the wrong which we did to him?"… "As for you, you meant evil against me, but God meant it for good in order to bring about this present result, to preserve many people alive. So therefore, do not be afraid; I will provide for you and your little ones," So he (Joseph) comforted them and spoke kindly to them.*

Paybacks can be a good thing. If a bank loans you money for an exciting home purchase, you pay it back. Or, if you have made a financial investment, then you will hopefully receive an amazing return on that investment, also known as a payback. But there is another kind of payback. It is what I typically think of when I hear this word. It is vengeance, retaliation or even a form of chastisement for wrongdoings, also known as a form of vindication. It is not uncommon for siblings to participate in ornery activities towards each other, to tattle on each other, have snarky sibling attitudes, or even play the game of payback if one does another wrong. This is the type of payback that Joseph's brothers feared. I cannot imagine the torment they felt, or the emotional weight they carried all those years for the decisions they made. How often did they think about Joseph? Did they whisper his whereabouts to each other, or was it a subject left unspoken, leaving each to silently lay at night wondering where he was? Regardless of this answer, it all came to a head when Jacob, who they felt protected any paybacks coming their way, died. Fear set in, and they began questioning if Joseph would begin playing the game of paybacks. Joseph could have easily sought revenge. But he ruled his soul. He forgave. He saw the big picture of God's handiwork. Once again, he reassured them of the 'God story' of their lives, and how they played a huge part in saving a nation. Joseph's answer to his brothers was full of God's love, grace, and hope, the opposite of the payback game. When we see the God story, we lay the payback cards down. And when we allow God to work in our hearts, we get to a place where we can even remind those who have caused pain to us about the power of God's redemptive love and grace. Showing this to others who know they have done wrong, though, will then set them up to reap the benefits of the first definition of paybacks, receiving a return on their investment with a revived heart of trusting in God and releasing fear.

Today's Challenge To Dig Deeper:
First, if there is anyone that you have wanted to play the payback game with in a vindictive way, ask God to help you forgive them. Ask Him to help you see the big picture. Work it out in your heart and ask God to show you how to respond to them through eyes of grace. And if there is anyone you come across today who is carrying the weight of past sins, be the vessel to lift them up and remind them of God's love.

Evening Reflection:
What did God speak to you today regarding paybacks? Also, did you have an opportunity to remind someone of God's love today?

RUN WITH HINDS' FEET
April 19

Morning Rinse: Habakkuk 1-3
Featured Verses: Habakkuk 2:2, 3:19 *Then the Lord answered me and said, "Record the vision and inscribe it on tablets, that the one who reads it may run"… Yet I will exalt in the Lord, I will rejoice in the God of my salvation. The Lord God is my strength, and He has made my feet like hinds' feet, and makes me walk on my high places.*

A student sits in class, confused about the lesson, and decides to bravely ask several questions to the teacher. While he thinks he is the only one with questions, he discovers that multiple students have those same questions. He also discovers from later conversations with these students, the reason they withheld raising their hands was because they lacked courage to do so. Therefore, they kept their arms frozen to their sides in anticipation of a fellow classmate being the brave one. Our faith journey can be like this scenario. In today's Morning Rinse, Habakkuk asked some tough questions that we may also have, but might be a little intimidated to ask. In chapter 1, he inquires to God about the evil in the world. He also asked why God allows some of it to even occur. The world seemed confusing to Habakkuk, and it was hard for him to see God at work in those moments. We may also feel this way at times. But God has an answer for us, just like He had an answer for Habakkuk. That answer is to seek a perspective of trust, being rooted and grounded in Him. God encouraged Habakkuk to be patient and wait on Him, trusting Him fully, even when he did not understand why certain things were occurring in his life. In answering Habakkuk's questions, God encouraged him to write down their conversations and document His response so he could remember what was said. When we write things down, it helps to keep our focus. It helps us remember what God has told us so when we do not see the end, or we get confused about the world around us, we can remember His words and keep trusting. This is what a hind, or female deer does when she runs. She can place her back feet exactly where her front feet just stepped, causing her to run securely, staying on track towards wherever she is going. This helps her trust the path. It helps her stay focused. God wants us to keep running towards Him like hinds' feet, with confidence, praising Him not just for what we see, but for the promises He has made. We must remember He is all knowing and no matter what our world looks like, or what questions we may have, God will do what is right and make His way straight. May we take one step in front of the other, staying on the path of trusting God, having freedom through Him even in times of uncertainty, crisis, and chaos. Run towards Him with hinds' feet and remain steadfast in His promises.

Today's Challenge To Dig Deeper:
Remember the things God has talked to you about. Whether they be visions, goals for your future, or promises He has made to you. Pray that your spiritual feet be like hinds' feet, sprinting towards faith and hope. Now, write down the vision in your heart, trusting Him as you write.

Evening Reflection:
Quietly reflect on what you wrote down today. As you lay your head down for sleep, talk to God about your life and goals. Ask Him to keep your hope and vision alive, trusting Him to wait on Him for the appointed time, no matter what your life may look like.

LIKE SIGNET RINGS
April 20

Morning Rinse: Haggai 1-2
Featured Verses: Haggai 1:14, 2:23 *So the Lord stirred up the spirit of Zerubbabel the son Shealtiel, governor of Judah, and the spirit of Joshua the son of Jehozadak, the high priest, and the spirit of all the remnant of the people; and they came and worked on the house of the Lord of hosts, their God… "On that day," declares the Lord of hosts, "I will take you, Zerubbabel, son of Shealtiel, My servant," declares the Lord, "and I will make you like a signet ring, for I have chosen you," declares the Lord of hosts.*

It is easy to believe that in our day and age, with technology and global resources, that we live in the busiest time of history. While that belief may actually be factual, the challenge to prioritize God's plans was even present back in biblical days. The short book of Haggai captures the rich and timely message of the importance of prioritizing our lives with God's 'to-do' list instead of our own agendas. There are consequences of not putting God first in our lives. During this biblical time, God wanted the temple to be rebuilt. Despite the people knowing this, they did not feel it was time, and prioritized their own agenda instead of the work to complete the temple. Due to their choices, they did not see the blessings in their lives. Haggai corrected them and reminded them to live with a heavenly focus, which at the time was to build the temple. The hearts of the people were stirred again to get their priorities straight, and they began walking in obedience. Of course, we see that God honored their obedience and immediately brought blessings to their households. Not only did God shower blessings on the people, but He spoke to Zerubbabel of his uniqueness in leading the people by comparing him to a signet ring. Signet rings contain an emblem unique to the king, and used to seal documents like a signature or notary. This message to Zerubbabel is something we can claim for our lives as well. We are unique to our Heavenly Father, just like personal signatures are unique, and He has chosen each of us for His kingdom. Whatever is in His plan for you to be a part of, you are worthy of the call. You are chosen, just like Zerubbabel.

Today's Challenge To Dig Deeper:
Today, pray that God will stir your heart to begin working on His 'to-do' list. Ask Him to show you what the list entails, and ask Him to help you write it, getting your priorities in line with His will. Have confidence knowing He has made you unique and your gifts and talents have a divine purpose. No one else is like you. Make the list and begin working on it.

Evening Reflection:
Did you feel your confidence rising today as you began owning the fact you are unique and chosen for heavenly purposes? What did God reveal to you today about His 'to-do' list? Did you make some changes in your priorities? Was your heart stirred for kingdom purposes?

3 - STAR REVIEW
April 21

Morning Rinse: Hebrews 1-3
Featured Verse: Hebrews 3:13 *But encourage one another day after day, as long as it is still called 'Today' so that none of you will be hardened by the deceitfulness of sin.*

My phone vibrated in my pocket, notifying me of a message coming through. I pulled it out and looked down. What came across the screen sent my heart rate from a calm level to a heightened panic. "Britney has given a 3-Star Review." "WHAT?" I said out loud. One of my businesses is renting out my basement as a short-term rental, through various hosting platforms. In the first year of allowing guests to come into my home and rent out this private space, no one has had any issues, until this day. In fact, all my other reviews received have been a 5-star rating. I work hard to make everyone comfortable, and to get feedback that someone was not happy with my services sent me into an immediate defensive mode. The reason for her 3-star review was unmerited, and of course I addressed the unfair ranking in my reply back to her. However, it did not change the fact that this rating was not connected to my hosting profile. In fact, I could feel myself starting to have ill feelings towards this individual for being so unfair. She had accused me of coming downstairs into the private space and 'straightening up' while they were still there. It is so vital to never be accusatory, even if something appears out of the ordinary. In my heart's state of heaviness, I complained to my son, Ezekiel, about the 3-star review. I could feel my heart battling the sin of bitterness towards Britney. However, my son became an example of living out Today's Featured Verse. "Mom, what is your average score now?" Still a little irritated, I answered that it was a 4.9 instead of my wonderful 5-star average. "Mom, that's a good thing. Anytime I see someone's rating is a 5-star, I think it's a bot. This will make your profile actually look better." He went on to say some other things to help my state of heart, and by the time our conversation was finished, he had encouraged me so much, my hard heart towards Britany had softened. Since receiving that 3-star review, I realized there will always be people around us ready to give unfair assessments of our services, or even our character. If this occurs, be like Ezekiel and encourage the hard heart away.

Today's Challenge To Dig Deeper:
As you go about your day today, look for opportunities to encourage someone. Even if it is a person with a hard heart, encourage them in Christ.

Evening Reflection:
Who crossed your path today that needed encouragement? Was it someone with a broken heart? Was it someone with a hard heart? Even if you did not see immediate change in them, write down the interaction.

HE SEES YOUR PILE OF KLEENEX
April 22

Morning Rinse: Hebrews 4-6
Featured Verse: Hebrews 4:16 *Therefore let us draw near with confidence to the throne of grace, so that we may receive mercy and find grace to help in time of need.*

A single mom cries alone in her bed after putting her child to sleep. The tears flow, not from feeling lonely or missing a mate. Her tear-stained pillow displays the overwhelming sense of pain for her daughter's broken heart. This mom cries out for help in a fatherless world, and longs for her child to believe she is loved by her earthly father. But instead, her child experiences a deep sense of rejection, and often cries many tears over the heartbreak of a father not present. Our Heavenly Father, though, is always present for us. When we go through hardships, it is common to feel a sense of loneliness, but He asks us to come boldly to His throne, bringing our needs to Him. When we take this step of faith toward His throne, this invites Him to walk WITH us through our valley. In this process, He offers grace to us to make it through to victory. The hope we have in Him must be the anchor of our soul. It must serve as our strength to keep pressing onward. The visual of this single mom is truly a reflection of us all. For we all experience loss at some point in our lives. Whether loss of a relationship, loss of a job, or even loss of a dream, none are exempt from this experience. When we feel these deep pains, what should we do? It is simple and yet often humbling. We must run to Him. This mom ran to Him in the stillness of the night, lying awake with a flood of tears streaming down the sides of her face. Next to her bed lay a pile of soiled Kleenex on the floor that she was too weak to pick up and throw away. How do you run to Him in your time of need? And when you run to Him, do you allow Him to help grow your trust in Him? Do you allow Him to secure the anchor in Him both stronger and deeper? What are you asking Him for? Let your trust in Him be your anchor, and do not let go. Keep believing He will supply what you need.

Today's Challenge To Dig Deeper:
Throughout your day today, ask God to help you walk to His throne, and ask Him for grace to see you through any struggles you may be experiencing. Ask Him to deepen and strengthen your anchor in Him, by helping you trust Him more through this process. Be assured He sees your pile of Kleenex.

Evening Reflection:
Write down what happened today in your heart in terms of your heartbreak or needs. Did you feel your anchor getting stronger and deeper as you went to Him with your needs?

STIMULATION
April 23

Morning Rinse: Hebrews 7-10
Featured Verses: Hebrews 10:1-2, 24-25 *For the Law, since it has only a shadow of the good things to come and not the very form of things, can never, by the same sacrifices which they offer continually year by year, make perfect those who draw near. Otherwise, would they not have ceased to be offered, because the worshipers, having once been cleansed, would no longer have had consciousness of sins... and let us consider how to stimulate one another to love and good deeds, not forsaking our own assembling together, as is the habit of some, but encouraging one another; and all the more as you see the day drawing near.*

Although we are constantly being made more and more perfect (or closer to the image of Christ), God cannot make us 100% perfect here on this earth. If we were perfect now, then maybe some, or all of our worship would cease. Yes, we worship in adoration of who God is. But also, in our praise, we are thanking Him for our need of repentance through His grace and mercy. During the time of the Law in the Old Testament, if God made the people perfect, they might not have made their annual sacrifices to Him in worship, nor would they have had a reason to sacrifice for the covering of sin. Could God love our worship so much that He chooses to not bring us to full perfection while we are here on this earth? If we cannot reach perfection here on this side of Heaven, we should stay committed to not only growing closer to the image of God, but helping others in their growth as well. How do we do this? One way is to stay faithfully involved in a local church! If we only go occasionally, we do not allow others to stimulate us in our growth, nor do we help others in their growth. This is one way we move as close to perfection as we can while on this side of Heaven.

Today's Challenge To Dig Deeper:
Have you found a local church to attend? If so, are you involved in it? Do you have a habit of attending on a regular basis? Are you actively encouraging others in your regular attendance of a ministry or small group? If you answered "no" to any of these questions, ask God to help you make some changes and commitments to yourself and your family today to be able to answer "yes" to them all.

Evening Reflection:
What changes did you make today within yourself or by commitments to your local church?

HOW DOES YOUR GARDEN GROW?
April 24

Morning Rinse: Hebrews 11-13
Featured Verse: Hebrews 12:14 *Pursue peace with all men, and the sanctification without which no one will see the Lord.*

Before heading to make her purchases, a gardener intentionally plans out the rows of her garden, selecting the best food to grow for her family. A good gardener understands that the chosen seeds, if watered and taken care of, will not only feed herself, but those around her. So she makes a trip to the local nursery and carefully selects the next season's harvest. What about the garden of our hearts? This garden, also known as our 'spiritual garden,' needs to be planted with intention as well. Exactly like the gardener growing food for nourishment for our bodies, what we plant in our hearts will be nourishment for the soul. When we grow and nurture the seeds of peace, for example, how we treat others will look completely differently than what we harvest from seeds of bitterness. Bitterness cultivates jealousy, anger, and ultimately immorality. But being intentional and planting peace will harvest unity and love, and is what God asks in a Christ-centered life. How do we do that? We let God heal our pain from bitterness, and instead, ask His help in pursuing peace with those around us. In other words, it is called forgiveness. This is being intentional with our spiritual garden. What we intentionally grow inside our hearts will absolutely affect others. What are people around you seeing from your garden? Are they experiencing peace, or are they experiencing bitterness? It is up to you as to what you grow in your 'spiritual garden.' If you do not have the strength to uproot any seeds of bitterness for your own good, get it out of your heart for the good of others. Be intentional and allow God to help you grow 'peace' seeds.

Today's Challenge To Dig Deeper:
Do you have ANY seeds of bitterness, unforgiveness, or resentment in your spiritual garden? Write on a piece of paper all the negative seeds you feel in your heart. One by one, ask God to uproot them, and then once you have felt the peace seeds take the place of what was uprooted, throw your piece of paper away. Finish your day walking with full forgiveness, nurturing the 'peace' seeds you just planted. Ask God to show you how to daily pursue peace with those around you.

Evening Reflection:
How does it feel to release the seeds of bitterness? Write down how your heart feels and any actions you took today to pursue peace with others.

POSSESSIONS FOR HIS KINGDOM
April 25

Morning Rinse: Hosea 1-3
Featured Verses: Hosea 2:8-9 *For she does not know that it was I who gave her the grain, the new wine and the oil, and lavished on her silver and gold, which they used for Baal. Therefore, I will take back My grain at harvest time and My new wine in its season. I will also take away My wool and My flax given to cover her nakedness.*

The love story of Gomer and Hosea is incomprehensible to most people. It is a story of the marital unfaithfulness and prostitution of Gomer, followed by Hosea's forgiveness of her. During the season of Gomer's sin, we read that she used the possessions given to her in irresponsible and sinful ways. These possessions were blessings given to her by Hosea while they were married, and are a picture of the blessings given to us by God. Peering into the life of Gomer, it is easy to judge how she abused the blessings and gifts given to her. And yet, are we guilty of this very thing in our lives? Do we take our blessings such as our money, our time, or our material possessions, and use them in ways that do not advance God's kingdom? Do we buy things we should not? Do we spend our time doing things we should not? Do we use our tithe money towards anything other than giving it back to God? If the answer is "yes" to any of these questions, then we are advancing the wrong kingdom with the very blessings God has given us. And just like Gomer, if we use our blessings for ways other than ways that honor God, we may make God regret giving us those blessings. May it never be.

Today's Challenge To Dig Deeper:
Sit quietly and scan your life with Jesus for 5-10 minutes. Celebrate the blessings of your life with Him. Now together, review how you use your blessings, like how you spend your money and your time. Watch in your mind's eye how you use your belongings. Is there any area you are using your blessings and gifts irresponsibly? What changes do you need to make?

Evening Reflection:
Becoming more responsible and trustworthy with our belongings is truly a unique way to give God glory. What changes did you make to use all your blessings for God's kingdom?

SILENT TEARS
April 26

Morning Rinse: Hosea 4-6
Featured Verse: Hosea 4:16 *Since Israel is stubborn like a stubborn heifer, can the Lord now pasture them like a lamb in a large field?*

A father yells at his son for not immediately obeying his repetitive instruction to do his chores. The scene is heart wrenching for everyone in the home, as it is uncomfortable to hear the screams from the father. The mother begins weeping, watching this scene too often acted out in her home by the display of her husband's uncontrolled anger. She quietly wipes her tears away so no one sees the pain in her heart. In this scenario, the question at hand is not whether the teenage son was guilty or not guilty of quick obedience. The question at hand is the behavior of the father. Why, you ask? It is simple. The question is so common from a heavenly perspective. Does this earthly father obey His Heavenly Father as quickly as he expects his son to obey? Or does God often shed silent tears like this mom, while watching the hypocrisy? How often does God ask us to do something, but the stubbornness in our hearts causes us to make it difficult for God to lead us? We often ask God to show us what to do in our lives, and yet, when He tells us through His Word or through the nudging of the Holy Spirit, we do not obey, or we take years to answer His calling. Why? It is not that we are bad people. But having stubbornness in our hearts causes a delayed obedience towards God, it is a protective barrier for our flesh. Yes, this son could have very well been stubborn. But we as parents, leaders, teachers, or anyone with influence, must make sure we keep ourselves obedient as we lead. We must first check our own hearts. Stubbornness is a lock on the gate to quick obedience, and can even cause us to run from God's help when we are in need. It is unfortunately linked to pride, which is sin. In Hosea's time, the nation of Israel had this kind of stubbornness towards God, causing heaven silent tears. Whether it be anger, bad habits, lack of tithing, or secret sin, may it never be that we expect our children, or those we lead, to obey us immediately, but we push God away when He instructs us with areas of our heart. May we never cause God to have silent tears from our lack of obedience.

Today's Challenge To Dig Deeper:
Stubbornness is a sinful shield that protects the fleshly areas of our heart from God. Where are you stubborn? What barriers or shields do you have that keep you from quick obedience towards God? Today, tear them down and begin a journey of quick obedience.

Evening Reflection:
What barriers did you tear down today? Did you begin a journey of quick obedience?

SQUELCH THE GLUTEN FEASTS
April 27

Morning Rinse: Hosea 7-8
Featured Verse: Hosea 7:2 *And they do not consider in their hearts that I remember all their wickedness. Now their deeds are all around them; They are before My face.*

When my son was little, he had an allergy to gluten. It was hard for him to see people eating things that he craved. So he would sneak food into his room and hide it under his bed until late at night, and then he would pull it out and have his own little gluten feast. I could always tell when this happened because he would wake up in the middle of the night with stomach pains, or he would be sick the following day. While this behavior is not considered sin, per se, he was hiding his behavior because he knew he was not supposed to do this. But God saw what he was doing. The stories in the Old Testament do not just capture the messages of prophets preaching to people we have never met, or stories of miracles that seem too good to be true. The pages of the Old Testament are full of rich, deep messages for us as well, including the words in the prophetic book of Hosea. In these short two chapters from today's Morning Rinse, we not only see Ephraim's iniquity, but we read how Israel reaps what they have sown from their sinful ways. How does this apply to us now? Or even to my son hiding his gluten snacks? Well, today's Featured Verse reminds us that God sees all that we are doing. Just like God saw how the people in the Bible behaved, and the sin they committed, He sees our actions too, just like when my son was eating things that would make him sick. There is nothing we do that is hidden from Him. The good, the bad, the ugly, the pretty, the wicked behaviors, and even the small things that could lead up to succumbing to sin. He sees it all. Today's reading reminds us of this fact. In our carnal minds, it is easy to forget this and think thoughts like "no one is watching" or "no one is home to see me do this." I am sure my son had these very thoughts. When we choose to do things that we would not want others to know we are doing, that is a good sign we should cease from those actions. And while some actions are not horrible, if we are hiding them, it could lead to further hidden behavior as we continue in life. Stay committed to keeping behavior in the light. If you are struggling with hidden behavior, remember that God sees what we are doing. I had to squelch the gluten feasts my son was having because it would make him sick. If we are not careful, our behaviors can lead to sin, making us sick as well. Are there any gluten feasts you need to squelch?

Today's Challenge To Dig Deeper:
While you were reading today's devotion, was there anything that came into your mind that God wants you to cease doing? Ask for His strength today to put those actions behind you.

Evening Reflection:
Did you repent and turn from the actions that God spoke to you about this morning? Celebrate forgiveness. Begin a new day.

KEEP YOUR WORD
April 28

Morning Rinse: Hosea 9-10
Featured Verse: Hosea 10:4 *They speak mere words, with worthless oaths they make covenants. And judgment sprouts like poisonous weeds in the furrows of the field.*

Have you ever known someone who made promises, or commitments, but they oftentimes did not keep them? Each time an unkept commitment was revealed, their integrity suffered. After multiple times of behaving this way, the value of their words begins to diminish rather quickly, leaving the recipient feeling frustrated, let down, and disappointed. One should never measure their integrity on the 'intent' to fulfill a promise, but rather by their actions. If our character was measured by intent, most of us would pass with flying colors. But intent is only as powerful as the actions behind it. If we speak, but have no action, then we speak with mere words, which are the same as worthless oaths. They are empty promises that cause our character to become untrustworthy. Oftentimes, we judge what comes out of our mouths, but only focus on whether our tongue formed a curse word or not. We can easily forget about the seriousness of a broken promise and the fact they are just as detrimental as cursing. It disappoints God when we are not true to our word. Are you guilty of this? This holds true to our commitments, not just to others, but our commitments to ourselves and even to God. Yes. Keep your word to all three.

Today's Challenge To Dig Deeper:
If you have broken any promises to God, to others or even to yourself, then ask for forgiveness. Start again and make those commitments right.

Evening Reflection:
Write about what God spoke to you today. Build a stronger foundation of integrity and keep moving forward in your walk with Christ.

DISPLAYS OF KINDNESS
April 29

Morning Rinse: Hosea 11-12
Featured Verse: Hosea 11:1 *When Israel was a youth, I loved him, and out of Egypt I called My son.*

Israel, God's chosen people to fulfill His plan and bring forth the lineage of David, was not always obedient. Just like parents must discipline their children when they misbehave, God had to discipline Israel. There are many examples of God having to discipline Israel throughout the prophetic books. But we must remember He still had love and kindness towards young Israel. This same kindness is in God's character for us as well, including young people needing correction and guidance. When God called the nation of Israel out of Pharaoh's hands, He called them "My son." We, too, are His children. His love for us is deeper and wider than we can even comprehend or imagine. He yearns to be with us, no matter what we have done. He longs to lead us, wrapping us in His loving arms. He longs to guide us, gently providing for us, calling us His own. God did not require Israel to obey by force, nor will He do this to us. But He does want to overshadow us with His kindness and love. May we all accept this from Him and reflect on the many times He has been gracious to us. May we pass this love and kindness on to others.

Today's Challenge To Dig Deeper:
Today, you have two challenges. First, reflect on your youth and thank God for His goodness to you in your childhood, no matter what choices you made. Second, look for someone, especially a young person, who needs to see the goodness of God. Maybe they are struggling. Ask God to use you today to shower some kindness and love in their life, despite how they may be behaving.

Evening Reflection:
Do you have a cool story from today where you showed kindness? Write down the experience. May this display towards others become part of your natural response to each other.

MAKE THE CALL
April 30

Morning Rinse: Hosea 13-14
Featured Verse: Hosea 14:4 *I will heal their apostasy, I will love them freely, for My anger has turned away from them.*

As we close on another book and another month, Hosea helps us end with a beautiful call to salvation and the promise that God will turn His anger away. It is not too late for anyone, no matter what choices they have made, to repent and return to God. No one is too far gone. There may have been years of someone living on a path of sin, but God can restore them in a mere second's notice. He longs for every sinner to receive His grace and mercy and come to know Him. The nation of Israel is a prime example of receiving this love through repentance. Yes, there were certainly people of this nation who were obedient. But oftentimes, the prophets of the Old Testament spent their lives preaching the message of God's love, longing for hearts to repent, and focusing on those who were not serving God. This included the prophet, Hosea. There's no greater feeling than restoration. No greater feeling than being able to express our heart of thanksgiving, the fruit of our lips, to Him for forgiving us. No one is too far gone in their actions to have the opportunity to experience the arms of God. No one.

Today's Challenge To Dig Deeper:
Do you know someone who needs to return to God through repentance? Do you know someone who needs to be saved? Today, pray for them. But not only that, if you know them personally, pick up the phone and call them. Ask them if they have any needs and let them know you are praying for them. In the conversation, ask them if they would like to be saved. What a way to end the month of April, with the opportunity to lead someone to Christ. Be brave. Make the call.

Evening Reflection:
Did you do this challenge? If you have not completed the call, do it right now. Write down the conversation.

May Rinsing

---※---

MEET A NEED
May 1

Morning Rinse: Isaiah 1-3
Featured Verse: Isaiah 1:17 *Learn to do good: Seek justice, reprove the ruthless, defend the orphan, plead for the widow.*

It was the Senior night ceremony for a high school softball team. After the game, the parents of each senior on the team began lining up to walk out onto the field as their daughter was being celebrated. The large crowd of family and friends, some who drove for miles, were waiting in anticipation for their favorite player's name to be announced so they could cheer with pride from the stands. This was supposed to be a momentous occasion. This particular school was a private school and did not meet the national average demographics of high school students with absent parents. In fact, each of the eight senior girls on the team showcased both her mom and her dad, one on each of her arms, escorting her onto the field. All except one. This young lady stood alone, with no parents to walk with her, no one to give her flowers, and no family members to cheer when her name was called. This obviously was upsetting. In fact, right before walking onto the field, one of the other softball families noticed her tears and grabbed onto her, claiming her as part of their family. They proceeded to escort both her and their softball daughter onto the field. This young lady cried the whole way to the mound where the coaches were greeting the players and shaking their hands for a job well done in the season. In fact, the tears never ceased during this ceremony meant to be an occasion full of joy. It was heart wrenching for the crowd to witness, and it was easy for everyone present to experience mixed emotions. The crowd wanted to cheer, whoop and holler, but also wanted to fix whatever issues were causing the tears. Come to find out, this young lady was fatherless. Her dad had left her family years prior, and now her mother had unexpectedly disappeared. It was also discovered that she was silently fending for herself at her older sister's place. She was in a state of survival. Not many knew the details about this young lady. But fortunately, an anonymous donor heard her parents had stopped paying tuition and stepped up to pay the bill so she could continue to attend this amazing school and stay in a good environment. In essence, this young girl was a modern-day orphan. As we begin reading the book of Isaiah, we see that Isaiah longs for the nations of Israel to do good, including defending the orphan. This is a community effort. It is about grabbing those in need by the arm and helping them. May we be vessels to heal those in pain and be Your outstretched arms in times of need.

Today's Challenge To Dig Deeper:
Look around you. Call your church. Call your school. Ask a close friend. Look for someone who is hurting, who is sad, who is hungry. Do not stop asking until you hear of a need today. When you discover a need, meet it.

Evening Reflection:
What need did you meet today?

FACES IN THE DARK
May 2

Morning Rinse: Isaiah 4-6
Featured Verses: Isaiah 6:1, 8 *In the year of King Uzziah's death I saw the Lord sitting on a throne, lofty and exalted, with the train of His robe filling the temple… Then I heard the voice of the Lord, saying, "Whom shall I send, and who will go for Us?" Then I said, "Here am I. Send me!"*

It was about the year 2000. I was singing in the choir loft one Sunday morning during worship service and had one of those moments where I literally sensed God gave me a vision. The worship team began leading the congregation in the song based off today's Featured Verse. I can still hear the choir voices around me singing in a melodious harmony, "I see the Lord seated on the throne." While I was worshiping, my eyes were closed and focused on the meaning of the words as my voice blended with the other vocalists. Out of nowhere, my mind's eye could clearly see a vision of a throne on the top of a mountain, and God sitting on it wearing a white robe with a long train. The train, or hem of His robe, extended all the way down to the bottom of the mountain. All over this mountain were other believers standing with me, all wearing white. Some were higher up on the mountain, while others were lower towards the edge. As I gazed at this magnificent view, God spoke to my heart and told me to walk to the bottom of His train and look over the edge. At first, all I could see was darkness. But as I focused my eyes, I began to see faces forming. There was a distinct difference between the white train that I stood on, and the sea of blackness on the other side of His train where these faces were. The sea was so thick that the faces were faint and hard to make out. I soon realized that the faces went on into the horizon, and made up this vast mass of darkness, stretching as far as I could see. The faces in the dark went on forever. Then I began to hear them, making it apparent they could see me too. The ones that were right below where I stood, had their arms stretched upwards towards me, screaming for help. The Lord told me to reach down and grab one. So I reached down and pulled one out of the darkness and tossed the person up the train. A Christ follower caught him and started wiping him off, and then passed him around for others to wipe off. I looked down at my hand and it had become dirty from the person's mess, but I saw the Holy Spirit, like an eraser, wipe my hand clean, and I reached for another hand to pull up. The Lord told me not every Christ follower would be called to do work on the 'edge' of His train, and that was okay. Each believer on the mountain had a different mission in soul winning and soul cleansing. In this moment, though, I knew He was calling me to go to the edge… or to be edgy for Him. Where does God want you on the mountain? Can He count on you to say "send me"? No matter where we are on God's mountain of purpose, we can count on staying 'ministry messy' if we keep working. May we all rise to the occasion.

Today's Challenge To Dig Deeper:
What did God speak to you about as you read this devotion? Pray that you answer with, "Here I am. Send me!"

Evening Reflection:
Share anything in your heart you might be called to do, that feels like it could be messy.

WHAT IF GOD WANTS TO GIVE A SIGN?
May 3

Morning Rinse: Isaiah 7-9
Featured Verses: Isaiah 7:11-12 *Ask a sign for yourself from the Lord your God: make it deep as Sheol or high as heaven. But Ahaz said, "I will not ask, nor will I test the Lord."*

Why did Ahaz respond like this to the instruction of God? God told him to ask for a sign and yet Ahaz refused to ask. Some believe that Ahaz wanted to give an appearance of righteousness when he replied, "I will not ask, nor will I test the Lord," but there had to have been an underlying motive. Maybe he really did not want to hear what God was wanting to say. Maybe he was afraid of what God would say to him. And yes, maybe he was even prideful and wanted to appear better than he really was. Appearing righteous like this keeps us from being close to God and hearing Him when He is speaking, therefore missing the beautiful moments of communion and community with our Heavenly Father. Do you answer when God wants to give you a sign?

Today's Challenge To Dig Deeper:
Do you ever feel God wants to give you a sign for your life? Write down what you think it may be. Ask God for confirmation today on what He is wanting to show you. Do not be afraid.

Evening Reflection:
What was revealed to you today? Write it down.

GO GET THE WOODEN SPOON
May 4

Morning Rinse: Isaiah 10-12
Featured Verse: Isaiah 12:1 *Then you will say on that day, "I will give thanks to You, O Lord; For although you were angry with me, Your anger is turned away. And You comfort me."*

When my kids were little, there were times we felt it necessary to spank them versus having a 'time out' or grounding them. My husband and I were not the type of parents, though, who spanked with freedom of the whipping hand or with lack of structure. Our kids always knew what the spanking routine would look like. Our guest bedroom was used for spankings, and then under the bed was the hated wooden spoon used for nothing more than swats. We modeled our routine from not only our past experiences and a few sermons we heard about the topic, but also what we did NOT want a spanking to look like in our home. To help us develop our structure, we adopted several simple rules for us as parents to follow, that the kids knew as well. Our first rule was to do our best to never use our hands for spanking, which is why we used a wooden spoon. We wanted our hands to be used for hugs, not hits. Another rule we adopted was the 'Three swat rule.' Three swats were our limit, and it was never on a bare butt. We also required the child to bring us the wooden spoon from under the bed, versus us grabbing it ourselves. No matter how angry the child was after the swat, we put them on our laps, talked to them about their behavior, and then prayed with them. Believe it or not, our swats were usually never harder than a pat on their rear. Nothing firmer was usually needed to get their attention. We knew we had their listening ear the moment that we said, "Go get the wooden spoon." Each time our kids heard us say this, their eyes would flood with tears, and they slowly walked to the room, wailing the entire distance. We would get this reaction more times than not, and it usually caused us to chuckle to ourselves as we tried to keep a straight face. Being reminded of this even as I write, makes me smile. As my kids became older, they eventually admitted that my spankings never really hurt. It was the process of getting into trouble that caused the tears. Still to this day, though, I have yet to receive a 'Thank you for the spankings, Mom.' Has Jesus ever told me to go get the wooden spoon? You bet. And I'm thankful. For in my correction, I become closer to Him.

Today's Challenge To Dig Deeper:
Thank God today for His correction. If you have any funny spanking stories, call your parents and thank them for the 'wooden spoon.' Make light. Have fun and chuckle, for I am sure your thankfulness will be unexpected.

Evening Reflection:
Write down how your conversations went with your parents, as well as with God.

WE WIN
May 5

Morning Rinse: Isaiah 13-15
Featured Verse: Isaiah 13:6 *Wail, for the day of the Lord is near! It will come as destruction from the Almighty.*

What if I wrote to you today and said that the Bible is never about destruction and always about hope? First of all, that would not be possible. For if there was no destruction, there would be no need for hope. Today's Morning Rinse captures Isaiah communicating about the judgement and destruction of several nations, including capturing a glimpse of what it will be like during the end times, or the Day of the Lord. Sometimes it is interesting and even difficult to read the conditions of life and what lies ahead. But we must remember the overall message of Isaiah, and other prophets of the Bible. That message is spoken over and over, and it is the message of hope, and to rely on God, not man. We should have hope even with the knowledge of what the last days will be like, and the destruction mentioned. Why? Because we win! Are you not grateful for this?

Today's Challenge To Dig Deeper:
Is there any area of your life that you are not relying on God? Do you find that the reason for not relying on Him is the fact that you are afraid in your heart? Dig deep. What is it that you are afraid of? Ask God to help you rid yourself of the fear, and stand on the hope we have in Christ.

Evening Reflection:
Write down the fear you had in your heart, and how God took that away.

NEVER IDOLIZE THE PLATFORM
May 6

Morning Rinse: Isaiah 16-18
Featured Verse: Isaiah 17:10 *For you have forgotten the God of your salvation and have not remembered the rock of your refuge. Therefore, you plant delightful plants and set them with vine lips of a strange god.*

"What I need from you is to never idolize the platform that I put you on." These are the words God spoke to me at the dress rehearsal for a play called "Tribulation Christmas," a narrative of the book of Revelation. These words still affect me to this day. I was walking across the stage preparing my heart for the next two weeks of performances, and as one of the leads that year, this night was a surreal moment for me. I had arrived early so I could have some quiet time before the rest of the cast arrived for our last pre-rehearsal meeting. The stage lights glared down on me as I gazed across the empty auditorium, knowing that in one day, most of the seats would be filled due to near sold-out performances. My conversation with God started out merely thanking Him for the opportunity to be in such an influential role as the one I was cast in. This play had been performed for decades prior, and my family had the honor of helping with ten of those previous years. There were always multiple performances each year, with ten scheduled this time around. As in years past, about ten thousand people were expected to come, traveling from hundreds of miles away, across multiple surrounding states. It was also estimated that fifteen hundred people would give their hearts to Christ during these two weeks. The role I was portraying was Lisa, a girl on the run due to her refusal to take the mark of the beast. I knew being in the spotlight was a huge responsibility, and therefore, I thanked God for trusting me and thanked Him for the lives that this play would change. While I was in this conversation with Him, I looked up to the lights and He told me to get out of the four walls of the church to pursue the world of film and commercials, but to never idolize the platform. I knew what He meant. I had, admittedly so, idolized the platform of the stage I was standing on. You see, while I was grateful for being used in ministry, I was also hoping I would be 'discovered' as an actress by playing in this lead role. My heart was pure in truly wanting to serve Him. But on the flip side, I also wanted to be noticed and grow in this craft. Unfortunately, I had, in essence, been worshiping the stage, the platform that God had put me on. The people of Moab, Damascus, and Assyria also had idols. Was my situation exactly like theirs? No. They had turned away from God. I had not. But no matter where we are in our faith, God encourages us to trust in HIM, not false attractions, false gods, or idols. These are anything that we value as higher than the one true God, even if that includes viewing ourselves as higher than we ought, like our own gifts and talents. Pride is even an idol, as well as the tangible things we put above our time with God, like electronics, work, and yes, even ministry. Let us put God in His rightful place in our lives and trust HIM instead of trusting the platform.

Today's Challenge To Dig Deeper:
Ask God to search your heart for any idols. You may be surprised at what He shows you. Be open to His voice. Listen. Then repent. Ask Him to help you put that area back in proper balance.

Evening Reflection:
What did God reveal to you about idols today?

WATCHMAN ON THE WALL
May 7

Morning Rinse: Isaiah 19-21
Featured Verse: Isaiah 21:8 *Then the lookout called, "O Lord, I stand continually by day on the watchtower, and I am stationed every night at my guard post."*

I used to attend a rather large church where, as we continued to grow, security became a priority for the leaders. A group of men formed a ministry called 'Watchmen on the Wall.' Many men in the church, including my husband, became a part of this secret security team. Each Sunday these men would meet prior to the service and get assigned a location on the campus to monitor during the service. They would don their walkie-talkies and 'hold their posts,' if you will. My husband loved being on this team. They were the 'watchmen' of our church. These men were the ones who kept an eye out for anything out of the ordinary, and then they would report it to the head of security. Honestly, knowing that these men were positioned all over the campus made me feel safer. I never knew where they were, and even though my husband was on the team, I did not even know who many of the other men were. I was not expecting things to go wrong, but there was a deeper sense of peace knowing that if something were to happen, the 'watchmen' were there to help at a moment's notice. These men were committed to looking out for not just trouble on the grounds, but they were also looking for anyone in need. Oftentimes I would see one of them surface to help a single mom get her kids to Children's Church, or help an elderly couple into their seats. They were watching and ready, with a plan to respond to any given situation that called for help. They were trained to respond versus reacting before it was too late. Our homes are also in need of a watchman. If we see something out of sorts, we need to report it to our Heavenly Father. We need to guard what is ours with indignation and righteousness, looking for things that are out of sorts. Making a habit to spiritually guard our household helps us keep our eyes open for when the enemy comes our way. He fights us at every angle. Do you watch for him?

Today's Challenge To Dig Deeper:
Where in your home or surroundings do you need to become a watchman on your wall?

Evening Reflection:
Write down the areas to become a watchman in your life.

THE HARVEST OF THE CHURCH IS ITS REVENUE
May 8

Morning Rinse: Isaiah 22-24
Featured Verses: Isaiah 23:2-3 *Be silent, you inhabitants of the coastland, you merchants of Sidon; your messengers crossed the sea and were on many waters. The grain of the Nile, the harvest of the River was her revenue; and she was the market of nations.*

Back in Bible times, Tyre was one of the most famous cities. It sat on the sea and was a place for major trading and business transactions to occur. It was probably very similar to a large city like our modern-day New York or Chicago. But while it was a city of wealth and growth, it was very evil. In fact, multiple prophets of the Bible rebuked the inhabitants of Tyre, and as we read in today's Morning Rinse, Isaiah speaks of its fall to destruction. Today's Featured Verses talk of the Nile housing the city's revenue. If only Tyre had listened to the heed of the prophets. If only they were focused on an eternal harvest versus a harvest for monetary gain. If only they took their wealth and used it to further God's kingdom. But unfortunately, this did not occur. Building revenue for God's kingdom includes an eternal harvest for the body of Christ. I am not talking about a monetary gain for the church. I am talking of eternal revenue. Souls. I am talking about bringing in people who need to be saved. If there is no harvest of people for salvation, there is no revenue for God's kingdom. Let us not be like the inhabitants of Tyre, where their revenue was broadly known, but not kingdom minded. Let us instead be kingdom minded, building God's revenue by pulling in the harvest of the lost.

Today's Challenge To Dig Deeper:
Ask yourself, "What am I doing to bring in a harvest for God's kingdom?" I know it can be a tough question, but ask God to help you position yourself to help pull in the harvest. Make a change today towards that positioning.

Evening Reflection:
Write down one thing you did today to help bring in the revenue for God's kingdom.

HISTORY MAKERS
May 9

Morning Rinse: Isaiah 25-27
Featured Verse: Isaiah 26:3 *The steadfast of mind You will keep in perfect peace, because he trusts in You.*

Lawrence Peter "Yogi" Berra, an American professional baseball catcher, was an 18-time All-Star, and won 10 World Series championships. He is widely regarded as one of the greatest catchers in baseball history. One of his famous quotes was "Baseball is 90 percent mental. The other half is physical."[15] I can vouch for this truth from watching my kids play sports, as well as playing myself growing up. My son, for example, plays soccer as his main sport, and my middle daughter plays softball. My daughter is left-handed and this often confuses a less seasoned pitcher who is used to pitching to right-handed batters. This results in her getting hit by wild pitches occasionally. One time, she was hit so hard while at bat, it knocked her to her knees, which stopped the game until she was able to recompose and claim the free first base. If you played sports, or know someone who has, you have probably experienced an injury or witnessed one. Take that thought a bit further and mirror it in your life. Have you experienced a curveball, or something unexpectedly happening in your life? Has a friend failed you, leaving you brokenhearted and knocked down for a few innings? Or on a deeper level, have you ever felt attacked from the enemy trying to knock you out for the entire game? Even amid these trials, you can still have perfect peace by trusting God. He ultimately has the last say, not your circumstance. After my daughter was knocked down from the wild pitch mentioned earlier, she got back up, and by the next inning, had recovered enough to take the mound and pitch for her team. We must get back up and keep running the bases. One thing I did not mention was that she, too, is a pitcher, and has hit multiple batters through her career of playing the sport. So we must remember that our own actions, can cause curveballs in other people's lives as well. It is not about the hard knocks that come, though. It is about how we respond to them. My daughter was the finishing pitcher in this game where she was hurt. She remained steadfast on the mound and not only won that game, but she led her team to break many records that season, becoming history-makers for her school. Remember, Jesus can give you perfect peace if you trust Him. Do not let the knocks of life keep you down. God needs you to be a history-maker in your world.

Today's Challenge To Dig Deeper:
Are you going through a hard time right now? Pray that God helps you stay steadfast, focused on Him, and ask for His perfect peace. Memorize the featured verse today and quote it all day.

Evening Reflection:
Write down the featured verse from memory, and journal how you are trusting Him through any struggles you may be having.

---

[15] https://www.usatoday.com/story/sports/mlb/columnist/bob-nightengale/2018/04/03/mlb-mental-health-coaches/482122002/

RECEIVING THE GIFT OF COMPASSION
May 10

Morning Rinse: Isaiah 28-30
Featured Verse: Isaiah 30:18 *Therefore the Lord longs to be gracious to you, and therefore He waits on high to have compassion on you. For the Lord is a God of justice; How blessed are all those who long for Him.*

According to *The Merriam-Webster Dictionary*, the definition of "compassion" is "to have sympathetic consciousness of others' distress together with a desire to alleviate it." In yesterday's Morning Rinse, we read the importance of having a steadfast trust in God, despite our circumstances or hardships in our lives. God watches our response in these situations and loves it when we long to be by His side through it all. He loves it when we trust Him with our lives, even if things are not perfect. He longs to bless us. So He watches and waits for the perfect time to show compassion on us during our time of need. We will all have times of suffering or misfortune due to living in an imperfect world. Our Father knows this, and so He waits, ready to alleviate our distress in a time of need. I can see Him now, excited to show us sympathy and concern when we need it most. When we sow trust in Him, we reap His compassion and intervention for us. It is one way He rescues us when we suffer. He is a loving God and longs to be there with us and for us.

Today's Challenge To Dig Deeper:
Yesterday, you reflected on a hard time that you are going through, and you asked God to help you trust Him through it. Today, look for His compassion in the situation. Keep your eyes peeled for how God is longing to serve justice on your behalf, and look for how He is showing up in your situation.

Evening Reflection:
How did God show compassion to you today? Reflect on the truth that He longs to show concern on your behalf. Write down how He showed it to you.

TRUSTING IN CHARIOTS?
May 11

Morning Rinse: Isaiah 31-33
Featured Verse: Isaiah 31:1 *Woe to those who go down to Egypt for help and rely on horses, and trust in chariots because they are many, and in horsemen because they are very strong, but they do not look to the Holy One of Israel, nor seek the Lord!*

The chapters in today's Morning Rinse are added to the many chapters and verses in the book of Isaiah focusing on the message of trusting in God. We learned today how Judah was relying and trusting on Egypt and other nations for protection and strength in times of war. I am sure it was very glamorous to have the resources of chariots and horsemen of those times. But God clearly wanted them to trust in Him instead of the things around them. When the Jews went to the battlefield, the chariots probably got them to their destination quicker, they had a form of protection and provided the upper hand when battling. Having chariots during war was probably like having the latest and greatest tanks, or other strong military pieces of equipment to tighten up their strategy. However, putting trust in the best pieces of equipment takes our trust away from God. Some people trust in the chariots, believing that will be their main source of protection. But, if God has called us to a battle, then we must fight the way HE wants us to fight, using the resources that HE gives us, even if that means that our weapons look different from what we expected them to look. This even applies to our tongue. How do we use this weapon? Do we praise Him through the storm, trusting Him all the way to the clear sky? Or do we pick up the phone and call our friends before even calling on His name?

Today's Challenge To Dig Deeper:
Are you trusting in your resources and other people around you more than you are trusting in God? Go to Him today with your needs. Pray through the struggle and see what God has to say about it. It may take you a few minutes to get an answer, or it may take you all day. But take this day to trust Him in a deeper way than before.

Evening Reflection:
How did you grow today in your trust in God for your situation? Did He give you peace? Write down what happened in your heart and in your situation.

<u>SALVATION IS FOR YOU</u>
May 12

Morning Rinse: Isaiah 34-36
Featured Verses: Isaiah 35:3-4 *Encourage the exhausted and strengthen the feeble. Say to those with anxious heart, "Take courage; fear not. Behold, your God will come with vengeance; The recompense of God will come, but He will save you."*

Most of the book of Isaiah so far has been Isaiah preaching a message of judgment to those who are disobedient. And he also spends time imploring the people to obey and walk by faith, trusting God despite what their surroundings and circumstances may look like. Bad circumstances are certainly something that could sway us from a faith in God. But in today's Morning Rinse, Isaiah takes a break amid these harder sermons he has been preaching and delivers a message of hope. The entire thirty-fifth chapter shows us a glorious picture of what we can look forward to once we get to Heaven. Oh, that will be the day for sure! It can be exhausting waiting for that day, especially as we endure trials and temptations. But Isaiah reminds us to keep running towards God with courage, letting go of our fear. Of course, while we are running, not only will we get tired, but it is evident that others running the race alongside us will get tired as well. So Isaiah prompts us to not only stay encouraged with this message of hope, but to encourage others along the way who are tired and feeble. Our journey to Heaven was never promised to be easy, and therefore should not be done alone. As we have learned in past devotions, we need reminders to keep our eyes on God, and we need each other for strength and support along the way. We can be confident that as we keep our eyes focused on Him, the author and finisher of our faith, He will save us from destruction, and prepare a place for us in His kingdom. But to get there, we must be saved.

Today's Challenge To Dig Deeper:
If you are not sure you are going to Heaven, take a moment right now and ask Jesus to forgive you of your sins and come into your heart to be your Lord and Savior. Whether you just received Jesus into your heart, or you have been saved for years, thank Him for the gift of salvation. While going about your day, meditate on what Heaven will be like.

Evening Reflection:
Did you notice a difference in your demeanor and overall perspective as you walked today with a spirit of thankfulness? Journal what you are looking forward to in Heaven.

ASK HIM
May 13

Morning Rinse: Isaiah 37-39
Featured Verses: Isaiah 38:1-5 *In those days Hezekiah became mortally ill, and Isaiah the prophet the son of Amoz came to him and said to him, "Thus says the Lord, 'Set your house in order, for you shall die and not live,'" Then Hezekiah turned his face to the wall and prayed to the Lord, and said, "Remember now, O Lord, I beseech You, how I have walked before You in truth and with a whole heart, and have done what is good in Your sight." And Hezekiah wept bitterly. Then the word of the Lord came to Isaiah, saying, "Go and say to Hezekiah, 'Thus says the Lord, the God of your father David, "I have heard your prayer, I have seen your tears; behold, I will add fifteen years to your life."'"*

As I sit down to edit this devotional before sending it to print, I am only a few days past a trip visiting my dad after he was critically ill only about a month ago. In fact, he told me while I was visiting, that he thought he was going to die. It was hard for me to hear and yet, when I prayed for him with my mom while he was hospitalized, I remembered the story of Hezekiah. So I prayed for God to extend my dad's life. Hezekiah had become so ill that he was nearing death. His condition was not recorded, but we know it had to be serious, just like my dad's condition was serious. Hezekiah was so distraught about it that he cried to God, begging Him to let him live. While reading this story, I noticed two things about Hezekiah that were noteworthy. The first is he lived for God with his whole heart prior to this prayer. He even reminded God of how he had lived for Him, using his life as part of his petition. I think that oftentimes we get in situations and want God to answer, but we have not done our part with our lifestyle before we do the asking. Now, do not get me wrong. I know there is grace and God is ready to bring us into His arms if we have swayed. But our lifestyle is most assuredly important. Otherwise, Hezekiah would not have mentioned it, nor would it have been something that God lent His ear to in the petition. The second thing I noticed about Hezekiah is that he took his illness, his heavy burden, to God, and was not afraid to beg for healing. Was he healed because of his righteous lifestyle? Or did he get healed because he asked for it? Maybe it was a combination of both, and God was just waiting to have an opportunity to show compassion. God's reasoning for healing is not recorded, but we know that God promised him another fifteen years. I asked God to extend my dad's life too. At the time of this writing, my dad is home from the hospital and getting stronger every day. We, too, can go to God with our requests. We, too, can ask Him for answers to our situations. What is it that you are wanting God to do for you? Do you have a burden or a situation in your life that appears bleak and surrounded by death? Is it a relationship? Is it an illness? Is it healing a heart wound? Whatever brings you to tears, take it to Him.

Today's Challenge To Dig Deeper:
Take your heavy burden to God today and ask Him for healing or answers for that issue. He may be waiting to hear from you.

Evening Reflection:
What did you ask God about? Did He talk to you about your request?

EAGLE'S WINGS
May 14

Morning Rinse: Isaiah 40-42
Featured Verse: Isaiah 40:31 *Yet those who wait for the Lord will gain new strength; They will mount up with wings like eagles, they will run and not get tired, they will walk and not become weary.*

When one gazes on the magnificence of an eagle, it is evident that its mere presence speaks of power and beauty. This majestic bird owns the sky with just a gaze of its piercing eyes or the turn of its sleek head. When an eagle lifts off its perch, putting its wings in motion, it presents a captivating scene. This flying bird is breathtaking with the wingspan of the bald eagle ranging from six to eight feet wide. Not only are an eagle's wings vast in size compared to the common flying bird, they are powerful. They have the ability to not only fly to an altitude of ten thousand feet,[16] but the eagle can glide with the current of storms. No other bird can weather storms like the eagle. And when it comes to storms, an eagle does not fear them. In fact, an eagle will oftentimes use the rushing winds and currents from the storm to lift him above the clouds. While other birds hunker down and hide, the eagle faces the storm head on. I wonder if the other birds know there is peace above the storm. I wonder if they know the storm is what gets the eagle to that peace. I think it is easy to forget storms can be a blessing. If we take the opportunity to learn from the storm, it could take us to a whole new level of faith, peace, and trust we never imagined before. May we cease to fight the storms in our life, and instead, ask God to use them to propel us to where He wants us to go. May we be like the eagles, using the storms to get closer to His peace. Put on your eagle wings.

Today's Challenge To Dig Deeper:
Take a look at any storms you have in your life. Whether they be small thunderstorms or tsunamis. Ask God to teach you how to use your faith, your eagle wings, to fly above the storm to His peace.

Evening Reflection:
Did you feel yourself putting on wings like eagles? Write what you felt today.

---

[16] https://www.animalfoodplanet.com/how-high-do-eagles-fly

CONDUCTOR OF NATURE'S CHOIR
May 15

Morning Rinse: Isaiah 43-45
Featured Verse: Isaiah 44:23 *Shout for joy, O heavens, for the Lord has done it! Shout joyfully, you lower parts of the earth; Break forth into a shout of joy, you mountains, O forest, and every tree in it; For the Lord has redeemed Jacob, and in Israel He shows forth His glory.*

When the song by MercyMe called "All of Creation" comes on my radio while I am driving, I cannot help but turn the music way up. There is something about this song that helps bring today's Featured Verse to life in a whole new way. I heard a pastor once state that he believes the atmosphere of Heaven will surprise us when it comes to nature. The Bible states nature praises God on this earth, so nature must have its own language that we do not understand or speak. This pastor also believes, as do I, when we get to Heaven, we will understand all the same languages and be able to hear what even nature is saying while it praises. How fun will that be?! This song is a mere reminder that nature truly does praise God and shout with joy. So when I hear it come on in my car, I cannot help but roll down my windows and blast the music for three minutes and fifty-five seconds, inviting the trees, the flowers in the fields, and all of nature to sing along with me. My kids will smirk at me when this happens, as I don my invisible, amateur conductor's hat and conduct a seemingly invisible choir with a waving free arm. (With the other hand on the wheel, of course.) I choose to believe the band members of MercyMe understand my silly actions. Here are the lyrics of the chorus to their amazing song:

> *And all of creation sing with me now,*
> *Lift up your voice and lay your burden down;*
> *And all of creation sing with me now,*
> *Fill up the heavens, let His glory resound.[17]*

If the mountains and forests can praise Him, all of nature can. For He is God. He not only is the Creator, but He is our Redeemer and our Savior. And I will also believe that God has another hat He wears, as the "Conductor of Nature's Choir."

Today's Challenge To Dig Deeper:
Look up the song "All of Creation" by MercyMe and listen to it. Ask God for a new perspective on how nature worships Him.

Evening Reflection:
Listen to the song from this morning one more time. Write down any new revelations you received about nature singing His praises.

---

[17] https://genius.com/Mercyme-all-of-creation-lyrics

REFINED LIKE SILVER
May 16

Morning Rinse: Isaiah 46-48
Featured Verse: Isaiah 48:10 *Behold, I have refined you, but not as silver; I have tested you in the furnace of affliction.*

One way a silversmith refines silver is to gently and with great care, put the metal through a heating process inside a silver furnace. The impurities of this metal, called dross, will then rise to the top when it begins to melt. The dross is carefully skimmed off the top and the process is repeated, but at a higher temperature each time until the refiner can see his reflection. In this moment, there are virtually no impurities left. When God refines us, and the 'heat' in our lives gets turned up, His plan is for our impurities, or dross, to be removed from our lives like the refinement of silver. And just as a silversmith refines silver, God gently puts us through scenarios to help us grow more like Him, so we eventually shine with God's reflection in our lives. The Jews, at several points in the Bible, were so sinful, God was saying if He refined them like silver, there would be nothing left of them because they were so full of impurities. I cannot imagine having nothing left to reflect Jesus even after my impurities are removed. But this is in essence what God was saying would happen to them. So God had to then allow them to go through the captivity of Babylon, what He called an affliction, to provide them with an opportunity to see their sinful ways and turn back to Him, so the refinement could begin again. God is the ultimate refiner, and takes great care in how He refines us. The added pressure in our lives, or challenges that come our way, are opportunities to help us grow closer to Him. Our response will make the difference. I am not saying that every bad thing, or negative detail in our lives is from God, but He will allow challenges that can be tough to walk through, so we can grow. Whatever way He lovingly chooses to refine us, whether through the 'heat' in our lives, or by some form of affliction, let us pray for two things. First, let us pray all our impurities will be removed as we yield to God's refining process. And second, as we grow in Him through His refining process, may we have purity left over, so we can be a true reflection of Him.

Today's Challenge To Dig Deeper:
As you go about your day today, reflect on your behavior and how you respond to the challenges that come your way. Are there any changes you need to make, due to the impurities that have surfaced? Ask God to help you mirror HIM in how you respond in life's challenges.

Evening Reflection:
Has your perspective of your challenge, or the 'heat' in your life, changed after reflecting today? Can you see God's handiwork in the challenges? Journal your thoughts and feelings.

A TATTOO KIND OF LOVE
May 17

Morning Rinse: Isaiah 49-51
Featured Verses: Isaiah 49:15-16a *Can a woman forget her nursing child and have no compassion on the son of her womb? Even these may forget, but I will not forget you. Behold, I have inscribed you on the palms of my hands.*

The relationship between a mother and her baby is one of the most beautiful expressions of unconditional love we, on this side of Heaven, can relate to. I have had the pleasure of not only birthing three children and experiencing this, but also watching my oldest daughter become a mother of three. Seeing her grow with this expression of unconditional love, is such a beautiful thing. But even with this pure relationship, not every scenario is perfect. One would like to think every mother loves her baby in a Christ-like fashion or puts her baby first. But this is simply not the case. Our world is an imperfect world. There are many imperfections, flaws, failures, and in some relationships, even sin. God knows this and He sent a message to the Jews, that we, too, can claim. He chose the purest relationship and compared it to His Son's love for us. Jesus loved us so much, our names are inscribed on the palms of His hands. What a beautiful foretelling of the Cross, and the promise of His love for us. People will often display their love for others by tattooing their names on their bodies. For example, a mom may tattoo the names of her children on her back, or a new husband will tattoo his bride's name on his forearm, both to show the world their love. In fact, my daughter's first tattoo was a picture of two figures, a child, and a mother. She did this to symbolize her and I. What a gift of love from your child. While tattooing is meant to be permanent, it can still be removed, written over, or even transformed to a new picture. The form of permanent writing Jesus has for us, though, is different. He loves us so much that He died for our sins and 'inscribed' our names on His hands with the nail scars. It was His way of 'tattooing' us on Him. Unlike our imperfect love on this earth, His love is perfect. And His love for us is permanent. No matter what we do.

Today's Challenge To Dig Deeper:
Watch today for Jesus to shine His perfect love on you. No matter what we do, He will always love us. Have you accepted this love yet? If not, ask Him to forgive your sins and be your Lord and Savior. Thank Him for inscribing your name onto His palm.

Evening Reflection:
Journal any revelations you received today about his love for you.

SHAKE AND WALK
May 18

Morning Rinse: Isaiah 52-54
Featured Verse: Isaiah 52:2 *Shake yourself from the dust, rise up, O captive Jerusalem; Loose yourself from the chains around your neck, O captive daughter of Zion.*

Several days ago, I called a friend of mine named Paula Wallace to get some counsel about a betrayal I am experiencing. This betrayal cuts deep and is fresh. It is one I would wish on no one, but admittedly, can assume it has happened to many others. It is the betrayal of a friend. When I use the word friend, I am not talking about an acquaintance. I am describing someone who I have confided in, prayed with, told my fears to, and even dreamed with. These are the relationships that are built on trust and time. This friend broke that trust by not only turning her back on me, but taking back her word and promise. Having had both occur has cut deep and caused trust issues that have been very difficult to repair. What makes my experience even more taxing to work through, is this person was a catalyst of a team of people pursuing a dream together, and I am all about dreams. However, after two years of working together in this pursuit, she made some choices which propelled me into living one of my biggest fears, being left behind. So my core has not only been bruised, but cut, and is now bleeding. I was knocked down. I am sure you can imagine the difficulty I have felt, but also the reality of being bound by chains of unforgiveness and bitterness. This has not been a healthy place to be, both spiritually and emotionally. I can imagine the Jews had to deal with this same kind of torment. They had been bound by chains as well. Those chains may look different. But I am sure they still had to walk through a process of forgiveness towards their captors who probably treated them wrongfully at times, making some of their issues relatable. So the advice I received from my phone call with Paula is some I will pass on to you. She told me to get the poison out of my heart by writing a letter to my now former friend. I spent about 1.5 hours writing down everything I wanted to say to her. All my pain, all my questions, all my hurts, and all my challenges with her choices. I wrote until I let it all out, even using a few curse words for my release. I cried until my head hurt. I thank God Paula told me to write. That letter allowed me to take my pain, my unforgiveness, my poison, and all the chains I had, and talk about it in a safe way. Writing that letter allowed me to point to the chains, and then begin the process of shaking them off. I did what God told the Jews to do. Shake. It is a way of healing. Of course, I also questioned God in that letter. And He listened. He answered. He began healing. And then He reached down and lifted me up. Just like the Jews became free, I worked towards freedom by shaking, and then rising to walk past my pain. After I wrote the letter, I followed Paula's advice and deleted it, never sending it to this lady. Instead, I allowed God to work in my heart as He read it with me. Will you rise with me by shaking and walking? It is freedom.

Today's Challenge To Dig Deeper:
Write a letter. Dig deep. Ask God to search your heart about anything you are struggling with. Then shred the letter if on paper, or delete it if it is in an email. If you do not have the ability to write it today, start preparing your heart, and write it in the next few days. Do not pass this up.

Evening Reflection:
What are your thoughts about shaking and walking?

MAY FLOWERS
May 19

Morning Rinse: Isaiah 55-57
Featured Verses: Isaiah 55:10-11 *For as the rain and the snow come down from heaven, and do not return there without watering the earth and making it bear and sprout, and furnishing seed to the sower and bread to the eater; So will My word be which goes forth from My mouth; It will not return to me empty, without accomplishing what I desire, and without succeeding in the matter for which I sent it.*

The popular poem, "April Showers Bring May Flowers," is often repeated in the springtime when storms begin to brew, and the ground is preparing for the colorful beauty that will come forth from the soil. It was originated by English poet and farmer, Thomas Tucker, back in 1557, and can be found in the April section of a collection of his writings titled, *A Hundred Good Points of Husbandry*. The original version of this line reads like this:

> *Sweete April showers,*
> *Doo spring Maie flowers.*[18]

Rain pours out nourishment for the hidden seeds just waiting to burst forth in the new season. Whatever version of this poem you prefer, whether the simple American one, or the original English version, the words remind us of the harvest we can anticipate from a refreshing, spring rain. It is an undeniable given. We expect to see the landscapes and crops across our land to manifest the fruit of that rain with flowers, trees and other plantations coming to life. Just like the rain cannot come down without producing fruit, God's Word cannot return to Him empty, without producing His purpose, or rather, His fruit. We can be assured of the purpose of His words being successfully completed for the reason that He spoke them. Is there anything He has promised you that you are still waiting for? Do you have unwavering faith in His Word? Do you have expectation in His promises? Do you have the same kind of faith in God's Word that you do in May flowers coming up after a spring rain? Or is God waiting on your faith to come forth? God has a harvest for your life. Believe in it!

Today's Challenge To Dig Deeper:
Have a conversation with God about His harvest for your life. Ask Him to show you any area you lack unwavering faith in His promises. Once He shows you, ask Him to help you tap into the faith inside you and put your faith into action to believe.

Evening Reflection:
Did you feel your faith growing today? Reflect on this message of harvest and God's promises to you. Write down any revelations you had today about God's May flowers for your life.

---

[18] https://en.wikipedia.org/wiki/Thomas_Tusser

FASTING AS A LIFESTYLE
May 20

Morning Rinse: Isaiah 58-60
Featured Verses: Isaiah 58:6-7 *Is this not the fast which I chose, to loosen the bonds of wickedness, to undo the bands of the yoke, and to let the oppressed go free and break every yoke? Is it not to divide your bread with the hungry and bring the homeless poor into the house; When you see the naked, to cover him; and not to hide yourself from your own flesh?*

From my observation for the most part, fasting is something that we, as Americans, have not adopted as a lifestyle. Yet scripture tells us of the power that lies in practicing it on a regular basis for not just spiritual growth, but also for physical benefits. Fasting not only helps us get closer to God, but it also helps reset our bodies, and it even provides us with an opportunity to give our food to the poor, as today's Featured Verses imply. According to every definition I have read, both from medical books and online research, fasting is merely withholding food and/or some type of drink for a designated time. Withholding food or drink is difficult, so I understand how hard it is to regularly choose to fast. As for how to get started, there are different types of fasts found in the Bible. These types include different numbers of days, as well as different reasons. For example, you can find examples of a one day, three day, ten day, twenty-one day, and even a forty day fast. One can fast privately or as a corporate fast that leaders, like Esther, asked the Jews to do with her. There is also a water only fast, and fasts where specific types of foods like deserts or meats are abstained from. Any fast done for spiritual growth, no matter the duration or the type, can lead to answers or direction from God. So why is it not a lifestyle in America for most Christians? I will admit, fasting is not easy. And Americans like to eat. When I first started fasting as a young adult, there were times when I did not feel I could even finish a one day fast, let alone a fast that was longer than that. You may not believe you have the strength to finish, but with God's help, you can do it. Through prayer and perseverance, God empowers us to not only finish the fast, but to rise to what He has called us to complete for His kingdom. Fasting gives us faith in not only Him and His promises, but in ourselves. Whatever the type and length of fast you are praying about doing, know the benefits are worth giving up the food for, not just for you, but for the body of Christ.

Today's Challenge To Dig Deeper:
Take today to plan a fast in the upcoming week. Ask God how long He wants you to fast, and what foods He wants you to abstain from. Ask Him if there is anything specific He would like you to fast about, or pray for. As part of your planning, please consult your doctor and get medical advice for yourself, especially if you are on medications. Some people are not physically able to fast, due to medical conditions. So please be safe and get advice from your doctor.

Evening Reflection:
Are you excited about fasting? What are you wanting from God through this fast? Journal your thoughts and then prepare spiritually for your fast in the upcoming week. Be sure to document what God shows you during your fast. If you have any breakthroughs, please write them down. Consider making fasting a regular part of your lifestyle.

BE THE RIGHT KIND OF RIPPLE
May 21

Morning Rinse: Isaiah 61-63
Featured Verse: Isaiah 61:3 *To grant those who mourn in Zion, giving them a garland instead of ashes, the oil of gladness instead of mourning, the mantle of praise instead of a spirit of fainting. So they will be called oaks of righteousness, the planting of the Lord, that He may be glorified.*

In scripture, we read about some of the rituals that were performed when people mourned in the Bible. One of those rituals is putting ashes on their foreheads. While this is customary for certain religions or cultures still to this day, it would not be standard to wear ashes for the rest of one's life, and remain in a state of mourning. There is a time for grieving, but Jesus gives the oil of joy in exchange for mourning. He gives a garment of praise in exchange for a spirit of heaviness. How does He do this and how long does this exchange take? Of course, one powerful way he makes this exchange is through His Word. Reading scripture and encouraging ourselves while we mourn is vital to receiving His oil of joy. He also uses His people to help heal one another's heartaches. Sharing our own personal testimony is one way He will use us. Also, our attitude, our counsel, our love, our encouragement, our time, our understanding, and our compassion, are other ways we can help someone going through grief. Having these godly attributes can make a huge positive impact on someone's life, and help guide them to a place of healing. Once that life is changed, God will ultimately be glorified through their testimony, creating even more of a ripple effect. What kind of ripple are you being? Is it ripples of joy? Is it kindness? Is it peace? Is it hope? It may take some people years to heal from grief, and each type of loss will affect everyone differently. So do not stop being God's hands and feet for those who need His comfort. Do not stop being a ripple for His kingdom.

Today's Challenge To Dig Deeper:
Examine the type of ripple effect you are spreading in your relationships, and consider how it is affecting those lives. Ask God to show you the intentional changes you need to make in the energy you are spreading from your ripple. Now ask Him to send you someone today that needs your ripple.

Evening Reflection:
What changes did you make in your ripple effect? Did you commit to being a ripple for those around you?

CHOICES
May 22

Morning Rinse: Isaiah 64-66
Featured Verses: Isaiah 66:2-4 *"For My hand made all these things, thus all these things came into being," declares the Lord. "But to this one I will look, to him who is humble and contrite of spirit, and who trembles at My word. But he who kills an ox is like one who slays a man; He who sacrifices a lamb is like the one who breaks a dog's neck; He who offers a grain offering is like one who offers swine's blood; He who burns incense is like the one who blesses an idol. As they have chosen their own ways, and their soul delights in their abominations. So I will choose their punishments and will bring to them what they dread. Because I called, but no one answered; I spoke, but they did not listen. And they did evil in My sight and chose that in which I did not delight."*

Today's Featured Verses sum up Isaiah's message to the people of Israel, and to us as well. His message captures choices. We can either choose a humble lifestyle, zealous for God while trembling in reverence at His Word, or we can choose a life of hypocrisy by living an outward appearance of sacrificial living, while nurturing sinful hearts. God knows our hearts and where our desires lie, so we must remember we cannot hide our hearts from Him. It makes Him sad when we make choices that He does not delight in, or when He calls us, and we do not answer. But oh, how it makes His heart joyful when He can turn and look upon His children and see us loving Him and obeying Him in return. He wants every area of our lives to turn His direction. Our creator is zealous for us. Choose Him in your choices.

Today's Challenge To Dig Deeper:
As we close out the book of Isaiah, ask God to show you where you are not reverencing His Word or trembling at His commands. Are there any areas of your life where you are still compromising or have not yet fully surrendered your will to His? Give it up today.

Evening Reflection:
Look back through your past reflections from Isaiah, and write down one big take away from our recent devotions.

GROWTH SPURTS
May 23

Morning Rinse: James 1-3
Featured Verses: James 1:2-4 *Consider it all joy, my brethren, when you encounter various trials, knowing that the testing of your faith produces endurance. And let endurance have its perfect result, so that you may be perfect and complete, lacking in nothing.*

When Haley, my firstborn, was around five or six years old, she began to endure pain in her legs. Although her legs would ache throughout the day, the most intense pain would hit her at nighttime while trying to go to sleep. At first, I thought she was trying to stretch her bedtime to spend a few more minutes with me. As a single mom at the time, it seemed a bit cute, and so I played along with her for several nights. But as time went on, I noticed the pain was consistent and real tears flowed from her eyes as she complained nearly every evening. I soon realized these tears were different from the tears a young child sheds when they want their way. So I began getting concerned. I would massage her legs to try and decrease the aching and eventually she would fall asleep, but I would wake up in the middle of the night with her crying out in pain again. This continued, so I sought medical advice. Her pediatrician explained that she was going through growth spurts. This is when muscles try to keep up with fast-growing bones, and of course, it causes pain as they stretch faster than what is comfortable. The book of James is all about growth spurts for Christians. Some believers even call this book the true *how-to* book. It is literally full of verse-by-verse instructions on how to live a Christ-centered life. James touches on many subjects such as faith, trials, temptation, anger, faith-driven works, gossip and slander, jealousy, selfish ambitions, arrogance, righteousness, peace, and wisdom. Just as my daughter went through growth spurts with her body, if we take to heart this little book, we as the body of Christ will no doubt have spiritual growth spurts. James tells us God uses trials and tests for our growth, and of course it may hurt to walk through them. But He assures us God is right there with us. Whatever way God chooses to walk us through a spiritual growth spurt, consider it joy, and realize it will produce endurance, or 'staying power,' in our faith. Just like I massaged my daughter's legs during her pain, the Holy Spirit massages us with God's love so we can endure these spiritual growth spurts, becoming exactly who God wants us to be. And just as my daughter had no choice in how fast her body grew, if we are moldable to God's plan, we will allow Him to grow us as fast as He wants us to grow.

Today's Challenge To Dig Deeper:
After reading today's Morning Rinse, did the Holy Spirit prompt you in any area He wants you to have a growth spurt in? Take time today to allow God to massage your heart into full growth, and ask Him for wisdom as you grow.

Evening Reflection:
Do you feel you had a major growth spurt today? If so, in what area?

NO MORE REGRETS
May 24

Morning Rinse: James 4-5
Featured Verse: James 4:14 *Yet you do not know what your life will be like tomorrow. You are just a vapor that appears for a little while and then vanishes away.*

In early 1999, my husband Nathan and I had a life changing conversation. That conversation is the reason for ten years, our kids and I attended church without him at least once a month. It is also the reason he missed many weekend events. It went something like this:

Me: "Do you have any regrets in life?"
Nathan: "Yes. I actually have two."
Me: "What are they?"
Nathan: "First, I regret not joining the military after college. Second, I regret not buying my football signet ring when our team went to nationals my senior year at Baker University."
Me: "Well, I don't know what to say about the ring, but I do not want to sit on our porch overlooking a white picket fenced yard when we are ninety and you say to me, 'We have had a good life except for these things.' The kids and I will be fine. Go join the military."
Nathan: "At my age?"
Me: "Yes. Go join. I do not want to be responsible for you not following what you want to do."

And that is exactly what he did. He was thirty-eight years old. He did not take the easy path by joining as an officer, either. He decided to go through basic, starting at the bottom. "If I am going to be a soldier, I am going to join the right way," he told me. He was the oldest guy at basic training and was called 'Grandpa' more times than he could count. But that did not stop him from becoming one of the top shoulders in his unit. He beat out kids that could easily be his son, in physical competitions and strategic games they trained in. As far as the signet ring, I uncovered the company who made it from years past. They required I obtain a letter from his coach confirming he was indeed on the team, giving them permission to make it from their original mold. The whole process of getting that special ring made took about six months, and I even had them engrave "No more regrets" on the inside of the band. I still remember the joy I had as I laid this gift under the Christmas tree that year.

Today's Challenge To Dig Deeper:
Our life is but a vapor. Today, ask God if you are to resolve any regrets. If He leads you to pursue it, then begin today. Also, have this same conversation with someone dear in your life. Ask God to use you to help them resolve their regrets if they list any.

Evening Reflection:
Write down what transpired today in your conversation with God about your regrets if any, and write down your conversation with your loved one about their regrets, if any. Are there any resolutions?

CONQUERING INSECURITY BY OBEDIENCE
May 25

Morning Rinse: Jeremiah 1-3
Featured Verses: Jeremiah 1:5-7 *"Before I formed you in the womb I knew you, and before you were born I consecrated you; I have appointed you a prophet to the nations." Then I said, "Alas, Lord God! Behold, I do not know how to speak, because I am a youth." But the Lord said to me, "Do not say, 'I am a youth,' because everywhere I send you, you shall go, and all that I command you, you shall speak."*

The book of Jeremiah begins with one of the most important areas of a Christian's life after salvation. This area is obedience. Jeremiah was called at a young age to be a prophet to the sinful nation of Israel, and he obeyed that call. God might not ask us to be a prophet like him, but He has a purpose for our lives that is equally important. The part that makes Jeremiah's life so powerful is he obeyed his call. Will you obey yours? As you read through this book, you will find Jeremiah's life exemplified obedience. In today's Featured Verses, you will see it was not the call of a prophet, though, that made him nervous. It was his age that caused him to be fearful. He told God he lacked the skill of speaking and initially focused on what he felt he could not do because of where he was at in his life. I am sure he wondered if people would even listen to him. This is an understandable concern. Many times, older people will not take younger ones seriously because, to them, the younger person may lack wisdom or life experience. This could be part of what Jeremiah was referencing when he spoke about his speaking skills. But God reminded Jeremiah that He called and formed him before he was even in the womb. This shows we all have a purpose even before we are born, and God can start that purpose at any age He wants. God promised Jeremiah He would be with him wherever he went and encouraged him not to be afraid, despite his youth, but to trust Him and obey. Can you relate to the insecurities that Jeremiah felt? Maybe yours are not age related, but skill related. I think we all have felt inadequate at some point in our lives. But God does not always commission us when we feel ready or when we think we are old enough. If this were the case, we might never even begin the journey of our purpose. Instead, God will often call us to our purpose with a commission to just begin by obeying. He will then equip us by telling us exactly what we need to do to fulfill that in our lives. Our job in the call is to obey, no matter our age or skill set.

Today's Challenge To Dig Deeper:
Are you feeling some insecurities or inadequacies about something? Take it to God today. Ask Him to give you one task to do today that will move you towards trusting in Him more in this area and conquering your feeling of inadequacy.

Evening Reflection:
What did God show you today? Write what is on your heart, and the action step to fulfilling what He is asking you to do.

SPIRITUAL CIRCUMCISION

May 26

Morning Rinse: Jeremiah 4-6
Featured Verse: Jeremiah 6:10 *To whom shall I speak and give warning that they may hear? Behold, their ears are closed (circumcised) and they cannot listen. Behold, the word of the Lord has become a reproach to them, they have no delight in it.*

The word "circumcise*"* literally means "to cut around." Under the law, it was a requirement for all of Abraham's descendants to be circumcised. This is a surgical procedure removing the prepuce, or foreskin, of a male. The purpose was to symbolize the covenant God made with them in Genesis seventeen. Of course, circumcision is no longer required spiritually, since we are not under the Law. But it is still chosen by many for reasons such as cultural and ethical standards, health benefits, religious beliefs, or a combination of several of these. In modern day scenarios, circumcision is done shortly after the birth of a boy, but men of the Bible were circumcised at all ages. In fact, in Genesis sixteen, Abraham was ninety-nine years old, and his son Ishmael was thirteen years old when they were circumcised. Understanding a little about circumcision can give a new perspective of today's Featured Verse with the word *closed* translated as *circumcision* in the King James Version. While it is not possible for females to be physically circumcised, and it is not chosen for some males, we can all be spiritually circumcised by cutting things off from our hearts and ears that keep us from fully hearing and receiving God's voice. First, we do this by cutting away the walls we have built around our heart that keeps us from being totally softened towards God and others. God wants us to love Him and love others with nothing hindering that love. But if we have unforgiveness, bitterness, grudges, or sin hidden inside the walls, we cannot love Him or others like He destined us to love. And the same goes for our ears. When we choose to put carnal 'ear plugs' over our ears, we close out God's voice as well as the voices of others who point us to Him, like pastors or mentors. When we circumcise our ears, we clear those voices away and choose to listen to God and to godly influence. We, in essence, cut off the things of the world. The truth is when our hearts and ears are uncircumcised, it is rebellion. This is the exact subject God wanted Jeremiah to preach to the Israelites about, avoiding it, and He wants us to avoid it as well. But when we choose to spiritually circumcise, like what Jeremiah asked of the nation of Israel, we position ourselves for a life of obedience and blessings from God.

Today's Challenge To Dig Deeper:
Ask God today to begin circumcising your heart and ears. Ask Him to show you any area that keeps you from loving Him and others, and from hearing His voice and obeying Him. Sit alone with Him and let Him do the surgery.

Evening Reflection:
Your heart may be raw tonight, and your 'ears' a little sore, but how do you feel after your spiritual circumcision?

CORPORATE WORSHIP
May 27

Morning Rinse: Jeremiah 7-9
Featured Verse: Jeremiah 7:2 *Stand in the gate of the Lord's house and proclaim there this word and say, "Hear the word of the Lord, all you of Judah, who enter by these gates to worship the Lord!"*

I remember when things started shutting down due to the global pandemic caused by Covid-19. It was around March of the year 2020. Some countries developed restrictions so tight, residents were confined to their home for months with the threat of being arrested if they left their premises. The United States left much of this decision up to our state and local principalities. For the first few months of this virus, here in America, one commonality, though, was the mass closings of businesses, restaurants and even churches. When this happened, life in America shifted tremendously, and people had to adjust to a changing environment. One of these major changes was when most of our churches ceased to meet in person. Therefore, many pastors developed a way to broadcast their services online. Probably somewhat comparable to Jeremiah standing at the gates and shouting for people to hear. Online services were great, and it worked for a while as we were all very unsure at first of how this new virus would corrupt society, and worse yet, our own families. But many people soon grew weary of not seeing their loved ones. In fact, there were several pastors who were so passionate about the importance of corporate worship and collectively hearing God's voice through praise, they were arrested due to their steadfast decision to continue to meet. Their arrests came even though they arranged to worship outside and took precautionary measures of safety for the people. There is just something special about the atmosphere during corporate worship. While I love singing in my car with the music blaring, and I love the sweet atmosphere between me and Jesus during these times, there is truly something different with how I feel in my car versus at church. I know we can have an atmosphere of worship anywhere. But there is a reason Jesus wants us to assemble in His house, or church locations. Being in a room full of fellow believers who are all unified in worship is so electrifying. I am convinced when we set up an atmosphere of worship, it truly does help us hear His voice easier.

Today's Challenge To Dig Deeper:
There is a beautiful song written by Elevation Worship called "Here as in Heaven." Look up this song on a music platform or YouTube, and listen to it with your eyes closed. Turn it on several times throughout the day today and take note of how you feel when you invite the Spirit of the Lord into where you are. If you do not attend a church in person, consider finding one.

Evening Reflection:
What are your thoughts regarding today's devotion? Write them down.

LIFE IS NOT ALWAYS FAIR
May 28

Morning Rinse: Jeremiah 10-12
Featured Verse: Jeremiah 12:1 *Righteous are You, O Lord, that I would plead my case with You; Indeed, I would discuss matters of justice with You: Why has the way of the wicked prospered? Why are all those who deal in treachery at ease?*

I imagine we have all had a situation in our lives when we have questioned the fairness of the circumstances surrounding it. My kids will tell you they have heard both my husband Nathan and I say to them countless times, "Life is not always fair." I can see their eyes roll even as I write this. I remember one Saturday night after a week of being on the road, Nathan wanted to take our teen son out for a 'guys' night to reconnect with him. He decided to take him to one of their favorite pastimes, the Indoor Go Kart course. We do not take our kids there often since it is a bit pricey. So you can imagine our son's excitement on the return of his father. When our middle daughter found out about this special event her brother received, she became upset and stated how unfair it was, claiming that he seemed to get all the fun. In moments like this, a kid's perspective can be a bit skewed. Kids seem to have a unique ability to notice, in detail, when a sibling receives something they missed out on, and yet forget the times where preferential treatment was given to them. The famous "Why" questions start at an early age for all of us, and continue through adulthood. Even Jeremiah had "Why" questions. He asked God why life seemed so unfair. It seemed the very people who had hurt God's heart were now prospering. So in his confusion about this, he questioned why no justice was given to them. These questions appear to be legitimate to ask, especially since he witnessed their sinful behaviors firsthand. And as a prophet, I am sure he felt the hurting heart of God, making what he witnessed a bit more challenging. I think we all have asked a similar question of God, if not verbally, in our hearts. But not all of God's answers to us about the fairness of life are nice and easy. Sometimes He must tell us as His children, "Life is not always fair."

Today's Challenge To Dig Deeper:
Are you going through a situation you feel is unfair? Have you asked God the "Why" question pertaining to your circumstance? Ask Him again today and see what His answer is.

Evening Reflection:
What answer did God give you when you asked Him the "Why" question pertaining to your 'unfair' circumstance?

HONESTY IS THE BEST POLICY
May 29

Morning Rinse: Jeremiah 13-15
Featured Verses: Jeremiah 15:18-19 *Why has my pain been perpetual and my wound incurable, refusing to be healed? Will You indeed be to me like a deceptive stream with water that is unreliable? Therefore, thus says the Lord, "If you return, then I will restore you – Before Me you will stand; And if you extract the precious from the worthless, you will become My spokesman. They for their part may turn to you, but as for you, you must not turn to them."*

To expect a prophet to be perfect in controlling not only his actions, but his emotions one hundred percent of the time, is unrealistic. Even one of the most obedient men, Jeremiah, got a little upset and claimed God did not help him at a dire time in his life. Even he, a powerful prophet, got a little off course in his attitude. But God can handle these times of venting. He is not afraid of our anger or accusatory words. In fact, He would rather us go to Him exactly how we feel, rather than hiding our true thoughts and feelings, burying them in the sand. It is always better to go to God authentically. Then God can meet us where we are, and a true healing and heart change can begin. God did this very thing for Jeremiah. He lovingly reminded him to change his heart back to full obedience to Him. God also reminded Jeremiah to be careful to not let others influence him, but to be the influencer. While Jeremiah had a heavy load to carry as a prophet, with a responsibility that not many are called to fulfill, it does not mean he walked the journey flawlessly. Even men of God get emotionally drained, and may need to get refocused and reminded of God's purpose. But it first begins with being honest and authentic, even if our feelings need adjusting.

Today's Challenge To Dig Deeper:
Be honest with God today. Take some time and tell Him everything that bothers you, and any anger you feel, even if it is towards Him. He can handle it. Do not hold back. Tell Him. Then listen.

Evening Reflection:
How did God respond to your anger? Write down what He talked to you about.

AM I CLAY?
May 30

Morning Rinse: Jeremiah 16-18
Featured Verse: Jeremiah 18:4 *But the vessel that he was making of clay was spoiled in the hand of the potter; so, he remade it into another vessel, as it pleased the potter to make.*

I am sure we have all either seen videos of a Master Potter molding clay on a pottery wheel, or we have had the privilege of witnessing this underrated art performed in person. The intricate machine these potters work on is designed to make circular ceramic pieces like vases, plates, and cups. Some even form extremely exquisite and unique creations. It is a long process and requires intentional patience from the potter. Creating with clay must first start with proper conditioning of the clay, called wedging. This is the process of getting the air bubbles out to help eliminate cracking, shattering or explosion later in the kiln. If wedging is done manually, it is very similar to kneading bread dough, by squeezing, pushing, and twisting the clay. This process can also help the potter find any hard spots to remove. Once all the preparation of the clay is completed, the potter gathers his tools. The next phase, called turning or throwing the clay, begins. This is the process of shaping the clay, starting from when the clay touches the wheel, to the time the wheel is stopped. Around and around the clay spins, as the potter gently molds and guides it, shaping, moving, squeezing, and sometimes even crushing it only to start all over again, in hopes of making that perfect ware. Once the masterpiece is created, the potter will set it aside to dry before firing it in the kiln. Firing hardens the clay and can sometimes take up to fifteen hundred degrees Celsius in the kiln. This is when the ceramic piece is converted from weak clay into a strong, durable form. The entire process of molding clay on a potter's wheel is no different from how our Heavenly Father wants to mold us. Stretching, pushing, removing our hardness, shaping, and putting us through the fire all sound familiar in a Christ-centered life, right? He desires to be our true potter by molding us on His wheel, creating the unique life He has for us. The question each of us must ask is, "Will we submit to His way of gently shaping us, even if that includes crushing and reshaping again and again? Are we willing to go with Him through the fire of life?" If we are, this allows God to make us into the vessel He needs us to be for His kingdom. But we first must be willing to be His clay.

Today's Challenge To Dig Deeper:
Recommitments are just a way of rededicating areas of your life to our Heavenly Father, so He can keep reshaping us. Ask God if there is an area you need to rededicate to Him. Ask Him to help you be His clay in EVERY area of your life.

Evening Reflection:
What area did He talk to you about today? Do you feel like soft clay? Or was there a small hard part He had to remove as He began to shape you?

DO YOUR BONES BURN?
May 31

Morning Rinse: Jeremiah 19-22
Featured Verses: Jeremiah 20:7-9 *O Lord, You have deceived me and I was deceived; You have overcome me and prevailed. I have become a laughingstock all day long; Everyone mocks me. For each time I speak, I cry aloud; I proclaim violence and destruction. Because for me the word of the Lord has resulted in reproach and derision all day long. But if I say, "I will not remember Him or speak anymore in His name," then in my heart it becomes like a burning fire shut up in my bones; and I am weary of holding it in; And I cannot endure it.*

The call of a prophet is not easy, especially when speaking to deaf ears. Jeremiah not only had an incredibly hard message to preach to the people of Israel, but they clearly did not like what he had to say. Unfortunately, in today's Morning Rinse, we even read how he was beaten for his prophetic message (20:2). He typically would ask the people to change their ways and repent, speaking directly to the matters of the heart. But the people refused to submit to his words. He prophesied that if they did not turn from their wicked ways, destruction would come to their lives consequently. I can imagine how frustrating and depressing it was to preach day after day, week after week, month after month, and not see the fruit of the words he was so passionate about. In fact, there were times when he felt so alone, he even claimed God had deceived him, leaving him to suffer through mockery and persecution. Even though his mission was extremely important, he admits there were times when he would refuse to prophesy, nearly giving up. But the words inside him would become like fire in his bones. They would burn so deep, he could not contain them any longer, and would begin prophesying again. Some of the messages seemed gloomy and full of despair for the people, but they were honestly a message of hope. Hope is what Jeremiah wanted for the people. Hope for a relationship with God. Hope for redemption. Hope for a blessed life. In the end, even though he did not see the people respond, and he did not feel God's presence at times, his heart would continually be drawn back to God. After this moment of complaining in today's Featured Verses, we read him giving thanks despite being mocked and persecuted.

Today's Challenge To Dig Deeper:
Do you have a message God wants you to speak? Is it like fire inside your bones, but you have kept it in? Or is there someone speaking out God's message, but you have refused to hear what they have to say?

Evening Reflection:
What did God speak to you about today regarding these questions?

June Rinsing

WHO IS INFLUENCING YOU?

June 1

Morning Rinse: Jeremiah 23-25
Featured Verse: Jeremiah 23:1 *"Woe to the shepherds who are destroying and scattering the sheep of My pasture!" declares the Lord.*

John Maxwell is an American author, speaker and pastor who focuses primarily on teaching about leadership for both businesses and churches. One of his top quotes states, "Leadership is not about titles, positions, or flowcharts. It is about one life influencing another." He also has stated, "A leader is one who knows the way, goes the way, and shows the way." Jeremiah's office as a prophet was not just for the people of Israel. His messages were also for leaders of that time, including the priests and those who were in a position of spiritual authority. It is natural to expect pastors and priests to hold a higher standard as they spread God's message of hope. However, Jeremiah also had to speak harsh words of correction to some of these leaders, due to false messages they were spreading. It is quite possible some of these leaders were even his friends. God takes it very seriously when people use His name in their messages, but lead people astray with error. This happens when pastors and teachers preach the Word of God by taking scripture out of context, do not study the Bible correctly, have wrong motives, or allow pride and even sin to take root in their lives. As people of God, we must learn to discern who these false teachers are. Just because someone stands behind a pulpit or speaks at a convention, that does not mean their words are automatically biblically sound, or that we should immediately deem what they say true. In fact, another quote from John Maxwell says, "It's not the position that makes the leader, it's the leader that makes the position."[19] We may never be given the responsibility to correct leaders like Jeremiah was called to do. But we do have the ability to hear God's voice and learn to discern whether a leader is truly speaking what is aligned with The Word of God. Yes, these false teachers and preachers will have to stand before God and give an account for leading people astray. But we also have a responsibility, as Christ followers, to flee from their leadership and influence. These influencers are clearly in the wrong.

Today's Challenge To Dig Deeper:
Is there an influencer in the wrong in your life? A pastor, podcaster, leader, singer, or an author, for example? Ask God today if you are to get out from underneath their influence. Begin steps to follow His direction and leading. If you are under safe leaders, then thank God for this in your life, and pray for them to stay grounded in The Word.

Evening Reflection:
What did God talk to you about today regarding influencers?

---

[19] Maxwell, John; *The 21 Irrefutable Laws of Leadership*; Zondervan Publishing; https://store.maxwellleadership.com/products/the-21-irrefutable-laws-of-leadership

GOD HAS THE LAST SAY
June 2

Morning Rinse: Jeremiah 26-28
Featured Verses: Jeremiah 26:14-15 *But as for me, behold, I am in your hands; do with me as is good and right in your sight. Only know for certain that if you put me to death, you will bring innocent blood on yourselves, and on this city and on its inhabitants; for truly the Lord has sent me to you to speak all these words in your hearing.*

In previous Featured Verses, Jeremiah was found complaining to God about his life being unfair. His perspective came from being mocked, scorned, and degraded by those he was called to minister to. Those who were mocking Jeremiah in his past caused frustration, and hence, he then complained to God about his feelings. But in today's Featured Verses, Jeremiah is a different man than the Jeremiah we previously read about. In today's passage, Jeremiah is faced once again with a challenging situation where he is surrounded by people who did not like what he had to say. However, he is not just faced with people mocking him. He is faced with a possible death sentence. After he gave a message to the people, most of them in the city were so upset they seized him and called for his death, based on what he was saying. This was truly a valid reason to talk to God. And honestly, I can safely say most of us would probably complain about life being unfair if we were faced with a similar situation. Jeremiah, though, had changed, and his response may surprise you. He appeared to be at peace with whatever happened to him, even though he had a front row seat to people plotting to kill him. He had become ready for whatever he faced, and therefore responded to the people with confidence, telling them to do whatever they wanted to him. Declaring this to a trusted foe is one thing. Yet giving this emotional freedom to an enemy is another. Even though he was restrained, he knew God was watching what was unfolding in this moment, and knew his ultimate destiny was still in God's hands. As you finish reading this story, we discover the people end up changing their minds and retracting his death sentence. Stay the course. When we face trials and setbacks from those around us, we must remember that God sees all we are going through. How will you respond differently in trials knowing this?

Today's Challenge To Dig Deeper:
Think in your mind's eye of any given situation where someone has detached from you, told lies, spread rumors, or even tried to defame your character. Plan your new response with the thought in mind that God will always have the last say. Ask for God's help in forming your response.

Evening Reflection:
What is your new response to character defamation, knowing God has the last say anyway?

HE THINKS GOOD THOUGHTS OF US
June 3

Morning Rinse: Jeremiah 29-31
Featured Verse: Jeremiah 29:11 *"For I know the plans that I have for you," declares the Lord, "plans for welfare (to prosper) and not for calamity (to harm you), to give you a future and a hope."*

Growing up as a pastor's kid, I heard literally thousands of sermons or teachings, and have an internal list of verses or stories that seem to be the most popular to get quoted from a pulpit. Today's Featured Verse is on that list. To know the Creator of the universe is thinking loving thoughts of me every day is beyond what my brain can comprehend, but it is true. God thinks of us, and longs for a relationship with us, and He longs for us to desire a relationship with Him in return. When hard things come our way, it is easy to think the opposite of this, and even blame God when struggles come. Comparably, when my kids were young and had a struggle about a situation or life circumstance, they would at times have the urge to question if we had a role in the issue they were facing. My husband would often chuckle and say to them, "I do not lie in bed at night asking myself how I can make things miserable for my kids." It is a funny statement, but there is truth in it. God, as well, does not sit on His throne wondering how to make our life hard. Instead, He thinks of us with love and compassion, longing for a relationship with us. And not only does He want that relationship, He believes in us. It can be challenging to remember this, especially if we have made a mistake in life. He truly does believe in our ability to carry out our life mission. He is our biggest fan and cheerleader. And since He believes in us, He gives us tasks to do, and sets us up for success if we follow His ways, versus setting us up to fail with unreachable accomplishments. He gifts us and calls us, knowing we can complete the tasks. And He has committed to walking through those plans with us, if we let Him. He is also right beside us, walking with us through the challenges we face in life. And we will face challenges, that is guaranteed. It is one thing to have a cheerleader like a friend with us, as we live life, but it is another to have Jehovah-Jireh, our provider, believing in us and longing to be with us through all the highs and lows. And not only is He with us, He also has a plan to build us up, to bless us, and to fill us with hope and a plan for our future.

Today's Challenge To Dig Deeper:
Do you truly believe God has loving thoughts for you and wants you to succeed in life? Do you truly believe He wants an intimate relationship with you as well? What about your struggles? Do you feel God's presence through them? Talk to Him today about these questions, and listen to His response.

Evening Reflection:
Write down the conversation you had with God today. Remember, He is near and wants a relationship with you. Write down your victory.

PURPOSE IN THE PURCHASE
June 4

Morning Rinse: Jeremiah 32-34
Featured Verse: Jeremiah 32:17 *Ah Lord God! Behold, You have made the heavens and the earth by Your great power and by Your outstretched arm! Nothing is too difficult for You.*

Jeremiah prayed this prayer shortly after purchasing a field from his cousin that had recently been captured by the enemy. He literally bought property in the middle of a war zone. Looking at the reality of this situation, it is easy to question why he would do such a crazy thing. It made no sense at all, and that opinion is also coming from me as a real estate agent. Jeremiah was known for his radical actions to prove a point, and this action was no different. He did not make this purchase based on a great business plan. He made it simply because God told him to do it. So out of an act of faith, and to provide hope to other people who were also about ready to lose everything to the Babylonians, he made the purchase. Logically speaking, circumstantial evidence showed one thing, but Jeremiah's faith in God and what He could do showed another. God wanted Jeremiah's actions to be a symbol to the Israelites that he would keep his promise of restoring them back to the land. Jeremiah died before he ever saw what happened to that field, but that was not the point. The point was, he obeyed God and bought it, standing on his faith that God had a purpose for the purchase, and that nothing was impossible with Him despite the surrounding circumstances. Now, if I were to say that Jeremiah was solid in his security about this purchase, I would not be fully accurate. He did get a little confused about why God asked him to buy it. His faith was completed in the purchase, but he struggled a little. So if you are confused about God's direction for your life, especially if you are making decisions that do not seem logical, just keep obeying. Nothing is impossible for God, despite the outward appearance looking too bleak to recover from. What is your impossible situation? Do you need to 'buy a field' as a symbolic act of faith? During hard times, make a declaration of faith to family and friends, that no matter what, you will trust in God. With the purchase of a 'field,' you may be creating a legacy and a faith story for your loved ones to pass on for generations to come.

Today's Challenge To Dig Deeper:
Is God asking you to make a radical move today? Is it an action? Maybe it is a purchase that will show your trust in Him, despite it not making sense. Maybe it is putting money in the offering plate, sponsoring a child, or helping a needy family with a meal. Or maybe you literally need to go buy a field in obedience to God's voice. What is He telling you to do today?

Evening Reflection:
What act of radical faith did God ask you to do today? How do you feel?

GOD ENCOUNTERS CANNOT BE BURNED
June 5

Morning Rinse: Jeremiah 35-37
Featured Verse: Jeremiah 36:23 *When Jehudi had read three or four columns, the king cut it with a scribe's knife and threw it into the fire that was in the brazier, until all the scroll was consumed in the fire that was in the brazier.*

During the writing of this devotional, there have been several times when my document was not saved properly, and I lost hours of work. After the first few times of this happening, I learned my lesson and began saving multiple versions so there would be backups if needed. Jeremiah did not have the luxury of a copier, a printer, or a computer to duplicate files. It is only by the grace of God that we have tangible words written, especially after his transcripts were destroyed. Whether in Jeremiah's century or in modern-day times, most people will struggle at some point when God speaks a harsh message of correction, like when Jeremiah spoke. It is humbling to be shown our errors or be given a perspective that causes us to look at ourselves in the mirror. God used Jeremiah to speak these messages, and unfortunately, he became an unpopular prophet for this reason. His prophecies made people uncomfortable, especially the leaders and priests of the land. In fact, some of the leaders went to great extremes to silence him, even restraining him so he could not go into the synagogues to speak. But God cannot be silenced, even by those in high authority. Since Jeremiah was kept away from the people, God instructed him to capture these messages on a scroll so the people would still be able to read what He had spoken to him. Upon learning of this scroll, the king sent Jehudi to obtain it and then read it to him. But when the king heard the calamities coming his way if the people did not obey God, he became angry and burned the scroll. I am sure there was panic, just like I get panicked when my files are not correctly saved, and I lose documents. But again, this did not stop God. He then asked Jeremiah to recite the messages to Baruch a second time. Jeremiah had encountered God so deeply, he had no problem remembering what God had spoken to Him, even from years past. When we encounter God, the messages we receive, the conversations we have, and the experiences we encounter with our Father, become so engraved in our soul, no one can destroy them, not even the enemy's weapons of destruction.

Today's Challenge To Dig Deeper:
Have there been God moments or encounters that are so etched in your memory, there is no chance of forgetting them? Today, begin writing your 'scroll.' Capture each encounter that comes to mind. Then make a commitment to continue adding to your 'scroll' in the days, months, and years ahead, so you will remember these God moments. Your journal begins today.

Evening Reflection:
Thank God for the encounters and God moments He has given you. Write down any nuggets you had today as you began writing. Keep your spirit open to more encounters in the days and months ahead. If something comes to mind, commit to a habit of spending a few minutes capturing it in your journal.

CISTERN SITUATIONS
June 6

Morning Rinse: Jeremiah 38-40
Featured Verses: Jeremiah 38:7-10 *But Ebed-melech the Ethiopian, a eunuch, while he was in the king's palace, heard that they had put Jeremiah into a cistern. Now the king was sitting in the Gate of Benjamin and Ebed-melech went out from the king's palace and spoke to the king, saying, "My lord the king, these men have acted wickedly in all that they have done to Jeremiah the prophet whom they have cast into the cistern; and he will die right where he is because of the famine, for there is no more bread in the city." Then the king commanded Ebed-melech the Ethiopian, saying, "Take thirty men from here under your authority and bring up Jeremiah the prophet from the cistern before he dies."*

Due to long periods of drought back in biblical times, it was common for cisterns to be dug. These were underground water reservoirs dug into the earth, and sometimes carved into rocks as well. They were large holes that would collect rainwater.[20] These holes were so deep, there was no way for a man to escape if they fell into one, or got dropped down into it, without the aid of those above ground. The leaders knew this when they dropped Jeremiah into it. With the rainwater and other moisture below the surface, one can visualize what the base of a cistern may have looked like. It is safe to say some cisterns may have been full of mud or slush, which could cause a quick death by way of sinking or drowning. If the water was limited in a cistern, then the next form of death would most likely be starvation, which seemed to be the concern in Jeremiah's situation. The people who threw him into this cistern hated his prophecies, and purposed in their hearts to do what they could to cause his death. However, one single man, Ebed-melech, felt an urgency to stand up against what was happening. He did not agree with these leaders and took measures to speak up to save Jeremiah's life. Some Bible scholars believe he was one of the king's favored servants, and used his influence to plead with the king to let him get Jeremiah out. Taking this bold step while so many people wanted him dead, was probably scary and possibly life threatening. But he chose to step out anyway with urgency and boldness. The king ended up granting Ebed-melech a team of thirty men to help tie ropes together and pull Jeremiah out. I wonder how deep this cistern death trap truly was, since there was a need for thirty men to assist. Do not be afraid to go deep with someone who needs saving. God will see your efforts and will bless you for your willingness to head into the cistern for others. We see later in the story that God spared Ebed-melech when the Babylonians came and captured Jerusalem (39:16-18). He saved a life and was ultimately saved himself because he dared to face someone's cistern situation.

Today's Challenge To Dig Deeper:
Do you feel a sense of urgency in your spirit to act on behalf of someone, so they can be saved from destruction? It just takes one bold person to stand in the gap for someone. What can you do today to be that one person to save someone from their 'cistern'?

Evening Reflection:
Did you act today on behalf of someone? Write down what you did and how you felt.

---

[20] https://www.growingchristians.org/devotions/broken-cisterns/

ARE YOU AN ACTOR?
June 7

Morning Rinse: Jeremiah 41-43
Featured Verses: Jeremiah 42:5-6, 10, 43:2 *Then they said to Jeremiah, "May the Lord be a true and faithful witness against us if we do not act in accordance with the whole message with which the Lord your God will send you to us. Whether it is pleasant or unpleasant, we will listen to the voice of the Lord our God to whom we are sending you, so that it may go well with us when we listen to the voice of the Lord our God."... Then Jeremiah said to them, "If you will indeed stay in this land, then I will build you up and not tear you down, and I will plant you and not uproot you; for I will relent concerning the calamity that I have inflicted on you."... Azariah the son of Hoshaiah, and Johanan, the son of Kareah, and all the arrogant men said to Jeremiah, "You are telling a lie! The Lord our God has not sent you to say, 'You are not to enter Egypt to reside there,' "*

The passage in today's Featured Verses is a classic example of hypocrisy. The word "hypocrite" is rooted in the Greek word hypokrites, which means "an actor."[21] When I think of a hypocrite, I think of negative behaviors. An example might be when someone is caught in an act that goes against what they have morally displayed. It is when someone says one thing about their beliefs, but acts completely opposite. It is probably not very often that we think of an actor as a hypocrite, though. When I first heard the origin of the word hypocrite, I was not very pleased, especially due to my personal endeavors as a film and commercial actress and filmmaker. When it is your profession to 'act,' you want people to see that ambition in a positive light. However, I can understand the origin. An actor puts on a mask, if you will, to portray a character. They are acting. And so is a hypocrite. I think it is safe to say we have all experienced a hypocrite, and some of us may even be guilty of hypocritical behaviors ourselves. The men in this passage were hypocrites. They went to Jeremiah and asked him to prophesy to them regarding their journey to Egypt. They told Jeremiah whatever God said, whether good or bad, they would obey. However, when God spoke through Jeremiah for them to not go to Egypt, these men called Jeremiah a liar. Instead, they continued to Egypt, disobeying God. We later read they were captured, which is exactly what God said would occur if they disobeyed Him and continued their journey. I hope and pray we as Christ followers listen to the voice of God, whether it be pleasant or unpleasant, and we follow through in obedience with our actions. I pray we are not acting in our faith and walk.

Today's Challenge To Dig Deeper:
Be courageous. Say to God, "Whatever you say to me, whether pleasant or unpleasant, I will do it." Ask Him to search your heart and clean out anything that keeps you from fully obeying Him, even if it means turning around from where you are headed, or stopping an endeavor you have started.

Evening Reflection:
Write down the conversation you had with God today. Were there hypocritical areas in your heart? Are you being an actor in some areas of your faith?

---

[21] https://www.merriam-webster.com/words-at-play/hypocrite-meaning-origin

KEEPING GOD'S BLUE FACE AT BAY
June 8

Morning Rinse: Jeremiah 44-48
Featured Verse: Jeremiah 44:16 *As for the message that you have spoken to us in the name of the Lord, we are not going to listen to you!*

Jeremiah's life was spent speaking to the people about their sinful ways. Time and again, they heard his pleas to obey God instead of worshiping idols. Time and again, he warned them of the consequences if they continued living a disobedient life. In today's Morning Rinse, we read Jeremiah even reminded the people of the sins from former generations, and the consequences of destruction from those actions of the past. He warned them against repeating history if they did not repent. Unfortunately, though, Jeremiah was a biblical example of *talking until you are blue in the face*. This popular saying references how one may feel if they must keep repeating themselves to an individual, feeling unheard. For example, parents may say this to their children when they give instructions, but do not see action. Unlike most kids, though, these people told Jeremiah to his face they were not going to listen to him. Some of these people may have been so heavily blinded by their idol worship that they no longer believed in God, completely gripped by witchcraft. Others may have known in their hearts that God was the way, but chose not to follow Him. We do not know details about each individual person Jeremiah spoke to. But we do know many of them were vocal about their rebellion. So God remained vocal about His plan to give consequences. God probably felt like He was blue in the face too. But His Word must remain true. We, at times, must suffer consequences for our poor choices and lack of following Him. Let us not be the cause of God's blue face. There are consequences for every choice we make. Let us all make good choices. That is why you are reading this devotional, right? To keep God's blue face at bay.

Today's Challenge To Dig Deeper:
Has God, your pastor, accountability partners, or leaders ever been *blue in the face* when talking to you about your choices? What comes to mind when I ask you that questions? Respond to God in repentance, and ask Him to help you make some corrections, beginning today.

Evening Reflection:
What corrections did God help you begin making today?

ARROGANCE IN THE MIRROR
June 9

Morning Rinse: Jeremiah 49-50
Featured Verses: Jeremiah 50:31-32 *"Behold, I am against you, O arrogant one,"* *declares the Lord of hosts, "For your day has come, the time when I will punish you. The arrogant one will stumble and fall with no one to raise him up; And I will set fire to his cities and it will devour all his environs."*

The word *arrogant* is seen in multiple places throughout the book of Jeremiah when describing sinful ways of both individual people and even entire nations. In fact, if you want to dig a little deeper into this, run a word search for *arrogant* or *arrogance* in Jeremiah and then underline each reference of them in your Bible. I did this and was amazed at how many times Jeremiah addressed this issue. One example was from the devotion we read two days ago about hypocrisy. The men who were hypocrites in that specific Morning Rinse were described as arrogant, and now we see it again in today's Featured Verses describing Babylon. *The Merriam-Webster Dictionary* definition is "exaggerating or disposed to exaggerate one's own worth or importance, often by an overbearing manner."[22] This type of person usually shows a sense of feeling superior over others, which is also a symptom of pride. Ultimately, pride leads to feeling superior in multiple areas, like talent, beauty, resourcefulness, and even possessions. When this happens, it can easily lead to demeaning others. These traits are repulsive to God, and are ultimately what led to the destruction of many lives that Jeremiah was trying to save. Being proud of oneself for a wonderful accomplishment is different than being arrogant and looking down on others. While this destructive pattern was a common theme throughout Jeremiah's messages, it is also a problem of modern-day living. It is very hurtful to be around an arrogant person. Equally damaging is to possess arrogance ourselves, because it is usually those closest to us we will hurt the most. To keep the Bible living and breathing in our own lives today, even a difficult book like Jeremiah, look at the steps below, allow God to search your heart and respond to this message.

1. Forgive those who display superiority over us through arrogance.
2. Set some boundaries for those who we feel are arrogant and have hurt us.
3. Search our own heart for arrogance.
4. Repent for any arrogance in our heart.

Today's Challenge To Dig Deeper:
Respond with the four steps today. Notice that two of the four steps point to the mirror.

Evening Reflection:
Reflect on today and what God spoke to you regarding forgiving others and looking in the mirror at our own lives.

---

[22] https://www.merriam-webster.com/dictionary/arrogant

COURAGEOUS LOVE
June 10

Morning Rinse: Jeremiah 51-52
Featured Verse: Jeremiah 51:15 *It is he who made the earth by His power, who established the world by His wisdom, and by His understanding He stretched out the heavens. When He utters His voice, there is a tumult of waters in the heavens, and He causes the clouds to ascend from the end of the earth; He makes lightning for the rain and brings forth the wind from His storehouses.*

Have you ever experienced a loved one who chose a destructive path for their life, despite your warning and imploration? I have, too. It is easy for their choices to cause our hearts to agonize daily in pain for what we see happening. Whether it be a child, a relative, or a close friend, watching them make choices that destroy their lives is literally one of the hardest things we can go through. While we cannot control their actions, we can control our responses. We can pray for them, speak words of wisdom over them, and love them every opportunity possible. These types of responses are examples of courageous love. Jeremiah was a true example of this deep kind of love, especially since all those around him denied his wisdom, and even rejected and abused him both verbally and physically when he tried to correct them. Even though he knew these types of rebellious responses from the people he loved would probably never stop, he continued. He never quit trying. Throughout the chapters of the book of Jeremiah, we read about him describing to the people consequences of their choices, as well as who God is as the King of Kings, making every effort to get the people to listen and change their ways. His heart agonized over the nations around him, because he knew their path of destruction was clear to see. Despite them ignoring his warnings and abusing him, he continued loving them anyway, by courageously speaking out. From the outside looking in, it may appear that he was unsuccessful in his mission to change lives. With every turn he made, every step he took, every prophecy he spoke, nothing seemed to make an impact in their rebellious hearts. With rejection, abuse, and name calling at his doorstep, it is easy to speculate his life of courageous love for the people was in vain, and he failed in his efforts to impact them towards a different path. But his success was not measured in whether the people responded to his prophecies. His success was measured by his obedience to speak what God told him to speak. It was measured by God, not man. Jeremiah obeyed his call to courageously love, and that, my friend, is success. Jeremiah comes to the end of his journey and still praises God for who He is. He knew from the beginning his ministry would be hard. But he loved the people enough to stay on the path of courageous love. Will you stay on your path of courageous love?

Today's Challenge To Dig Deeper:
Is God asking you to follow Jeremiah's example of a life of courageous love? You may never live to see the changes in their lives, but your tangible acts of obedience are key. Living a life of courageous love will be difficult. But do it anyway.

Evening Reflection:
Write what God spoke to you today about tangible ways He wants you to courageously love someone in your life.

WORSHIP THROUGH WOUNDS
June 11

Morning Rinse: Job 1-4
Featured Verses: Job 1:20-22 *Then Job arose and tore his robe and shaved his head, and he fell to the ground and worshiped. He said, "Naked I came from my mother's womb, and naked I shall return there. The Lord gave and the Lord has taken away. Blessed by the name of the Lord." Through all this Job did not sin nor did he blame God.*

In today's Morning Rinse, we read about the revolving front door of Job's home. It seemed the moment one person came through it with bad news, the door immediately revealed someone else scurrying inside to bring him yet more heart wrenching news. Multiple people crowded into his living room, each sharing a traumatic story of how they nearly escaped death. But the news they brought showed that nothing or no one else survived their specific calamity. Job's possessions, employees, and his children were gone in a moment's notice. One by one, the survivors reveal the catastrophes, which was Satan's plan to destroy Job's livelihood. For starters, a strange fire consumed his sheep and the servants tending them. Then the rest of his livestock and servants were attacked by the Sabeans and Chaldeans. Tragically, on top of these losses, a tornado-like wind crushed the home that all his children were in, killing everyone inside except the person delivering this horrific news. Anyone experiencing just one of these great loses would obviously be overwhelmed with grief and depression. But how does Job respond with the surmounting news of multiple losses? Much to our amazement, he worships through his wounds. We know God gave Satan permission to destroy Job's possessions. But Job worships anyway. And God did not give Satan permission to hurt Job just once. We see in chapter two in today's Morning Rinse, Satan went back to God a SECOND time and received permission to continue his plan to destroy Job's life. This time was to obtain permission from God to destroy his health. We often forget there was not just one round of perceived defeat. There were TWO. The second round came while Job was still grieving the loss of his children, probably shortly after he buried them. This would literally be the lowest of low points in anyone's life. This time around, Satan attacked Job's health with boils, making Job's body nearly unrecognizable. Job was not only enduring his recent heart pain, but he was now in extreme physical pain as well. This physical pain was so intense, he would scrape his skin with broken pottery to try and find relief. Even in the midst of a wounded heart and body, Job worshipped God, never sinning with his lips. Satan tried to use Job's pain and grief to tempt him to turn his back on God. But Job pushed through his wounds and continued worshiping anyway. We must remember the ploys of the enemy. Just like Job, we must keep worshiping despite the wounds from attacks.

Today's Challenge To Dig Deeper:
Are you experiencing any emotional or physical pain? Today, when you feel the pain hit you, worship. Every time an ache surfaces, worship. Worship Him anyway, through your wounds.

Evening Reflection:
Journal your experience, worshiping through your wounds.

JOB'S FRIENDS
June 12

Morning Rinse: Job 5-8
Featured Verse: Job 6:14 *For the despairing man there should be kindness from his friend; So that he does not forsake the fear of the Almighty.*

And so it begins! Job's friends. It is safe to assume Eliphaz, Bildad and Zophar were in Job's inner circle, and probably had possessions and wealth like Job. I am sure these four men had many lengthy conversations with each other that included subjects like politics, social trends, religion, and the ins and outs of running a business. It appeared they had a place in Job's life that allowed them access to his front door at any given time. This group of men could have been accountability partners, in a sense. If this were the case, one would expect these men to be Job's strongest encouragers and partners in prayer through this time of loss. But instead, they were harsh to Job, thinking the worst of him, and claiming this destruction was caused by sin in his life. Their accusations were so cruel, Job boldly warned them to be kind to those in despair, stating that unkindness could even cause a grieving person to leave their faith. After warning them, he defended himself, and asked these 'friends' to give examples where he had sinned. He even committed to listening in silence, if they would tell him (Job 6:24). But they had no proof of any wrongdoings of Job. Only false assumptions and half-truths. While Eliphaz was correct when he stated, "Behold, how happy is the man whom God reproves" (Job 5:17), his advice did not apply to Job, making what he said a half-truth. And while Bildad was correct when explaining God's justice, he was incorrect in his belief that God would never allow the righteous to go through hardships. Bildad also went so far as to accuse Job's children of sinning, causing their death (Job 8:4). He also claimed Job suffered from generational curses (Job 8:8), and was hopeless because he was godless (Job 8:13). He then accused Job of putting trust in his possessions for security instead of trusting in God, causing his house to fall (Job 8:15). Finally, Bildad attacked Job's character and integrity (Job 8:20). These men were close to Job and knew he was a righteous man. But in a fleshly effort to have the answers, they grabbed at straws. This gave Job the opportunity to defend himself. Through it all, Job stood firm in his righteousness and defended his heart, guarding it against the accusations of his friends.

Today's Challenge To Dig Deeper:
Sometimes it is okay to stick up for yourself. Guarding our heart is not just about keeping it away from things that could harm us. It could also mean vocalizing a defense. Do you need to vocalize something today to defend your heart? If so, do it in a loving, bold way.

Evening Reflection:
Did you defend your heart to a friend today? Were you loving? Write about it.

GOD IS GOD
June 13

Morning Rinse: Job 9-12
Featured Verses: Job 12:16-19 *With Him are strength and sound wisdom, the misled and the misleader belong to Him. He makes counselors walk barefoot and makes fools of judges. He loosens the bond of kings and binds their loins with a girdle. He makes priests walk barefoot and overthrows the secure ones.*

In today's Morning Rinse, Job begins with a pity party. Pain can tempt the brokenhearted to lean towards self-pity, but this is when we, as a friend, can encourage. However, once again, one of Job's friends had other plans. Zophar, the third friend, had been listening to the exchange between the other two men and Job when he finally broke his silence. He was angry at Job's defense of his righteousness, and called him 'false,' accusing him of hiding wrongdoings and sins (Job 11:11). This spurred Job, once again, to lay down his self-pity and defend himself. In the beginning of chapter twelve, Job answers Zophar with sarcasm and boldly tells him he is not inferior to him, despite his affliction. While Job admits he does not know the reasoning behind his losses, Job reminds his friends that he, too, knows about God. That he, too, has a foundation of faith. In fact, Job ends chapter twelve with declaring the greatness of God. He speaks of His power, and reminds his friends he is fully aware that God owns it all. God is God and can do what He wants, whether it is restraining the oceans or taking speech away from man. He can take strength away from the strong, or mental clarity from the old. He can bind kings and make fools of judges. God is God and does not owe man an explanation for His choices. Even amid a storm, as Job's body was becoming weaker with the thought of nearing death, he shows his true godly character by sticking up for the One True King.

Today's Challenge To Dig Deeper:
Albert Einstein once said, "Adversity introduces a man to himself." How do you respond to adversity or trials? Are there character adjustments needed? Today, search your heart and resist old ways. Take Job's position and declare that no matter what, God is God. Reread Job 12:13-25 to encourage your heart, and claim this passage through your trial. Embrace 'God is God.'

Evening Reflection:
Was your heart lifted today after taking Job's position? Did you get a different perspective when you focused on 'God is God'? Journal where your heart was and where it is now.

SORRY COMFORTERS
June 14

Morning Rinse: Job 13-16
Featured Verses: Job 16:1-5 *Then Job answered, "I have heard many such things; Sorry comforters are you all. Is there no limit to windy words? Or what plagues you that you answer? I too could speak like you, if I were in your place. I could compose words against you and shake my head at you. I could strengthen you with my mouth, and the solace of my lips could lessen your pain."*

The boxers rise from their corners in the ring and begin Round Two. This is exactly what happened in today's Morning Rinse. Eliphaz threw the first punches in this new round with his disapproval of Job's defense, and these punches hit even harder than Round One. Job is amazed at these friends, and gives them the title 'Sorry Comforters.' He is not weakened, though, by these first few punches from Eliphaz. In fact, Job stands up to all three men and gives some underlying advice that we, too, can glean from if we have a friend going through something. Here are the valuable steps to follow from Job's words:

1. Watch what you say to those in grief. Do not let your words be windy or useless.
2. If they vocalize confusion in their situation, or you hear them asking questions, realize you may not be the one with the answer. Staying silent with them may be more powerful.
3. Put yourself in their shoes.
4. Do not criticize.
5. Strengthen them with your words by giving hope and encouragement.

Today's Challenge To Dig Deeper:
Do you have a friend going through a tragic situation? Ask God to help you follow Job's advice. Contact your friend today and speak life into their life. Ask God to never allow you to be a 'sorry comforter' to anyone ever again.

Evening Reflection:
Write down what happened with your conversation today. Did you follow the 5 steps above? Write down how the conversation went.

PROVE SATAN WRONG
June 15

Morning Rinse: Job 17-20
Featured Verse: Job 19:25 *As for me, I know that my Redeemer lives, and at the last He will take His stand on the earth.*

WOW!! Job's love for God, despite thinking He had abandoned him, is such a beautiful picture of faithfulness. Interestingly, Job did not even know about the conversation between God and Satan before Satan struck him. In that conversation, Satan claimed Job loved God due to the blessings God gave him. So God gave Satan permission to send destruction to Job to prove him wrong. God knew no matter what happened, Job would remain true to his faith. Despite all the calamities, and the things Bildad said to him, Job held true to his faith and proved Satan wrong. Here is a recap of what Bildad said:

1. He told him he was wicked (18:5).
2. He claimed Job's light, or influence in life, was dimming because of wickedness (18:6).
3. He said he had schemes against others who turned on him (18:7-8).
4. He claimed traps have caught up to him and grabbed him (18:9).
5. He declared more calamity was headed his way (18:12).
6. He listed the bad things that had happened to Job, such as his boils, his kids' deaths, and how he was driven from his home due to the boils (18:13-14).
7. He reminded Job he had no offspring or clout, and told him many people were appalled by him (18:19-20).
8. He said he did not know God (18:21).

Can you imagine being told these things from a friend? Even though Job had no explanation as to why he was going through these things, he continued to stand firm in his faith. He remained hopeful in God, his Redeemer. This proved Satan wrong. When you face trials, will you be a Job and prove Satan wrong too? Will you declare 'I know my Redeemer lives,' no matter what you are going through or what people are saying about you?

Today's Challenge To Dig Deeper:
Today, prove Satan wrong with your praise. Repeat all day, no matter what has happened to you, "I know my Redeemer lives."

Evening Reflection:
Did you feel a heart change today? Did you feel an increase in hope just by repeating this short phrase? Did it feel good to be a part of proving Satan wrong?

20/20 VISION WITH GOLD-FRAMED GLASSES
June 16

Morning Rinse: Job 21-24
Featured Verses: Job 23:10-11 *But He knows the way I take; When He has tried me, I shall come forth as gold. My foot has held fast to His path; I have kept His way and not turned aside.*

Four months after production ended on a short film I produced and starred in, I sat across the table from the director at a local coffee shop. We had worked countless hours on this film and had high hopes for it. I knew something was wrong, though, when this director called me, stating there were some challenges, and asked to meet face to face. My fears unfolded as I sat across from him and heard the words that initially crushed me. "Anita, we have to reshoot the film." My heart sank as I listened to his explanations while sipping on my apple flavored latte. My taste buds were no longer feeling sweet, though. My hopes and dreams for this project diminished as each word flowed from his mouth. I initially was angry. It is easy to be bitter when things don't go our way. It is easy to throw a tantrum and cry, "Me, Me, Me. What about Me?" But life is more than just about us. It is about others. It is about community. It is about doing life with friends and family and those surrounding us, with God's point of view. There were roughly seventy-five people who helped us make this little movie. From actors to crew, to sponsoring businesses, to kids and more. The decision for this director to reshoot this film affected many people. I had to choose to shift my perspective and begin to see a small glimpse of God's 20/20 vision, through HIS perfect lens. God's glasses are so much better than my own. I may not have all the answers, just like Job. But that was a trial I wanted to come forth as gold. After praying and putting on HIS gold-framed glasses, asking Him to help me see with 20/20 vision, I was able to offer some godly solutions and we never did have to reshoot the movie. I would never have been able to offer sound solutions if I had not put on those gold-framed glasses, and seen our challenges through God's eyes. And now, that little movie is an award-winning piece, changing lives of the viewers. When I go through trials, I want to come out wearing those gold-framed glasses. Don't you?

Today's Challenge To Dig Deeper:
Do you need to put God's gold-framed glasses on to give you His 20/20 vision for your situation? Put them on today. Ask Him to help you.

Evening Reflection:
What did you see today that was different from yesterday?

TESTING THE SPIRIT OF OUR WORDS
June 17

Morning Rinse: Job 25-27
Featured Verse: Job 26:4 *To whom have you uttered words? And whose spirit was expressed through you?*

"You need to change your spirit," said my friend to her two-year-old son. He had been misbehaving and said something that needed to be corrected. So she pulled him away from his playmates and with a firm, motherly tone, gave him this instruction. The first time I heard this type of correction from her, I was thrown off a bit. I did not grow up hearing my parents use this phrase, so at first it made me uncomfortable. But after reading today's Featured Verse, it made sense. Job was basically saying the same thing to his friends, that my friend said to her son. What if we all tested the spirit of our words before we spoke those words? I would like to propose that a lot less offense would be in the world, and a lot fewer wounds in the hearts of men would be present.

Today's Challenge To Dig Deeper:
Before you speak today, test the spirit by which your words come from. In every conversation, test them. See if you notice a difference in what you say.

Evening Reflection:
Were you more cautious today with your words? Did you say everything out of the right spirit? If you did not, be sure and apologize for it.

GOLD-FRAMED SUNGLASSES WITH PEARLS
June 18

Morning Rinse: Job 28-30
Featured Verses: Job 28:16-19 *It cannot be valued in the gold of Ophir, in precious onyx, or sapphire. Gold or glass cannot equal it, nor can it be exchanged for articles of fine gold. Coral and crystal are not to be mentioned; And the acquisition of wisdom is above that of pearls.*

After writing the devotion a few days ago titled "20/20 Vision With Gold-Framed Glasses," I decided to buy a pair of sunglasses with gold frames. My mission is to wear them as a symbol to remind me to keep God's perspective in my life, and strive to come out as gold no matter what I go through. So yesterday, I went shopping at our local Target, and began the hunt through their large display of summer eyewear, in hopes of finding that perfect pair. I walked back and forth by the display three times, touching, trying on, and gazing at the different styles available for purchase. On that third trip, there they were. Gold-framed sunglasses. But they weren't just any gold-framed sunglasses. They had 'Anita flare,' with pearls adorned on the outer rim, adding the perfect balance of bling. He knows me, as I love pearls and bling! It was like a little added message from God that I was His queen. But His plan for these glasses did not end at the checkout counter. There was purpose, just for me, in the very specific style I fell in love with at first sight. Fast forward to this morning as I read today's Morning Rinse chapters and prepared to write this devotional entry. Job was explaining to his friends how difficult it is to find wisdom, and how acquiring it cannot even be compared to precious gems, including... you guessed it... pearls. I had to smile at God. God used a pair of sunglasses to tell me what I would learn though trials and challenges would be far greater than pearls, if I kept His glasses on. So coupled with the 20/20 vision devotion, if we keep God's perspective, we will come forth as gold in our character AND have wisdom that cannot even be compared to precious gems, stones, or pearls.

Today's Challenge To Dig Deeper:
Swing by the store or search online, and buy something to remind you that gaining wisdom will be greater than pearls. It can be anything to remind you to keep God's perspective as you embrace the trials you go through.

Evening Reflection:
What did you purchase today to remind you of having wisdom? Write down why it meant something special to you.

INACCURATE WISDOM
June 19

Morning Rinse: Job 31-33
Featured Verses: Job 33:32-33 *Then if you have anything to say, answer me; Speak, for I desire to justify you. If not, listen to me; Keep silent, and I will teach you wisdom.*

If we thought the three 'friends' giving their false words of 'wisdom' were extreme, a fourth enters the picture. His name was Elihu. He sat in silence, listening to the entire conversation between Job and the three others, boiling in his arrogance. When Job defended his integrity for the last time, this fourth could no longer stay silent. His pride was a complete contrast to Job's character, and he basically told Job to quit talking so he could teach Job a thing or two about wisdom. I wonder if these four 'friends' could defend their own personal lives like Job could. Job was able to speak with integrity about these things about his life. Can we?

1. He had not looked on women lustfully (31:1).
2. He did not lie nor was he deceitful (31:5).
3. He never committed adultery (31:9).
4. He never withheld pay to servants (31:13).
5. He never ignored or wrongly treated the poor, widows, orphans or those in need (31:16-20).
6. He lacked pride, and did not trust in his possession (31:24).
7. He never wanted revenge on his enemies (31:19-20).
8. He was hospitable to those who needed a place to stay while traveling (31:32).
9. He was a 'real' man of faith, being very open about his life, with nothing to hide (31:34).

Elihu had a false picture of Job's trials and claimed he heard from God regarding them. I am thankful Job did not listen to anyone around him, but remained steadfast in his faith and in his integrity towards God. If we all have a close relationship with God, like Job did, we will be able to tell if a friend is wrong in their assessment and counsel. Be steadfast in your faith so you are not swayed by 'inaccurate wisdom.' And live a life of integrity like Job.

Today's Challenge To Dig Deeper:
Have you ever received counsel from a friend that left you feeling unsettled? Ask God to free you from any emotional ties you have with what your friend has stated to you. Love your friend. But remember, God is the ultimate counselor.

Evening Reflection:
After evaluating your friendships, do you feel at peace with your confidence in God, even if your stance is different from your friend's position regarding your life and your situation?

REFINED WITH SILENCE
June 20

Morning Rinse: Job 34-36
Featured Verses: Job 34:35-37 *Job speaks without knowledge, and his words are without wisdom. Job ought to be tried to the limit, because he answers like wicked men. For he adds rebellion to his sin; He claps his hands among us and multiplies his words against God.*

When will these verbal attacks cease against Job? Today's Featured Verses are more examples of things spoken to Job by his 'friends.' These words are just more examples of things spoken out of arrogance by those who thought themselves wise, in a situation they knew nothing about. These examples are also more stories of Job sitting through hours of erroneous scorning, waiting for his turn to continually defend his righteousness. As I read through this book, I wonder if Job allowed his friends to finish their thoughts without interrupting them, because he had to reserve his strength for the times he spoke. Remember, he is sitting with boils and other discomforts causing extreme pain and exhaustion. On the other hand, maybe he waited for the scribes to document all that was said, so he could appropriately address the accusations of sin. Were these men sitting at a distance from him, which forced documentation and pauses? Regardless of Job's reasonings for not interrupting, he sat there in silence, waiting for each man to finish the attacks. Waiting for each to state his case. Listening. He was being refined, and we have front row seats through his process. What made Job a good candidate for the struggles God allowed to happen? Was Job used to sitting in silence? I would like to propose that he was. I believe he had already been through a refining process, which gave God the confidence in him to begin with. We do not know Job's early struggles in life. But I believe he learned the wisdom of speaking wise words at the appropriate time. Job was not perfect. But he was refined.

Today's Challenge To Dig Deeper:
It can be extremely hurtful when someone has talked erroneously about our character. But today, choose to let God be your defense, and forgive them. Choose to be refined with silence.

Evening Reflection:
Name a time that you were silent, not interrupting, while someone in your life was accusing you of something. Build on that moment, and resolve to keep silent in future moments like this.

GOD IS GOD. WE ARE NOT
June 21

Morning Rinse: Job 37-39
Featured Verse: Job 38:1 *Then the Lord answered Job out of the whirlwind and said...*

God speaks with a thunderous entry with a voice out of a whirlwind, so Job and the men could hear. When it is God's turn, one cannot help but listen. He did not answer Job's specific questions, but instead reminded Job He is in control of the entire world. He is God, not Job. Here is a list of the things God stated in response to Job's questions:

1. God was there from the very beginning. Job was not (38:4).
2. God made the sea and the clouds. Job did not (38:8-10).
3. God commands the morning, including the dew. Job does not (38:12).
4. God is all through the earth. Job is not (38:16).
5. God has full knowledge of hell. Job does not (38:17).
6. God has full understanding of the universe. Job does not (38:18).
7. God made the rain and the path for it down the mountains to nourish crops. Job did not (38:25-27).
8. God can move the stars. Job cannot (38:31-32).
9. God causes the clouds to bring rain. Job does not (38:34-35).
10. God feeds all the wild animals. Job does not (38:39-41).
11. God sees when all animals give birth. Job does not (39:1).
12. God makes homes for the wild animals. Job does not (39:6).
13. God watches over the eggs of ostriches. Job does not (39:14).
14. God gives horses their power. Job does not (39:19).
15. God gives the survival instinct to hawks and eagles. Job does not (39:26-27).

When we fully embrace that God created and designed the universe and all that is in it, it will help us see the heavenly 20/20 vision for our lives.

Today's Challenge To Dig Deeper:
Are you dealing with something and need the same reminder Job received in God's response? Look around you today. Open your eyes to all God has created. Remind yourself all day that God made the universe and all that is in it. Be comforted knowing He sees you too.

Evening Reflection:
What was something that stuck out to you today about God's creation? Did your perspective change about your situation at all? Write it down.

WE THE PEOPLE
June 22

Morning Rinse: Job 40-42
Featured Verses: Job 42:10-11 *The Lord restored the fortunes of Job when he prayed for his friends, and the Lord increased all that Job had twofold. Then all his brothers and all his sisters and all who had known him before came to him, and they ate bread with him in his house; and they consoled him and comforted him for all the adversities that the Lord had brought on him. And each one gave him one piece of money, and each a ring of gold.*

The three high profile friends had condemned Job publicly, making it easy for the people to watch in agreement. They probably knew Job better than anyone in his life, so it is easy to understand why the people in the land believed what these men were saying, and joined with the condemnation. But on the flip side, when God rebuked these men and they publicly repented of their false accusations with a sacrifice, it was also easy for the people to follow suit and be a part of Job's restoration. There is power in unification, both for good and for bad. We, the people, can bring harm in our words and actions. And yet, equally so, we the people, can bring restoration. Soon after his friends brought public sacrifices, Job prayed for them, and God began restoring Job. This showed the world the truth. We may not know how all his wealth was restored, but many blessings were brought to Job by the people. And it was not just a few who brought money and gold to Job. It was EVERY SINGLE PERSON that knew Job. Each one responded in this fashion of giving. Can you imagine if every single person who knows you gave you these types of gifts? The very people who had cast Job out, from the lowest to the highest in status, were part of his restoration. It was the people who condemned him, and it was then the people who God used to restore him with double the amount of wealth he had before. No one withheld their gifts. Not one person. The power of 'We, The People' is shown here for the world to see.

Today's Challenge To Dig Deeper:
Do you know of someone who needs to be restored from false accusations? Could God use you to bring about that restoration? Today, choose to be a part of 'We, the People.'

Evening Reflection:
What has God spoken to you today about being a part of 'We, the People'? Is there someone that God brought to your heart to give to?

SOUND THE ALARM
June 23

Morning Rinse: Joel 1-3
Featured Verse: Joel 2:1 *Blow a trumpet in Zion, and sound an alarm on My holy mountain! Let all the inhabitants of the land tremble, for the day of the Lord is coming; Surely it is near.*

I have a friend who repeatedly writes a simple post on social media. All he writes is "JESUS IS COMING," and he will tag as many friends to that post as the particular social media platform will allow. Although I do not see all of what my friends say on social media, I see these, as I am usually one of the friends he will tag with the post. He is sounding an alarm and wanting the world to hear it. In today's Morning Rinse, we read that Joel also was sounding an alarm. It was like that of my friend, which was repeating words, telling of what would lie ahead with the coming of the Lord. Both men use their platform to speak a message or sound an alarm. The exciting thing is, we all have a platform on which to speak to those around us. God has given all of us a voice, and we can all sound an alarm to our sphere of influence, and anyone who will listen. If we use each of our own personal platforms for His glory, we can spread the news God has asked us to share. We are not to idolize those platforms, but use them to be a messenger.

Today's Challenge To Dig Deeper:
Has God been speaking to you about using your platform and influence to sound an alarm? Has He been asking you to share news that makes you uncomfortable? Be brave today and sound the alarm He wants you to vocalize.

Evening Reflection:
How did you sound the alarm today? What did you say?

DEHYDRATING GOD
June 24

Morning Rinse: John 1-3
Featured Verses: John 3:16-17 *For God so loved the world, that He gave His only begotten Son, that whoever believes in Him shall not perish, but have eternal life. For God did not send the Son into the world to judge the world, but that the world might be saved through Him.*

The day I wrote this Morning Rinse marked three weeks of fighting an illness. I believe it was a lingering sinus infection, causing extreme weakness and severe dehydration. During these past three weeks, I experienced a constant thirst, and could not keep enough water in me to compensate for my endless runny nose. My excessive thirst seemingly never got quenched, as my fatigued body was longing for something it needed. This literal example is such a small picture of the unceasing thirst Jesus has for each of us. He longs for all of us to be saved, and He thirsts to have a deep relationship with us. He craves our companionship. Today's passage is a reminder that His thirst for us is so much bigger than even what I underwent in my illness. The question is, though, do we do our part to quench His thirst for us? Do we answer His nudging to spend time with Him? Or do we contribute to His dehydration? We contribute when we ignore His prompts, make excuses for lack of time to read His Word, or even choose to not be a part of our local church. May we all cease from causing our Heavenly Father dehydration.

Today's Challenge To Dig Deeper:
If you have not given your heart to Christ, today is a good day to do that. Go to the back of this devotional and say the Salvation Prayer. He longs for us to have companionship with Him. He thirsts to love on us. If you are already a Christ follower, but have not been spending quality time with Him, start today. Repent for being a part of dehydrating Him. His thirst for you is constant, and He will not rest as He longs to love you even more through His word.

Evening Reflection:
How did this devotion speak to you today?

ARE WE THIRSTY? ARE WE HUNGRY?
June 25

Morning Rinse: John 4-6
Featured Verses: John 4:13-14, 6:35 *Jesus answered and said to her, "Everyone who drinks of this water will thirst again; but whoever drinks of the water that I will give him shall never thirst; but the water that I will give him will become in him a well of water springing up to eternal life."... Jesus said to them, "I am the bread of life; he who comes to Me will not hunger, and he who believes in Me will never thirst."*

In yesterday's Morning Rinse, we learned God is thirsty for us. He desires to commune with us and longs to be in a relationship with us. But are we thirsty for Him? Jesus explains to the woman at the well, whoever thirsts for the water HE provides will have eternal life. He is the living water. He is the way. With any thriving relationship, both parties must have a desire to be with the other. So how do we develop this eternal thirst for Jesus? How do we have a hunger for the Bread of Life He offers? You might be surprised to know that even if you do not feel thirsty or hungry, the desire is truly inside of you. Just like we may not always feel hunger pains at lunchtime, we know it is time to eat. In several stories from today's Morning Rinse, Jesus gives us lessons and easy steps to build the hunger inside of us for Him.

1. The first step is believing, just like the woman at the well. If we believe in our hearts He is the way, the truth, and the life, we will have the eternal well quenching our thirst.
2. The second step is telling Him we believe, like the woman at the well, and asking for eternal life to come into our hearts and be saved through Him.
3. The third step is to keep eating His Word. Keep studying every day. His Word will fulfill that hunger. Jesus showed this example when He fed the five thousand.

God hungers for a relationship with us. In most cultures, when mealtime is coming near, we make plans to eat. Most do not wait until they are starving. Making time to eat from His Word is key to staying fed.

Today's Challenge To Dig Deeper:
If you have not given your heart to Christ, read the Salvation Prayer at the back of this book. Ask God to help you stay committed to reading his Word and spending time with Him. If you are already a Christ follower, but haven't been spending time with Him as often as you would like, begin today. Stay committed to eating His Word. He will quench and fill you.

Evening Reflection:
Did you feel your hunger and thirst for Christ grow today?

HE IS LOOKING FOR YOU
June 26

Morning Rinse: John 7-9
Featured Verse: John 9:35 *Jesus heard that they had put him out, and finding him, He said, "Do you believe in the Son of Man?"*

Jesus continues his journey of being a life changer with the story of the blind man. I love this story. Can you imagine being a grown man, never to have seen the light of day, but in one moment you are healed? We do not know much about this man other than he was a beggar, which probably means no one was willing to care for him, no one could afford to, or maybe his entire family was frowned upon due to his blindness, so they rejected him. Regardless of why he was there, we know he was alone in a dark world. Yet when Jesus walked by him, He found healing. Jesus asked him to go wash in the pool of Siloam. I am not quite sure what my response would have been to this strange request. But this man believed enough, and had hope enough, to do what Jesus asked of him. He was desperate for change. My assumption is this man had to have heard of Jesus before, and had enough faith that he, too, could see a life change. Even if his faith was the size of a mustard seed, it was enough to follow the request of Jesus and he was healed. After he was healed, he began sharing his story throughout the city, causing a stir amongst the people. So the Pharisees called him to the synagogue and questioned both he and his parents about the healing. However, when he asked them why they did not believe, he was thrown out of the synagogue. His parents became worried they, too, would get kicked out, so they chose to remain neutral in their answers. Once again, he was alone and rejected, even by those who should love him the most. When Jesus heard the Pharisees kicked him out of the synagogue, He went looking for him. His concern for this man's heart is equal to His concern for us. Whether we have been rejected, abandoned, hungry or feeling alone in life, He is looking for us. He longs to give us our own life changing miracles every day.

Today's Challenge To Dig Deeper:
Are you feeling alone, rejected, or afraid? Do you just need to talk to God about your heart? Find a place where you can be away from all distractions and play the song "Jesus" by Chris Tomlin. While the song is playing, close your eyes and put your heart in your hands. When you are ready, hand your heart to Jesus. Give Him all of your hurts, pains, disappointments, and struggles. Tell Him what they are, and watch Him gently take your heart and hold it. Let Him heal your heart just like He healed the blind man's eyes.

Evening Reflection:
Write down what happened today and how you are feeling. May this moment forever be etched in your memory.

WHAT THIEF IS TRYING TO KILL YOUR TESTIMONY?

June 27

Morning Rinse: John 10-12
Featured Verse: John 10:10 *The thief comes only to steal and kill and destroy; I came that they may have life and have it abundantly.*

As a pastor's kid, I have attended many conferences, youth conventions, camps, and services where teachers, and even pastors, have misquoted John 10:10. Many people, when quoting this verse, say, 'Satan' comes to steal and kill and destroy. Read it again. It does not say Satan. It says THIEF. Now, while Satan is a thief, he is not the only thief in our lives. The reality is, ANY voice or distraction that moves us away from Jesus is a thief and a robber. Later in our Morning Rinse, we read about the chief priests trying to kill Lazarus because he was a living witness, a testimony of Jesus' power. We all have a testimony, a 'Lazarus story,' if you will. It is a moment that has brought something to life in us. Whether it is our salvation story, a healing, a time of protection, or an answered prayer, we all have one. And something, or someone, is trying to shut down or kill our voice, so our testimony is not heard. Maybe it is the daily distractions that rob us of our daily quiet time to hear God's voice over the voices of the thieves in our lives. Maybe it is the voices of loved ones who do not want us talking about our faith, robbing us of living in courage. Or maybe it is even our own voice in our head saying, "I do not have anything to offer the world. I have made too many mistakes." This voice, too, robs us of the grace to share our 'Lazarus story.' Whatever voices we hear that are not moving us towards God's plan for our lives, are the voices robbing us of our destiny, and trying to destroy or kill our testimony. Jesus knows we have thieves in our lives. He is here to give us power to keep them at bay.

Today's Challenge To Dig Deeper:
Are any thieves in your life trying to kill your 'Lazarus story'? Write them all down. As you write, ask God to help you close your ears to each voice trying to destroy your testimony and voice, and ask Him to give you boldness to keep it alive. Ask Him to show you how to protect it, just like Jesus protected Lazarus.

Evening Reflection:
Write down any changes you are going to make to keep your testimony alive, and keep the thieves in your life at bay, whether the thief is your own voice and insecurity, or other voices in your life.

SELECTIVELY SERVING WITH A BASIN AND TOWEL
June 28

Morning Rinse: John 13-15
Featured Verse: John 13:5 *Then He poured water into the basin, and began to wash the disciples' feet and to wipe them with the towel with which He was girded.*

It was August 28, 1999, the day of my wedding. Nathan and I wanted the ceremony to be a picture of not only what Heaven might be like visually, but who Jesus is as well. So we filled the sanctuary with décor using some of the colors that describe Heaven found in the book of Revelation. My seamstress even glued little colored gems all over my dress to match the décor and the colors we chose. We also used flowers mentioned in the Bible, like lilies, and our program was printed to look like a scroll. Amidst these details of our special 'heavenly' day, Nathan washed my feet to depict the very scene from today's Featured Verse. On the queue of Michael W. Smith's song "Basin and the Towel," he removed his tuxedo jacket, carefully grabbed a borrowed basin and towel, and knelt in front of me. While the song played, he slowly and gently washed my feet, causing tears to not only run down my face, but the faces of many of our guests. This moment remains one of the most special memories from our ceremony, and despite it being decades ago, I still receive comments from some of the guests, proving it is still etched in many minds. Although Nathan did not wash anyone else's feet on our wedding day, and rightfully so due to the context, Jesus wants us to live our lives ready to use our personal 'basin and towel' in our daily lives to serve those around us. Jesus wants our hearts to be open to serve, regardless of who the person is or what they have done. It is easy to forget Jesus washed ALL the disciples' feet, despite knowing one of them would betray Him, another would deny knowing Him, and then all of them would desert Him for a time. He still lowered Himself to a servant's position. I am convinced the disciples were embarrassed by His washing their feet, since they often argued with each other about who was the greatest among them. Do you live a life of servanthood? Or do you selectively pull out your 'basin and towel' and serve only those you want? Jesus did not live an example of selective serving. It was His life to carry around a 'basin and a towel.'

Today's Challenge To Dig Deeper:
Allow God to search your heart and reveal to you any area of your life you are selectively serving in. Ask Him to help you get to the root of why you lay your 'basin and towel' down at times, instead of being willing to serve. Ask Him to reveal ways you can serve those around you where you are not. Commit to living a new lifestyle of carrying around your personal 'basin and towel'.

Evening Reflection:
Write down what God showed you about being a servant.

JESUS PRAYED FOR US
June 29

Morning Rinse: John 16-18
Featured Verses: John 17:20-23 *I do not ask on behalf of these alone, but for those also who believe in Me through their word; that they may all be one; even as You, Father, are in Me, and I in You that they also may be in Us, so that the world may believe that You sent Me. The glory which You have given Me I have given to them, that they may be one, just as We are one; I in them and You in Me, that they may be perfected in unity, so that the world may know that You sent Me, and loved them, even as You have loved Me.*

John chapter 17 is one big prayer. First, Jesus prays for himself, knowing what is about to happen to Him. He then prays for His disciples, knowing what they will go through during the crucifixion. And finally, He prays for future believers, you and me, knowing what future struggles the church body will have. I wanted to highlight the part where Jesus prays for us, because it is evident Jesus desires us to be unified as His followers. The fact He included us in this prayer is humbling, but shows His great love for us as the body of Christ. He thought of us before the Cross, on the Cross, and after the Cross. It is overwhelming, but true. We were on His mind, and He wants His children to be one unified force to further His kingdom. Many will come to know Him through our testimony, or our words. But we also must stay unified through our words. We can be so heavenly focused when sharing our testimony, but when distractions come, it can lead to gossip, disunification, tearing others down, being critical, and arguing. Our words can easily change from focused testimony to murmuring, if we are not careful. Unification comes when we cease to gossip, avoid pride, tithe, and commit to praying for each other.

Today's Challenge To Dig Deeper:
Pause for a moment and thank Jesus for thinking of us, and praying for us as believers. Now, ask yourself, "Am I one of the answers to Jesus' prayer of unity? Am I praying for other Christians? Do I avoid gossip? Am I serving in the church and helping others? Do I offer encouragement and hope? Do I tithe?" All these are ways to help the church stay unified. Ask God to show you areas you need to work on.

Evening Reflection:
How do you feel about Jesus praying for us? How do you feel about Him praying for unity? What did you learn about yourself today regarding it?

A CONDUIT OF CHANGE
June 30

Morning Rinse: John 19-21
Featured Verse: John 21:17 *He said to him the third time, "Simon, son of John, do you love Me?" Peter was grieved because He said to him the third time, "Do you love Me?" And he said to Him, "Lord, You know all things; You know that I love You." Jesus said to him, "Tend My sheep."*

In yesterday's Morning Rinse, we read that Peter denied Jesus three times. I can only imagine how Peter must have felt after he realized what he had done. Jesus even told him he would deny Him three times that night before the rooster crowed, and it was indeed fulfilled. Did Peter carry shame and guilt? How did he feel around the other disciples knowing they knew what he had done? The beautiful part of this story is, even though Peter denied Jesus at the most crucial part of Jesus' ministry, his relationship with Jesus became stronger through repentance. Jesus forgave him and changed his life by showing forgiveness, which further deepened Peter's faith and call. It is interesting that Peter denied him three times, and Jesus then had to ask him three times whether he truly loved him. But in this moment, Peter's occupation changed from being a fisherman to an evangelist. In this moment, Peter became a 'rock.' It took Jesus coming to him, asking deep questions, and digging deep into Peter's heart to help Peter fully understand this love Jesus was asking about. In this moment, Peter fully understood Jesus' love for him, despite his imperfections. Peter, in this moment, became fully aware of the truth behind all of Jesus' words He had previously spoken regarding His death and resurrection. Peter was changed that night. Despite where we are in our walk with Jesus and despite our many mistakes, Jesus forgives. He is ready to show His love and grace to us. He is ready to launch us into a full understanding of this love so we can further be changed. Are you ready for this change? Once you understand this love, you will then become an even greater conduit of change for others as you tell your story.

Today's Challenge To Dig Deeper:
Take all of your mistakes, shame and guilt to Jesus. Ask for forgiveness for any actions not Christ-like, and let Him take your burdens away. Whether they be a bad attitude, fear-filled choices, or even other sins not mentioned, take them to the Cross. Accept His forgiveness and see what Jesus does with your life. Let all your burdens and shame go and accept His love. Now run, as you live a life of being a conduit of change in others.

Evening Reflection:
How were you changed today by the act of repentance? What did Jesus speak to you about?

July Rinsing

DO YOU KNOW HIM?
July 1

Morning Rinse: 1 John 1-3
Featured Verse: 1 John 3:23 *This is His commandment, that we believe in the name of His Son Jesus Christ, and love one another, just as He commanded us.*

Several of the devotions in this book have focused on the importance of our names, reminding us God knows each of us by our name. One example is the Morning Rinse from 1 Chronicles 1-2 titled "Every Person Behind a Name is Important." On that day, I reiterated the importance of every name in the Bible, and how God sees each of us as valuable. But there is one name above all names. That name is Jesus. The name every knee will bow to. It is awe-inspiring and breathtaking to take a moment and meditate on who He truly is. What a perfect place to pause, halfway through the year, and reflect on Him. Do we really know who He is, and who John declares us to believe in? And not just to believe in, but to love others as He loves? His name is powerful and majestic. His name… is Jesus. Look at just some of His names and characteristics:

- Jehovah Jireh: The Lord will Provide (Genesis 22:14)
- Jehovah Tsidkenu: The Lord our Righteousness (Jeremiah 33:16)
- Elohim: Creator, Mighty and Strong (Genesis 1:1)
- Yahweh-Elohim: LORD God (Genesis 2:4)
- YWHW: LORD (Deuteronomy 6:4)
- El Elyon: Most High (Deuteronomy 26:19)
- Adonai: My Great Lord and Master (Genesis 15:2)
- El: The Strong One (Nehemiah 9:17)
- El Shaddai: Lord God Almighty (Genesis 17:1)
- El Olam: The Everlasting God (Psalm 90:1-3)
- El Roi: The God Who Sees Me (Genesis 16:13)
- El Gibhor: Mighty God (Isaiah 9:6)
- Shiloh: Peacemaker (Genesis 49:10)
- Jehovah Rapha: The Lord Who Heals (Isaiah 53:5)
- Jehovah Nissi: The Lord our Banner (Exodus 17:15)
- Jehovah M'Kaddesh: The Lord Who Sanctifies and Makes You Holy (Ezekiel 37:28)
- Jehovah Shammah: The Lord is here (Ezekiel 48:35)
- The Captain of the Host of the Lord (Joshua 5:14)
- Jehovah Shalom: The Lord our Peace (Judges 6:24)
- Jehovah Sabaoth: The Lord of Hosts (1 Samuel 1:3)
- The Rock of my Salvation (2 Samuel 22:47)
- My Strong Rock and Fortress (Psalm 31:2, 3)
- My Redeemer (Romans 8:28)
- My Hope (Psalms 39:7, 119:147)
- My Helper (Psalm 121)
- My Physician (Jeremiah 8:22)
- My Refuge from the storm (Isaiah 25:4)
- My Resting Place (Ezekiel 34:23)
- Crowned with a Crown of Pure Gold (Psalm 21:3)
- The Prince of Princes (Daniel 8:25)
- He who sitteth King Forever (Psalm 29:1)
- Jehovah: I AM the One Who Is (Revelation 1:8)

- Jehovah-Roi: The Lord is My Shepherd (Psalm 23:1)
- The Holy One of Israel (Isaiah 49:7)
- Giver of Hope (Jeremiah 29:11)
- My Restorer (Psalm 23:3)
- The King of Glory (Psalm 24:10)
- The Rock that is higher than I (Psalm 61:2)
- The Rock of my strength (Psalm 62:7)
- Protector (Psalm 91)
- My Comforter (2 Corinthians 1:3-4)
- My Strength (Proverbs 3:5-6)
- The Friend that Loves at all Times (Proverbs 17:17)
- Wisdom (Romans 16:27)
- A Strong Tower (Proverbs 18:10)
- A Friend that is closer than a brother (Proverbs 18:24)
- The Rose of Sharon (Song of Solomon 2:1)
- The Lily of the Valley (Song of Solomon 2:1)
- The Chiefest Among Ten Thousand (Song of Solomon 5:10)
- Yes, He is altogether Lovely (Song of Solomon 5:16)
- He is my Beloved and my Friend (Song of Solomon 5:16)
- HOLY (Isaiah 6:3)
- A Sanctuary (Isaiah 8:14)
- The Great Light (Isaiah 9:2)
- The Mighty God (Isaiah 9:6)
- Mighty El Gibhor (Isaiah 9:6)
- The Father of Eternity (Isaiah 9:6)
- The Prince of Peace (Isaiah 9:6)
- A Strength to the poor (Isaiah 25:4)
- My Deliverer (Psalm 18:2)
- The Rock of Ages (Isaiah 26:4)
- God's Son (Luke 1:35)
- A Crown of Glory and Beauty (Isaiah 28:5)
- A Stone (Isaiah 28:16)
- As Rivers of Water in a dry place (Isaiah 32:3)
- As a Hiding Place from the wind (Isaiah 32:2)
- The Ruler (Micah 5:2)
- My Approver (Zephaniah 3:17)
- He sings over us in delight (Zephaniah 3:17)
- A Refiner's Fire (Malachi 3:2)
- My Purifier (Malachi 3:3)
- Yeshua: Salvation (Matthew 1:21)
- Emmanuel, God with us (Matthew 1:23)
- King of the Jews (Matthew 2:2)
- The Bridegroom (Matthew 9:15)
- The Horn of Salvation (Luke 1:69)
- A Savior, Which is Christ the Lord (Luke 2:11)
- The Word (John 1:1)
- The True Light who was made flesh (John 1:14)
- The Only Begotten Son (John 1:18)
- The Lamb of God (John 1:29)
- Messiah (John 6:33)
- The Way, The Truth and The Life (John 14:6)

- He is my Hope (Romans 15:13)
- Faithful (2 Timothy 2:13)
- The Foundation (1 Corinthians 3:11)
- A Servant who Humbled Himself to death (Philippians 2:8)
- The Creator of All Things (Colossians 1:16)
- The Head of all principalities and powers (Colossians 2:10)
- My All in All (Colossians 3:11)
- God of Miracles (Hebrews 2:4)
- The Same Yesterday, Today and Forever (Hebrews 13:8)
- The High Priest (Hebrews 3:1)
- The Sinner's Savior (1 Timothy 1:15-17)
- The Author and Finisher of faith (Hebrews 12:2)
- Compassionate (1 Peter 3:8)
- Precious Cornerstone (1 Peter 2:6-7)
- The Life (1 John 1:2)
- The Savior of the world (1 John 4:14)
- He is Love (1 John 4:19)
- The True God (1 John 5:20)
- Jesus Christ (Revelation 1:5)
- The Alpha and Omega (Revelation 1:8)
- The Tree of Life (Revelation 2:7)
- The Lion of the Tribe of Judah (Revelation 5:5)
- The Lamb that was slain (Revelation 5:12)
- Lord of Lords (Revelation 17:14)
- Crowned with many Crowns (Revelation 19:12)
- I am the root of and the descendent of David, the Bright and Morning Star (Revelation 22:16)
- Abba (Galatians 4:7)
- He is Risen (Matthew 28:1-7)
  And He is COMING BACK!

Today's Challenge To Dig Deeper:
Is your faith strengthened by reading these names? Read this list 3 times during the day today, and lean on the name(s) you need most in this moment of your life. Copy these pages and post these names where you can easily reference them. If you would like to visually see some of these words spoken, go watch this 6-minute video of friends of mine manifesting these words: https://youtu.be/LCXPTlcNpMc

Evening Reflection:
How do you feel about these names? What characteristic(s) stuck out to you the most today?

A MATTER OF THE HEART
July 2

Morning Rinse: 1 John 4-5
Featured Verse: 1 John 5:3 *For this is the love of God, that we keep His commandments; and His commandments are not burdensome.*

People often state kids will do what you say until they get old enough to do what you do. I believe in most situations, children want to do what their parents ask of them, if it is not illegal or immoral. They like pleasing their parents. At some point in a child's life, though, they start to make choices of their own free will. It changes from doing what their mom and dad say, to making their own choices based on what they individually want to do. We all desire for our children to live a life of good choices out of love for us as parents, coupled with doing what is right, both lawfully and morally. Each person will come to this pivotal moment in life, making a conscious choice to obey our parents, not necessarily because we agree, but because we love them. This same choice is given to us as Christ followers, when God asks us to obey His ways for our lives. Our flesh does not usually agree with our spirit, which gives us the opportunity to obey because we love Him and have a heart to live for Him. Obeying Him because we love Him and want to do His will is a matter of the heart. And obedience and loving God is two-fold. Yes, God wants us to obey and keep His commandments. But notice the second part of today's Featured Verse. It states, "*... and His commandments are not burdensome.*" A burdensome action can also be described as tough, oppressive, or even unbearable. Mother Theresa acted in love because it was in her heart. Yes, some of the things she had to go through were hard. But she never complained or called her mission a burden. It is the same in loving God and obeying His voice. Loving God is not just about obeying His voice and doing what He asks us to do, like a kid obeying his parents when they are young. It is also about having a unified heart in God's purpose WHILE we obey. Loving God is truly a matter of the heart, and it should not be a burden to live a life for His kingdom.

Today's Challenge To Dig Deeper:
Is there anything in your life you are begrudgingly obeying? Are you obeying God merely because He says to do something, instead of having your heart in it because you love Him? Ask God to show you where your heart needs to be corrected so you will begin to obey not just because He asks that of you, but because you WANT to obey no matter what He asks.

Evening Reflection:
What did God show you today regarding the matter of your heart?

ROW, ROW, ROW YOUR BOAT
July 3

Morning Rinse: 2 John and 3 John
Featured Verses: 3 John 3 *For I was very glad when brethren came and testified to your truth, that is, how you are walking in truth.*

Life is not always gentle, and it is not always a dream, like the childhood song declares in "Row, Row, Row Your Boat." Case in point, a lady was driving down an Interstate in Chicago, and began oddly swerving between two of the lanes on the highway. She quickly lost control of her pickup, hit the concrete median, and began spinning in circles, coming to a complete stop on the highway facing the oncoming traffic. A trucker following behind her, fully loaded with cars, watched as the horrific scene unfolded before his eyes. Unable to maneuver around her, he did his best to minimize the impact of the head-on collision. Upon impact, the engine compartment was crushed into the windshield, causing the trucker to lose the ability to see. He swerved to his left, crashing into the same concrete median she had hit just seconds before. Obviously, this accident totaled both vehicles, including all the vehicles being hauled. Despite this horrific life event, I know of at least seven miracles associated with the wreck, including how God spared the lives of both the lady and the trucker, who also happens to be my husband, Nathan. Initially, there was fear and frustration, and our loved ones watched how we responded. There is no argument that can stand against the fact that we are watched by others all the time. So how do we respond in both the great moments of life, and during life's challenging situations? Do we continue to live out a testimony of truth and faith for others to see? What do people say about our responses in ALL situations? I compare our daily lives to being on a river, as we ride in our 'life canoe.' The childhood song describes rowing gently down the stream, but our life is not always gentle. Sometimes we can feel our boat knocked around by the waves or bumped by unseen rocks underwater. When this happens, I can get nervous, wishing I could see around the river bend and see the hardships ahead to properly prepare for them. I will sometimes say to God, "God, could you row just a little faster? Or could you just give me a glimpse of what I might face ahead? I am not sure my faith can handle the surprises." Jesus then responds to me, "The testing of your faith makes you grow. Trust Me as I row." Life is not always a dream, as stated in this merry song. So despite hard times and the unknown future, do we still live a life of truth, faith, and trust? What do other people see in you as you journey down the river, even in the bad times?

Today's Challenge To Dig Deeper:
Have you ever gone through a hard time and had a rotten attitude? First, repent if you have. Then ask God to help you change your responses. Today, memorize the Featured Verse, and let it be a reminder to you, that you are being watched. Your faith and living out God's truth will ultimately change the lives of others.

Evening Reflection:
What did God show you today about how you respond to life's challenges? Was there an area that God wants to help you with in your growth?

JONAH'S TANTRUM
July 4

Morning Rinse: Jonah 1-4
Featured Verses: Jonah 3:10, 4:1-2 *When God saw their deeds, that they turned from their wicked way, then God relented concerning the calamity which He had declared He would bring upon them. And He did not do it. But it greatly displeased Jonah and he became angry. He prayed to the LORD and said, "Please LORD, was not this what I said while I was still in my own country? Therefore, in order to forestall this, I fled to Tarshish, for I knew that You are a gracious and compassionate God, slow to anger and abundant in lovingkindness, and one who relents concerning calamity."*

The book of Jonah does not paint a picture of what was going on in Nineveh, but we do know some facts about this wicked city from other prophets. Nahum wrote that the people were guilty of evil plots against God (Nahum 1:9). He also documented that they exploited the helpless (2:12), and practiced idolatry, prostitution, and witchcraft (3:4). In the story of Jonah, God declared that He would destroy this city, and wanted the people to be warned of their coming judgment, to give them a chance to repent. So He asked Jonah to be the messenger. However, Jonah did not want to go to the city. In his time, the Jews did not want to share the good news with the Gentiles. He knew that if they heard the good news and repented, God would indeed show His mercy on the city. Knowing this trait of God, Jonah did not want that, as seen in our Featured Verses. After Jonah finally obeyed and preached to the city, the people of the city repented. He then realized God was not going to destroy the city, so He threw a tantrum and decided he wanted to die (Jonah 4:3). What a dramatic response! He had forgotten the fact that God gave him grace and mercy while in the belly of the whale. He was certainly happy that his life was spared, and yet angry when Nineveh was saved. Why? I would imagine it had something to do with his upbringing. The Jews were taught to hate the Assyrians. The root of hate and unforgiveness was so strong, he did not want them to receive God's mercy. After Nineveh's salvation, God asked Jonah if he had a good reason to be angry, to which Jonah replied that he still believed he did (4:9). Maybe he was angry because of how wicked the people were. Maybe he felt that they did not deserve God's mercy. Despite how Jonah felt towards the people, they listened and repented. We, too, can have our tantrums in life. And yet, God will still use us to change the lives of others if we let Him.

Today's Challenge To Dig Deeper:
Have you ever wished for God's judgment on others due to their behaviors, instead of wishing grace and mercy? What caused you to feel this way? If there are any seeds of hate or anger towards anyone, causing you to want them judged, ask God to remove those feelings.

Evening Reflection:
Did God show you anyone you need to release your anger towards? What did God show you? How can He use your voice to spread the good news?

WINDOWS, THE ARK, AND RIVERS
July 5

Morning Rinse: Joshua 1-5
Featured Verses: Joshua 2:17-18, 3:17 *The men said to her, "We shall be free from this oath to you which you have made us swear, unless, when we come into the land, you tie this cord of scarlet thread in the window through which you let us down, and gather to yourself into the house your father and your mother and your brothers and all your father's household."... And the priests who carried the Ark of the Covenant of the Lord stood firm on dry ground in the middle of the Jordan, while all Israel crossed on dry ground, until all the nation had finished crossing the Jordan.*

Rahab's story has been repeated for generations, to all ages alike. It is a perfect story of how God will use us to be a part of His plan of salvation, so long as we are willing and have faith to act on our willingness. When Joshua took on the role of the new leader succeeding Moses, God told him three times to be courageous (1:6, 7, and 9). He commissioned Joshua for what was ahead, commanding him to have faith. Joshua then prepared the people to take the Promised Land, and he sent spies into Jericho to bring back a report. Rahab gave these spies room and board while they were in the city, hid them when the king's officials came looking for them, and then helped them escape by using a rope to climb out of her window and down the city wall. This same window was the window she tied the scarlet thread to, which saved herself and her family during the battle soon to come. When the spies made it back to the Israelites' camp and spoke to Joshua of their findings, Joshua immediately began making plans to cross over the Jordan River to capture the city. He and all the sons of Israel set out the following morning, leading the people towards this new land. As they marched, the Ark of the Covenant was carried before them, displaying God's presence and power. Once the people reached the Jordan River, the priests who carried the ark touched the water in faith, and the waters were pushed back like a dam, much like when Moses parted the Red Sea. This allowed the people to cross over water safely for a second time, headed towards a victorious battle. Windows are not made to crawl down, and rivers are not created to walk through. Yet when we live in faith, it sparks God's power, or 'ark,' and miracles will occur through us for the world to see. I urge you to carry God's presence and power every day. Be strong and courageous, like Joshua and Rahab. Your faith holds the key to unlock 'windows' to save others, and to dry up 'rivers' to be crossed over to a Promised Land of destiny.

Today's Challenge To Dig Deeper:
Has God spoken to you about how He wants to use you? Have you picked up the 'ark' of His presence with courage yet? If not, ask Him to help you. Repent of fear in your life, and look for the 'windows' and 'rivers' to help save others.

Evening Reflection:
What did God speak to you regarding the opportunities He has for you? Are you committed to be courageous?

COLLECTIVE SILENCE OR COLLECTIVE SHOUTING
July 6

Morning Rinse: Joshua 6-8
Featured Verse: Joshua 6:10 *But Joshua commanded the people saying, "You shall not shout nor let your voice be heard nor let a word proceed out of your mouth, until the day I tell you, 'Shout'! Then you shall shout!"*

Warfare looks different, depending on where we are in the battle, and it will look different depending on God's direction during the fight. It is easy to pull scriptures from the Bible to confirm how important it is to shout, lift our hands, and do battle using our speech and verbal praise. But what about the silence? Being collectively silent during a war can make some nervous, because it can be perceived as no manifestation of action. The truth is, we ARE witnessing action. We ARE witnessing battle. Silence is a tool of spiritual warfare, and it takes discernment to know when to fight with it. I do not know why God has us silent at times and then shouting at other moments during our battles. Could it be to intimidate the enemy? Could it be to show obedience? I can only imagine the feeling of intensity the Israelite men felt during those seven days of marching around the city of Jericho, being mocked the entire time by those living there. And I can only imagine how intense it felt for the ladies to sit at their campsites, longing to speak to each other, but instead obeying in silence while listening to the mockery from a distance. I am convinced the atmosphere was palpable. The energy or the sheer 'wonderment' had to be incredibly extreme, and yet, we know from our Morning Rinse that they had the power and strength to war this way and overcome. Silence can be a manifestation of faith, trust, discernment, and inward prayer. Did they wonder what day 7 would look like? Yes. I am sure. And yet their pondering did not cause doubt to overshadow their faith. Everyone was instructed to be quiet, and they collectively obeyed. We must remember the battle is not fought only on the battlefield with our weapon in hand, but it begins way before the swords are drawn. It begins with training in our prayer closet, in learning to submit to leadership, in studying our enemy, in obedience, in growing our faith, and yes, even practicing silence. When we, as Christians, unify in our spiritual battles, whether collectively shouting in victory, or battling in a unified silence, we are stronger in the fight against our enemy. May we learn to be collective and unified, to fight as God instructs us, despite how it may appear and despite being mocked by the world.

Today's Challenge To Dig Deeper:
Ask God to teach you not only when to be silent, but how to pray during your silence. Discern the timing of silence today, and practice it like the Israelites did. The warfare is real, but the victory is ahead. Be prepared for your time to shout victory.

Evening Reflection:
Write down an example from today of what happened during your silence. How did you feel? How do you think you were battling in the spirit? Did you feel God speaking to you in the silence?

FIGHTING FOR YOUR PROMISED LAND
July 7

Morning Rinse: Joshua 9-12
Featured Verse: Joshua 11:23 *So Joshua took the whole land, according to all that the Lord had spoken to Moses, and Joshua gave it for an inheritance to Israel according to their divisions by their tribes. Thus the land had rest from war.*

By now we know that Joshua and the Israelites were already IN the Promised Land. They were eating off the land, living in a base camp, and knew they were where God had destined them to be. This was their heritage. While they were physically IN the Promised Land, they did not POSSESS the Promised Land until after they destroyed the enemy living there. In today's Morning Rinse, the scriptures documented all of the cities and kings that Joshua's army had to battle in order to possess their land. They did not just cross into Canaan, introduce themselves to the inhabitants, and then watch the enemy just hand over the land to them on a silver platter. Quite the contrary. Instead, God needed them to fight for the land that was promised to them. Why? Because just like the promises are real, so is our enemy, and he seeks to kill, steal and destroy those promises. It took approximately seven years of fighting, but through it all, Joshua conquered thirty-one kings, cleared out enemy occupied areas, and took back the land promised to the Israelites through Moses. Joshua did not stop until this mission was complete. And just like the Israelites had to fight for their Promised Land, we must also fight for those things God wants us to have. Fighting the good fight of faith is using our faith to claim those promises God has given us. Our fight may not look like Joshua's military strategy. But our battles can be just as intense and lengthy. We cannot please God without faith, and with that faith, we fight. We fight through prayer, quoting scriptures and claiming promises in The Word. We fight through action and living a holy life. We fight by our word and testimony. The Christian walk is not just sitting in our comfy chair waiting for those promises to manifest. We must do our part too, which requires faith and focus. God has so much for our lives, but He needs us to rise and do what it takes to receive those gifts.

Today's Challenge To Dig Deeper:
Write down in faith, the promises you are claiming for your life and for your family's lives. Then write a scripture next to each item on the list and remind God of what The Word says about that item. Memorize the verses you have selected, and say them out loud today. Rekindle your faith in those promises, and ask God what your battle plan will be. Is it memorizing more scripture? Is it more consistent quiet times? Maybe it is fasting and prayer, or a combination of all of the above. Begin battling for those promises and have faith they will come to pass.

Evening Reflection:
Write down what God told you about your promises and your battle plan. Be brave as you begin your fight to victory. And DO NOT GIVE UP!

GIANT SLAYING FAITH
July 8

Morning Rinse: Joshua 13-16
Featured Verses: Joshua 14:11-12 *I am still as strong today as I was in the day Moses sent me; as my strength was then, so my strength is now, for war and for going out and coming in. Now then, give me this hill country about which the LORD spoke on that day, for you heard on that day that Anakim were there, with great fortified cities; perhaps the LORD will be with me, and I will drive them out as the LORD has spoken.*

Today's Morning Rinse covers the onset of the distribution of the Promised Land amongst the tribes of Israel, after many of the giants in the land were destroyed. Once the Israelites gained control of an area, Joshua would then give that area to one of the tribes, so the responsibility of possessing the remainder of that area fell upon that specific tribe. Caleb was part of the Levites, who did not receive a portion of the land. However, God remembered his faithfulness when he spied on the land forty-five years prior, and gave him a personal inheritance, promising him a portion of the land as his own. When Caleb went to claim his portion, he was eighty-five years old. He knew there were still giants in the land, and just like forty-five years prior when he went in to spy, he did not focus on the giants. His faith-filled spiritual eyes focused on the fact that God had promised this land to him, and he knew God would keep His promise. Faith kept Caleb moving forward to possess the land. I am convinced Moses needed leaders with 'giant slaying faith,' that would help him lead the Israelites through the wilderness. While in the wilderness, the giants they fought for forty years were more internal like fear, and not external like the enemy's military. When it came time for Joshua to distribute the land, Caleb patiently waited his turn to ask for God's promised portion. When he received it, did that mean he was free to rest? No. Absolutely not. Why? Because there were still giants in the land that he had to clear out. Despite his age, his 'giant slaying faith' remained as strong as the day he went in to spy out the land. What do you need 'giant slaying faith' for in your life?

Today's Challenge To Dig Deeper:
As you were writing your list from yesterday, did you realize you may already be IN your Promised Land, but there may be giants that you need to clear out? What are those giants? Could they be unwise counsel? Could they be attitudes within your heart? It can be anything that is keeping you living in fear of the giants around you. Ask God to show you ALL giants keeping you from your Promised Land, and wisdom on how to clear them out. Then go grab the Sword of the Spirit with your 'giant slaying faith' and clear them out.

Evening Reflection:
What were the giants God showed you today and how are you clearing them out of your Promised Land? Keep your 'giant slaying faith' on every day, and keep clearing out the brush.

GO CLAIM YOUR INHERITANCE!
July 9

Morning Rinse: Joshua 17-20
Featured Verse: Joshua 18:3 *So Joshua said to the sons of Israel, "How long will you put off entering to take possession of the land which the LORD, the God of your fathers, has given you?"*

A kindergartener walks into her classroom on the first day of school. She is frightened by this new adventure and clings with a deathly grip to her mother's hand. Even though her parents prepared her for this anticipated day, she is still not fully embracing the excitement in the air. Now that she is facing this long-awaited moment, the inward fear of the unknown has her stuck to her mother's side. She gazes across the room at her newly acquired classmates as they excitedly grab their seats, show off their new outfits to a nearby neighbor, pose for pictures and kiss their moms and dads goodbye. She watches as parents wipe away tears that display the realization that their baby is growing up. These tears cause her to unconsciously grip her mother's hand just a little tighter. Suddenly, her teacher walks over and breaks her gaze. Bending down to the little girl's eye level, the teacher kindly asks, "Don't you want to take YOUR seat?" The teacher points to a clean desk with her name beautifully displayed on a brightly colored card. The child looks back at her teacher and slowly nods her head. Through eyes glossed with a few tears of fear, and yet a strange excitement, she hugs her parents, and reaches for her teacher's hand before timidly walking across the room. Once they arrive at her desk, she reaches for her chair, and the feeling of ownership takes over as a small smile captures her face. This was her desk now. Her inherited space as a kindergartner. Just like this child, we have things God wants to give us. We are children of the King, and that means we have inheritances for our journey. Why do we live without claiming them, though? Joshua asked this same question, when he discovered seven of the tribes had not yet claimed their land. After he asked them how long they were going to wait, he told them to go scope out the land so he could divide it amongst the tribes. Why do we sit and wait? Is it because of fear? Is it because of laziness? Could it be a lack of discipline in our prayer time or time management overall? Or are we simply disobeying God and not claiming what is rightfully ours? May this discovery be the spur we all need to receive what God wants to give us. Go claim it.

Today's Challenge To Dig Deeper:
Amid instructing the tribes to go scope out the land, Joshua made them write down the territory for him so he could divide it up. Ask God today to show you what is rightfully yours as a child of the King.

Evening Reflection:
What are the inheritances you are claiming? Write down what God showed you and what He wants you to do to claim them.

SETTING YOURSELF UP
July 10

Morning Rinse: Joshua 21-24
Featured Verse: Joshua 21:45 *Not one of the good promises which the LORD had made to the house of Israel failed; all came to pass.*

The book of Joshua is a wonderful book about promises kept by our Heavenly Father. It is a book of hope given and hope received, and is an example of what happens when we obey and live a life of faith. From the story of Rahab, to the Israelites obtaining the Promised Land and conquering giants and more, this book is full of ways to learn how to claim our personal promises from God. Twice, it is documented where Joshua states to the people, not any of the good promises God made had failed. The first time is in today's Featured Verse, and was right after the Promised Land had been secured in its entirety. The second time is when Joshua reiterated this truth right before his death (Joshua 23:14). During the second time, he reminded the Israelites of the importance of obedience. Just like all the good promises are kept when we obey and follow His voice, God must also keep the threats He makes if we disobey. We, in general, do not always like the word threat. But those threats are merely God letting us know the consequences of disobedience, just like a parent would tell a child, or a teacher a student. Joshua's leadership helped the people make decisions to receive the good promises. But we will see in a few days when we begin reading the book of Judges, the people began a journey of disobedience after he died, which set them up to receive the consequences of those choices. Stay the course of obedience. For obedience commands a blessing. Stay under good leaders. Stay in the Word. Stay humble and accountable. Set yourself up for the good promises, and have faith your life will be full of receiving them all.

Today's Challenge To Dig Deeper:
As we close out the book of Joshua, quickly review the other devotions from this book. Meditate and chew on what God is speaking to you about the good promises for your life. Are there any changes you need to make to set yourself up for more of these good promises?

Evening Reflection:
What did God talk to you about today? What changes will you make to set yourself up to receive more good promises? Write them down and keep these changes close to your heart.

BEING A WITNESS
July 11

Morning Rinse: Jude 1
Featured Verses: Jude 1:20-23 *But you, beloved, building yourselves up on your most holy faith, praying in the Holy Spirit, keep yourselves in the love of God, waiting anxiously for the mercy of the Lord Jesus Christ to eternal life. And have mercy on some who are doubting; save others, snatching them out of the fire; and on some have mercy with fear, hating even the garment polluted by the flesh.*

In today's Morning Rinse, Jude wrote about three examples of rebellion. One of those examples was the Israelites and their lack of faith when they originally did not want to go into the Promised Land. I had to smile at the weaving of scripture into even the timing of this devotion, especially since we just finished the book of Joshua. Jude used this example to bring home the truth that we, as Christ followers, can make a difference in the lives of those living in rebellion or doubt. How do we do this? We first need to build OURSELVES up by The Word, making sure our own footing is solid. We also need to pray in the Spirit, getting deeper in tune with God and His daily leading. We must take the responsibility to keep OURSELVES in the love of the Lord. Then we start living it out by witnessing to those living in rebellion, or who are caught in the act of ungodly behavior. How? To some we will need to give mercy, knowing we received it ourselves through salvation. We may rescue others by snatching them out of darkness if they cannot save themselves. These may be frontline ministers near the edge of darkness, like those rescuing trafficked victims or those caught in other domestic or abusive situations. And still to others, we may need to sternly teach about the consequences of their actions, even if it causes them to tremble upon hearing the truth. Ultimately, we must live a life of hating sin. This is what Jude encouraged us to do as believers. Some of those we witness to will never choose a heart change. Our job is not to be the one to change them. Our job is to be a witness, pointing them to Christ, and allowing God to work through us as HE changes hearts.

Today's Challenge To Dig Deeper:
We all know people who are not saved, or people caught in ungodly acts. Whether you know a handful, or are exposed to the masses, each of these people are in different stages of bondage and need witnessing in different ways. They may be in the early stages of making poor choices, and merely need a stern warning. Or they may be so entrapped they need a strong hand to pull them out. Ask God to show you who these people are in your life, and how He wants you to play a part in their salvation. Meditate today on His answers and begin to act.

Evening Reflection:
Did God mention any names to start witnessing to? Write them down and write anything God told you in regard to them and the actions He wants you to take.

WEAKNESSES AS STRENGTHS
July 12

Morning Rinse: Judges 1-3
Featured Verses: Judges 3:15-16 *But when the sons of Israel cried to the LORD, the LORD raised up a deliverer for them, Ehud the son of Gera, the Benjamite, a left-handed man. And the sons of Israel sent tribute by him to Eglon the King of Moab. Ehud made himself a sword which had two edges, a cubit in length and he bound it on his right thigh under his cloak.*

According to commentary, being left-handed during this time in history was a perceived weakness. Yet, God used this trait about Ehud to bring deliverance to the Israelites. Prior to Ehud entering the story, the Israelites had been living in the Promised Land for at least sixty-six years, not including the years of peace under Joshua's leadership. Out of those sixty-six years, they were in bondage for the first eight, until Othniel rose to deliver them. For the following forty years, the Israelites had peace in the land again. Once he died, though, the Israelites started disobeying God again. So God kept His Word and allowed them to once again be held captive. This went on for the next eighteen years, until the people called out to God, repented of their evil ways, and asked Him for help. God responded to their cries and brought Ehud, another hero, to rescue the people from King Eglon. King Eglon had just conquered part of Israel and had taken control of the city of Jericho. So Ehud went to offer a gift to him for winning the war. According to historians, the proper side to mount a sword for a left-handed warrior was the right thigh. Since most of the warriors were right-handed, their swords were mounted on their left thigh. Ehud knew this and covered his right thigh with his cloak, giving the appearance he was unarmed, since the king did not know he was left-handed. Once Ehud built the trust of Eglon after presenting the gift, he excused his servants and told Eglon he had a message for him from God. Eglon then excused his servants as well, making him vulnerable for Ehud to draw his hidden sword and kill him. Ehud used this perceived weakness as a hidden strategy to save the nation and lead them into the next eighty years of peace in the land.

Today's Challenge To Dig Deeper:
God sees us through 'kingdom eyes.' He does not view our characteristics, His creation, as weak. Sometimes we allow the viewpoints of others to supersede God's view of us, causing insecurities. Once we realize this, what characteristics do you have that you have viewed as a flaw or weakness, that you need to embrace and allow God to use as a strength for His kingdom? Take today to ponder this challenge.

Evening Reflection:
Did God begin to change your heart regarding character traits you have often thought were flaws? How do you feel now?

GOD MEETS US WHERE WE ARE
July 13

Morning Rinse: Judges 4-7
Featured Verse: Judges 6:37 Behold, I will put a fleece of wool on the threshing floor. *If there is dew on the fleece only, and it is dry on all the ground, then I will know that You will deliver Israel through me, as You have spoken.*

Do you ever hear God's voice so clearly there is no doubt it is His voice? Whether that be through His Word, through someone else confirming a prodding in your heart, or even just the still, small voice speaking inside, we learn to know His voice as we grow closer to Him. However, just because we hear His voice, that does not mean we listen or believe each time He speaks to us. We all know this story of Gideon. Like many of us today, he was someone, a leader nonetheless, who needed signs of confirmation from God that he was hearing His voice. In today's Morning Rinse, we read of several examples where he asked for these signs. The first example was when God called him to be a warrior and fight for the people of Israel. In his reply, Gideon used two excuses. His first excuse was, his father's family was not very influential in the city. And the second excuse was, he was the youngest in his family (Judges 6:14-22). Gideon clearly heard God telling him to go deliver the people because he answered Him. And yet he still asked for a sign. The second example was when God told him to go fight Mideon, and He assured Gideon he would win. Gideon, for reasons probably due to fear, asked for yet another sign. He put a fleece of wool outside and asked God to keep the fleece dry while the ground all around would remain wet with dew. Even though God answered this request, Gideon again asked for another sign by requesting the following morning, the fleece then remain wet with dew and the ground dry. Sometimes we ask for signs from God to boost our faith. But sometimes we ask for signs due to fear or lack of commitment to what God is asking of us. God will give us what we need as we are growing in Him. But if we continue asking God for signs, even after God has told us something, it can be a sign of doubt or unbelief. God was not mad at Gideon for asking for these signs of confirmation. In fact, He met Gideon where he was, giving him what he needed to grow in his faith.

Today's Challenge To Dig Deeper:
Are you afraid of something God is asking you to do? Do you feel you have heard God's voice, and still have a hard time believing? Today, take this to God, and ask Him to help you overcome fear and trust His voice. He will answer.

Evening Reflection:
Did you learn anything today about your level of faith? Are there any seeds of doubt inside your heart? Write down how your day went in these areas of growth.

EMOTIONAL VOWS
July 14

Morning Rinse: Judges 8-11
Featured Verses: Judges 11:30-31 *Jephthah made a vow to the LORD and said, "If You will indeed give the sons of Amon into my hand, then it shall be that whatever comes out of the doors of my house to meet me when I return in peace from the sons of Ammon, it shall be the LORD's, and I will offer it up as a burnt offering."*

Making futuristic vows to God, other than our commitment to daily serve Him, can sometimes be foolish, especially in the heat of extreme emotion. But this is what Jephthah did. Even though he was a warrior, a leader, and an amazing negotiator with his enemy, he made a vow to God that he, no doubt, regretted. He told God if God helped him win the battle against Amon, he would offer whatever came out to greet him when he returned home from the battle as a sacrifice to Him. He did not even consider the fact that it could possibly be his only child that would come out first, versus one of his animals. I will not offer a debate on what was possibly going through his mind when he made this vow, or how he kept it, because even Bible scholars are divided on this topic. Some believe his daughter was literally sacrificed on an altar, while others believe, since human sacrifice is not something God condoned, his daughter was instead forever separated to life as a virgin, never marrying (11:39). This gave Jephthah no inheritance or way of having grandchildren. Either way, Jephthah had to make a choice to keep his word by sacrificing his daughter in a way he had not planned for his family, which grieved him deeply. While he had many strengths and is even listed in Hebrews 11, the 'Hall of Faith' chapter, he also had weaknesses. His vow made from emotion, was one of those weaknesses. Despite making this foolish vow, he took responsibility for his words and kept the promise he made. He was a man who could be trusted. Do you keep your word despite how difficult it may be? Do your children, friends, co-workers, and family know you can be trusted with your words? Or do you make excuses as to why you do not have to keep a past vow? How well we take responsibility for what we say, is a direct correlation to how much we can be trusted, and it bleeds into our personal integrity. God would much rather have our daily obedience to Him versus making futuristic promises driven by emotion. When we keep our emotions at bay and focus on daily obedience, our words will remain steadfast and steady, minimizing vows we may regret.

Today's Challenge To Dig Deeper:
Have you made the mistake of promising something you regret, or making a foolish vow, and now must make the choice as to how to keep it? Make it right with God today and commit to living each day in obedience to God, instead of making idle promises for the future out of emotion.

Evening Reflection:
What did you resolve today in your heart? What did you learn about today's lesson regarding keeping your word?

PREPARE BEFORE THEY ARE BORN!
July 15

Morning Rinse: Judges 12-15
Featured Verse: Judges 13:8 *Then Manoah entreated the LORD and said, "O, Lord, please let the man of God whom You have sent come to us again that he may teach us what to do for the boy who is to be born."*

Introducing Samson! From childhood stories all the way to adulthood sermons, Samson is a name most of us know. His supernatural strength and power baffles our understanding, and his feats are incomprehensible to our natural mind. God's will was for Samson to use this strength to deliver Israel from the hands of the Philistines. So He sent an angel to instruct and prepare his mom for this lifelong journey. Out of the many sermons I have heard about Samson, this part of the story is often overlooked. We focus on the adult Samson, but forget about the angel instructing his parents before he was even born. In this first heavenly interchange, the angel let his mom know she would conceive a son, and gave her instructions on how to prepare herself for him. Preparation began with a change in her diet. I can imagine how hard it was, but she obeyed this first step. This meeting caused Manoah, her husband, to also want more instructions on how to care for their coming baby boy. So Manoah asked God to send the angel back to them for further guidance. Oh, if only all parents sought more godly wisdom on how to raise their children. Manoah even asked the angel what Samson's vocation would be as an adult, so they could begin training him as a child (13:12). It is easy to say we desire godly wisdom as parents. But do we really? What if the instruction is hard to hear? What if God asks us to change ourselves first as we prepare to guide our kids later? Are we willing to change our ways for God's purpose? Samson's parents were. Samson did not always make wise choices in his life, and sometimes he would respond to life's challenges with anger, using his God-given strength for revenge, as we read about today. And sometimes he would act prideful after his feats, like when he killed a thousand Philistines by himself with merely the jawbone of a donkey (15:16). But his parents laid a foundation for Samson's life, preparing for him before he was even born.

Today's Challenge To Dig Deeper:
If you have children, or want children in the future, are you preparing for them? Ask God to send you earthly angels who will pass on godly wisdom to you as you prepare. If you do not have children, or your children are grown, ask God for godly wisdom in other areas of your life.

Evening Reflection:
Did God put anyone in your path with godly wisdom to glean from? Who is it? And did God ask you to make any changes in your pursuit of wisdom?

PROTECTING THE SECRETS FROM GOD
July 16

Morning Rinse: Judges 16-18
Featured Verse: Judges 16:18 *When Delilah saw that he had told her all that was in his heart, she sent and called the lords of the Philistines, saying, "Come up once more, for he has told me all that is in his heart." Then the lords of the Philistines came up to her and brought the money in their hands.*

Samson loved Delilah, but allowed his heart to be blinded by the fact she did not love him in return. In fact, she deceived him, contributing to his demise. The lord of the Philistines wanted him captured, so she accepted a bribe of eleven hundred pieces of silver to help in this quest. She faked her love for him and enticed him to reveal the secret of his strength. One would think Samson would discern the deception of Delilah, after her repeated attempts. But he was blinded. He knew his secret should remain private, which is why he did not initially tell her the truth. Each time he told her a fake reason to the origin of his strength, and each time she would test it. Three times she tried and three times she failed. First, he told her if he was tied up with seven fresh cords that were not dried, he would lose his strength (16:7). He also told her if he were bound with brand new ropes, he would lose his strength (16:11). And finally, if his hair was weaved and fastened with a pin, he would lose his strength. Each time, Delilah would try what he said with men ready to capture him, but of course it would fail. Her daily nagging and fake love finally broke him down and he caved to her prodding, revealing his lifelong secret of his long hair (16:13). The power of the deceiver over the blind can be fatal. While he slept, she had a servant shave his hair, then invited the lords of the Philistines to enter her room. Once they entered, they gouged out his eyes, blinding him, and then put him in prison. During a city-wide party, Samson was brought out and put on display to be mocked. I wonder if Delilah was in the crowd laughing with everyone, priding herself with her recently gained riches. While on display, Samson's final request to God was to receive strength one more time. God answered him, and Samson pushed the pillars down that held up the venue, killing three thousand people. If God gives us a secret, no matter how much we are enticed by others, we must keep those secrets protected. For if we share, we run the risk of changing the perfect plan of God for our lives.

Today.s Challenge To Dig Deeper:
We must be careful who we open our heart to. It can be difficult, especially if we have loved ones who are gossipers or deceivers. Ask God to reveal who to be more careful around. Ask Him to help you keep the secrets in your heart protected.

Evening Reflection:
How do you feel about your inner circle becoming tighter? Is there anyone in your life you need to cease revealing your secrets to?

STAY HUMBLE
July 17

Morning Rinse: Judges 19-21
Featured Verse: Judges 21:25 *In those days there was no king in Israel; everyone did what was right in his own eyes.*

Throughout the time of the book of Judges, we read many stories of what happens to the heart of man when there is no godly king, or when the people of Israel do not put God first. Yes, God is a God of mercy. But we must remember He is also a God of judgement. Every choice has a consequence, and in some cases, many consequences. Good choices reap good consequences and bad choices reap bad, forcing God's judgement to be a risk. During this timeframe in the book of Judges, the people of Israel became their own authority and did what was right in their own eyes, versus what was right in God's eyes. These poor choices led to horrendous consequences on so many accounts. The tragic story we read about today with the concubine being raped all night long and then dying from the abuse, is just one example of the disintegration of their faith and unity as a nation (19:25). It is easy to be mortified at the behavior of the abusers, but we must realize that ultimately, the responsibility of her death is equally on her husband for choosing not to protect her. Instead, he selfishly thought of himself when the abusers came. This horrific story, though, is not the worst offense or byproduct of the nation of Israel turning from God. Even worse is the fact that the nation did not establish a government based on godly principles. The nation of Israel became disunified and lawless, resulting in terrible crimes ignored and the laws not enforced. The damaging consequences continued when the leaders of Gibeah did not turn over the men who raped the concubine, which then led to a civil war where thousands of soldiers died (20:13). Why do we choose to live with pride instead of humbling ourselves and repenting of our evil ways? When we live in pride, we in essence are doing what is right in our own eyes. This is sinful and affects not just us individually, but also those around us. Pride allows lawlessness to rule in our hearts, a crime against our creator Himself. May we be determined to live our lives with the kingdom of Heaven as our standard. Let us choose to guide our home with a standard of faith, pure morals, humility, godly truths, and convictions from the Word of God. The only way to do this is to stay in The Word. So keep reading. Keep repenting. Stay humble.

Today's Challenge To Dig Deeper:
Do you ever feel a nudge from the Holy Spirit to quit doing something, but have not yet stopped? This is 'doing what is right in your own eyes.' If God is nudging you about anything right now, ask Him to impress on your heart the desire to follow HIS ways and not your own. Search your heart today, and choose to put His kingdom first in every area of your life.

Evening Reflection:
What did God nudge you about today? How did you respond?

BIRTHDAY WISH FOR WISDOM
July 18

Morning Rinse: 1 Kings 1-3
Featured Verse: 1 Kings 3:9 *So give Your servant an understanding heart to judge Your people to discern between good and evil. For who is able to judge this great people of Yours?*

Whether it be birthdays, Christmas, or other holidays, it is normal for gift exchanges to occur amongst family members and close friends. My wish list for these occasions usually consists of tangible items. Sometimes it is things to replace things broken in my home. Other times, it is a little treasure I have had my eyes on in a cute boutique. Sometimes I will even ask for help with a project as a gift of service to me. My love for gift giving makes me want to believe our story today was possibly centered around Solomon's birthday. I have no proof of this, or even if it was during another gift giving season, but I do know God asked Solomon in a dream, "Ask what you wish me to give you" (3:5). Was his birthday on the horizon? I would like to think maybe it was. Instead of asking for tangible things or help around his newly acquired kingdom, though, he asked for wisdom on how to be successful in this position of grandeur, and he asked for an understanding heart with which to judge the people. When God heard this humble request, He was pleased and not only honored it, but He made Solomon more wise than anyone before or after him from that day on. A prideful heart is ruled by a title or position. But a humble heart knows the need for our Savior's help to carry out a position successfully. Let us not ask God for more possessions and wealth for the future, but may we ask for wisdom with what He has given us in the present. Today, July 18th, happens to be my real birthday. It never ceases to amaze me the timing of these devotions. So as I lean into Him on my special day, instead of asking for tangible things from God, I ask for even a small portion of the wisdom Solomon was given. I pray, "God, grant me the wisdom to live my life for you, making every decision throughout my day, one You would have me to make. Whether it be how I lead my kids, how I love my husband, how I run my businesses, or even how I spend my time and money, I want wisdom from You. May I receive the whisper in my ear, a dream in my sleep, or any creative way as an answer to this birthday wish from You. I love You all the days of my life."

Today's Challenge To Dig Deeper:
Ask for wisdom today in every area of your life. As He shows you this, act upon that wisdom, and commit to asking for wisdom every day throughout the rest of your life.

Evening Reflection:
Were there any golden nuggets of wisdom from God today? What were they? Keep seeking wisdom all the days of your life.

FAMOUS INFLUENTIAL REACH
July 19

Morning Rinse: 1 Kings 4-6
Featured Verse: 1 Kings 4:31 *For he was wiser than all men, than Ethan the Ezrahite, Heman, Calcol and Darda, the sons of Mahol and his fame was known in all the surrounding nations.*

Through the years, the word *famous* has grown to have a negative connotation in many Christian circles. In fact, those in the spotlight tend to avoid this reference, even if it is true. I believe this is because of the ties this word has to Hollywood, especially when entertainers purposefully seek out fame in a non-authentic fashion, or use their influence to take advantage of people. However, scripture uses this word to describe King Solomon in a very positive light. The Bible states he became a famous man, not by his own pursuits, but from naturally manifesting the God-given wisdom he possessed. His character was known far beyond his own territory, positioning him to have trustworthy and respected relationships with not just those around him, but with kings in distant lands. In fact, many came to hear his wisdom, including these kings (4:34). Due to his reputation, Solomon was able to negotiate a deal with King Hiram to hire his people, the Sidonians, to cut down timber for the forthcoming temple construction (5:6). This negotiation showed while he used wisdom with his wealth, he also used wisdom in his relationships. He not only offered to pay King Hiram's people, but to pay them a fair wage, making a wise investment into this international relationship. He paid these workers what they were worth, instead of negotiating a lower salary. This showed respect and honor. Wisdom is the act of doing what we know is right in all areas of our lives, including possessions, finances, and even relationships. King Solomon excelled in all these areas, which explains how his fame and influence passed even beyond his own borders. Solomon influenced people in such a positive light, there was even peace in the land far and wide. His influence was great. His fame stretched far. Are you willing for this to occur in your life?

Today's Challenge To Dig Deeper:
God has given you a platform of influence, a voice to display your wisdom and love for Him, and living a life of influence. Pray today to have the courage to expand the reach you have, even if it makes you famous across the land.

Evening Reflection:
This golden nugget about being famous, or influential, can stretch our minds and can make us even a little uncomfortable. But if we keep our eyes on Christ, it will allow Him to use us for whatever He wants to use us for. What did He show you today about your influence?

KING DAVID OR KING SOLOMON? WHICH ARE YOU?
July 20

Morning Rinse: 1 Kings 7-10
Featured Verse: 1 Kings 8:19 *Nevertheless you shall not build the house, but your son who will be born to you, he will build the house for My name.*

Have you ever had a burning desire to do something great, and the idea of this vision was so strong it kept you up at night? Lying in bed for hours on end, planning with your mind's eye, envisioning it accomplished, and even sharing with close friends about the idea, can be the norm when a strong urge like this is inside of us. I believe the desire to build the temple burned inside King David so strong, this scenario may have been what he experienced. However, due to the wars going on during his time, God told him he would not be the one to build this massive temple, but his son Solomon would be the one to bring it to life. Even though he was not part of the actual construction of the temple, I believe he was instrumental in laying the foundation for it. This foundation was not the concrete structure of the building, but the foundation of the vision. I can imagine the many conversations Solomon and his father had while sitting around the dinner table or walking around the palace. I can imagine the excitement spewing as ideas were shared, plans were exchanged, and even names of people who could be pivotal in helping were listed. Whether true or not, I am convinced Solomon had his father's help in laying the foundation for when the time was right to begin construction. The role of a visionary foundation layer is extremely vital to help build the momentum needed for completion. And then, the person who takes on someone else's vision and adopts it as their own, is equally important. These are two different roles with the same vision. Where do you fit in? Do you have something inside your heart that may not come to fruition in your lifetime, but you are laying the foundation? Or do you have an opportunity to take on someone else's vision, and run with it like Solomon did? King David was not afraid to let go of his vision, and King Solomon was not afraid to pick it up and run with it. Whether you are in King David's shoes or in King Solomon's shoes, do not be afraid, but go.

Today's Challenge To Dig Deeper:
Are you a King David or a King Solomon regarding a vision in your heart? Seek God today for answers on what role you play. Ask God for the needed peace to move forward in whatever capacity that may look like.

Evening Reflection:
What did God speak to you about today's devotion and your life?

STAND ON CONFIRMATIONS, NOT CONTRADICTIONS
July 21

Morning Rinse: 1 Kings 11-14
Featured Verses: 1 Kings 13:17-19 *"For a command came to me by the word of the LORD, 'You shall eat no bread, nor drink water here; do not return by going the way which you came.'" He said to him, "I also am a prophet like you, and an angel spoke to me by the word of the LORD, saying, 'Bring him back with you to your house, that he may eat bread and drink water.'" But he lied to him. So he went back with him, and ate bread in his house and drank water.*

In today's Morning Rinse, there are two stories where the voice of contradiction was adhered to instead of the voice of God. These two stories pertained to the disobedience of Solomon and the disobedience of the prophet from Judah. Two stories which included the same outcome, death in disobedience. In the story of Solomon, God confirmed His Word to him several times, imploring him to live a godly life. Solomon had the wisdom of the Lord. And yet, instead of living in this wisdom, he ended his life in disobedience by allowing the voice of his flesh and the voices of his wives to contradict God's voice. Sadly, he began doing evil in God's sight (1 Kings 11:6). The second story is about the prophet from Judah. God gave him strict orders to travel to Bethel and warn Jeroboam about his ungodly ways of worship. God also specifically instructed him not to eat, drink or stay overnight in that land, but to return immediately home. Another prophet heard about the warning, and after self-reflecting, realized some of the warning pertained to him as well. So he sought out the prophet and lied to him so he would stay in his home. Instead of remembering God's voice, the prophet from Judah followed the man and ultimately died due to disobedience. Solomon should have known better than to listen to his wives and his flesh. And equally so, the prophet from Judah should have known this man's voice was a contradiction to what God had told him. Solomon's disobedience caused a nation to fall, and the prophet's disobedience caused his own personal death. Listening to the voice of contradiction will be fatal, whether physically or spiritually, and can also affect the lives of others. Choose God's voice.

Today's Challenge To Dig Deeper:
Has God given you a word, or confirmed some things to you, and yet there are voices contradicting His, causing confusion? Today, stop listening to the voices of contradiction. Go back to the very beginning when God spoke to your heart. Remember what He said and commit to standing on the confirmations, not the contradictions.

Evening Reflection:
Write down the promises and instructions God gave you in the very beginning. Write down His words along with His confirmations to you. When voices of contradiction come your way, commit to remembering what God said, and follow that path, not the path of destruction. Purpose in your heart to stand against the voices of contraction.

TSUNAMI FAITH
July 22

Morning Rinse: 1 Kings 15-18
Featured Verses: 1 Kings 17:11-12 *As she was going to get it, he called to her and said, "Please bring me a piece of bread in your hand." But she said, "As the LORD your God lives, I have no bread, only a handful of flour in the bowl and a little oil in the jar; and behold, I am gathering a few sticks that I may go in and prepare for me and my son, that we may eat it and die."*

A couple walking hand in hand on a beach notice the ocean water had receded more than usual from the shore, leaving the appearance of the ocean drying up. What they did not know was, a tsunami was approaching the land. When a tsunami forms, it draws back the beach water, which helps to feed the massive wave. In every life situation, we can choose what to focus on. Our lives are all about perception. Are we focused on the dry ground in our life, or on the miraculous wave headed our way? Elijah's ministry began with a literal drought in the land. It had not rained for several years, which of course, caused a famine. While traveling on a journey, he met a widow gathering sticks to make the last meal for herself and her son. Her plan was to use the last of her flour and oil, and then prepare to die of starvation. She was focused on the dry area in her life. However, Elijah saw a tsunami coming for her, and knew a breakthrough was headed her way if she had faith. Breakthroughs come when we use our faith and trust that God will not leave us in our 'dry' places. While she was gathering the sticks, Elijah told her not to fear, but prepare a bread cake for him first. He assured her there would be enough food for her and her son as well. And as we read in the story, she obeyed Elijah in faith, and God provided her with an overflow of oil for a very long time. Neither her bowl of flour nor jar of oil became empty (17:15-16). Her tsunami came, providing her with exactly the provision she needed in the area most dry in her life. Could the dry ground in our lives be the ground God needs us to build our faith on? Just like the gigantic wave needs the water from the beaches to build strength, could our faith be exactly what God needs to feed our coming tsunami? Yes. It is called tsunami faith.

Today's Challenge To Dig Deeper:
List on paper all areas in your life that are dry, or appear dry and empty. Pray, and with faith, begin to feed the tsunami of provision God is forming on your behalf. Call out your miracle and see the tsunami coming with eyes of faith. Now, go to the store or find a little empty jar in your home. Set this jar somewhere to remind you of the widow's faith in her dry place. If she can have faith on her near death bed, you can have faith too in your dry place. Pray over the tsunami coming and with faith, feed your miracle!

Evening Reflection:
Write down what your tsunami looks like. What is it bringing to you or your family?

BE THE RIGHT KIND OF MESSENGER
July 23

Morning Rinse: 1 Kings 19-22
Featured Verses: 1 Kings 22:13-14 *Then the messenger who went to summon Micaiah spoke to him saying, "Behold now, the words of the prophets are uniformly favorable to the king. Please let your word be like the word of one of them, and speak favorably." But Micaiah said, "As the LORD lives, what the LORD says to me, that I shall speak."*

In a meeting between Jehoshaphat, the King of Judah, and Ahab, the King of Israel, Ahab asked to join forces in a battle against Ramoth-gilead. Jehoshaphat was willing, if he received a word from the Lord. Ahab called all four hundred prophets together and they unanimously voted to go to battle, claiming that the Lord would prevail. However, Jehoshaphat knew these prophets were false. So he asked Ahab if there were any prophets of the Lord in Israel so he could hear God's true voice. This did not make Ahab happy. Micaiah was the only true prophet of God in the land, and each time Ahab called him for a word, the messages were repeatedly about destruction coming to him (22:18). Therefore, he hated Micaiah. However, he complied with Jehoshaphat's request and sent a messenger to get him. This messenger asked Micaiah to speak only what the king wanted to hear, and to agree with the other prophets. However, Micaiah stated he would be a messenger of God and only Him. When Micaiah arrived in the king's presence, he appeared to be sarcastic in his response to the king's question, mocking the pagan prophets (22:15). His tone let everyone know the word from God would be different from that of the pagan prophets. Micaiah's one voice of disagreement stirred the kingdom and stood out amongst the four hundred false prophets. Of course, Ahab became angry and put Micaiah in prison. We later read that what Micaiah spoke from God did indeed come to pass. Ahab lost the battle and his life. What kind of messenger are you? Are you one who follows the crowd? Or one who courageously speaks what God wants you to speak? Can God trust you to be the right kind of messenger for Him?

Today's Challenge To Dig Deeper:
God has given each of us something to say to the world around us. Whether that be a warning, or a message of hope, we are to use our voice to share it. If we stay silent, we are not fulfilling our part of The Great Commission, but instead are becoming the wrong type of messenger for God. If you have been silent or compliant, repent. Then ask God to help you share what is on your heart. Whether through social media, a phone call, or a prophetic word to a group of people, be brave and share it. Today. NO MORE DELAYS!

Evening Reflection:
Write down what you shared today. Commit to living a life as a messenger from this day forward, every day using your voice for Him.

THE "ARWEN RIDE" (PART 1)
July 24

Morning Rinse: 2 Kings 1-4
Featured Verse: 2 Kings 4:24 *Then she saddled a donkey and said to her servant, "Drive and go forward; do not slow down the pace for me unless I tell you."*

One of my favorite scenes in the *Lord of the Rings Trilogy* is called the "Arwen Ride." Frodo is close to death as he has not only been nearly taken over by the ring, but he has been wounded. Arwen, the Half-Elven daughter of Elrond and Celebrian, puts him on her white stallion and races through the land to the elves. This scene is the ride of her life. This is the moment where death is on her heels, where the evil Wraiths are trying to steal the life of Frodo and the destiny of the land. She does not have a second to spare, and has no room for error, as she desperately heads for safety in hopes that the elves can save Frodo's life. The journey becomes extremely intense when these evil Wraiths catch up to her. But she has ridden this path many times before, as she learned to be skilled in horseback riding. She knew each twist and turn on the tree engulfed path. And she never gave up on her ride. This movie scene is what comes to mind when reading the story of the Shunammite woman. This woman's son began complaining of a painful headache that came on with such speed, that by noon it caused him to die in her arms. But this woman did NOT accept his death. An 'Arwen' kind of desperation rose in her. A warrior kind of faith she had inside her already. I can imagine her heavy breathing as she rushes to gear up for her own 'Arwen ride.' It would also be the ride of her life. Just like the scene in the movie, I can see the Shunamite woman racing for miles on her donkey through the land to where Elisha was. With focus, determination, and a fighting spirit in her, she rode with full speed, very similar to the scene of Arwen's. Death had just gripped her son, so she mustered up every ounce of faith she could, and she rode! FAST! She rode full force, never stopping, straight to Elisha. When she found him, she grabbed hold of his feet and begged him to heal her son. She even refused to leave Elisha's side until he personally came back to her home. Arwen had learned how to ride. Arwen's skill for her ride did not come overnight. She practiced her skill and became excellent. Faith is the same. We must practice it through prayer and believing. One day, we will need intense faith for hard situations. May we be faith filled for our 'Arwen ride,' whether it be for ourselves or for someone else.

Today's Challenge To Dig Deeper:
Google the "Arwen Ride" scene in the *Lord of the Rings Trilogy* and let it stir your faith. Now rise on your prayer stallion and race to the throne of God with this same kind of intense faith for your situation. Believe God for your answer and take your 'Arwen ride' in faith.

Evening Reflection:
What did you learn from your 'Arwen ride,' and what answers are you believing for? What did God speak to you regarding your situation?

THE "ARWEN RIDE" (PART 2)
July 25

Morning Rinse: 2 Kings 5-8
Featured Verse: 2 Kings 6:17 *Then Elisha prayed and said, "O LORD, I pray, open his eyes that he may see." And the LORD opened the servant's eyes and he saw; and behold, the mountain was full of horses and chariots of fire all around Elisha.*

Once again, we read a story where death is at the heels of someone's life. The story surrounding today's Featured Verse is around the time Elisha warned the King of Israel to stay guarded while at a certain location. The reason for this warning was because the King of Aram was out to kill him. When the King of Aram heard Elisha was helping the King of Israel, this made him furious. So he planned to capture him by sending an army of horses and chariots to surround the city he and his servant were lodged in. When Elisha's servant woke up the next morning and saw the enemy's army, he panicked. But Elisha saw something different on the horizon. His eyes were not on the enemy's army. They were on chariots of God's army filling the mountainside. Yesterday, we watched the "Arwen Ride" scene from the *Lord of the Rings Trilogy*. Just like Arwen believed in the power of the water coming to help her save Frodo in the end of the scene, we must also believe in the power of our Father. We must begin to open our eyes to the spiritual realm, and see where our help comes from. May we see the mountains full of horses and chariots of fire ready to go to battle for our lives. Help us, Lord, to see you at work, even amid hard situations in our lives. Help us to see your provision when the enemy is at work to destroy us or our loved ones.

Today's Challenge To Dig Deeper:
Watch the "Arwen Ride" scene again from the *Lord of the Rings Trilogy*. Take note of the water horses coming to kill the enemy in the eleventh hour of the scene. As you watch it, ask God to help you see His chariots battling for you in your situation. Then some time today, either go to a store or go online. Buy something tangible that will remind you to keep your eyes focused on God's chariots. I purchased a T-shirt with a picture of Arwen holding her sword. This T-shirt reminds me I have an 'Arwen' kind of faith inside me.

Evening Reflection:
What stuck out to you about this scene that may have been different from yesterday's devotion about this clip?

WHAT IS YOUR PLACE IN GOD'S PLAN?
July 26

Morning Rinse: 2 Kings 9-12
Featured Verses: 2 Kings 11:1-2 *When Athaliah the mother of Ahaziah saw that her son was dead, she rose and destroyed all the royal offspring. But Jehoshabeath, the daughter of King Joram, sister of Ahaziah, took Joash the son of Ahaziah and stole him from among the king's sons who were being put to death, and placed him and his nurse in the bedroom. So they hid him from Athaliah, and he was not put to death.*

For the third day in a row, we read a story where death is prevalent. The story surrounding today's Featured Verses shows the tragic murders of the offspring of Ahaziah, the King of Judah. These deaths were ordered by his mother Athaliah, when she found out he was killed by Jehu (9:27-29). Due to his death, one of his sons was to become the heir to the throne. But Athaliah wanted the throne to herself, and killing his offspring was the only way she could accomplish this plan. For six years, her evil mission was successful because the nation believed all the offspring were dead. Therefore, she sat on the throne ruling Judah. However, God had made the promise to His people that Jesus would be born from the line of David, which was from Ahaziah's lineage. Despite his mother trying to destroy Ahaziah's lineage, God's promises never fail. Ahaziah's sister Jehoshabeath, and the wife of Jehoiada the high priest, hid Ahaziah's baby boy, Joash from deaths grip. For six years, he lived with them in the synagogue, while Athaliah ruled the land. Can you imagine, though, the feeling of despair in the land at the thought the promises God had made seemed dead? Can you imagine how hopeless the people must have felt believing the only way the Messiah would come to them was destroyed? But in the seventh year, Jehoiada secretly revealed to the rulers of the military, that Joash was still alive (11:4). I can imagine the hope that began to stir in their hearts, knowing this reveal would change the course of Judah back to God's timetable. During the reveal, a plan was set in place for Joash to be surrounded by guards for protection, as the rulers anticipated Athaliah would be full of rage. When Joash was revealed to the public and crowned as king, Athaliah was put to death, and Joash reigned in her stead. What is your place in bringing God's promises to life? Is it to be a secret bearer protecting God's promise for His perfect timing? Is it to be a guard that protects the truth when it is being revealed? Or is it to personally be willing to walk into God's calling, and allow others to protect you as you fulfill the position God has for you? Whether a secret bearer, a guard, or the one being guarded, allow God to use you for His will and purpose.

Today's Challenge To Dig Deeper:
Meditate on the questions above and ask God what your place is in bringing His plan to fruition.

Evening Reflection:
What did God speak to you today about your place in His plan?

ANNOINTED BONES
July 27

Morning Rinse: 2 Kings 13-16
Featured Verse: 2 Kings 13:21 *As they were burying a man, behold, they saw a marauding band; and they cast the man into the grave of Elisha. And when the man touched the bones of Elisha, he revived and stood up on his feet.*

"WHAT?" you ask? Anointed bones? For the fourth day in a row, death has been the subject. We have seen death at the heels of others as they are trying to be saved. We have also read how death hovered over a family to try and destroy its legacy. Death is often viewed in a negative way, and in the correct context, death does have a sting. Often, though, we forget to focus on how someone's death can influence a person's life BECAUSE they have died. Today's Featured Verse shows a glimpse of the impact Elisha's death had on the life of another dead man. As this deceased man was being buried, a 'marauding band,' which is a group of people looking to attack, was spotted on the horizon. I have two thoughts on what could have been the scene on the day of this man's funeral. My first thought is, those burying this man probably panicked a little and had to quickly find a tomb to bury him in so they could defend themselves against the band. Elisha's tomb may have been the closest one to use. Another thought of why they were using Elisha's tomb could have been that this man was part of Elisha's family, and it was part of the plan to bury him in this tomb alongside those related to Elisha. Maybe the tomb was already open and ready for the burial, but in the moment, the funeral became a rushed situation with no time for proper honor and placement. Regardless of the reasons for using Elisha's tomb and who this dead man was, his body touched the bones of Elisha, and he miraculously came back to life. WHAT A LEGACY! If Elisha had not died before this man's death, Elisha's bones would not have been available to bring him back to life. Elisha made an impact in his living years, and even with his anointed bones after his death. While our bones will most likely never touch another dead person and have this kind of impact, our life can. What kind of impact is your life legacy going to leave? Are you positioning yourself to carry on a message of hope even after you are gone? Will your 'bones' be anointed for those around you?

Today's Challenge To Dig Deeper:
Elisha's life was all about following God. His godly choices set him up to be impactful even after his death. What can you do while you are living to allow your impact to carry on past your life on this earth? Are there changes you can make with your choices? Or things you can do to make sure your voice is heard for many years to come?

Evening Reflection:
What did God speak to you today about your legacy?

FERVENT PRAYER OR FERVENT SHARE
July 28

Morning Rinse: 2 Kings 17-20
Featured Verses: 2 Kings 20:4-6 *Before Isaiah had gone out of the middle court, the word of the LORD came to him, saying, "Return and say to Hezekiah the leader of My people, 'Thus says the LORD, the God of your father David, "I have heard your prayer. I have seen your tears; behold, I will heal you. On the third day you shall go up to the house of the Lord. I will add fifteen years to your life, and I will deliver you and this city from the hand of the King of Assyria; and I will defend this city for My own sake and for My servant David's sake."'"*

Once again, and for the fifth day in a row, we study an impactful story centered around someone facing death. Hezekiah, the King of Judah, became mortally ill, and it appeared there was no hope of his survival. In fact, Isaiah the prophet came to pay him a visit on his deathbed, which did not appear to be a good thing. I am guessing this scene is very similar to our modern-day hospice scenario of a loved one. I am sure Hezekiah was hoping Isaiah would give him a prophetic diagnosis of hope and miraculous healing. However, Hezekiah received the instruction from Isaiah to get his house in order because he would die soon (20:1-2). This grieved Hezekiah so much he began fervently praying to God, begging for healing. Imagine having a reputation for having a fervent, or passionate, prayer life. Hezekiah's reputation was exactly this and this trait was even seen on his deathbed. Prayer was how he responded in life and what he leaned on, and is a trait that can be learned by all of us, not just something kings and prophets in the Old Testament did. When we learn to live a life of faith and fervent prayer, it will be the first thing we do, versus the last thing. God heard Hezekiah's prayer and quickly changed His mind, even before Isaiah left the area where Hezekiah lay. God spared his life and added another fifteen years. How do you respond to situations of despair? Do you fervently pray to God? Or do you fervently share with your friends first? Remember Hezekiah's situation. God turned the situation of death to a situation of life for Hezekiah, and He can do the same for you.

Today's Challenge To Dig Deeper:
Is there a situation in your life where fervent prayer is needed? If so, instead of fervently sharing with your friends about it, commit to fervently praying to God today.

Evening Reflection:
What did you learn about fervent prayer today? Did you go to God first and did anything change for you in your spirit?

SET OUT FOR GOD
July 29

Morning Rinse: 2 Kings 21-25
Featured Verses: 2 Kings 23:3, 25 *The king stood by the pillar and made a covenant before the LORD, to walk after the LORD, and to keep His commandments and His testimonies and His statutes with all his heart and all his soul, to carry out the words of this covenant that were written in this book. And all the people entered into the covenant… Before him there was no king like him who turned to the LORD with all his heart and with all his soul and with all his might, according to all the law of Moses; nor did any like him arise after him.*

Out of all the kings of Judah, there were no kings like Josiah before or after him. He purposed his life to be set out for godly ways. At the young age of eight years old, his father Amon died, and he took over the throne. Despite both Amon and his grandfather Manasseh doing evil in the sight of the Lord, Josiah purposed in his heart to be different. He had a heart for God. I am sure the scribes read the law to him, just like they read it to his father and grandfather. And he had access to the priests just as they had access. The resources and scenarios for him to learn God's ways were similar. But his choices and what he was set out to pursue made him different, which also changed what those around him were set out to pursue. He made a covenant before the Lord to keep His commandments, and Josiah kept that covenant, becoming the most godly king of Judah in all of history. He talked the talk and walked the walk, putting his faith into action. During his reign, he made choices that began changing Judah as a nation, including removing everything ungodly from the temple, such as the idolatrous priests (23:3). He even did away with the horses that were used in processions to worship the sun (23:11). He also reinstated the Passover celebration, and revived obedience to God's Law. Josiah purposed in his heart to be obedient, and then the people followed suit. He set out to pursue holiness. He set out to pursue God's ways. Many kings came after him who did not make these same choices, which caused God to remove His hand of protection on Judah during their reign, allowing their enemy to capture them as slaves. Our choices of what we set out to pursue will influence not just our lives, but the lives of those around us. Are you set out for God in every area of your life?

Today's Challenge To Dig Deeper:
Do you know someone who is not set out to pursue God? Pray for them to be set out for God's ways, and if you can contact them, call them today and let them know you love them. Put your faith into action. It will change someone's world and set them free. The people followed Josiah. You will have people follow you too. Set out to pursue the right path.

Evening Reflection:
Who did you pray for today? Did you call them? How did that go?

BREAK MY HEART FOR WHAT BREAKS YOURS
July 30

Morning Rinse: Lamentations 1-2
Featured Verse: Lamentations 2:11 *My eyes fail because of tears, my spirit is greatly troubled; My heart is poured out onto the earth because of the destruction of the daughter of my people, when little ones and infants faint in the streets of the city.*

If one only read today's Featured Verse without the context of the book of Lamentations, it would not be obvious why Jeremiah, the author of this book, is crying. But reading the entire first two chapters makes it very clear. The people of Jerusalem turned their hearts away from God, causing the destruction of Jerusalem. Jeremiah is often remembered as the "weeping prophet" because his written words capture the deep grief his heart bore. We can feel his burden jumping right off the pages of these chapters. Making his grief and lament sting even deeper is the fact that he warned the people about these consequences of sin for many years. However, they chose to not listen. In fact, their sin became so rampant, God removed His protection from them, and eventually the people were taken into captivity (1:1). The book of Lamentations begins with Jeremiah reflecting on the captivity, looking back on their sin, and documenting his grief. Do we grieve over the things God grieves over? Does our heart break knowing eternal destruction will come to sinners? Do we grieve deep enough to warn them? When we grieve, the burden we feel helps us to warn with love. When we judge, we can easily fall into speeches based on pride. May our hearts break for what breaks His, and when it breaks, may we warn with love. For God is love.

Today's Challenge To Dig Deeper:
Be extremely honest with yourself. Do you deeply care that people are headed to Hell? Does your heart truly break for what breaks the heart of our Heavenly Father? If it does not, ask God to give you a deep grief and help you begin to warn with love. Lives are at stake, and God needs you to lead souls to Him. Just like most of the people did not listen to Jeremiah, you may not be heard either. But God is ready to welcome those who will listen to your voice.

Evening Reflection:
Did you feel God answering your prayer throughout the day? Did you feel your heart begin to break for what breaks His? If you already have a burden for the lost, did it grow deeper? Write about it.

IN THE GAP OF OUR LAMENT
July 31

Morning Rinse: Lamentations 3-5
Featured Verse: Lamentations 5:21 *Restore us to You, O LORD, that we may be restored; Renew our days as of old.*

Jeremiah knew God had turned His back on the people, and he knew why this happened. For years, he warned the people about the consequences headed their way, if they did not turn their hearts back to God and repent of their sins. One of those consequences was when God removed his hand of protection from over their lives, followed by the destruction of Jerusalem. It grieved Jeremiah so much, he wrote the book of Lamentations, recording his grief as he recalled the sad story that brought the people to this troublesome time. Throughout the book of Lamentations, Jeremiah vented to God about his feelings regarding the story, and God lovingly listened. He did not say anything back to Jeremiah, but instead, was just present. As we follow Jeremiah's words, we know he used his grief and prayed for the people. He stood in the gap for them, praying for their restoration back to God. You may be grieving and lamenting over choices others have made. You may have even been directly affected by those choices, just as Jeremiah was. However, Jeremiah did not lament out of bitterness, but out of love. In your lament, love the people. Pray for them, despite how they have behaved. Someone needs you to stand in the gap for them, even while you lament.

Today's Challenge To Dig Deeper:
Challenge yourself to do some soul searching. Is there any area of your heart that has bitterness towards someone for their behavior? Ask God to change your heart to a heart of love for them. Now, stand in the gap today for them. Pray for them and be okay if God just sits and listens to your heart's cry. Do not expect an answer. But know that God will hear.

Evening Reflection:
Did you have a heart change towards someone in your life today? Who was it, and how did you stand in the gap for them?

August Rinsing

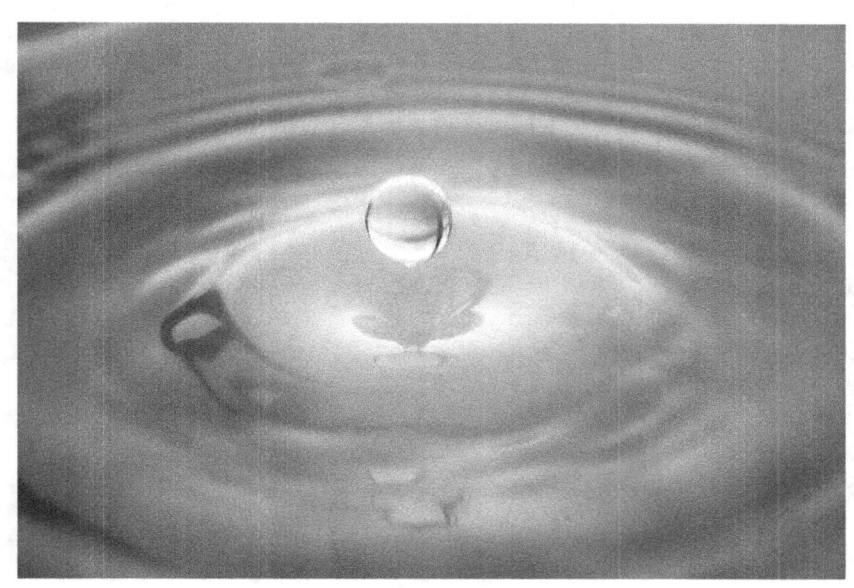

SALTY WORSHIP
August 1

Morning Rinse: Leviticus 1-5
Featured Verse: Leviticus 2:13 *Every grain offering of yours, moreover, you shall season with salt, so that the salt of the covenant of your God shall not be lacking from your grain offering; with all your offerings you shall offer salt.*

Worship is an expression of reverence. In the time of Moses, these expressions to God were manifested by offerings. The five offerings he wrote about to begin our study in Leviticus were the burnt offering, the grain offering, the peace offering, the sin offering, and the guilt offering. While the modern-day expressions of worship are different from the ancient Eastern civilizations in the Old Testament, we can still glean nuggets from their practices. Worshiping God should be a lifestyle. In all we do, we should strive to worship Him. That includes living holy by daily decisions we make, people we date, the friends we have, where we live and more. Of course, the obvious ways to worship Him include things like going to church, serving in a ministry, and tithing. Regardless of the type of worship we are talking about, seasoning our worship with salt is still a biblical principle. As Christians, we are called the salt of the earth (Matthew 5:13). God wants our lives of worship to be seasoned with Him so much it affects the world around us for His purposes. For that to occur, we must accept the responsibility of being salt for God in all we do, and then live our lives with salty worship. Just like Moses' offerings had salt in them for a purpose, our lives of salty worship have purpose. If we point to God in all we do, He will be the spotlight for others to run to.

Today's Challenge To Dig Deeper:
Our lives should be an act of worship to God, seasoned in such a way that it causes the world to hunger for what we have. Is there any area of your life not seasoned with God? If there is, you do not have salty worship in that area. Ask God to help you make changes in that area to have salty worship for Him, and to make others thirst for God. This could be in our responses to life, how we talk, what we do in our spare time, and many other examples, just to name a few.

Evening Reflection:
What did you change today to have salty worship in every area of your life?

BURNING AND BUILDING THE FIRE
August 2

Morning Rinse: Leviticus 6-9
Featured Verse: Leviticus 6:12 *Fire shall be kept burning continually on the altar; it is not to go out.*

The offerings we read about yesterday were focused on offerings and sacrifices the people made. In part of today's Morning Rinse, the focus is on the offerings the priests made. Symbolically, it is no wonder God instructed the priests to keep the fire on the altar burning. This fire was the base of their offerings. It was what burned their sacrifices made to God. And just like this fire was the foundation of the altar, the fire of God inside of each of us must be kept burning as the foundation of our faith. It must be kept alive, burning daily as we strive to live for Him in all we do. We all have an individual responsibility to keep it burning, not just our pastors and teachers as they lead us. To effectively accomplish this, we must each choose to do things like reading our Bibles, staying in an attitude of prayer, and making daily decisions that are Christ-led versus self-focused. The more we are centered around the burning fire of God, the more our lives will be strong, living sacrifices for Him. While the fire in Leviticus may not be literal in modern-day times, it is symbolic of the fire that can grow inside each of us. You may ask, how do I get this fire inside of me? It starts with repentance. We all must stay in a state of humility, so our lives will burn for God and not for the things of this world. Not only will being humble keep the flame burning, but humility will also help this fire build in intensity. The fire of God is what consumes things in our lives that take us away from His holiness. Is your fire burning and building?

Today's Challenge To Dig Deeper:
Examine your walk with the Lord. Examine your heart. Is the fire, or passion of God burning? Repent for letting it die down, or even go out. Let your repentance reignite the flame of love towards Him.

Evening Reflection:
What did you change in your life to grow your flame?

BE A RESOLVER
August 3

Morning Rinse: Leviticus 10-13
Featured Verses: Leviticus 10:19-20 *But Aaron spoke to Moses, "Behold, this very day they presented their sin offering, and their burnt offering before the LORD. When things like these happened to me, if I had eaten a sin offering today, would it have been good in the sight of the LORD?" When Moses heard that, it seemed good in his sight.*

Nadab and Abihu were Aaron's two oldest sons, and they were priests under his leadership. In today's Morning Rinse, it is suggested they brought coals of fire from an outside source to keep the altar fire burning for their sacrifice (10:1). This would have made the sacrifice unholy, since the fire on this altar was never supposed to go out, as we learned yesterday. These two men became lazy and indifferent to the holiness of God by not keeping this fire holy. Therefore, their consequence was death. Their two younger brothers, Eleazar and Ithamar, were next in line for positions of priesthood. I can only imagine how they must have felt. With emotions high, I am sure they were angry at their brothers for becoming indifferent. They were potentially also a bit fearful of making a mistake themselves, worthy of death. And understandably so, they probably did not want to finish their brother's job of this sacrifice by eating from it, which was part of the sacrificial ritual. With confusion and some chaos surrounding the situation, Moses got angry at Eleazar and Ithamar for not eating from the sacrifice their older brothers had started. Aaron defended Eleazar and Ithamar with a reasonable explanation, calming Moses down and ultimately diffusing the entire climatic situation, bringing order back to the atmosphere. Do I think Moses got a little too angry at times and jumped to conclusions? Probably so. He killed an Egyptian, hit a rock too many times causing his fate, and got angry in this situation. I believe Aaron learned the skill of being a resolver of conflict when emotions were high. We, too, will be around others that may get angry occasionally. Can we be an 'Aaron' during those moments of conflict? Can we be a resolver?

Today's Challenge To Dig Deeper:
Is there someone in your life who often responds in anger? No doubt, this can cause more conflict than the actual conflict itself. Today, look online for an article with tips on how to resolve conflict, and learn two skills to be a resolver. Be prepared to use what you learned in case an opportunity comes your way today, or in the near future. Commit to being a resolver.

Evening Reflection:
What two skills did you learn today in the article you read? Did you use those skills today? How did it end up?

THE GREAT GATEKEEPER
August 4

Morning Rinse: Leviticus 14-17
Featured Verse: Leviticus 16:30 *For it is on this day that atonement shall be made for you to cleanse you; you will be clean from all your sins before the LORD.*

Throughout today's Morning Rinse, multiple instructions were written pertaining to sacrificial rituals, cleansings, and what to do at the altar. In these specific instructions, God listed the animals required, the order of the rituals, and what the ceremonies needed to look like for the people to receive cleansing. These directions all link straight back to two things, the heart of worship and the forgiveness of sins. In the Old Testament, an animal's life was the cost of man's sin. These sacrifices, or acts of worship that the priests conducted, gave the Israelites an open door to God. The priests were the gatekeepers. It is important to remember that even though we do not conduct these types of sacrifices under grace, God still takes our sin very seriously. Sin has a cost. It has a price. God wants us to be holy, and the good news is, He gave us a way to be holy. He wants ALL to be forgiven when we mess up, not just the Israelites. We know the sacrifices in the Old Testament were temporary. What became permanent was when God canceled all requirements for them, and sent His Son to pay the price for the sins of the world. He became the ultimate sacrifice on the Cross. He became the Great Gatekeeper. His name is Jesus.

Today's Challenge To Dig Deeper:
Do you know anyone who needs Jesus? Reach out to them today. Tell them you are praying for them, and Jesus loves them. You may be the hand that guides them to Jesus.

Evening Reflection:
Did you reach out to someone today? Who was it?

A FRESH START TO BEING SET APART
August 5

Morning Rinse: Leviticus 18-22
Featured Verse: Leviticus 20:26 *Thus you are to be holy to Me, for I the LORD am holy, and I have set you apart from the peoples to be Mine.*

As the softball game is about to begin, the pitcher takes the mound and begins her warmup regimen. There is no intimidating stance or form, no 'beastly' facial expressions, no muscles bulging and no special magic glove. She is a person, just like you and I, who has worked tirelessly to learn how to master this skill. Many hours of sweat, tears, dedication, and getting back up after failure, led to her being set apart from other pitchers. Even though some have teased her, and others have hated her for taking their previously held spot in the lineup, she continues pursuing this position with excellence. This young lady is one of my daughters, Micaiah. I have watched her growth in this sport and witnessed each step of her journey that got her to where she is now. At the time of writing this devotion, she is one of the starting pitchers for the varsity team at college, as a FRESHMAN. Yes. Wow. Her dedication to athleticism and perseverance earned this spot in the lineup. This is how God wants us to be in our walk with Him. He wants us to be willing to persevere in our journey of holiness. Even through failures, He wants us to get back up, dedicating our lives to being set apart for Him. Today's Morning Rinse begins the last part of Leviticus, and covers the clear standards God set for the Israelites on how to live a life of holiness. Despite living in pagan nations, God wanted them to be set apart, and He wants the same for us. He wants us to live holy and BE holy. While we do not offer sacrifices and are not bound by the rituals of biblical times, there are plenty of moral standards in these chapters to help us live holy. These chapters include standards on family responsibilities, including reverence (admiration) for our parents (19:3). Also included are rules on sexual conduct covering child abuse, incest, adultery, and even the sin of sexual acts with animals (18:6-24). God also instructed the people to stay away from divination, witchcraft (19:26), and from the worldly standards of living (18:3). Being set apart is a journey that begins with repentance and salvation. After salvation, we will face choices every day, whether to live holy and be holy. Why is God wanting us to be holy? Because He is holy, and we are His.

Today's Challenge To Dig Deeper:
After reading today's Morning Rinse, is there any part of your life that needs to be set apart? Even little things, like returning the toilet paper the store did not charge you for? Or ceasing to laugh at a friend's sexual joke? Repent and make a fresh start to being set apart.

Evening Reflection:
Was there anything you had to address today to continue being set apart for God? What was it? Do you feel God's forgiving touch on your life? Receive it and go live holy.

GOD'S FINANCIAL SYSTEM
August 6

Morning Rinse: Leviticus 23-27
Featured Verse: Leviticus 27:30 *Thus, all the tithe of the land, of the seed of the land or of the fruit of the tree, is the LORD'S; it is holy to the LORD.*

Do you want to know about God's financial system? It is simple. Give. Under the Law, which is covering most of what we read about in today's Morning Rinse, it is about rituals. Tithing was part of the rituals then, and it is still expected from us today. Throughout the book of Leviticus, we learn about God's character through the Law, and the principles of holiness He asked of the Israelites. When Jesus came and died for us, His death gave us grace, which released us from the Law. But the God-given principles of giving remain. There are three ways God asks us to give:

1. Tithe: Today's Featured Verse says all 'the' tithe. It is THE tithe, and the tithe is the Lord's. It is not even our money. This is universal and is the first ten percent of our increase. We rob God when we do not tithe back what is His.
2. Free-will offerings: 2 Corinthians 16:1-2 and Deuteronomy 12:11-14 talk about offerings above the tithe. Offerings are other ways God wants us to give, but it must be outside of the tithe. Offerings are given from our heart, freely, to causes, individuals, organizations, or places we want to bless and help. When we remain open to God's voice, He will guide us on where to give these offerings.
3. Alms (to the poor): Acts 10:31, along with many verses in the Bible, implores us as Christ followers to give to the poor. Jesus is very clear on this. We must remain open to helping the poor and those in need.

God's financial system is different from ours. But when we begin giving to God, He begins to bless our household. One of my favorite pastors, Pastor George Westlake, Jr, used to say almost every week in church, "You cannot out-give God." Test Him. Challenge Him. Give and follow His financial system. You will not regret your life-changing choice.

Today's Challenge To Dig Deeper:
Out of the three points in God's Financial System, do you follow them all? Or are you lacking in one or more of the areas? Ask God to help you trust Him with your finances. Tithing MUST come first. So start there. If you are a tither, begin giving. Start today and watch God begin to pour out His blessings on your life.

Evening Reflection:
What changes did you make today to get in line with God's Financial System? How do you feel about those changes?

FAVOR IS FOR PURPOSE
August 7

Morning Rinse: Luke 1-3
Featured Verse: Luke 1:30 *The angel said to her, "Do not be afraid, Mary; for you have found favor with God."*

When God gives us favor, it is for a purpose. In today's Morning Rinse, we read about several people who had God's favor. The first was Zacharias. He was a priest who became the father of John the Baptist. When the angel came to visit Zacharias to tell him he and his wife, Elizabeth, would have a son, he was doubtful and questioned the angel (1:18). His doubtfulness caused him to become mute until his son, John, was born. Mary is another person we read about today who had favor for a purpose. Mary, on the other hand, answered her purpose with faith (1:45), and was an example to the world as she walked this faith journey out. And lastly, Jesus was the ultimate example of someone with favor for a purpose (2:52). If Jesus grew in purpose, will not our purpose grow as well? When we walk out God's will for our lives, our favor and purpose will affect generations to come, blessing many lives for years if we rise to the call. God wants us to be a part of the big plan, and He desires that we have the faith for our purpose. Will we believe like Mary, or will we have doubt like Zacharias? Either way, we have the favor of the Lord, and we have a purpose. It is our job to be willing to walk it out in faith.

Today's Challenge To Dig Deeper:
Today's Challenge includes three parts. First, look up the song, "The Blessing" sung by Kari Jobe. Listen to it several times, letting it sink into your spirit to build your faith. Second, write Luke 1:45 on a card, and put your name in the place of 'she' where it is referencing Mary: ie "And blessed is (your name)." Place this card where you will see it on a regular basis. Third, ask God to call you for His purpose and give you faith to walk it out, so generations can be blessed.

Evening Reflection:
What golden nugget did God speak to you about today regarding His favor over your life?

THE CHALLENGE
August 8

Morning Rinse: Luke 4-6
Featured Verses: Luke 6:27-29 *But I say to you who hear, love your enemies, do good to those who hate you, bless those who curse you, pray for those who mistreat you. Whoever hits you on the cheek, offer him the other also, and whoever takes away your coat, do not withhold your shirt from him either.*

Recently, I found out someone had been continually saying cruel and untrue things about me to try and undermine my character as a Christ follower. When things are declared in this fashion, it is a curse, and can wound to the very core of our hearts. This wound did just that to me. It cut so deep, I have struggled with bitterness and unforgiveness, especially due to the position this person held in my life. The overwhelming feeling of betrayal has been so strong, I have not even wanted this person's name mentioned around me. It has been a horrible feeling to believe I must defend myself with no vindication from the Lord. After pouring my heart out to a wise friend two days ago, she gave me The Challenge. In love, she encouraged me to forgive him, release him from the awful things he said about me, and accept that I may never hear an apology from him for his wrongful behavior. "The truth of the matter is," she said, "he is probably going about his merry way, and has forgotten about you and things he said. Anita, it is eating you alive. You must lay it to rest and bury it in the ground." She was right. There was no skirting the issue. So as difficult as it was, I accepted The Challenge. For the last two nights, I laid in bed with my hand over my heart asking God, "How? How do I forgive him, Lord? Show me how." For two nights straight, I did this with no real feeling of release. That is, until this morning while writing today's devotion. Even though forgiveness is a choice, sometimes we need practical ways to help us make a deep heart change to forgive. How am I using The Word to help me forgive? Simple. Read today's Featured Verses again. While I do not think this man is on my 'enemies list,' he did curse me and mistreat me with his words. The light bulb of how to forgive became a little brighter for me this morning. God reminded me in a very practical way that I am to bless him, pray for him and treat him as I want to be treated. My heart began feeling the release of unforgiveness and bitterness. I now pass on to you The Challenge.

Today's Challenge To Dig Deeper:
Do you need to take The Challenge towards someone who wrongfully mistreated you? Begin praying prayers of blessings over them. Any time they come to mind, bless them. Watch the unforgiveness melt away.

Evening Reflection:
Who did you bless today? How did it feel?

HE TURNED
August 9

Morning Rinse: Luke 7-9
Featured Verse: Luke 7:44 *Turning toward the woman, He said to Simon, "Do you see this woman? I entered your house; you gave Me no water for My feet, but she has wet My feet with her tears and wiped them with her hair."*

When this woman heard Jesus was at the Pharisee's house eating, hesitation had no place in her footsteps. Despite not receiving an invitation for this dinner gathering, she headed His way with her alabaster jar in hand. I can see the scene playing out in my mind's eye. She arrives at the Pharisee's home, scurries inside and desperately runs past the servants who were unsuccessful in their efforts to stop her. It was customary for dinner guests to recline on a couch with their heads at the table as they ate. She scans the room and finds Jesus with the other men at the table. She courageously approaches Him, fighting her extreme intimidation. With her face hanging with shame, she weeps in repentance at His mere presence. She is used to being looked down on, so she has nothing to lose in this act of desperation. With her hair hanging over her face, she stands behind Him, ready for her mission. Her eyes focus on His feet and her alabaster jar of oil to wash them with. She keeps her face covered by her hair, avoiding Jesus' eyes, as well as everyone else's at the table. Her shame is too great to reveal herself, or so she thought. I can only imagine the awestruck wonder this woman felt when Jesus paused his conversation with His disciples, and turned His attention towards her. This moment was life changing. She was a sinner, desperate for a healing touch for her soul. Her touches with oil-soaked hands did not startle Jesus. He did not create a scene or move His feet away so she could not touch Him any longer. Instead, He turned towards her and gave her forgiveness. This woman was not the only woman who He turned to in today's Morning Rinse. The woman who had a hemorrhage for twelve years touched the bottom of His robe, and He turned to her. Pushing through a large crowd to get to Him, she, too, was desperate for healing. The faith of both women caused Jesus to turn and take note. It was not because of anything other than the position of their hearts. They were desperate for Him. And so, He turned. And He turns to us as well.

Today's Challenge To Dig Deeper:
What specific thing are you desperate for today? Reach out to Him. Tell Him what it is. He WILL turn to you.

Evening Reflection:
What specific thing did you pray for today? Did you feel Jesus turn to you?

HAIR COUNTING TIME
August 10

Morning Rinse: Luke 10-12
Featured Verses: Luke 12:6-7 *Are not five sparrows sold for two cents? Yet not one of them is forgotten before God. Indeed, the very hairs of your head are all numbered. Do not fear; you are more valuable than many sparrows.*

Ever since I was a child, I have been intrigued by this passage. I remember reading it or hearing it, being taught and having a hard time wrapping my brain around the fact God knows how many hairs are on my head. One day, while in elementary school, I decided to try and count the hairs on my head to get an idea of this number. Using my bathroom mirror for assistance, I sectioned off my hair into parts and began the count. I counted and counted until my arms were so tired, I had to cease my mission. I do not remember getting much higher than a few hundred, but it opened my eyes to the vast knowledge God has of us. He created us. So why would He not know? I even remember in my quest to understand this passage, plucking a few hairs and then secretly telling God He needed to recount my head. Oh, the silliness of a child. I am sure this scenario is not the first or only time God had a few chuckles on my behalf. He tells us repeatedly in His Word that He cares for us and knows us. He remembers the sparrows. How much more will He remember and think of us? Be encouraged. He sees us. He loves us. He knows us. My son-in-love, Dre, who is married to my daughter, Haley, has Alopecia. It is an autoimmune disease that caused all of his hair to fall out. There was no warning on the onset, and it has never grown back. My point in saying this is, you do not have to have hair for this verse to be applicable. Dre lives a life still knowing that God sees him and cares for him. Whether it is counting our hair, or knowing every vein inside our body, we are still seen by God.

Today's Challenge To Dig Deeper:
Are you struggling with feeling like God has forgotten you? Memorize today's Featured Verses and take them to heart. Let God speak to you through this passage.

Evening Reflection:
Is your heart comforted after letting this passage soak into your heart all day? Write about what it means to you.

THE SHEEP, THE COIN, AND THE SON
August 11

Morning Rinse: Luke 13-15
Featured Verses: Luke 15:6-7 *And when he comes home, he calls together his friends and his neighbors, saying to them, "Rejoice with me, for I have found my sheep which was lost!" I tell you that in the same way, there will be more joy in heaven over one sinner who repents than over ninety-nine righteous persons who need no repentance.*

The entire chapter of Luke 15 is dedicated to the story of Jesus speaking to a crowd full of tax collectors and sinners. He knew His audience, and knew once again that there were Pharisees and scribes nearby listening to Him, who were trying to trap Him. Therefore, the three parables He shared back-to-back were timely messages of redemption, falling on the ears of those trying to accuse Him of blasphemy. These three stories, the wandering sheep, the lost coin and the prodigal son, simply show how important sinners are to our Father. Why would the shepherd in the first parable leave his ninety-nine sheep to go find the one separated from the flock? Because that one sheep was important to him. Caring for the sheep was not only the shepherd's way of life, but he had a sentimental connection to them, willing to defend them even against wild animals. Why would the woman search her entire home for one lost coin, instead of going about her day safeguarding the other nine coins? Because the one lost coin was important to her. Some Bible scholars even state that when a woman got married during this time, she was given ten coins of high value. They were not only of worth, but held sentimental value connected to her wedding day. The same is true with the prodigal son. He was of value to the father no matter how he had behaved. The shepherd, the woman and the father longed for what was lost, and are a mirror of how Jesus longs for those who are lost and need His mercy. He chases us, desires for our presence, and longs for a relationship with us. And oh, when we are found, He hosts a huge celebration party in Heaven. No matter how someone is lost, God's love covers it all. Stay encouraged. The accuser has been silenced with this message.

Today's Challenge To Dig Deeper:
Who do you know that is wandering, lost or rebellious? No matter how they got to where they are, Jesus loves them. Reach out to them today. Tell them this message and pray for their return.

Evening Reflection:
Who did you pray for today? Did they respond to the message you sent them?

STUBBORN FAITH
August 12

Morning Rinse: Luke 16-18
Featured Verse: Luke 17:5 *The apostles said to the Lord, "Increase our faith!"*

Right before the apostles made this request to Jesus, Jesus tells them to forgive. My guess is they are asking for more faith to have the power to forgive. Even if someone sins seven times in a day and asks seven times for forgiveness, Jesus wants us to keep forgiving. This can be very challenging and take more faith than we have, in and of ourselves. So I believe the apostles asked Jesus for what I call 'stubborn faith.' Multiple times in today's Morning Rinse, the message of stubborn faith is embedded into the stories. Repeatedly forgiving someone takes stubborn faith, especially when it logically does not make sense. Other words that help describe what stubbornness looks like are tenacious, perseverance and determination. These traits can be needed while forgiving someone who repeatedly behaves in offensive or sinful ways. We must stay the course, though, and remain focused on what Jesus asks of us. We also read today about the ten men with leprosy (17:11-19). They were probably outside the city due to their condition. So when they saw Jesus, they yelled out to Him for healing. Despite what others might have said to silence them, they kept yelling until they got His attention. Being stubborn can be uncomfortable because it can take us outside of our comfort zone. But having stubborn faith can cause God to hear our cries. This parallels the story of the widow who kept going to the judge for legal protection. At first, the judge did not fear God and was not interested in helping her. But she had stubborn faith and would not give in to him. The judge even admitted she might wear him out with her persistence (18:5). Jesus wants us to go to Him and not give up in our requests. He wants us to have stubborn faith for our situation. It wears the enemy out and moves mountains. Among the multiple stories we read in today's Morning Rinse, we close out with the blind beggar who also had stubborn faith. This man cried out to Jesus for mercy. Those around him were sternly telling him to be quiet, but he continually cried out for mercy from Jesus (18:35-43). We are to keep on forgiving, keep on asking, keep on seeking, and keep on knocking. If all these people we read about today, with odds stacked against them, can have stubborn faith, then we can too. Will Jesus find stubborn faith in you?

Today's Challenge To Dig Deeper:
What do you need stubborn faith for? Is it to forgive someone? Is it to keep asking God for provision for something? Is it for healing? Direction? Ask God for some stubborn faith, and then go to Him with your situation. Be stubborn.

Evening Reflection:
What did you learn about your faith today? Do you now have stubborn faith?

YOU COME DOWN!!!
August 13

Morning Rinse: Luke 19-21
Featured Verse: Luke 19:5 *When Jesus came to the place, He looked up and said to him, "Zacchaeus, hurry and come down, for today I must stay at your house."*

When I was a child, one of my favorite songs in Children's Church was about Zacchaeus. I still remember the dramatic line in the song where a room full of kids would shout out "ZACCHAEUS! YOU COME DOWN!" My friends and I would point to each other with one hand, with the other hand on our hip. We would giggle and display silly facial expressions. Zacchaeus brought out the sass in us with that song. He was limited by his height, but not limited by his hope. I think, even as a child, we wanted his hope. It is what caused him to sprint ahead of the crowd and climb a tree to see Jesus. Despite his height, he became taller than anyone in the crowd. He found a way to surpass his limitation. Jesus noticed him, and not only did He tell him to come down from the tree, He agreed to have dinner with him. We know in that interchange, Zacchaeus' life was forever changed. Whether it was Jesus' acceptance of him or something He said while dining, we know his heart changed. He even committed to giving half of his possessions to the poor and paying back four times to anyone he defrauded (19:8). We may also have limitations that cause challenges in our lives. But Jesus wants us to put forth effort to combat those limitations. Zacchaeus did not complain about his height. It was his reality. So he found a way to get past it. What can you do to creatively get past your limitations to fulfill the plans He has for you? Our efforts will allow Jesus to then say to us, "YOU COME DOWN! For I'm going to your house today!" Here are the words to this childhood song:

> *Zacchaeus was a wee little man and a wee little man was he;*
> *He climbed up in a sycamore tree for the Lord he wanted to see.*
> *And as the Savior passed that way, He looked up in the tree;*
> *And He said, "ZACCHAEUS, YOU COME DOWN!*
> *For I'm going to your house today.*
> *For I'm going to you house today."*[23]

Today's Challenge To Dig Deeper:
List two things you can do today to creatively combat a limitation you have. Put forth the effort and go do something today to turn it into a strength. Ask God how, and He will show you.

Evening Reflection:
Can you sense excitement growing in your heart about how you will now handle your limitations?

---

[23] https://en.wikipedia.org/wiki/Zacchaeus_(song)

7 MILE ROAD
August 14

Morning Rinse: Luke 22-24
Featured Verse: Luke 24:32 *They said to one another, "Were not our hearts burning within us while He was speaking to us on the road, while He was explaining the Scriptures to us?"*

Today's Morning Rinse covers the entire story of the crucifixion and resurrection of Jesus. This is the foundation of the Christian faith. The Featured Verse centers around the part of the story that happened three days after Jesus died on the Cross. Two believers were walking on a seven-mile road to a village called Emmaus (24:13). On their trip, their conversation naturally consisted of all the events that occurred over those last three days. To add to their points of conversation, breaking news had just been released that morning. It was the news that the tomb where Jesus' body was laid was now empty. I am sure every conversation across the land was consumed with people sharing details of what they knew or heard, including their feelings about this part of the story. While these two men were walking, a man appeared to them on that road. Unbeknownst to them, though, it was Jesus Himself. When He met up with them, He already knew the condition of their hearts and their lack of faith in His resurrection. But sometimes He wants to hear us say what is in our hearts, so He can correct it. As they spoke, He pretended to not know about the current events, which shocked them. I wonder if He smiled to Himself, knowing how they would soon respond to His reveal. Or maybe His heart was a bit grieved at their lack of faith in His resurrection. As He listened to them share the news of the empty tomb, Cleopas mentioned in disappointment how they had hoped Jesus would redeem Israel. They knew the tomb was empty, though, and still did not believe it. After Cleopas shares his perspective and feelings, Jesus calls them both foolish for not believing the prophets and scripture. They were believers who really did not believe. But when Jesus spoke, their hearts began to burn, so they begged Him to stay and have dinner with them. When He began breaking the bread, their hunger consumed them in their hearts, and their eyes were opened to who He was. They became believers who truly believed. I can only imagine their excitement on their journey back to where they started. It had to have been electric as they, no doubt, ran to share with others about the interchange on their seven-mile road.

Today's Challenge To Dig Deeper:
Reread Luke 24:13-35 some time today. Ask Jesus to help your unbelief on whatever your seven-mile road looks like. Be ready for a heart change and excitement to fill the air.

Evening Reflection:
What did God reveal to you today?

WATERMELON SEED RESET
August 15

Morning Rinse: Malachi 1-4
Featured Verses: Malachi 3:10-11 *"Bring the whole tithe into the storehouse, so that there may be food in My house, and test Me now in this," says the LORD of hosts, "if I will not open for you the windows of heaven and pour out for you a blessing until it overflows. Then I will rebuke the devourer for you, so that it will not destroy the fruits of the ground; nor will your vine in the field cast its grapes," says the LORD of hosts.*

"Obedience commands a blessing." This is a common statement I would repeat as I raised my children. I pray they remember and act on this quote throughout their entire life. When we obey, God blesses us. When we reset, He takes note. This also includes how we handle our finances. God sees what our priorities are in our spending, and knows what our bank accounts look like. He does not need a secure password to view our online account. Do we handle our spending the way He wants us to? Or do we need a reset? I am not talking about purchasing that flavored coffee on the way to work each day, or splurging at a dining establishment. I am talking about tithing what is His anyway, and giving back in other ways as well. Tithing is an act of holy obedience that God never released us from when He ended the Law and moved us under grace. It should be a 'given' as a Christ follower. When my husband and I got married, we made some non-negotiable lifestyle decisions as a couple, and tithing on all our increase was one of them, which we have never regretted. God asks us to test Him. It is not about the money. It is about our obedience. Tithing is His anyway, and it is a return of what He is owed. We rob Him when we do not tithe. On top of tithing, there are grace offerings, which include gifts to causes of our choice. And then the third way of obedience with our finances is giving to the poor. When we give back, we sow into God's kingdom of financial planning, not man's way of doing it. Each of the sowing choices I mentioned will truly bring a harvest of blessings, especially if we practice all three on a regular basis. If you are not seeing a harvest in your finances, there could be a sowing problem. A wise man once stated, "It is not how many seeds are in a watermelon, it is how many watermelons are in a seed." When we reset, we adjust something in a new or different way. Does your watermelon seed need a reset?

Today's Challenge To Dig Deeper:
In the area of tithing, grace offerings, or giving to the poor, do you need a reset? God wants us to have these three areas of financial decisions be a priority and to trust Him. Commit to a financial reset. No turning back.

Evening Reflection:
Did you have a financial, or watermelon seed reset?

BEING AN *IMMEDIATELY* FOR GOD!
August 16

Morning Rinse: Mark 1-4
Featured Verse: Mark 4:20 *And those are the ones on whom seed was sown on the good soil; and they hear the word and accept it and bear fruit, thirty, sixty, and a hundredfold.*

John Mark, the author of the Gospel of Mark, witnessed many stories of Jesus, and as he documented these stories, he also captured the reactions of people who encountered Him. Some people received Him while others sadly rejected Him. Despite how each person responded, a common word Mark used to describe their reactions is the word "immediately." In just the first four chapters of this gospel, Mark captures seventeen *immediately* occurrences, along with another moment as equally dynamic, a *just then* moment. *Instantaneously*, *right away*, *abrupt*, and *without delay*, are other descriptive terms to portray this narrative. If you would like to look at all the references again, and even underline them in your Bible, here they are:

> 1:10, 1:12, 1:18, 1:20, 1:21, 1:28, 1:29, 1:30, 1:42, 1:43, 2:8, 2:12, 3:6,
> 4:15, 4:16, 4:17, 4:29
> 1:23 "Just then."

The question is, are we an *immediately* for God? Do we respond to Him without delay? Most of the examples above are stories of positive responses to Jesus, but even the Pharisees had an *immediately* moment when they hurried to conspire against Him. How do we become an *immediately* for God versus an *immediately* for the kingdom of darkness? We find the answer in Mark 4:23. Right after Jesus explains the parable of the four soils, He states if you have ears, then hear. When we choose to hear and obey the Word, we choose to be the good soil that Jesus references. The condition of our heart and how we obey the Word is what defines what kind of soil we are, and sets us up for our *immediately*. It is a choice to hear the Word, accept it, and then ultimately bear fruit.

Today's Challenge To Dig Deeper:
If you have been one of the other three soils besides the good soil, seek God about this. Ask Him to help you be the type of Christ follower that bears fruit that expands to thirty, sixty or a hundredfold. Set out to be an *immediately* for Him in all you do.

Evening Reflection:
How was your day? What nuggets did God give you about the soil you have been?

IMMEDIATELY MOMENTS OF CHRIST

August 17

Morning Rinse: Mark 5-7
Featured Verses: Mark 6:48-50 *Seeing them straining at the oars, for the wind was against them, at about the fourth watch of the night He came to them, walking on the sea and He intended to pass by them. But when they saw Him walking on the sea, they supposed that it was a ghost, and cried out; for they all saw Him and were terrified. But immediately He spoke with them and said to them, "Take courage; it is I, do not be afraid."*

In today's Morning Rinse, there are yet eleven more *immediately* moments, just in case you are continually underlining the words in your Bible. These verses are 5:2, 5:29, 5:30, two in 5:42, 6:25, 6:27, 6:46, 6:50, 6:54, and 7:25. Today's Featured Verses capture one of those moments with Jesus sitting on the mountainside, watching His disciples struggle in a windstorm. Despite not being physically in the boat with them, He was still present. But after all the miracles the disciples had witnessed up to this point, it amazes me they did not have this knowledge engrained in their spirit yet. In fact, just hours before this storm, they had witnessed one of those miracles when Jesus fed the five thousand with just the five loaves and two fish. But they still did not have the faith to call out to Him for help, or to even calm the winds themselves. Unfortunately, fear and unbelief remained strong in their hearts. When Jesus decided it was time, He entered the storm and walked on the water to go past them. But what do they do? Instead of the disciples recognizing their Savior, they scream out in fear and terror, thinking they were seeing a ghost. Sometimes during our storms, something happens that causes us to freak out and think it is the works of the enemy, when instead, it is really God's hand moving past us. Jesus knows all about the storms we go through. And He will sometimes set Himself up for His own *immediately* moment as another way to teach us faith. He may allow things to get uncomfortable, and maybe even scary, to help us realize His presence is already with us. Then at just the right time, He will have His *immediately* moment. He will calm our fears and grow our faith. Do not underestimate the *immediately* moments of Christ.

Today's Challenge To Dig Deeper:
Are you going through a struggle? Look for God to walk past you and have an *immediately* moment. What will He tell you in that moment? Will He need to tell you to have courage? Will He need to remind you He is there? Look for Him today.

Evening Reflection:
How did God reveal Himself to you today amid a struggle?

THE LESSON IN THE *IMMEDIATELY*
August 18

Morning Rinse: Mark 8-10
Featured Verse: Mark 8:10 *And immediately He entered the boat with his disciples and came to the district of Dalmanutha.*

Are you beginning to see a theme of *immediately* moments in the Gospel of Mark? In today's Morning Rinse, there are five more times this word is used, 8:10, 9:15, 9:20, 9:24 and 10:52. This brings the total to thirty-four times in just ten chapters, including the added verse when Mark used *just then*. Right before the *immediately* moment in today's Featured Verse, Jesus had just finished feeding four thousand people with seven loaves and a few fish. The disciples witnessed this miracle, as well as the feeding of the five thousand in yesterday's Rinse. In both stories, the crowds were in desolate places, making it very difficult to find food. After Jesus fed this second crowd, He and the disciples immediately got into a boat, heading on a round trip journey across the lake. However, they forgot to grab leftovers, and only had one loaf of bread with them in the boat. I would like to think Jesus had something to do with this scenario. Did He scurry them onto the boat and purposefully not make mention to pack for their next meal? Did He use this *immediately* moment to rush them, so He could set them up to reveal their hearts to them? Well, it worked. When the disciples realized they had literally nothing to eat, they began making this a point of discussion. Were they arguing? Were they worried? Whatever the discussion led to, Jesus interrupted them and pointed to their hardened hearts (8:17). Why were they not able to believe Jesus would feed them in this desolate place out on the water, after witnessing the miracles of feeding two huge crowds? Jesus sometimes takes us to a desolate place, so he can show us an *immediately* miracle while revealing our lack of faith. I am convinced He fed the disciples in this moment, just like He provided for both crowds, and just like He wants to provide for us in our desolate times. Oh, Lord, help us to learn in our *immediately* moments to have faith.

Today's Challenge To Dig Deeper:
Are you needing something right now? Maybe Jesus has taken you to a desolate place, so you can watch His miracle of provision. Trust. Believe. Watch. And pray for provision.

Evening Reflection:
What did God provide for you today?

IMMEDIATELY RESPONDING
August 19

Morning Rinse: Mark 11-13
Featured Verses: Mark 11:2-3 *… and said to them, "Go into the village opposite you, and immediately as you enter it, you will find a colt tied there, on which no one yet has ever sat; untie it and bring it here. If anyone says to you, 'Why are you doing this?' You say, 'The Lord has need of it'; and immediately he will send it back here."*

My husband, Nathan, has a gift for handyman skills. In fact, our family has a running joke where we often say with a chuckle, "He can fix just about anything." He seems to be able to problem solve with nearly any needed household repair, while others are challenged in this area. It is extremely fun to watch him use his gifts. In fact, one of the times we visited my sister's family and my parents in Virginia for Thanksgiving, we all had the opportunity to watch his skills in action. He installed a new garage door opener for my sister. Also, on this trip, he moved some furniture around for my parents, set up their TV, installed a dog ramp for their dog who has hip issues, arranged their garage so their cars could fit inside, and installed a new garage door opener for them as well. He has helped them on past visits by repairing a damaged door and a damaged ceiling for my sister. My family knows he is very gifted at this type of work, and sometimes feel guilty at asking for help when we are in town. But Nathan is always willing to bless them with the knowledge and skills he has for repairing things around a home. He does not necessarily love doing the work, but he loves helping others with his giftings, and is quick to offer his services to bless them. I believe the owner of the colt in today's Featured Verses had that same heart. He did not hesitate to give what he had, for what was needed to bless Jesus. And blessing others is part of having a kingdom mindset to fulfill kingdom purposes. This man immediately offered his colt, just as Nathan immediately offers his talents when the need arises.

Today's Challenge To Dig Deeper:
What does God need of yours for kingdom purposes? This could be your talents, money, or even items to give towards a need. As you evaluate what you have to offer, the bigger question becomes, are you willing to immediately respond when God asks for it? If you find yourself hesitating, ask God to give you a heart to immediately respond. Watch for opportunities to arise today.

Evening Reflection:
Were you made aware of a need today that you can meet? Did you respond immediately? And by the way, the *immediately* moments in Mark are now up to thirty-six, with the two from our Featured Verses added to the count.

IMMEDIATELY KISS OF BETRAYAL
August 20

Morning Rinse: Mark 14-16
Featured Verse: Mark 14:45 *After coming, Judas immediately went to Him, saying, "Rabbi!" and kissed Him.*

In our final Morning Rinse from the Gospel of Mark, we read another four *immediately* moments. These four times are found in 14:43, 14:45, 14:72, and 15:3, bringing the total number to forty in this book. Just like God uses our *immediately* moments for His kingdom purposes, He uses the *immediately* moments of our enemies as well. This is not something we always like hearing because these life examples can cause deep pain. Judas' kiss was not only a betrayal that ran deep against Jesus, but it was also against all the disciples. He lived with them for three years. He traveled with them, ate with them and yes, even witnessed miracles with them. But his heart was full of deceit and the love of money. In fact, he was not only their treasurer, continually stealing from the money box (John 12:6), but he accepted payment for this *immediately* kiss of betrayal (Luke 22:48). Jesus knew all along that this *immediately* moment would be part of the story of His death and resurrection. So while it was a betrayal, it was also a purposeful action in saving the world. This *immediately* kiss was shocking to the disciples, I am sure. "Will I be betrayed next?" they may have thought as they ran (14:50). Then Peter, in his moment of denying Jesus three times, realized he, too, betrayed Jesus, as did all the disciples at one point. I wonder if they later compared themselves to Judas in their time of repentance and reflection. Thankfully, they all experienced Jesus' forgiveness. If I had to guess, we have all been betrayed by others, and unfortunately, probably betrayed others as well. But just like the disciples, we too must use the *immediately* kiss of betrayal in our lives for kingdom purposes, by living out the gift of forgiveness, forgiving others. Forgiveness is the whole point of the Cross and the result of the *immediately* kiss of betrayal we read about today.

Today's Challenge To Dig Deeper:
If you have not underlined or highlighted the word *immediately* throughout the Gospel of Mark, including where *just then* was written, do that today. The references are listed in each of the past five devotions. Now, write down any experience of an *immediately* kiss of betrayal in your life, whether one was against you, or you against another. Forgive those who committed the betrayal, even if it was you. Let your heart heal today as you receive and offer deep forgiveness, and seek out how God will use that *immediately* kiss for His purposes in your life.

Evening Reflection:
How does your heart feel today? Go use your healing for kingdom purposes.

CHRISTMAS PEACE IN THE MIDST OF CHAOS
August 21

Morning Rinse: Matthew 1-3
Featured Verses: Matthew 1:19-20 *And Joseph her husband, being a righteous man and not wanting to disgrace her, planned to send her away secretly. But when he had considered this, behold, an angel of the Lord appeared to him in a dream saying, "Joseph, son of David, do not be afraid to take Mary as your wife; for the Child who has been conceived in her is of the Holy Spirit."*

The snapshot through a camera lens shows a moment of peace the night Jesus was born, for He is the Prince of Peace. Can you imagine the scene? The smiles on Mary and Joseph light up the manger area as they peer down on baby Jesus' tiny face. The camera lens captures the calm atmosphere under the brightly lit star of Bethlehem, just as the words from the popular song "Silent Night" play softly in the background. But the months prior to, and after this special night, portray another part of the story that is not this peaceful and still. Let us peer into the camera lens again. Months before Jesus was born, Joseph and Mary were an engaged young couple planning a wedding. Can you imagine the shock and stress when loved ones began learning the news of her pregnancy? Once a couple is 'betrothed,' it is as serious as the actual marriage, and according to their custom, getting pregnant before the actual wedding day not only would cause the family humiliation, but could cause the bride to be stoned to death. Trying to protect her, Joseph decides to secretly send her away, causing a form of divorce. Can you imagine the tears and heartache in Mary's home? God, though, brought peace back to the story by instructing Joseph in a dream to continue with their wedding plans. Of course, then there is the stress of traveling to Bethlehem for the census, including trying to find a place to stay in the city, with Mary being nearly nine months pregnant. Again, peace comes when the cave-like stable area is offered to them, setting up the birthing scene. However, after the birth, another climactic turn in the story occurs when Joseph, Mary and baby Jesus must escape to Egypt in the middle of the night. God informs Joseph in yet another dream, that Herod had set out to kill all the boys two years old and younger (2:13-16). He wakes Joseph and tells him to "Get up" and go to Egypt. This mass murder plot caused more chaos than we can even imagine. However, looking back on that original scene of baby Jesus in the manger, we know that Christmas peace is obtainable amid any chaos. And this peace, if we pursue it, can surpass all chaos, all year long.

Today's Challenge To Dig Deeper:
If you are in a stressful situation in your life, look for the Christmas peace. Close your eyes, think of the scene of Jesus' birth, and believe for God to bring you the peace that passes all understanding. Trust Him.

Evening Reflection:
Did you get the peace you need for the situation in your life?

WILDERNESS TESTING
August 22

Morning Rinse: Matthew 4-6
Featured Verse: Matthew 4:1 *Then Jesus was led up by the Spirit into the wilderness to be tempted by the devil.*

I do not think my childhood family vacation to White Sands National Park would count as a desolate wilderness, despite the miles of white sand dunes stretched across the horizon. True wildernesses, though, as beautiful as they may be, are great to visit, but not ideal to remain in. While they are naturally beautiful for wildlife, the chance for human survival is low, and the idea of spending any length of time away from porta-potties makes me anxious. My mind's eye shows a neglected, undisturbed area with a stark need for food and water, which seems to be very similar to that of the wilderness Jesus was led to. While I cannot relate to spending multiple days camping out in one, I have experienced other kinds. I have battled a wilderness mentality, for starters. This is when we are trapped in a negative mindset, and our circumstance is centered around lack, with no direction, no way out, and a sense of hopelessness. This mindset may even cause us to view our circumstance as worse than it really is. I have also been through other types of wildernesses, like financial, relational, and spiritual, just to name a few. And I am sure you can name more from your life experiences. When there is an area with a deep sense of dryness, hopelessness, or a battle to thrive, it can be a personal wilderness. But Jesus is here to give us hope and provide a way out. Wildernesses are not designed for us to stay in. He knows what a wilderness feels like. He has experienced hunger, temptation, and has even heard the lies of the enemy whispered in His ear. Sometimes we are in a wilderness due to our choices. But other times, it is because the Holy Spirit has led us into one to grow us. Just as Jesus was led into the wilderness to be tempted, we too may be in a wilderness so we can pass the tests ahead and come out stronger for the next leg of our journey. Jesus started His ministry after the wilderness, and we also may have a ministry waiting on the other side of ours. Whether you are in a wilderness due to your own choices, or your negative mindset, or even if God has led you there, be confident that God is close by to bring you out and begin something new.

Today's Challenge To Dig Deeper:
If you are in the wilderness right now, pray you can conquer and overcome any tests, so you can step into a new level of ministry. Have faith God will bring you out.

Evening Reflection:
Did you receive new, fresh hope regarding your wilderness? Write about it.

A SIMPLE TOUCH OR A SINGLE WORD
August 23

Morning Rinse: Matthew 7-9
Featured Verses: Matthew 8:15-16 *He touched her hand, and the fever left her, and she got up and waited on Him. When evening came, they brought to Him many who were demon-possessed; and He cast out the spirits with a word, and healed all who were ill.*

A slumber party consisted of six tween girls celebrating a birthday. Right before snuggling into their sleeping bags for the night, they sat in a circle to play one last game. The Whispering Game. It is simple to play. The first girl in the circle whispers a short story or phrase in the ear of the girl sitting next to her. Then that girl whispers what she heard to the next girl in the circle, until the story makes its way around to all the participants. When the last girl gets the message, she shares what she heard to the others and the laughter ignites the room, after they realize how dramatically different it is from the original story. Exaggeration is at its finest around that circle. But unlike the Whispering Game, Jesus does not need exaggeration when performing miracles or telling stories. This truth can go against our carnal thought process when we read stories in the Bible. We, as humans, like dramatization, and we sometimes even enjoy creating it. From the perception of an actress, it is easy for me to develop dramatic scenes in my mind when I read stories of Jesus healing someone or casting out demons. I can picture in my mind's eye large crowds around Him and can hear the whispers amongst the people. I can feel the energy as they rise on their toes, peering over their shoulders, hoping to be the first to witness His next miracle so they can pass on what they observed. Maybe their carnal minds, like mine, anticipate something big and even exaggerate the story a bit. But when it comes to Jesus, exaggerations are not what changes lives. It is His simple touch and a single word. In today's Featured Verses, He touches the lady's hand, and she is healed. Then He casts out the spirits with one single word. No exaggeration is needed, just a touch or a word. In this story we do not know what His simple word is. But later in this same chapter, He casts a legion of demons into a herd of swine with a single word, "Go" (8:32). I have a hunch this is a simple word He used frequently when casting out demons. Another example of His simple touch of healing is when He touches the leper (8:3), or when He simply touches the blind men (9:29). Both times, healing them. And of course, we must remember the story of the bleeding woman who only needed to touch the fringe of Jesus' cloak to receive healing (9:20). A simple touch and a single word are all we need, to be changed forever. No drama, and certainly no exaggerations.

Today's Challenge To Dig Deeper:
Do you need a simple touch or a single word? Close your eyes and see Jesus in His simplicity. His simple moments can bring the biggest change.

Evening Reflection:
What simple things did you experience today?

YOKE CHOICE
August 24

Morning Rinse: Matthew 10-12
Featured Verses: Matthew 11:28-30 *Come to Me, all who are weary and heavy-laden, and I will give you rest. Take My yoke upon you and learn from Me, for I am gentle and humble in heart, and you will find rest for your souls. For My yoke is easy and My burden is light.*

A yoke is a wooden bar, of sorts, that is placed over the necks of two animals. The bar is then attached to a plow or cart so they can pull it. The connotation, or symbolism, when the reference of a yoke is used is that it has a sense of toiling in life because of circumstances or trials. God never said the life of a Christ follower is always easy. In fact, Jesus warns us of tests, trials, and even persecution that may come our way. So knowing this, it may be easy to view today's Featured Verses as a contradiction. But on the contrary, Jesus knows there are many types of 'yokes' or bondages in life that cause a lack of peace. There is the yoke of sin, the yoke of listening to false teaching, and even the yoke of bad decisions that lead us from His will, just to name a few. The wrong type of yoke will cause distress, exhaustion, worry and even sin. This is why Jesus tells us to take up HIS yoke. When we choose to do this, we become bound to Him, bringing on a new way of living in exchange for the needless toiling. We put on HIS peace. We put on HIS forgiveness. We put on HIS acceptance and guidance. And we put on HIS rest. That is, IF we choose to put on His yoke. This choice is more than asking Him to be our personal Lord and Savior. While this is the first and most important step, putting on His yoke is a daily choice for the rest of our lives. It is waking up each morning, allowing Him to guide our every footstep throughout the day, and trusting Him on our journey, even when we face bumps in the road. It is a choice. What will your yoke choice be today?

Today's Challenge To Dig Deeper:
Do you need peace in a situation? Are you needing to lay down the yoke of worry, or the yoke of a bad decision? Take it to God. Ask for forgiveness and then pick up HIS yoke. Trust Him to guide you. Listen to His voice. Then obey.

Evening Reflection:
What yoke did you lay down today in exchange for His yoke? How do you feel? Write about it.

REMEMBER THE MUSTARD TREE
August 25

Morning Rinse: Matthew 13-15
Featured Verses: Matthew 13:31-32 *He presented another parable to them, saying, "The kingdom of heaven is like a mustard seed, which a man took and sowed in his field; and this is smaller than all other seeds, but when it is full grown, it is larger than the garden plants and becomes a tree, so that the birds of the air come and nest in its branches."*

AH! The mustard seed parable. This scripture is one of the most widely known in the Bible about faith. In this parable, Jesus shows us we do not need faith the size of mountains, but only the size of a mustard seed. Around .039 to .079 inches in diameter, this seed is one of the smallest of all seeds. Yet it ends up growing into the largest of all garden plants, becoming over ten feet tall, depending on the climate. It is common for Christ followers to ask God for faith the size of this seed. But we can admittedly be guilty of only asking for the faith to get us past our situation. What about seeing the actual mustard tree? In Jesus' parable, the seed is used for the sowing, but the tree is the result, not the seed. After studying about mustard trees, I learned they have many uses, making this parable a great example of what our fruit can look like after sowing. The most well-known use of this tree is the fact birds can nest in this garden plant, providing shelter and livelihood for them. Do you have the ability to provide shelter for others, or provision for those in need? If not yourselves, do you sow to churches or ministries with this mission? This is another reason why tithing is so important. Along with this benefit from the mustard tree, there are many other uses. The flowers from it can be tossed into salads or dried into a delicate spice. The mustard greens can be eaten as well, and are rich in fiber. Also, once the mustard seeds are harvested from the tree, they can be ground into a spice or made into a powder for making prepared mustard, which includes antioxidants and other beneficial compounds. There is also mustard oil, which has the properties to improve hair root health, if used as a root scalp treatment. Parallel with the many benefits of a mustard tree, when we sow into God's kingdom with our faith and resources, the reaping will be far greater than we can even imagine.

Today's Challenge To Dig Deeper:
Ask God to show you where to adjust your sowing. Pray all your seeds of faith and resources will reap every possible benefit they can bring. Just like the mustard tree provides multiple uses, pray your seeds will too. Remember the mustard tree.

Evening Reflection:
What did God speak to you about your mustard tree today?

70 x 70 FOR THE 1

August 26

Morning Rinse: Matthew 16-18
Featured Verses: Matthew 18:21-22 *Then Peter came and said to Him, "Lord, how often shall my brother sin against me and I forgive him? Up to seven times?" Jesus said to him, "I do not say to you, up to seven times, but up to seventy times seven."*

Pain from the offenses of others can come from many different situations, and can keep us stuck emotionally and spiritually until we conquer the sins unforgiveness and offense. Years ago, I was trying to recover from this type of deep pain, but it felt my efforts of forgiveness were in vain. I was frustrated about how long my battle to forgive was taking, and could not figure out why I remained stuck, with no true healing in my heart. At the time, I was attending Sheffield Family Life Center, a mega church in Kansas City where Sunday night services were part of the regular weekly schedule. These Sunday night services were a bit different in structure than Sunday mornings, in that the pastor allowed extra time at the end of sermons for anyone needing prayer. For months, it seemed, I would go down to the altar nearly every week, get down on my knees, and take my pain to God. I would repeatedly ask Him to help me forgive this person, but the reminders of the pain would not go away. I could not seem to overcome my unforgiveness. One Sunday evening while on my knees, I distinctly remember asking Him about today's Featured Verses. "If I keep forgiving, then why does my pain keep surfacing?" He answered me in a way I will never forget. He told me He never said to forgive seventy times seven for that many different offenses. "Instead," He said, "you may need to forgive a person seventy times seven times for the same offense." Shocked and yet enlightened, I asked, "WHAT? That many times for the SAME ONE?" It finally made sense. Satan is the master of reminding us of the failures of others, to keep us bound by unforgiveness and bitterness. From that point forward, each time Satan reminds me of the wrongdoing of this person towards me, I forgave him for that instance. I was intentional about being specific for each offense, instead of praying a general, blanket prayer of forgiveness. Seventy times seven for each offense. Over and over, I forgave until finally my heart healed. Sometimes our imperfect heart requires seventy times seven for the one. Oh, the freedom we would walk in if we would forgive seventy times seven for EACH of the many sins of others towards us. May it be so.

Today's Challenge To Dig Deeper:
Do you feel stuck on your quest to forgive someone? Search your heart and forgive seventy times seven for the one.

Evening Reflection:
How do you feel about the seventy times seven for the one?

EVICTION TIME FOR THE CHIEF PRIEST AND SCRIBE

August 27

Morning Rinse: Matthew 19-21
Featured Verses: Matthew 21:15-16 *But when the chief priests and the scribes saw the wonderful things that He had done, and the children who were shouting in the temple, "Hosanna to the Son of David," they became indignant and said to Him, "Do You hear what these children are saying?" And Jesus said to them, "Yes; have you never read, 'Out of the mouth of infants and nursing babies you have prepared praise for yourself?'"*

One of my favorite songs is "Old Church Choir" by Zach Williams. When it first came out, a video circulated on social media with a children's choir performing this song. When the music started, a little girl in the second row began dancing, releasing her inward jig with no cares in the world as to who might be watching. Children have a way of expressing joy and praise that is contagious, and if we grasp it, we can experience that same joy. Children have a sweet ability to trust God without doubt, and praise Him without reservation. But as we get older, this ability often leaves us, causing our faith to decrease and our praise to become more refined. Jesus wants us to have the freedom of praise like a child because He knows it brings us joy, which in turn gives us strength. Another example of children praising is in today's Featured Verses. A group of children witnessed Jesus healing the blind and the lame and started shouting praises and singing in the synagogue. This made the chief priests and scribes very angry. Why? Their praise was loud, breaking the formality of the synagogue rituals while also bringing attention to Jesus, the very person they were trying to destroy. "Where are the parents and why are they not controlling these disruptive kids?" they may have asked. In my opinion, the parents were probably followers of Christ and part of the crowds that witnessed miracles. Maybe even a few of them experienced healings of their own, giving these children front row seats to their parent's healing, and even more cause for praise. When a healing occurred of any kind, I believe they witnessed and learned from the adults. Jesus set people free while teaching them, including children, and the importance of praise outside of the rituals was something I believe they became used to. Shouts of praise or doing a jig may make people upset, especially those who are comfortable in their structured form of worship. But Jesus allowed the children to break the rituals of the synagogue, and He asks us to do the same. So why are we, as adults, afraid to shout and dance like children? Why do we hesitate? Could it be we have allowed a 'chief priest' or 'scribe' to take residence in our heart, squelching our jigs and shouts of praise? It is eviction time.

Today's Challenge To Dig Deeper:
Look online for the video I referred to above. Watch the joy in the little girl in the second row. Evict anything in your heart that squelches this kind of joy. Find the little dancing child inside of you today.

Evening Reflection:
Did you find the child inside of you? How did it feel to do a jig?

100% RETURN
August 28

Morning Rinse: Matthew 22-25
Featured Verse: Matthew 25:15 *To one he gave five talents, to another, two, and to another, one, each according to his own ability; and he went on his journey.*

Even though we all have equal worth, we do not have equal abilities. However, we can be confident whatever we receive from God, He trusts us to manage it. I cannot emphasize enough how amazing this is. God, the Creator of the universe, trusts us and values us. In this parable, the man, a picture of God, divides his possessions amongst his servants based on their individual abilities. The man leaves on a journey and expects his servants to manage those possessions, or the 'talents,' until his return. When the man in the parable returns from his trip, he asks the last servant where the return was. The servant began making excuses and even disclosed that he hid them. This makes the man angry, and he calls the servant wicked and lazy. Then unfortunately, he takes the talents back from him and gives them to another servant to manage. God knows what each of us are capable of, and He gives us resources to manage according to that potential. When He gives us our 'talents,' that does not only include our abilities and natural gifts, but it also includes things like our time, money, relationships and even ideas or pursuits on how to use those resources. While God is the provider of our 'talents,' it is our responsibility to bring the return of those 'talents' by using what He gives us for His kingdom. We may not achieve a 100% return every day, but God does expect something, and excuses on why we are not using them is not how He expects us to respond. God does not accept excuses. He expects a return. When we use what He gives us, this allows Him to then trust us with even more, instead of putting Him in a position to take them away and give them to someone else to use. May we play our part in the investment of bringing 100% return to God's kingdom.

Today's Challenge To Dig Deeper:
Be honest. If you have not allowed God to see a 100% return on what He has given you, repent. Do not walk in shame. Walk in change. Ask God to help you begin now with using all He has given you for a 100% return.

Evening Reflection:
What baby steps did you make today to begin giving God a 100% return on His investment in you?

LITTLE GRANDPA
August 29

Morning Rinse: Matthew 26-28
Featured Verses: Matthew 28:19-20 *Go, therefore, and make disciples of all the nations, baptizing them in the name of the Father, and the Son, and the Holy Spirit, teaching them to observe all that I commanded you; and lo, I am with you always, even to the end of the age.*

I wish I'd had the opportunity to see my grandpa from Oklahoma one more time before he left this earth. I miss his gentle words and warm smile. We called him 'Little Grandpa' because he was small in stature compared to my other grandfather. While he was a shorter man, though, he was a giant in God's kingdom. He was so impactful, and his legacy as a pastor, a mentor, and an example of how to love people will forever be etched in my heart. But greater than any of our loved ones' last words, are the last words of Jesus while on this earth. Today's Featured Verses are those words. They are not just idle words, but are His last commandment to us, and what we call The Great Commission. We are to 'GO' and make disciples for Him. If we are to fully live a Christ-filled life, ignoring this instruction is not an option. How do we do this, though? What does it mean to put this commandment into practical action? My little grandpa was one individual whose life can explain how. He lived his life on purpose. We can too, by being intentional with our daily choices for Him, choosing to be a disciple like my little grandpa. It begins by hearing and reading The Word, and then living out what the Bible says. When we get The Word in our hearts, this creates a powerful domino effect that will bring about not only our destiny, but the destiny of others, hence developing disciples. The steps are simple to understand. When we read The Word, it changes our thinking to a kingdom mindset. This mindset will then help our emotions be more Christ-centered. When we are controlled by kingdom emotions, this will guide our decisions and ultimately form our habits. It is a domino effect because once we have developed habits, our character is formed. Once our character is formed to be more like Christ, our destiny will come to life, and it all starts with reading The Word. Through this entire process of growth as a disciple ourselves, people are watching. They see the decisions we make, how we respond to life when the trials come our way, and who we are as a person. Mentoring and being an example are part of fulfilling The Great Commission. We become changed personally and live it out for others practically, just like my little grandpa did for me and so many others.

Today's Challenge To Dig Deeper:
Where in your life can you change to be more of a disciple, and then make more disciples? Is it your mindset, decisions, habits, or other areas?

Evening Reflection:
What do you feel is something you can do for The Great Commission?

LOVE AND HATE COMBINED

August 30

Morning Rinse: Micah 1-4
Featured Verse: Micah 4:5 *Though all the peoples walk each in the name of his god; as for us, we will walk in the name of the Lord our God forever and ever.*

God hates sin, and we must acknowledge that He is the righteous Judge. And yet, He is a loving God. He loves us so much, He sent His Son to die on the Cross for our sins, and to save the world from eternal damnation. In this short book, Micah presents the true picture of God. This true picture shows us He loves the sinner, but hates the sin. Much of today's Morning Rinse is devoted to God's judgement of Israel. Micah lists the loathsome sins they committed, including fraud (2:2), theft (2:8), greed (2:9), oppression (3:3), hypocrisy (3:4), blasphemy (3:5), and injustice (3:9), to name a few. God does bring judgement to those caught in sin, and those who are unwilling to turn from it. Sometimes it is hard to accept this side of Him because we only like seeing the side of mercy and grace. However, the truth is, He will bring judgement if we do not obey after He gives us numerous attempts to repent. Israel did not heed these opportunities, though. So while Micah predicts the judgement upon Israel, he does not leave us with a doom and gloom message. He also gives us hope. He gives us the truth of God's redeeming love for us. When we accept that love and repent of our sins, we will walk in His name forever, spending eternity with Him in Heaven.

Today's Challenge To Dig Deeper:
Be thankful today. Thank Him for hating sin so much, He sent His Son to die for us, and save us from our sin, so we could live with Him forever. If you have not accepted Him as your Lord and Savior, say the prayer at the back of this devotional.

Evening Reflection:
Write down your thoughts about God's combination of love and hate from today's devotion.

GOD'S WISH LIST
August 31

Morning Rinse: Micah 5-7
Featured Verse: Micah 6:8 *He has told you, O man, what is good; And what does the Lord require of you but to do justice, to love kindness, and to walk humbly with your God?*

A young child walks up to his dad and asks, "What do you want for Christmas, Daddy?" The desire to give our loved ones items from their wish list is joyous to all ages, but especially the young at heart. There is such purity in this act of love. That same pure desire of a child can be implemented even in our relationship with God. It is easy to discover what is on His wish list when we read The Word. Today's Featured Verse reveals three things on God's wish list that we can gift Him every single day.

1. When others act unjustly, we can act justly.
2. In situations of setbacks, we can show kindness and mercy.
3. In a world driven by pride and self-centeredness, we can walk humbly with God.

Oftentimes, when we fulfill the desires of others, it does something special in our own heart. Gifting items off God's wish list through our actions, is no different. Our own hearts will be changed. He desires us to act justly, love kindness, and walk in humility. For when we give these things from His wish list, it ultimately will affect our homes, our community, and our world. This is the bigger picture, to transform our world by our actions.

Today's Challenge To Dig Deeper:
Are you fair in your dealings with people? Do you show kindness to those who have reacted to you with wrongdoings? Are you walking in humility? Correct any areas that need correcting, and become an expert at gifting from God's wish list.

Evening Reflection:
What did God show you about His wish list?

September Rinsing

MAN YOUR FORTRESS
September 1

Morning Rinse: Nahum 1-3
Featured Verse: Nahum 2:1 *The one who scatters has come up against you. Man the fortress, watch the road; strengthen your back, summon all your strength.*

At the time Nahum wrote this book, Assyria was the most powerful nation on earth, and Judah's greatest enemy. Just one hundred years prior to this time frame, Jonah preached in the streets of Nineveh, the capital of Assyria, and the Assyrians turned from their evil ways. But once again, evil lurked in this city and nation. In fact, Nineveh is called the "bloody city" (3:1), as well as an "evil city" (3:19). The entire nation reeked with pride, using their powerful military to oppress, plunder and slaughter their victims. Can you imagine the fear of the Israelites? Nahum, though, had a message of hope. He spoke of the judgement coming to the Assyrians due to their evil (1:11), idolatry (1:14), murder (3:3), and continuous wrongdoings (3:19). But while the book of Nahum speaks of this judgement, Nahum also predicts and prophesies the restoration of Judah from the oppression they had endured. We all have personal battles and struggles. We may have bosses, friends, family members, or those in our lives that oppress us and cause us to feel vulnerable at times. So what did Nahum instruct that we, too, can do? *Man your fortress.* Put up boundaries around our hearts and homes if need be. Strengthen yourself with the Armor of God and protect what God has given you. And ask for wisdom as you guard your lives, including relationships. Guarding your lives can even mean you keep your eyes on the road around you for those who want to hurt you. Stay strong in the Lord. Do not stop living for Him during the storms around you, and remain courageous in what He wants you to do. Even if you are in a battle, be encouraged and know He sees you. He will restore. Nahum's prophecy of the destruction of Assyria did indeed come true about fifty years after writing this book. Be comforted knowing God sees all we go through, and His power and justice will conquer our enemies. In the meantime, *man your fortress*, and stay strong.

Today's Challenge To Dig Deeper:
Do you feel discouraged or oppressed? Rise up in your strength and *man your fortress*. Guard what God has given you, and commit to growing in your faith during your trials. Be encouraged that God will see you through what you are going through. Do not give up.

Evening Reflection:
Do you feel stronger in the Lord today? What hope do you have?

PRE-PRODUCTION OF YOUR CALL
September 2

Morning Rinse: Nehemiah 1-2
Featured Verses: Nehemiah 1:5-6 *I said, "I beseech You, O LORD God of heaven, the great and awesome God, who preserves the covenant and lovingkindness for those who love Him and keep His commandments, let your ear now be attentive and Your eyes open to hear the prayer of Your servant which I am praying before You now, day and night, on behalf of the sons of Israel Your servants, confessing the sins of the sons of Israel which we have sinned against You; I and my father's house have sinned."*

One of my favorite businessmen in the Bible is Nehemiah. Today's Morning Rinse gives us insight into how he did his pre-production work on the huge task of rebuilding the wall, and he even outlines his business plan for us. If you have a task or a call on your life, and need a plan, follow his steps on how to accomplish it. The first 5 steps below begin with how Nehemiah prayed. The remaining steps are practical, action steps he took to complete the rebuilding of the wall. So here we go together, on our own journey with Nehemiah:

1. Praise God and make sure He is in His rightful place of honor in your heart (1:5).
2. Ask God to hear and see your prayers (1:6).
3. Confess and take responsibility for whatever is applicable. In my case, it is lack of movement and obedience (1:6-7).
4. Remind God of His promise and word (1:8-9).
5. Ask Him for favor with those you need it from (1:11).
6. Know how much time you need to work on it. Begin making those preparations, and even prepare your boss for the time you'll need off in the future (2:6).
7. Prepare a list of needs and include a budget (2:8).
8. Make your 'networking list,' and write letters to those on the list. Ask for help with their resources (2:7-8).

Back before computers or phones were a way of life, business owners and project leaders kept important data at their fingertips, including their 'networking list.' This is a basic business concept from as far back as Nehemiah's time, if not before. A networking list includes contacts, relationships, and people of trade. Just as it was vital for the success of Nehemiah's mission, it is vital for ours as well. It is used for connecting with others on our journey, especially when we have a need. With strategic planning, Nehemiah was able to rebuild a wall around the entire city of Jerusalem. You have this same ability to do what God has put into your heart. It is time to begin pre-production on what is burning in your heart to fulfill.

Today's Challenge To Dig Deeper:
Make Nehemiah's business plan your own. Today, begin pre-production by following the steps above.

Evening Reflection:
What steps did you take today?

PRODUCTION PART 1: HAVE A MIND TO WORK
September 3

Morning Rinse: Nehemiah 3-5
Featured Verse: Nehemiah 4:6 *So we built the wall and the whole wall was joined together to half its height, for the people had a mind to work.*

If I were smarter, I could… ! If I had more money, I would… ! If only I had a specific skill set, I might… ! Let us be honest, we are all guilty of making excuses. Excuses are a crutch we lean on to place blame on something or someone. They do not help us further our call or purpose in life. STOP IT! Right now! Instead, begin taking responsibility. While the rebuilding of the wall of Jerusalem was for protecting the city in moments of war, it was a project with a business plan, and we can all learn from that plan. Here are what I call the 'Production Steps' in Nehemiah's business plan:

1. Make a list of fifty-two tasks needing completed (Chapter 3).
2. Each day, pray against anything in your way (4:4-5).
3. Set your mind to work and divide up your list (4:6).
4. Celebrate your accomplishments along the way, even if you are only half done. It all still has a purpose (4:6).
5. Keep praying. Then adjust your plan when obstacles or people come against you (4:9, 21).
6. Organize your 'networking list' and know who your support system is (4:13, 5:16).
7. Tell yourself to not be afraid (4:14).
8. Take needed breaks, but do not live lazy (4:22).
9. Set your mind to never take advantage of people, and guard against others who do. Make fair trades, or pay (5:12).
10. Trust God for your provisions as Nehemiah did. He was the governor, but did not take a salary due to the high demand of the task on the people (5:14, 18).

In chapter three of today's Morning Rinse, I counted around fifty-two sections of the wall that were repaired. Does that number sound familiar? I hope so because there are fifty-two weeks in a year, making it easy to divide up our tasks! The people divided and conquered as well. And yes, some were not even qualified for the work. In fact, Nehemiah had a jewelry maker and a perfumer each in charge of a section (3:8). So no more excuses! Today, begin your production!

Today's Challenge To Dig Deeper:
Make a list of fifty-two tasks for your business, your call, or your purpose. Divide those fifty-two things up, one for each week of the year, and assign each item to your next year. Be flexible, but set your mind to start working. This will take a while, so spend some time working on it.

Evening Reflection:
What did you do today in your production steps?

PRODUCTION PART 2: STRENGTHEN MY HANDS

September 4

Morning Rinse: Nehemiah 6-8
Featured Verse: Nehemiah 6:9 *For all of them were trying to frighten us, thinking, "They will become discouraged with the work and it will not be done." But now, O God, strengthen my hands.*

This is too hard! They are lying about me! I am afraid! What if Nehemiah had bowed to fear? What if he had listened to those trying to distract him or lie about him? I will tell you what would have happened. The wall would not have been completed. The production would have halted. Opposers were so angry about what he was doing, they tried everything they could to stop him (6:1-4). They started rumors about him (6:5-8), and even tried to destroy his testimony by getting him to sin (6:13). There WILL be opposition doing the work of God. Will you bow to fear, or will you ask God to strengthen your hands? Here is part two of the Production Steps in Nehemiah's Business Plan:

1. Be mindful of any distractions. STAY FOCUSED (6:2-3).
2. Discern the lies about you. Do not stop the work (6:6-8).
3. Spontaneously pray when making decisions. Ask for strength to finish (6:9, 14).
4. Discern wrong counsel and stay on course (6:11).
5. Live with integrity in all your decisions to protect your character (6:13).
6. Do not let fear stop you (6:14).
7. Finish your list of 52 things. Side note: 52 days (6:15).
8. Set in motion to praise God (7:1).
9. Protect your work (7:2-3).
10. Begin the real work: the legacy of homes, renewed hearts, and restored peace (7:4, 8:1, 17).

After your project is completed, this does not mean you are finished. Once the wall was completed, the true legacy began. Homes needed to be built for the people, and the life of how God intended for them to live was set in motion. It was a new beginning of reformation in their hearts, as well as restoration of customs and traditions, all bringing praise to their hearts. This included a protection plan for the wall, by having each family guard the section in front of their home. Their legacy was set in motion, and it was all because of one man's obedience.

Today's Challenge To Dig Deeper:
What legacy are you building? God's plans for you are not just for the now, but for the future. Ask God to strengthen your hands as this legacy is built.

Evening Reflection:
What did you do today to keep your plans in motion?

A FAITHFUL HEART
September 5

Morning Rinse: Nehemiah 9-11
Featured Verses: Nehemiah 9:7-8 *You are the Lord God, who chose Abram and brought him out from Ur of the Chaldees, and gave him the name Abraham. You found his heart faithful before You, and made a covenant with him to give him the land of the Canaanite, of the Hittite and the Amorite, of the Perizzite, the Jebusite and the Girgashite – to give it to his descendants. And You have fulfilled Your promise, for You are righteous.*

Once the wall of Jerusalem was built, and various feasts and celebrations were restored to the lifestyle of the Israelites, the hearts of the people were also restored to a right relationship with God. This was manifested in several ways. First, they fasted (9:1). Second, they 'separated themselves from all foreigners' (9:2), which usually indicates getting new friends who are aligned with living a life of faith. The people began confessing their sins (9:2), and listened to the book of the Law of the Lord (9:3). Since the Bible was not in print, the people gathered to listen to it being read by one of the priests. Each day, for one fourth of the day, The Word was read (9:3). In today's Morning Rinse, the story of Abraham was read to the people. The priests read the history of his life, highlighting the fact he was not only chosen by God, but was faithful to answer the call. God found his heart faithful to Him. Therefore, God was able to fulfill His promise of the covenant. We need to be reminded of the faithfulness of others to stay encouraged to live our lives with a faithful heart. Faith without works is dead. We must do our part so God is able to do His. May our hearts be found faithful, just as Abraham's heart was found faithful.

Today's Challenge To Dig Deeper:
Is there any area of your life that inhibits your heart from being found faithful? Ask God for forgiveness, and take steps to correct it. Strive to have a faithful heart in all you do.

Evening Reflection:
What did God speak to you today about being found faithful?

THE MAKING OF A LEADER
September 6

Morning Rinse: Nehemiah 12-13
Featured Verses: Nehemiah 13:30-31 *Thus I purified them from everything foreign and appointed duties for the priests and the Levites, each in his task, and I arranged for the supply of wood at appointed times and for the first fruits. Remember me, O my God, for good.*

Once things were set in place, after the wall was rebuilt, Nehemiah went back to the king in Babylon. There are no clear reasons why he did not stay in Jerusalem, but we can assume either Artaxerxes needed him, or he wanted to keep his word by returning to his previous job. It is not clear how long he was there before turning around and going back to Jerusalem, but by the time he returned, corruption was rampant. Eliashib, one of the priests, had cleared out a room inside the temple and given it to Tobiah, one of the original opponents of the rebuild (4:3, 7, 6:1). To make matters worse, Tobiah was forbidden to even enter the temple due to being an Ammonite. Nehemiah also discovered some of the staff had to return to their old jobs because they were no longer getting paid, nor was the Sabbath being honored. This, among other things, slowly steered the customs of the people away from God's design. Of course, and rightfully so, this displeased Nehemiah (13:8, 10, 15). Leaders get accolades for the great accomplishments that come with their position, but oftentimes we forget the hard decisions they must make at times. Nehemiah was faced with making some of those hard decisions. He had to kick Tobiah out of the temple, bring back all the utensils and offerings, reprimand the officials for not paying people, and restore the Sabbath. His focus, honesty, integrity, ability to make tough decisions, and his life of constant prayer, provides us a picture of the qualities of a true, godly leader. Everything Nehemiah did glorified God. Being a leader is often a lonely lifestyle, and it is filled with opportunities to compromise one's values and standards. But if we surrender our lives to our Heavenly Father, He makes us into the leaders He needs. Nehemiah showed us this through his entire journey rebuilding the wall, including how he handled the opposition he faced after the rebuilding. A true leader relies on God, prays often, and builds others up through the journey. And through the journey of being a leader, he even shows us it is okay to ask God to remember the good choices we make when leading.

Today's Challenge To Dig Deeper:
Is God raising you up as a leader? Are there some hard decisions you need to make? Put those decisions into action today and watch God move on your behalf.

Evening Reflection:
Did you make any tough decisions today? What were they?

YOUR NAME IS IN HIS PLAN
September 7

Morning Rinse: Numbers 1-3
Featured Verse: Numbers 1:17 *So Moses and Aaron took these men who had been designated by name.*

The first time I read today's Featured Verse, my eyes read it to say, 'destined by name.' When I went back and reread it a second time, I felt a twinge of disappointment, I must admit. I like the word 'destined.' It feels more impactful or purposeful. But that is where I was wrong. Whether the word is written as 'destined' or 'designated' or 'specified,' as the NIV reads, we can be assured God took note of them and called them by name. The book of Numbers is a book that helps us see the side of God that is very orderly, systematic, and very intentional with details. We see these qualities in Exodus, as well, when He reveals the design plan for Moses and Aaron on how to build the tabernacle. In fact, God is a master mathematician, engineer, and leader. When reading the book of Numbers, we immediately see His orderly trait as He begins to instruct Moses and Aaron how to prepare the people to enter the promised land. The leaders that Moses and Aaron designate by name play a big part in helping prepare the people. This bigger plan included taking a census (1:2), implementing the layout of their camping site, and detailing where people stayed (2:2). It also included assigning tasks of responsibilities in how the tabernacle was managed. God is orderly and detailed, and He desires us to be as well, especially when we are preparing for our purpose. Preparation, just as we studied in Nehemiah, is vital to the success of our business plan, and God will show us how to do it. As we read through the book of Numbers, do not be tempted to skip over the details. Do not be tempted, like I was, to view words as less significant than they really are. Instead, take note of the detail and the fact that God is in it all, even in all the numbers listed throughout this book. The leaders mentioned in today's Morning Rinse had a purpose in the preparation. They were called out by name and set apart. Their names were in God's plan, just like yours is in His plan.

Today's Challenge To Dig Deeper:
Are you guilty of ever feeling insignificant in God's overall big plan? Today, take note that God is orderly, and He is intentional in His plan. He has designated your name to be a part of it. He has not forgotten you. Rest today knowing this, and get excited for your journey, for you are designated to have a role!

Evening Reflection:
What did God speak to you today about your name in His plan?

HEAVENLY RIPPLE EFFECT
September 8

Morning Rinse: Numbers 4-7
Featured Verses: Numbers 6:24-27 *The Lord bless you, and keep you; The Lord make His face shine on you, and be gracious to you; The Lord lift up His countenance on you, and give you peace.*

Today's Featured Verses include a prayer of blessing that reaches past a family bloodline. It is about heavenly blessings. With God's directive, Moses instructed Aaron and his sons to pray it over the Israelites when they were preparing the people to take the Promised Land. We all have an impact beyond our physical womb, and it is called a spiritual womb, which is a direct reflection of a 'Heavenly Ripple Effect.' This is when our lives impact people and generations far and wide. When we bless others, we are asking for God to give them favor, and impart kindness and mercy on their lives that is greater than what is due or even usual. It is favor beyond what we can imagine, and runs deeper than just a discount at a store or a decreased electric bill. If we truly grasp the blessings God has for us, we will walk in greater faith, stand with increased boldness, and speak with more power. This ultimately changes lives around us, expands our territory, and sets the Heavenly Ripple Effect in motion. This prayer that Aaron and his sons prayed over the Israelites can be prayed over our lives as well. Here are the five parts to this amazing blessing.

1. Bless and keep us (protect us).
2. Make His face shine upon us (be pleased with us).
3. Be gracious to us (kind and merciful to us).
4. Lift up His countenance (turn His face to us for approval).
5. Give us peace.

Today's Challenge To Dig Deeper:
Today's challenge is four-fold.

1. Look up the song "The Blessing," and listen to it as many times as you can. Get the words into your spirit.
2. Write today's Featured Verses on a card. Post it where you will be reminded of it.
3. Say this prayer over at least one person today.
4. Commit these verses to memory.

Evening Reflection:
Write about this blessing.

70 TO CARRY THE BURDEN
September 9

Morning Rinse: Numbers 8-11
Featured Verses: Numbers 11:16-17 *The Lord therefore said to Moses, "Gather for Me seventy men from the elders of Israel, whom you know to be the elders of the people and their officers and bring them to the tent of meeting, and let them take their stand there with you. Then I will come down and speak with you there, and I will take of the Spirit who is upon you, and will put Him upon them; and they shall bear the burden of the people with you, so that you will not bear it all alone."*

There is an old quote that says, "It's not what you know, but who you know." Another popular way to say this is "It's not who you know, but who knows you." Some view these statements with disagreement to their validity of truth, while others base their entire life on the merits of one or both. Regardless of the position you take, one thing is true. We must surround ourselves with those who are willing to help us carry our burdens. Moses complained to God about his burden of taking care of the people alone (11:14), and so God asked him to appoint seventy leaders who were prepared to help him. I do not know how many leaders were already established in his life, but out of those leaders and elders, seventy were gathered. God moves when we move. We must put action to our steps. Moses' first action was asking for help. His second action was obeying God's direction to make a list of the seventy. God then took the burden that was on him and divided it amongst those leaders. Who are your *seventy*, or *twenty*, or even *ten*, and are you a part of someone else's *seventy*? God asks all of us to help move His kingdom forward, and we cannot do it alone. What we are called to do will impact the world around us, whether that is to rise as a politician or start a business. Maybe it is to go into teaching or become a mechanic. God may be asking you to go overseas as a missionary or quit your career to be a stay-at-home mom. Whatever journey He has you on, you cannot do it alone. Nor can your friends do what they are called to do alone. Not only do we need our own *seventy*, but our friends do, too.

Today's Challenge To Dig Deeper:
Make a list of seventy people, or as many as you can, from your network who can help you with what is in your heart. Authentically connect with each of them over the next week. In your conversations with them, vocalize what is in your heart and the needs you have. Also, make yourself available to be on their list of *seventy*.

Evening Reflection:
Did you reach out to anyone on your list yet? If so, who was it and how did it go?

UNSTICK YOUR STUCK
September 10

Morning Rinse: Numbers 12-15
Featured Verse: Numbers 13:30 *Then Caleb quieted the people before Moses and said, "We should by all means go up and take possession of it, for we will surely overcome it."*

I once heard a sermon on faith centered around the story of the twelve spies. In that sermon, the pastor, whom I cannot remember his name, quoted, "A faith that can't be tested, can't be trusted." God pre-told Moses He was going to gift the land to the Israelites (13:2). This gift was a known promise and a distinct word from the Lord, and it was going to take a trustworthy faith to receive it. As we grow, God pushes us to move further with Him in our lives. He will test our faith, including testing us to see if we will do what it takes to receive what He has for us. Is our faith test-worthy, and ultimately trustworthy? Right before the people went in to possess the land, God instructed Moses to send twelve spies into the land to bring back a detailed description of what the land and the people there were like. Upon their return, after forty days, ten of the twelve spies brought back a report so bathed in fear, it caused a major setback in God's plan of gift giving. The message of these ten spies revealed they were stuck. Their bad report even described the Israelites as grasshoppers in comparison to the size of the inhabitants of Canaan (13:33), instilling their own fear onto the people. They were stuck in fear of the task of conquering the giants, instead of focusing on the gift and the gift Giver. Oh, how easy it is to let our mind forget the promise and wonder of the challenge, or focus on the giants instead of how big God is. But when we rely on God, our problems become the grasshoppers and we 'unstick our stuck,' passing the test of faith. Caleb and Joshua were the only two spies with test-worthy and trustworthy faith. We can see this in Caleb's message to the people in today's Featured Verse. These two men relied on God's Word and His promise, not on the hurdles to jump over to receive it. Be like Caleb and Joshua and remain unstuck when your faith is tested, even if everyone around you gives a different report, and their opinion is followed instead of yours.

Today's Challenge To Dig Deeper:
Are you going through a test of faith right now where the promise of God seems too big to receive? Commit to getting your faith unstuck. Believe God for His promise and what He has put inside your heart. Repeat today's Featured Verse several times today.

Evening Reflection:
Did you get unstuck today by your words and growth in faith?

WHAT COLOR IS YOUR BOW?

September 11

Morning Rinse: Numbers 16-19
Featured Verse: Numbers 18:6 *"Behold, I Myself have taken your fellow Levites from among the sons of Israel; they are a gift to you, dedicated to the Lord, to perform the service for the tent of meeting."*

From the short lessons in Sunday School to the deep sermons as an adult, we are taught the powerful story of Moses delivering the children of Israel out of Egypt. This story encompasses many challenges and hurdles he had to face, including Pharaoh and the plaques. We read of even more hurdles Moses had to overcome once the Israelites made it to the wilderness, like how to find food or a place to camp. Challenging moments were not new for Moses. But being used to them did not make it easier for him to face. His whole life seemed to encompass obstacles. He had to be keenly aware and wise with each decision he made. He also had to know the voice of God, and remain humble when obeying His voice. Despite being obedient to God's voice (17:11), and despite God declaring him as the humblest man on the whole earth (12:3), Moses had a ton of opposition from the Israelites, adding to the obstacles he had to overcome. At one point, two hundred and fifty leaders rebelled against him (16:2), accusing him of trying to overpower the people. Time and time again Moses faced challenging things. But oh the sweetness of God continually came through for him. How? God gave Moses people to help carry the load, calling them 'a gift.' When we obey God, walk in our giftings and talents, and use them for His glory, we are the gift. When we live for Him, we benefit the kingdom no matter what we do. Our giftings help carry the load, solve problems, and fulfill God's plan in the bigger picture. The question is, will you answer the call? Will you allow your giftings to be used to help your church and further the kingdom of God? Or will you stay on the pew or at home under the bushel. God wants to use you as a gift for someone else. When you are used, you allow the unwrapping of YOU as a gift. What color will your bow be? Mine is yellow.

Today's Challenge To Dig Deeper:
Have you been a pew sitter for far too long? Do you have gifts that are not being fully used? If so, ask God where He wants you to be used, and make steps to begin. Maybe that means calling a ministry leader and offering help. Start today and commit to being a gift.

Evening Reflection:
Write down your insecurities of using your giftings, but include your excitement about the journey.

WILL WE HEAR YOU ROAR?
September 12

Morning Rinse: Numbers 20-23
Featured Verse: Numbers 23:19 *"God is not a man, that He should lie, nor a son of man, that He should repent; Has He said, and will He not do it? Or has He spoken, and will He not make it good?"*

Today's Featured Verse is part of the blessing spoken over Israel by Balaam. Parts of this blessing is often quoted in sermons reminding us He is for us, too. Several days ago, we read examples of hurdles that Moses had to get past. As the story of his journey to the Promised Land continues to unfold, even more hurdles are revealed. First, the Israelites' hearts became sinful, and they began to loathe God's provisions. Thankfully, they repented, but the fact Moses even had to deal with these actions from the people is beyond grievous. There were also two separate kings who would not let the people pass peacefully through their land, causing physical roadblocks against the Israelites, leading to a battle. On top of these challenges Moses endured, there were some behind the scenes events occurring. Balak was bribing Balaam, a man known for his effective blessings and curses, to place a curse on Israel so they would not take his land. When Balaam arrives for this anticipated curse, instead of following through with what Balak requested, Balaam obeys God and blesses them. In that blessing, Balaam declares not even divination or curses can come against the Israelites, and he declares the people will rise as lions and lionesses and devour their prey (23:24). This makes Balak upset, and he tries to get Balaam to quit speaking. But God will not be silenced, nor his people cursed. In fact, He wants His people to claim this same blessing and roar. No matter what you may have done in your past or if you feel unworthy or inadequate, God has blessed you and will not revoke that blessing. Receive it and roar as the lion or lioness you are.

Today's Challenge To Dig Deeper:
Memorize Numbers 23:19-24.

Evening Reflection:
Did your spirit roar today as you claimed your blessing?

5 SISTERS AS LAW CHANGERS AND LEGACY MAKERS
September 13

Morning Rinse: Numbers 24-27
Featured Verses: Numbers 27:3-4 *"Our father died in the wilderness, yet he was not among the company of those who gathered themselves together against the Lord in the company of Korah; but he died in his own sin, and he had not sons. Why should the name of our father be withdrawn from among his family because he had no son? Give us a possession among our father's brothers."*

It may take only one act of courage to transform the legacy of your family and the legacy of even a nation. The case that Moses took before the Lord was a case brought to him by five sisters: Mahlah, Noah, Hoglah, Milcah and Tirzah (27:1). Moses had just completed a census of the men of Israel and their households. This was in preparation to divide up the land of Canaan for their inheritance based on the size of each tribe. According to the Hebrew law, only sons had the right to inherit. Since these five sisters had no brothers and their father had died, the law did not allow them to receive any land. Therefore, they had no place of inheritance. So they appealed this law and asked Moses to consider changing it. These five women courageously used their voice. Their request allowed God not only to guide Moses in changing the laws of inheritance for situations like theirs, but changing the laws in situations beyond what they brought to Moses. Their bravery influenced the laws also affecting men with no children at all (27:10), men with no brothers to give their inheritance (27:10), and even men with no children, brothers, or uncles. These five women were influential in changing legacies for all families who did not have a direct lineage of sons to receive their inheritance. We have not because we ask not. Has God placed a burden on your heart that could change the legacy of your family and families in your world for generations to come if you only asked Him? Be brave. Be like the five sisters.

Today's Challenge To Dig Deeper:
Be brave and ask God for something big and specific today. Ask Him.

Evening Reflection:
What did you ask God for today?

5 STEPS TOWARDS CONFLICT RESOLUTION
September 14

Morning Rinse: Numbers 28-32
Featured Verses: Numbers 32:5-6 *They said, "If we have found favor in your sight, let this land be given to your servants as a possession; do not take us across the Jordan." But Moses said to the sons of Gad and to the sons of Reuben, "Shall your brothers go to war while you yourselves sit here?"*

This scenario sounds like an argument is brewing. The children of Israel were on their last leg before crossing into the Promised Land. This was it! The eleventh hour. The moment they had been waiting for. Moses was ready to send the warriors over the Jordan River to begin the takeover. However, a curveball was thrown causing conflict in the camp that needed to be resolved. Here are the five simple steps to resolve conflict, found in this situation:

1. **Define the source of the conflict:** Moses had spent years preparing the children of Israel to take the land God had promised them. But the sons of Gad and the sons of Reuben wanted to live where they were currently camping (32:5).
2. **Look beyond the conflict and listen:** It appeared these men were not interested in helping the rest of the Israelites conquer their piece of the inheritance, which was unfair. Moses reminded them their fathers, from forty years prior, had discouraged the people from entering the land, which appeared to be exactly what these men were doing (32:8-13). Despite these concerns, Moses listened to them.
3. **Find solutions:** Sometimes finding solutions is easiest when you clear your head or take a break from the situation or conversation. We do not know how long the parties conversed with each other. But we do know the men left to privately problem solve and then returned to complete the conversation with Moses.
4. **Come up with acceptable solutions for both parties:** Upon the return to Moses, the sons of Gad and the sons of Reuben gave their word they would help conquer the rest of the land in exchange for inheriting the piece of land they were asking for (32:16-19).
5. **Agreement:** The contract negotiation, including the terms of breaching it, was agreed upon, showing both sides moved to a workable solution (32:21-25).

Today's Challenge To Dig Deeper:
Are you in a conflict, or a situation that needs resolving? Follow these five simple steps modeled by Moses, and strive towards peace.

Evening Reflection:
Did you make any headway towards a resolution with your conflict?

42 CAMPSITES
September 15

Morning Rinse: Numbers 33-36
Featured Verse: Numbers 33:48 *They journeyed from the mountains of Abarim and camped in the plains of Moab by the Jordan opposite Jericho.*

The book of Numbers covered thirty-nine years, and ends with the Israelites camping near the banks of the Jordan River. The Promised Land was in sight, and they were getting their final instructions from Moses before crossing the Jordan and taking the land. Based on the recordings of Moses (33:2), the journey up to this point included forty-two campsites (33:3-38). This was forty-two moves! Sometimes the Israelites would camp for a very short period, while other times they stayed at a location for potentially several years. For instance, it took quite a while to build the temple. Camping in one location for that entire season made the temple construction easier. But forty-two different moves is a lot of stops, and many were avoidable. If the ten spies had not sinned in their doubt of God's Word about possessing the land and caused doubt in the people, they would have been able to take the Promised Land earlier and avoid many of these campsites. So how is this applicable to us? We can use this entire book to learn lessons on how to avoid taking so long to receive God's promises in our lives. Unbelief is ruinous, sinful pleasures will be tragic, complaining causes grievances, and compromise leads to disaster. Receive your promise faster by trusting God, staying holy, being grateful for all you have, and commit to an unwavering life focused on God's standards and values. Avoiding mistakes like the Israelites made, will help us avoid nearly forty-two campsites in our life. I wonder how many campsites God had originally intended for them as He mapped out their journey. I wonder how many campsites we have created in our lives due to acting like the Israelites.

Today's Challenge To Dig Deeper:
If you have any doubt in God's promises or plans for your life, ask forgiveness. If you are struggling with any sinful pleasures, repent. If you are guilty of complaining, bite your tongue and speak gratefulness over your life. And finally, if there is any area in your life that you are compromising, turn from those ways and commit to having a godly focus. You changing your choices may very well circumvent avoidable campsites.

Evening Reflection:
What are some things about today's devotion that spoke to you and caused you to ponder some changes in your life that may be needed?

QUIT THE GLOAT
September 16

Morning Rinse: Obadiah 1
Featured Verse: Obadiah 1:12 *Do not gloat over your brother's day, the day of his misfortune. And do not rejoice over the sons of Judah in the day of their destruction; Yes, do not boast in the day of their distress.*

AH! Gloating can be so malicious. Especially if someone has satisfaction in the misfortunes of others. In today's Featured Verse, God warned the nation of Edom about their behavior, which included gloating when crisis hit Israel. Edom's hatred towards the people of Israel was so strong, they wanted the entire nation destroyed (Amos 1:11-12). So they betrayed Israel and assisted her enemies, even looting them and aiding in disaster. However, God warned them about their arrogance and treatment of His people, and He is very clear about His judgement towards them for their behavior (1:15). I tell my kids they can be confident there will most likely be someone in their lives who will not be a raving fan. There may even be someone who has evil intent for their lives. We cannot please everyone with our decisions, and we may even have some enemies who gloat when we struggle, or even aid in things going wrong in our lives. We may not ever experience the hatred Israel received from Edom, but anyone hating on and aiding in destroying a child of God is doomed for destruction. When enemies behave this way towards a Christ follower, God sees it and He will judge them. On the flip side, God asks us not to gloat when our adversaries struggle, even if they deserve it due to sin. It is no laughing matter when evil rules in someone's life. God does not like our adversaries gloating at us, nor does He want us to gloat at the enemies of His kingdom. If we stay focused on God, we will naturally refrain from this. Keeping our eyes focused on Him will help us remember God's heart, and remain confident those against His people will be judged.

Today's Challenge To Dig Deeper:
Do you have experience with gloating, whether someone has gloated over your misfortunes, or you have gloated over theirs? Follow God's heart and refrain from this practice. Repent and then let go of any bitterness towards anyone who has done this to you. Commit to keeping your eyes on Jesus and watch Him work in your life.

Evening Reflection:
Write down any thoughts about gloating from today's Morning Rinse.

FAITH MORE PRECIOUS THAN GOLD

September 17

Morning Rinse: 1 Peter 1-2
Featured Verses: 1 Peter 1:6-7 *In this you greatly rejoice, even though now for a little while, if necessary, you have been distressed by various trials, so that the proof of your faith, being more precious than gold which is perishable, even though tested by fire, may be found to result in praise and glory and honor at the revelation of Jesus Christ.*

One of the oldest methods of purifying gold is by melting it. This process is critical because it removes the impurities through heat. The temperature of the fire needed to accomplish this must be higher than a standard fire, which makes today's Featured Verses contain deep meaning for a Christ follower. There are several different methods of refining gold. Whatever method is used accomplishes the same thing in the end, pure gold. Pure gold is practically indestructible because it resists breakdowns by acids and other chemical reactions. Only a few things, such as chlorine water or bromine water, can corrode gold, and even then it takes a very long time. Since gold does not react to oxygen, it does not blemish, rust, or even deteriorate, reinforcing that there is no known natural substance that can destroy it. One fascinating thing about pure gold is it can be remelted and used repeatedly, reshaping it for new uses. No matter the use, though, it must go through the refining process to obtain purity. It must go through the fire to be melted and then shaped for its intended use. As valuable as pure gold is, God sees the testing of our faith as more precious than this metal, comparing it to the refining process of gold. Our faith will be put through the fire. We will experience trials and extreme pressure, or heat at times in our lives. This is the refining process of our faith, giving God an opportunity to remove impurities in our heart, such as fear, doubt, and unbelief. During our refining process, God will grow us. If we keep our eyes focused on Him and trust Him, our suffering and trials will not crush or destroy us. They will, instead, increase our faith. We were never promised a life void of hardships and challenges. We were, however, promised God would be with us through them. Will our faith pass the test of being tried?

Today's Challenge To Dig Deeper:
Each disappointment, test, trial, challenge, or hardship we face will be an opportunity for us to choose a response. Will we respond with trust? Or will we respond with frustration, gossip, and bitterness. Ask God to forgive those times of reacting in error. Choose to allow your faith to pass the test.

Evening Reflection:
What did God reveal to you about the testing of your faith?

HOSPITABLE INFLUENCE
September 18

Morning Rinse: 1 Peter 3-5
Featured Verse: 1 Peter 4:9 *Be hospitable to one another without complaint.*

One of my desires is to have a home my kids and their friends choose to hang out at, even in their adult years. My husband and I would rather create an environment they want to be in versus always hanging out at someone else's home. As they have grown up, we have learned how to make this happen. We have not always been successful, but we have gotten better through practice. When our kids became teenagers, this desire of ours as parents, grew. We knew our plan was working when their friends began driving to our house by choice. In fact, my son Ezekiel, has a group of six friends who enjoy hanging out together. They will often plan sleepovers which entail playing online games, eating pizza, munching on snacks, and falling asleep around 4 am. Much to our delight, this group of boys enjoy doing this at our home. During nice weather, it can be several times a month, making this long standing wish a reality. You would think I would be grateful. However, I recently found myself complaining to my son. Not because they come over, but because they are teenagers and have minimal regard to picking up. Shocking, right? Now, I understand it is perfectly acceptable to expect frequent guests to have some level of standards when in your home, like throwing trash away or putting blankets back where they were found. Reminding my son to help keep those standards with his friends is not being anti-hospitable. But complaining in an annoying fashion while reprimanding him in an unloving demeanor is. And that, I was guilty of. Boys will be boys. And just as this is true, a parent needs to be a parent. That means teaching standards in a loving way, and remembering the value of being hospitable, no matter the situation. Being hospitable is not about the host, but about the guest. You never know the influence you will have by creating a warm, hospitable, welcoming environment bathed in love and acceptance of those walking through your door. Cease from complaining and embrace your influence. You never know the environment your guests are coming from.

Today's Challenge To Dig Deeper:
Invite a person or family over to your home, not for a social gathering, but for a casual time of fellowship. Do not stress in the preparation, but keep your spirit open to the little things you will learn through this process.

Evening Reflection:
Write down who you are inviting, and any thoughts you have about the planning process.

8 CHARACTERISTICS OF GUARD DUTY
September 19

Morning Rinse: 2 Peter 1-3
Featured Verses: 2 Peter 3:17-18 *You therefore, beloved, knowing this beforehand, be on your guard so that you are not carried away by the error of unprincipled (wicked) men, and fall from your own steadfastness, but grow in the grace and knowledge of our Lord and Savior Jesus Christ. To Him be the glory, both now and to the day of eternity. Amen.*

Today's Featured Verses are Peter's last words communicated in all his letters. This great warrior knew how to fight, and he knew what it takes to faithfully end well. He had firsthand experience of pitfalls and temptations that can trip believers up. He knew how to stand guard, protecting from a moral or spiritual fall. This book conveyed many warnings to the church regarding these pitfalls, with his last two sentences summing up his entire message. Be on guard so you do not fall into evil, and keep growing in Christ until the very end. How do we guard against pitfalls like a warrior guards a city on his daily watch? How do we keep growing in Christ? In this little book, Peter shows us eight godly characteristics to guard in our walk with Christ (1:5-7). If we practice these things daily, and guard against temptation, we will not stumble (1:10):

1. Diligence (Guard against a lack of faith.)
2. Moral Excellence (Guard against lower standards than biblical ones.)
3. Knowledge (Guard against laziness in gaining spiritual understanding.)
4. Self-control (Guard against lack of discipline.)
5. Perseverance (Guard against giving up.)
6. Godliness (Guard against temptation.)
7. Brotherly Kindness (Guard against isolation.)
8. Love (Guard against not loving your neighbor as yourself.)

If we want to keep growing, guarding these characteristics must be our daily guard duty as a Christ follower. Allow God to work in these areas, while remaining humble and repentant.

Today's Challenge To Dig Deeper:
Imagine being dressed in warrior's armor. That is what it looks like in the spiritual realm. Put yours on. Ask God how He wants you to battle today. Is there a temptation to overcome? Is there a person He needs you to pray for or show kindness to? Be ready for His answer.

Evening Reflection:
Write down what God showed you about your daily duty of guarding.

HEART CHANGE
September 20

Morning Rinse: Philemon 1
Featured Verses: Philemon 1:8-9 *Therefore, though I have enough confidence in Christ to order you to do what is proper, yet for love's sake I rather appeal to you – since I am such a person as Paul, the aged, and now also a prisoner of Christ Jesus.*

What is Paul strongly appealing to Philemon about in this letter? He is asking for a heart change. Philemon was a wealthy man who owned slaves, one being Onesimus. Onesimus had stolen from him and ran off to Rome, which is where Paul was imprisoned at this time. Somehow, Onesimus connected with Paul, and in that interchange, Paul led him to Christ from his prison cell. The crime Onesimus committed against Philemon was worthy of death. However, Paul appeals to the heart of Philemon in this letter and asks him to forgive Onesimus. Paul was an elder and an apostle and could have easily used his position and authority to order Philemon to forgive him and accept him back. But Paul not only appealed to Philemon to do this, but he also asked Philemon to forgive Onesimus and see him as a brother in Christ. Paul requested a heart change of action in his forgiveness. He did not make this request because of who he was as a leader, but because of who Philemon was in Christ. Not everyone we forgive will be invited back into our inner world. But there are times when God will ask that. This is not the point of Paul's letter. The point is a heart change through forgiveness, even in those moments worthy of death. The heart change in this story is two-fold. The first heart change is with Onesimus when he became saved. The second heart change for us to celebrate is Philemon's when he forgave. Whatever side of the heart change you are on, celebrate it and surround yourself with those who celebrate the heart change with you.

Today's Challenge To Dig Deeper:
Do you need to forgive someone? Ask God to help you make a complete heart change through forgiveness. Ask God if they are to be part of your life again and in what capacity.

Evening Reflection:
Write down your heart change and what God spoke to you about regarding your relationship with the one you forgave.

THE BLESSING OF THE GIVER
September 21

Morning Rinse: Philippians 1-4
Featured Verses: Philemon 4:15-19 *You yourselves also know, Philippians, that at the first preaching of the gospel, after I left Macedonia, no church shared with me in the matter of giving and receiving, but you alone, for even in Thessalonica you sent a gift more than once for my needs. Not that I seek the gift itself, but I seek for the profit which increases to your account. But I have received everything in full and have an abundance; I am amply supplied having received from Epaphroditus what you have sent, a fragrant aroma, an acceptable sacrifice, well-pleasing to God. And my God will supply all your needs according to His riches in glory in Christ Jesus.*

The promise of God supplying all our needs is a promise made to the giver. We must give to receive. The Philippian church gave when no one else did. They sacrificed in helping Paul's ministry when no other church felt the need to do so. We cannot claim a promise to givers when we, ourselves, do not practice giving when there is a need. This type of giving is above our tithe. It is a lifestyle. May we all position ourselves to receive the blessing that Paul spoke over the Philippian church.

Today's Challenge To Dig Deeper:
What act of giving can you offer up today to meet a need? Find a need and supply it today. Is it paying for someone's lunch? Is it offering to watch the kids of a single mom so she can go to the grocery store alone? Is it sending money to a ministry? Be a giver and watch yourself, instead, become the receiver of God's blessings.

Evening Reflection:
What did you give today? In return, what did you receive?

LIFE-GIVER LEGACY
September 22

Morning Rinse: Proverbs 1-3
Featured Verse: Proverbs 3:18 *She is a tree of life to those who take hold of her, and happy are all who hold her fast.*

As each new year begins, it is quite common for people to individually claim an encouraging word that represents that year to them. Several times I have even claimed two words for my year. This word, or words, help mold and shape the attitude behind that year, and is meant to be an inspiration. But have you ever considered giving yourself a word to encompass your entire life? Today's Featured Verse is that verse for me. I have declared it as my life verse, or motto, and have claimed the word *life* as the word to be my life motto, or mission. I want this verse to be the center of who I am. A life-giver. I understand the 'she' Solomon is describing is wisdom. But that's just it. How do we pass on heavenly life to others without godly wisdom? Despite Solomon's failures, we can learn from him. This book we are now embarking on is full of wise instructions to not only adopt for ourselves personally, but to pass on to others. We do this by sharing the good news and what God has done in our lives. Solomon was not perfect, but the good news is that no matter what we have done in our past, we can start living a life of wisdom today, passing on life to others and forming our legacy. How? We can be an example in how we handle daily decisions, including struggles. Some examples would be in health, mentorship, and emotional support. We can also use wisdom to spread life by being an example of spiritual maturity, business aptitude and yes, even by being physically fit. Spreading life to others is a way of life. Being a life-giver is a legacy.

Today's Challenge To Dig Deeper:
First, do you have a word for your life mission? If not, pray God gives you one. Second, what are your ways to pass on godly wisdom and spread life and hope to others? Ponder these questions throughout your day.

Evening Reflection:
Did you come up with a life word for yourself? If so, write it down. Did you challenge yourself to be a life giver? How?

HE HELPS US RUN
September 23

Morning Rinse: Proverbs 4-7
Featured Verses: Proverbs 6:16-19 *There are six things which the LORD hates, yes, seven which are an abomination to Him: Haughty eyes, a lying tongue, and hands that shed innocent blood, a heart that devises wicked plans, feet that run rapidly to evil, a false witness who utters lies, and one who spreads strife among brothers.*

One of the quotes my children grew up hearing me say is "Live a life to where if anyone talks about you, no one believes it." How do we live this kind of a life? We seek wisdom and understanding, following God's heart in all our decisions. Solomon writes in the book of Proverbs how to do this. In this book, he lists fourteen behaviors God hates, and he warns us to run from these sins. When we run from them, we set the foundation to live a life of holiness and a life that speaks for itself, rather than a life spoken about in a negative fashion. Today's Featured Verses list seven of the fourteen. They include haughtiness (arrogance), lying, murdering, wickedness, eagerness to do evil, being a false witness, and stirring up strife. An eighth behavior God hates that we read in yesterday's Morning Rinse is violence (3:31). Knowing what to run from is the first step. While Solomon lays it out with simplicity, we still must fight our flesh against these things. We may not struggle with murder, but we may struggle with stirring up strife among fellow Christians. We may not struggle with arrogance, but may struggle with lying, or exaggerating stories to make someone look bad, or even have violent tendencies, even in our words. We may not struggle with pride, but we may struggle with sexual sin. God is present and longs to free us from behaviors that will hold us captive. He is here to help us run.

Today's Challenge To Dig Deeper:
Are there any behaviors you need to ask God to help you run from? If so, repent of those behaviors and ask God to help you run today.

Evening Reflection:
Were there any moments today where you had to run from a past behavior you knew would not please God? Maybe you were with fellow believers, and they began stirring up strife and gossip. Maybe you were tempted to lie about a situation to make yourself look better. Write down the situation and praise God for your running shoes.

ANSWER WISDOM'S PHONE CALL
September 24

Morning Rinse: Proverbs 8-10
Featured Verse: Proverbs 8:1 *Does not wisdom call, and understanding lift up her voice?*

I must admit, this morning when I got up to read the Morning Rinse and write this devotion, I wanted to skip. You see, today is a HUGE day in my life. Today is the day I am taking a test for my real estate Broker's License for the state of Missouri. It is a test that includes national questions as well as state law scenarios, and is not an easy test. I got up this morning hoping to immediately jump right in and keep studying for it. However, the nudge to stay faithful to my devotions would not shake. The Word kept calling me. So I laid my computer down and grabbed my Bible. I had to chuckle when I started the chapters for today. The first verse of the day was today's Featured Verse, and it speaks of wisdom calling us. God does not ever stop chasing us. No matter how full our day is, He will not stop trying to help us gain more insight into who He is. That is, if we ask for it. He wants to teach us wisdom and understanding, and He is everywhere. If we seek who He is, and seek His wisdom, we will find it. As we grow and learn each day, wisdom helps us live more righteously. And I am happy to report I passed the test, and now have my Broker's License in Missouri. Choose wisdom, answer its call, and your life will change.

Today's Challenge To Dig Deeper:
Look for opportunities to gain wisdom today. Wisdom is present whether in big decisions you need to make, or in small conversations in passing. Remain wise in all you do and say. Listen to His voice. You will learn what to do in each and every situation.

Evening Reflection:
Did any situation arise today that caused you to ask God for wisdom? Be known for seeking Him. It starts each day.

GOD'S CIRCLE OF LIFE
September 25

Morning Rinse: Proverbs 11-14
Featured Verses: Proverbs 13:12-13 *Hope deferred makes the heart sick, but desire fulfilled is a tree of life. The one who despises the word will be in debt to it, but the one who fears the commandments will be rewarded.*

My husband would often make a statement to our children during the years of raising them saying, "Every choice has a consequence. Depending on your choice, it will either be good or bad." Our choices determine where we are headed in life, and can often be predicted by the people we hang out with, the things we watch and the words we speak. If our choices are centered around God's ways, we will rotate around 'God's Circle of Life.' His ways will bring peace and joy instead of frustration and hopelessness. To hop in God's circle and begin this glorious rotation, the instructions are simple:

Step 1: Read The Word and learn God's ways on how to live.
Step 2: Obey God's instructions about what we read in The Word.
Step 3: Guard our mouth. One who is not careful, or has no filter, is setting themselves up for ruin (13:3).
Step 4: Blessings will come our way in our obedience, including desires of our heart being fulfilled.

Out of the four steps in the rotation of God's Circle of Life, three of them are controlled by us. We gain life through obedience and practicing wisdom. We then PRESERVE this life by guarding our mouth. Preserving our life is not just about living a long life. It is also about preserving our foundation of holiness, our testimony, and our integrity. Blessings will then come in our life from our obedience. The circle will keep rotating back around as we continue, repeating step one again. Daily reading, learning more, and living out God's ways on His Circle of Life is truly what this devotional is all about. Keep rotating, friends, and choose the blessed consequences.

Today's Challenge To Dig Deeper:
Purchase a blessing journal today. As you receive blessings from the Lord, begin writing them down every day. Look for even the little blessings God is passing your way.

Evening Reflection:
What are your thoughts about a blessing journal? Do you feel blessed?

WAITING AND WEIGHING
September 26

Morning Rinse: Proverbs 15-18
Featured Verse: Proverbs 15:28 *The heart of the righteous ponders how to answer, but the mouth of the wicked pours out evil things.*

So much of having wisdom links to how we use our mouth. Repeatedly, the book of Proverbs addresses how important it is to be careful what we say. The righteous wait on God and ponder what to say, being slow to speak. However, the wicked pours out evil from their mouth without thinking. This reminds me of a dam. Oftentimes, if a dam has a leak or even breaks, the damage from the released water can destroy lives, homes and even cities. We must learn to wait and speak what God would have us say, knowing the weight of our words will affect those who hear. We all have important things to say. But weighing our words is equally as important, making it better at times to stay silent. Think of the impact we would have if we all waited and weighed what we speak.

Today's Challenge To Dig Deeper:
Ask yourself the hard question, "Do I wait and weigh my words, or do I speak what is on my mind with little or no concern for the impact my words have on others?" This can be a hard question. If you have not mastered waiting and weighing, ask God to begin convicting you when you are tempted to leak or pour out words that need not be stated.

Evening Reflection:
Did any opportunities arise today that gave you the chance to wait and weigh? If so, describe what happened.

HEART IN A LOCKED BOX
September 27

Morning Rinse: Proverbs 19-21
Featured Verse: Proverbs 21:1 *The king's heart is like channels of water in the hand of the LORD; He turns it wherever He wishes.*

We often hear that God is in control of worldly leaders, and He is ultimately the one who puts them in their authoritative position to fulfill His plan and will. While this is often widely accepted, many believers still have a hard time understanding how God wants to take care of and guide our individual hearts. Yes, He absolutely gives us free will. But He is very concerned about our hearts, and wants to help mold them. Years ago, I made the free choice to enter a relationship with someone God had not approved of. I was disobedient. My heart ended up broken, hurt, and in need of much repair and healing. For several years, I battled trust issues, hopelessness, and unforgiveness. One morning, I was laying on my couch praying and asking Jesus to heal my pain. My mind's eye then saw a vision of Him sitting next to me listening to my prayers. I knew He heard my heart's cry. After He listened, He then asked me to do something very difficult. He asked me to hand Him my heart. I had already given Him my heart through salvation. But this was different. He was asking me to fully surrender in areas I had not yet done. I hesitated, not fully ready to do this. However, through His gentle guidance, I slowly released my heart and placed it in His outstretched hands. I then watched Him gently take my heart and put it in a box, lock the lid, and pull it close to His chest. I saw Him lovingly hug that box, as if to show me how much His heart cared for mine. That day began the onset of making better choices and trusting Him with my life. That day began my receiving God's healing ointment over my brokenness. That day was a springboard to a deeper trust in His big plan for me and my life's journey. If we believe God has the power over worldly leaders, and to move them if He wishes, how much more does He want to be a part of our individual lives? God is an individual God. He cares for you and me more than we will ever know, and He desires for us to fully surrender to Him. Give Him a chance to hold your heart in a locked box.

Today's Challenge To Dig Deeper:
Search your heart today. If God reveals any brokenness, unforgiveness, or hopelessness, hand your heart to Him in a moment of prayer. This will show your surrender to Him and help you trust Him with your life.

Evening Reflection:
Did you give God your full heart? Did you let go? How did it feel?

GUIDING THE BENT

September 28

Morning Rinse: Proverbs 22-25
Featured Verse: Proverbs 22:6 *Train up a child in the way he should go, even when he is old he will not depart from it.*

It is easy to view today's Featured Verse as an instruction to teach our children biblical truths. It is easy for a parent to use it as a foundation to study Bible stories together, encourage Bible memorization, and for staying faithful to church attendance, knowing we are training up our children. This verse can even be encouraging for a parent with a wayward child who is believing for the promise of their return to a heart of faith. While this meaning can be accurate to an extent, it goes deeper. I believe it means parents are to help discover a child's true 'bent,' or strength, and use their influence to call it forth, encouraging opportunities to train in it. When I was growing up, my dad would often call my siblings and I to the stage, handing us a microphone for various opportunities to serve. He would ask us to sing a song, play our instruments, give a testimony, or even to pray. I was the introvert of our family and did not always feel comfortable in large crowds or having the spotlight. Even to this day, I get nervous before crowds at times. However, I now see how God used my dad to bring out the bents inside of me, even from an early age, that guided my aspirations in adulthood. My dad probably never knew his influence with this verse, because our stage presence was part of what we did as a pastor's family. Now that I am an adult, I realize even more that we as adults have a responsibility to speak into the younger generation and bring out their giftings, bents, or strengths, just like my dad did for my siblings and I. My brother now is a pastor, I am a speaker and entertainer, and my younger sister is a teacher. When we are bringing out the bents of the younger generation, it will obviously include any children we have, but should also extend to youth we mentor or speak into in any capacity. Getting to know the younger generation is not just about knowing them as a person, but learning what their strengths are so they can use them for God's kingdom. May we take our responsibility seriously in guiding the bent of youth.

Today's Challenge To Dig Deeper:
What youth do you have in your life that you can help guide to know their bent? Today, reach out to them and tell them what you see in them. If you have a strong influence over their lives, begin a dialogue with them about how they can use these giftings for the future, and help start creating a path for excellence in that area.

Evening Reflection:
Write down any conversations you had today with the youth in your life.

SHARPENED SHARPENER
September 29

Morning Rinse: Proverbs 26-28
Featured Verse: Proverbs 27:17 *Iron sharpens iron, so one man sharpens another.*

Sharpening materials such as iron, is typically done by grinding the rough or dull parts away. When it comes to our Christian walk, we too can become sharper by allowing rough or dull parts of our lives to be ground off. How is this done? Of course, by reading The Word and allowing it to change our lives. But it can also be done when we, as believers, help each other grow in faith by living an example through our actions, words, and deeds. This is iron sharpening iron in our faith walk. How we live our lives will make a powerful impact in sharpening others in the Lord. Not only can we do this by our personal example, but by words of encouragement, speaking truth, and lovingly correcting when others are living with sinful choices, bad habits or negative thought patterns. The sharper and more polished we are individually for God's kingdom, the brighter we will shine His light to the world. And as we grow individually, ultimately this will spread to the entire body of Christ, making us stronger as a sum. It is known when iron sharpens iron, both subjects are changed. So just as we must be willing to be an example to others, we must be willing to be sharpened ourselves. We must remain teachable and humble, staying open to godly correction and wise counsel. Being the recipient of sharpening as well as being the sharpener are true examples of how God desires us to be in community. We need each other. Being in community will strengthen, encourage, instruct, and ultimately help us all stay sharp until we finish the race set before us. Commit to being a sharpened sharpener.

Today's Challenge To Dig Deeper:
Has there been a recent interchange with someone who tried to sharpen you, but you did not receive it with humility? Did you get offended, inhibiting a full correction from the Lord? Quickly repent and ask the Lord to help you make it right. Commit to being a sharpened sharpener.

Evening Reflection:
Write down any thoughts about becoming a sharpened sharpener.

THE BEAUTY OF CHARACTER
September 30

Morning Rinse: Proverbs 29-31
Featured Verse: Proverbs 31:10 *An excellent wife, who can find? For her worth is far above jewels.*

It is wonderfully appropriate for Solomon to end the book of Proverbs by describing the characteristics of the infamous Proverbs 31 Woman. I have witnessed some people viewing her as compliant, domestic, and homely. However, this is simply not true. In fact, this woman is not only a fantastic family member (31:10, 21), but she is trustworthy (31:11), loves to work (31:13), looks for good deals (31:14), makes wise financial investments (31:16), strives to live a healthy lifestyle (31:17), and gives to those in need (31:20). She is also a fashion designer (31:22), an entrepreneur (31:24), has a positive attitude (31:25), speaks with kindness and uses her words wisely (31:26), is not lazy (31:18, 27), and is known for her creative ideas (31:31). While she may live a life full of fascinating achievements, her honor does not come from her accomplishments. It comes from her fear of the Lord (31:30), witnessed from her lifestyle of wise choices. Another thing to note in the description of the Proverbs 31 woman, is her appearance is never mentioned. Her beauty comes entirely from her character. I love that this woman is a visionary and constantly looks for ways to better not only her life, but the lives of those around her. Through the years of studying Proverbs 31 and striving to be like her, I am continually reminded I am a work in progress, never fully achieving all areas described in these verses. However, there may be several areas I have mastered on my journey, and of course, there are women in my life who also excel in areas listed in her description. Back in 2017, I began a list. This list encompassed each verse from Proverbs 31:10-31. Not all verses have a name next to it yet, but those that do, have the name of a woman in my life who exemplifies the characteristics of that verse. The Proverbs 31 woman is truly a picture of a community of women compiled together with their strengths completing the big picture of what a godly woman should look like. The list is not a list of dos and don'ts, but a list of women who focus their lives on looking to God. May we all be on The List.

Today's Challenge To Dig Deeper:
Make a list of the verses from Proverbs 31:10-31. Write the names of women in your life who fulfill that specific verse by their lifestyle. Contact them and let them know they are on your list and what verse you connected them with. Give them honor for their godly characteristics. Then if you are a woman reading this devotion, think of one or two verses that you want to strive to excel in.

Evening Reflection:
How did it make you feel, or make the women in your life feel, as you shared with them their name is on your list?

October Rinsing

KINGDOM REVELATION
October 1

Morning Rinse: Psalms 1-3
Featured Verses: Psalm 1:1-3 *How blessed is the man who does not walk in the counsel of the wicked, nor stand in the path of sinners, nor sit in the seat of scoffers! But his delight is in the law of the Lord, and in His law he meditates day and night. He will be like a tree firmly planted by streams of water, which yields its fruit in its season and its leaf does not wither; And in whatever he does, he prospers.*

What a way to start our journey in the Psalms. These first few verses give us powerful insight into obtaining a kingdom revelation encompassing wisdom and knowledge. These insights are:

1. Do not walk in the counsel of the wicked.
2. Do not stand in the path of sinners.
3. Do not sit in the seat of scoffers.

Imagine sitting in a seat surrounded by friends and associates who do not live by God's word. Maybe they openly go against biblical standards, steal from the office, or are having an affair. At this meeting, you are explaining to them about a business decision you must make and are seeking advice. While having this meeting, an attendee begins to make subtle suggestions that go against the moral compass of God's word. Another makes a rude remark about faith and standards. And then, another begins to speak with ill will of those who follow rules. If one is sitting at the feet of those living with ungodly standards, they cannot also be sitting at the feet of Jesus obtaining His advice. We must choose our friends and those who counsel us wisely. Humbly sitting at the feet of Jesus and being counseled by those living a godly life, will set us up for staying on a righteous path. His peace will overshadow any confusion in our decision making. As we live out wise choices, we will learn to delight and love God's Word and standards, setting us up to prosper in all we do. This does not mean we will be rich or famous. This does mean, however, we will see God's fruit manifesting in our lives. This fruit is the by-product and result of living a life pleasing to Him, gaining His approval.

Today's Challenge To Dig Deeper:
Do you have any friends or associates that you need to reconsider accepting counsel from? Even if they are Christ followers, sometimes they can still scoff and gossip. Have a heart-to-heart with God about your friends, and begin making changes if He leads you in that way.

Evening Reflection:
How did this first day of reading Psalms help guide you on a path of kingdom revelation, gaining wisdom and understanding?

WHO OR WHAT ARE YOUR FOES?
October 2

Morning Rinse: Psalms 4-6
Featured Verse: Psalm 5:8 *O Lord, lead me in Your righteousness because of my foes; Make Your way straight before me.*

I have never experienced someone hunting me down to kill me, nor do I personally know anyone in this situation. I have felt threatened for my safety a few times, but nothing this severe. This does not mean I do not have enemies or foes in my life. Anything that tries to keep us from God's perfect will, whether that is Satan himself, distractions in life, or our bad habits, can be considered a foe. Other examples are unnecessary tasks, toxic relationships, or worrisome burdens. These all can cause us to turn our focus away from the peace and direction of God. They can be our enemy when trying to do God's perfect will. Recognizing these types of foes can be life empowering and life enriching. Once we recognize that they are sucking God's plan from our lives, we can work to gain the victory over them, praying the dynamic prayer that David prayed, "Make Your way straight before me."

Today's Challenge To Dig Deeper:
Keep your spirit open to the prompting of the Holy Spirit. Ask Him to reveal any foes that are distracting you. Maybe it is a toxic relationship. Maybe it is laziness. Maybe it is something on your to-do list. Whatever God reveals, ask Him to rid you of the foe, and give you clear vision for the straight path ahead.

Evening Reflection:
Write down the revelation God gave you about foes in your life and the action today of getting rid of them. What changes have you made to keep yourself on the straight path?

A LOVE SONG AND A PROMISE
October 3

Morning Rinse: Psalms 7-9
Featured Verses: Psalm 9:1-2 *I will give thanks to the Lord with all my heart; I will tell of all Your wonders. I will be glad and exult in You; I will sing praise to Your name, O Most High.*

It is strongly speculated that David wrote the words in today's Featured Verses after winning a battle with the Philistines. It is certainly easy to express gratitude to God after moments of victory such as this. God wants us to succeed, and it is okay to be joyful about great achievements in life. Just like David, having a heart of praise should be a way of life. When our hearts convey an attitude of thankfulness to God, it expands our love towards Him, developing into a daily love song. You do not have to win a large battle or complete a successful event for this love song to be sung. A habit of praise can be developed even in celebrating the smaller blessings that may easily go unnoticed. For example, a song of praise can be sung when victories come such as finding lost keys or finishing a walk right before a thunderstorm begins. Forming a habit of thanking God for even the little things in life that He does for us, will ultimately increase our understanding of who He is. We will then become more aware of His presence around us. This is the ultimate love song. If we take this daily love song one step further, we can be like David and promise to sing this song no matter what we go through. Is this a promise we are willing to make to our Creator? God sent His Son to die for us. In that death, we have life. There is nothing more honoring than praising the One who gave that life to us.

Today's Challenge To Dig Deeper:
As you go through your normal everyday formalities, be mindful of God's presence, and thank Him for even the little blessings in life. Become faithful in singing a love song to Him, and make a promise to continue to give thanks to Him. Also, start today by telling two people of something He has done for you.

Evening Reflection:
Did you find yourself intentionally thanking God more frequently today? After thanking God for the blessings He has given you, did you find yourself more grateful, more positive, more hopeful, and more faith-filled?

HONEST EMOTIONS
October 4

Morning Rinse: Psalms 10-12
Featured Verse: Psalm 12:1 *Help, Lord, for the godly man ceases to be, for the faithful disappear from among the sons of men.*

As my oldest daughter, Haley, was walking through the dining room one afternoon, the sound of an impact caught my attention. I quickly turned and saw her wrenched in pain, and realized she had collided with the table, stubbing her little pinky toe. Captured in that two-second movie being displayed before my eyes, she yells while holding her foot, "JESUS!" She chuckled with a semi-smile on her face, merely because that is how she often handles tension. After the pain subsided, we giggled together, and she was able to resume assisting me with dinner. I have always loved the fact that, amid her agony, her first response was calling out His name. All through today's Morning Rinse, we read about David's honest emotions through his agony. His emotions ranged from pain, to doubt, fear, and despair. These same emotions can be seen throughout the entire book of Psalms, no matter who the psalmist was, and is a prime example of why the psalms are so powerful. These honest emotions show us what a wonderful friendship we can have with God, never having to hide our feelings when we are struggling. Despite our fear or doubt, we can see throughout the psalms, the writers are still very comfortable crying out for help, knowing God is always there. Time and time again, God meets them where they are and answers their cry. Along with the honest emotions of despair, we see another common reaction. No matter the outcome of their struggles, the psalmists sing in praise for who He is. Their honest emotions eventually turn to joy, praise, and thanksgiving for who God is. So while we may be struggling, do not forget to do what David did during his honest emotions. May we never forget to cry out "Help, Lord!"

Today's Challenge To Dig Deeper:
Be honest today with your struggles. Find a quiet place and sit alone with God, sharing how you are feeling and do not hold back. Ask for help and let Him answer your cry.

Evening Reflection:
Were you completely honest with God today? Did you ask Him tough questions, or share with Him your hurts? How did it make you feel?

TIGHTEN THE SHIP
October 5

Morning Rinse: Psalms 13-15
Featured Verses: Psalm 15:1-5 *O LORD, who may abide in Your tent? Who may dwell on Your holy hill? He who walks with integrity, and works righteousness, and speaks truth in his heart. He does not slander with his tongue, nor does evil to his neighbor, nor takes up a reproach against his friend; In whose eyes a reprobate is despised, but who honors those who fear the Lord; He swears to his own hurt and does not change; He does not put out his money at interest, nor does he take a bribe against the innocent. He who does these things will never be shaken.*

While following the Ten Commandments is a common standard of living and sets guidelines for the foundation of obedience, the bar of living with integrity as a Christ follower is actually higher than these commandments. God wants more for our lives than just following those ten basic rules, and it starts with the little decisions we make in life. I use the analogy of a ship. When a captain makes the slightest turn of the wheel, it changes the angle of the rudder, turning it in a direction that could lead to miles away from the original destination. Each day, we can keep our ship on the right path by making the right choices. In these five little verses, David wrote ten guidelines to help keep our ship tight:

1. Walk with integrity (be blameless in everything).
2. Live righteously.
3. Speak truth.
4. Do not verbally slander (smear or insult).
5. Do not do anything wrong to a neighbor.
6. Do not criticize a friend.
7. Honor those who fear the Lord.
8. Keep your promises, even if it is hard.
9. Do not charge interest to the needy.
10. Do not take a bribe against the innocent.

We all can do better. It may mean adjusting who is in our inner circle of friends, or making that promise from years ago right again. The little decisions we make provide us the opportunity to either stay lukewarm with our standards, or tighten the ship we steer. Which will you choose?

Today's Challenge To Dig Deeper:
Do you need to tighten your ship? Underline these ten guidelines in your Bible and ask God how you can begin the tightening process.

Evening Reflection:
Did God show you areas to tighten your ship? Write how that conversation with Him went.

AFFIRMATIONS OF FAITH
October 6

Morning Rinse: Psalms 16-18
Featured Verse: Psalm 18:49 *Therefore I will give thanks to You among the nations, O Lord, and I will sing praises to Your name.*

Our words have the power to not only transform the lives of others, but also transform how we think and feel about ourselves and our faith in God. Studies show our brain will eventually begin to believe and affirm the words we speak, despite whether they are based on lies or truth. When facing challenging circumstances or roadblocks, if we are not faith driven in our words, we can destroy relationships, and hinder our faith in God. Nearly every psalm shows us the writer faced challenges, and yet it is also very clear they believed in positive affirmations. Simply put, a positive affirmation is a statement to challenge a negative thought. Along with the two in today's Featured Verse, here are a few more positive affirmations in the psalms:

1. I will surely tell the degree of the Lord (2:7).
2. I will not be afraid of ten thousands of people (3:6).
3. I will order my prayer to You and eagerly watch (5:3).
4. I will be glad and exult in You (9:2).
5. I have trusted in your lovingkindness (13:5).
6. I have set the Lord continually before me (16:8).
7. I have purposed that my mouth will not transgress (17:3).

How does one develop a positive affirmation?

1. Identify your personal roadblocks.
2. Create a positive statement challenging your roadblocks.
3. Write it down in present tense.
4. Begin with the word 'I' to make it personal.

A positive affirmation, for example, to challenge the roadblock of stress and lack of peace would be, "I feel at peace today no matter what I face."

Today's Challenge To Dig Deeper:
Skim through the last 18 psalms, and underline all the positive affirmations you can find, including the nine I have provided for you. Continue underlining the affirmations as we read through the psalms. Now, write ten affirmations for yourself. Say them out loud several times. Repeat and add to the list as often as you need.

Evening Reflection:
Say your personal affirmations one more time before you go to sleep. This daily practice will teach you how to become an affirmer of faith for both yourself and for others. Write down your thoughts.

A CHANGE OF HEART
October 7

Morning Rinse: Psalms 19-21
Featured Verse: Psalm 20:4 *May He grant you your heart's desire and fulfill all your counsel (purpose)!*

Have you ever prayed your heart's desire, but later discovered the prayer you so fervently took to God was different from HIS desire? I have. As I looked through my notes from the psalms from former studies, I came across a prayer from decades ago that I am not proud of. There was someone in my life who caused me a great deal of pain. I had been studying the book of Psalms during that time of trial, and admit that my past notes revealed I had prayed for this individual to be completely removed from my life. I even connected today's Featured Verse to the desires of my heart, writing it down in my three-ring binder. The reality is, while this individual is no longer embedded into my world, my heart's desire from years ago did not get met by a complete removal. Instead, my heart's desire changed. While I wrote that prayer out of a pure heart and was living for God, what I wrote grieved me as I read it years later. It was a harsh prayer, and one I would not want my children reading if they found my notes after I go to heaven. Now, I am fully aware that David prayed for his enemies to be destroyed. But those enemies were out to kill him. Most people in our lives do not send an army to hunt us down, or chase us across deserts, over mountains, and through caves. There will probably always be, however, people who hate God, and will remain at an arm's length to us. Are we to have the heart's desire for their complete removal from our lives, or will there be times that God wants something different? In my case, the removal was not feasible, and over time, God graciously changed the desire of my heart. I have evidence of that change. Does that mean I was wrong years ago? I cannot say. But I know now that it would have been wrong to have received my heart's desire, and God knew that. As we stay in The Word and continually live a life for Jesus, He changes our heart's desire to take the shape and desire of His heart. This will ultimately leave the fleshly parts in the past. I crossed out that former prayer, and now my heart's desire is for the salvation of this individual. Let us pray the desires of our hearts mold into what His desires ultimately are for our lives.

Today's Challenge To Dig Deeper:
Pray today that every desire in your heart aligns with God's desire, even if changing your mind about a situation is hard.

Evening Reflection:
Did God reveal any changes in your heart's desire He wants to do in your life? It may seem hard at first, but truly as He molds your heart, the desires will become easy as you align with what God wants for your life.

PRETENDER TO A SURRENDERED ASCENDER
October 8

Morning Rinse: Psalms 22-24
Featured Verses: Psalm 24:3-4 *Who may ascend into the hill of the Lord? And who may stand in His holy place? He who has clean hands and a pure heart, who has not lifted up his soul to falsehood and has not sworn deceitfully.*

I looked down at the call log on my phone and discovered my conversation had lasted over two hours. Through pain, tears, heartache, and discovery, a dear friend had helped me work through several challenging issues that had led to my low self-worth. Admittedly, I had allowed someone to be a pretender to me. I had shunned God's signals and still, small voice that whispered words of warning. Yes, this friend is a Christ follower. However, her struggles of insecurity slowly became a lack of loyalty coupled with the pretense of a faithful friend. I should have surrendered to the signs. Jesus knows this feeling of heartache. Many people claiming to be Christ followers are, in actuality, a pretender of the faith. Pretenders will never reach the top of the hill of the Lord, or the Mount of God. Why? Because pretenders allow things in their life that keep them from a complete surrender to God. But there is another way. There is the way of the surrendered ascender. Pretenders allow the deception of lies to overtake friendships, purpose, and pure love. Ascenders walk in truth, living authentically, real, and honest. Pretenders live for selfish gain, idolizing those who they think will further their cause, and they will trample on those who seem to be in their way. Ascenders live with a pure heart, allowing instead for God to clear the path for them. Pretenders bruise relationships with insecurities and lies. Ascenders walk in love and truth, valuing people. Pretenders gossip. Ascenders take thoughts captive. Pretenders live a life of pride. Ascenders live a life of humility, repentance, and prayer. Who do others say you are?

Today's Challenge To Dig Deeper:
What changes do you need to make to become a surrendered ascender? Do you need to wean from a friend like I did? Is there something else you need to do? Ask God for help in becoming a surrendered ascender.

Evening Reflection:
What changes did you begin making today in your life as a surrendered ascender?

KEEP SINGING
October 9

Morning Rinse: Psalms 25-27
Featured Verse: Psalm 25:8 *Good and upright is the Lord; therefore He instructs sinners in the way.*

Simply put, God teaches us to be good and upright because He is good and upright. Daily, He longs to teach us and mold us, especially when we mess up. Of course, we will not be able to learn His way of living if we are not willing to listen and obey. So He will teach us IF we are teachable. It is easy to condemn ourselves when we sin or do something that displeases Him. But He has committed to guiding us even when we mess up. There have been moments in my growth when I have felt like I messed up so bad I was not worthy or 'holy' enough to even worship on a Sunday morning. I remember a few times I felt like I did not even have a right to lift my hands or sing the songs with the worship team. These negative thoughts are lies of our soul and keep us from staying connected to God and accepting His love. But He knows our struggles. He knows we may have times of feeling insecure. He knows we are not perfect and will mess up occasionally. So David reminds us that God will keep instructing us in the right way. God desires to stay close to us, His children. Do not let the enemy of your soul tell you anything different from this truth. Keep accepting God's love, even when you mess up. Stay humble. Stay teachable. Stay committed to learning His ways. Keep singing.

Today's Challenge To Dig Deeper:
Have you recently messed up and feel you are not worthy to accept God's love or even sing the songs in church? Even if your error was small, it has the potential to affect your heart if you let those lies speak louder than the truth of God. Lay shame aside, sing a worship song today, and feel God's love.

Evening Reflection:
How was your singing today? Just as Jesus loved those who followed Him during His time on earth, He loves us.

EYES TO HEAR AND EARS TO SEE
October 10

Morning Rinse: Psalms 28-30
Featured Verse: Psalm 29:5 *The voice of the Lord breaks the cedars; Yes, the Lord breaks in pieces the cedars of Lebanon.*

During David's time, the mountains of Lebanon were filled with cedars of the best quality. He used them to build his palace (2 Samuel 5:11, 7:2). They were also acquired when building the temple (Ezra 3:7), as well as when Solomon built his Palace of the Forest of Lebanon (1 Kings 7:2). These cedars were a source of wealth, and symbolized power and prosperity, making them a coveted resource as a magnificent source of timber. They could reach as high as 130 feet and as large as 8 feet in diameter. But no matter what we value on the earth, such as the extreme value that cedar trees had, God's voice is still more powerful. David reminds us His voice can even split these enormous cedars in half. Can you imagine having a voice that shakes the earth, or causes mountains to move? If we listen, we can hear His voice throughout nature, and we can see His wonders across creation. David tells us of many ways we can hear Him. We hear His voice in the clapping of waves or the crashing of thunder. We hear Him in the birth of a baby animal or the many sounds of the forest. His voice is everywhere. Do you hear it? Can your eyes see the presence of it? Whether God speaks with a whisper or a shout, everything He says has meaning and purpose, even in nature. Sometimes God wants us to open our eyes so we can *hear* His voice around us more clearly. And sometimes we are to open our ears and hear the clapping of those waves, so we can *see* more of His glory. May we open our ears and see, and may we open our eyes and hear.

Today's Challenge To Dig Deeper:
Look around you today with a new set of ears and eyes. Be intentional and seek out the majesty of God in everything around you. Hear His voice. See His voice.

Evening Reflection:
Write down instances from today where you noticed His voice in the things around you that you did not notice before. Was there anything you learned about His voice while listening and seeing?

REJOICE WITH PROTECTIVE WEAR
October 11

Morning Rinse: Psalms 31-33
Featured Verses: Psalm 33:20-21 *Our soul waits for the Lord; He is our help and our shield. For our heart rejoices in Him, because we trust in His holy name.*

The enemy lifts his oversized bow and fires a steel arrow at Wonder Woman. She happens to see the thrusted weapon shot at her and lifts her shield, protecting herself from what could have killed her. When she does this, she blocks the very sight of the weaponry, but trusts her shield. I also think of other shields, like a metal helmet and padded vest that an umpire wears during my middle daughter, Micaiah's, softball games. I have, on more than one occasion, witnessed an umpire getting struck with a softball launched in their direction. Even though they are wearing protective gear, those rapid whacks to their head or chest can still cause a jolt of pain. While these examples of protective shields stop the full impact of an object from doing deep damage, both the protective gear worn by Wonder Woman and the shields worn by umpires help safeguard from a detrimental injury. God is like these shields. He is ready to protect us from increased damage the enemy wants to inflict on us, as Christ followers. We can still feel pain when life throws a curveball at us, or the enemy shoots a dart our way. There are still times when our armor takes a hit, causing suffering or discomfort. We are not promised a life free of struggles. But we are promised He will be present, shielding us and easing our pain. When we are faced with grief, life's challenges, and even attacks from the enemy, He sees us and hears our cries, just like He heard the cries of David. If we keep our eyes on HIM, though, just like Wonder Woman hides her eyes with her shield, we will often be protected from even seeing the darts our eyes are not meant to see. Despite the darts that are meant to hurt us, rejoice in Him for He is holy. Rejoice in Him because His lovingkindness is upon us. Rejoice in Him because of the hope He gives us. Be like David and rejoice.

Today's Challenge To Dig Deeper:
Do you feel the enemy's weapons trying to hurt you? The challenge today is to rejoice, no matter the darts heading your way. Turn your eyes to God and rejoice in Him for who He is. Even if you are having a hard time feeling rejoiceful, rejoice anyway.

Evening Reflection:
Write down how it felt to rejoice despite what you are going through. Write down what it felt like to rejoice because of who God is.

PRAY FOR YOUR JIMMY
October 12

Morning Rinse: Psalms 34-36
Featured Verses: Psalm 35:11-14 *Malicious witnesses rise up; they ask me of things that I do not know. They repay me evil for good, to the bereavement of my soul. But as for me, when they were sick, my clothing was sackcloth; I humbled my soul with fasting, and my prayer kept returning to my bosom. I went about as though it were my friend or brother; I bowed down mourning, as one who sorrows for a mother.*

A quiet sixth grader sits alone on the playground swing, when the school bully, Jimmy, walks up with his two minions and gruffly declares, "You're next. Meetin' you in the alley after school today." For the remainder of the day, fear grips her heart and worry engulfs her every thought. After school, she gathers her younger sister and the kids her mother babysits, and leads them on their walk home. She is the timid one of this group of young kids. But she is also the oldest, and is responsible for getting them safely through the fence of her yard each day after school. As they approached the dreaded alley, Jimmy and his friends appear from behind a bush. With sleeves rolled up and determination on his face, he begins harassing her with the intent of harm. He throws his first punch, knocking her down on the ground. With the adrenaline rushing inside of every cell in her body, she rears one of her legs up into the air and kicks him with as much strength as she can muster, causing him to retract his attack, but only for a moment. More hits come. Jimmy's minions cheer him on while the kids scream out in fear. I will never forget that day. That quiet sixth grader was me. I have no idea why I was next on Jimmy's target list. But thankfully, a neighbor heard the commotion and ran up the street. He waved his belt in the air and warned Jimmy and his friends of the consequences if they ever tried to harm any of us again. And of course, when my dad heard about it, Jimmy's parents were contacted. Scholars believe that David wrote today's Featured Verses when he was being hunted down by Saul (1 Samuel 24). Throughout the psalms, David never tries to bring revenge himself, but prays for God to bring justice to his enemies. In fact, he prays for his enemies like they are his friend or brother. He even prays for them in the same way one mourns for their own mother. He does not just say a one-time prayer either. He is burdened to pray for them continually. I have often wondered what became of Jimmy. What about the Jimmies in your life?

Today's Challenge To Dig Deeper:
I think we all have a Jimmy or two. Maybe your Jimmy has not physically attacked you like mine did. But maybe he has condemned you, gossiped about you, or has tried to halt your blessings. Today, pray for your Jimmy like you would pray for a friend or close family member.

Evening Reflection:
Who did you pray for today, and how did it make you feel?

IF TODAY WAS YOUR LAST
October 13

Morning Rinse: Psalms 37-39
Featured Verse: Psalm 39:5 *Behold, You have made my days as handbreadths, and my lifetime as nothing in Your sight; Surely every man at his best is a mere breath.*

Some of today's Morning Rinse breathed heaviness and sorrow from David's heart for the sins he had committed. He wrote about the pain he felt, his confession for what he had done, and the anxiety he felt from his choices (38:18). David knew the grief sin causes, and he also knew we have limited time on this earth to make it right when we sin. His hope in God is undeniable and his passion for running after Him, despite his wrongdoings, is contagious. We all fail at times. Some of those failures and wrong choices will weigh heavier on our hearts than others, and we will all have to face the consequences for those choices. David understood this and yet he also knew the freedom of God's grace and forgiveness. He nailed it when he wrote today's Featured Verse describing our limited time on this earth. Our time to make an impact is temporary. In the grand heavenly scene, we are here on this side of heaven in the same amount of time needed to take a breath. What would we do differently if we knew today was our last day to live? Would we humble ourselves and ask forgiveness? Would we make one last plea to a loved one to live for God? What would we want our final conversation or last memory to be with those around us? Would it be a memory of anger, gossip, frustration, and bitterness? Or would it be a last memory full of love, grace, and encouragement? We are not promised a future breath, and David helps us understand this through his writings. If we all truly caught the depth of this truth in our hearts, I believe we would change how we live our lives, moment by moment, with the world around us.

Today's Challenge To Dig Deeper:
Ask yourself today, "If I passed today, is there anything in my life that is out of order that I do not want to leave my family with to clean up?" Living a life with a clean heart sometimes means putting tangible things in order as well.

Evening Reflection:
Today's was not necessarily a 'feel good' devotion, but one we all must realize is a true reality. How did it make you feel? Was there anything you need to do to put your life in order for the day when you cross into heaven?

SOUL SURGERY
October 14

Morning Rinse: Psalms 40-43
Featured Verse: Psalm 41:4 *As for me, I said, "O Lord, be gracious to me; Heal my soul, for I have sinned against You."*

Yesterday was a time of repentance, reflection, and restarting. It was a day to make any revisions to our legacy regarding how people will remember us. It was about being intentional and striving to make every moment and every decision count, especially when interacting with others. Just as a doctor will oftentimes prescribe medicine to complete the healing of an infection, Jesus must also complete the healing of our soul when we repent from sin and grow in our walk. Sometimes the healing from our choices is immediate, but sometimes the healing takes a little time to walk through. Whether our healing is short lived, or we must take a longer journey, God is the master surgeon. He knows exactly what 'tools' to use to bring the complete healing we need so our lives will be of greater impact for His kingdom. If we surrender to Him, His spiritual scalpels, forceps, scissors, and clamps will be used for the soul surgery that will ultimately heal us. And soul surgery is not just for restoring our heart when we sin. While it is the focus of today's Featured Verse, it is not the end to God's surgical procedures. Our soul can also be damaged from the sin and disobedience of others, causing us to need Him to work on those areas of our heart. God is the master surgeon. This question is for all of us, though, "Will I surrender to the operating table?"

Today's Challenge To Dig Deeper:
Are there some things in your soul that need healing? Maybe you are experiencing the consequences of your actions. Maybe it is pain inflicted on your soul by others. Make an appointment with God today, and ask Him to reveal to you what area of your heart needs surgery. As you pray, surrender to His operating table.

Evening Reflection:
Did you allow God to perform soul surgery today? What did it feel like and what did God talk to you about?

HE IS A VERY
October 15

Morning Rinse: Psalms 44-47
Featured Verse: Psalm 46:1 *God is our refuge and strength, a very present help in trouble.*

The sons of Korah were temple assistants and wrote eleven of the psalms, including all of today's Morning Rinse. The sons, or probably grandsons, of Korah were spared destruction from Korah's rebellion against God (Numbers 26:9-11). But God still had a plan for the line of Korah, and rose leaders up from his lineage of future generations to join King David. Some scholars speculate that the heart of the music from their psalms came from a deep gratitude of being spared the destruction Korah experienced. We know God is present when we need Him. God is with us through all we go through. But there is a little word in this verse the sons of Korah wrote, that can be easily overlooked. *Very.* God is a *very* present help in trouble. What were these sons of Korah reflecting on when they wrote these words? I do not know. But what I do know is regardless of where the root of their words came from, even if it was reflecting on some of their descendant's destruction, they knew God is *very* present to those who love Him. While reading today's Featured Verse, I noticed there was a notation next to the word *very* in my Bible. The note defined the word as *abundantly*. Abundantly present! Wow. But if this is not powerful enough, I found more words that describe *very. The Merriam-Webster Thesaurus* gives even a clearer picture of this word by describing it as extremely, incredibly, exceptionally, exceedingly, extraordinarily, lavishly, and fantastically.[24] God is fantastically present. He is lavishly present. He is incredibly present. He is a very.

Today's Challenge To Dig Deeper:
Do you need to feel the *very* concerning anything you are going through? Ask Him to be a *very* today for your needs.

Evening Reflection:
Did God show you anything special today about Him being a *very*?

---

[24] https://www.merriam-webster.com/thesaurus/very

THE CATTLE IN OUR STABLE
October 16

Morning Rinse: Psalms 48-50
Featured Verse: Psalm 50:10 *For every beast of the forest is Mine. The cattle on a thousand hills.*

Back in 2018, I began a nonprofit called *I Will Rise*. The purpose was to provide a platform for ways to give back to the community, especially regarding the needs of children and teens. The need for resources to hire videographers or buy equipment is a constant necessity when I am marketing or even creating films to expose these needs to the community. In fact, there have been times I have admittedly been guilty of praying, "Lord, you own the cattle on a thousand hills. Could I have one of those hills?" While I have justified the asking by using humor, I now shake my head and have a 'face palm' moment when thinking of those conversations. The reason for my asking was pure, but the context was not necessarily in line with the heart of God. He knows our needs, but He does not walk around with a silver platter, handing out resources just because we throw scripture at Him. I have also been admittedly guilty of reminding Him of the sacrifices I have made, trying to build my ministry. When Asaph wrote today's Featured Verse, the people were sacrificing out of habit. At one point, they did indeed follow God with their whole heart, living a life of authenticity and true love for Him. Asaph's words are a reminder to us all, no matter what we sacrifice to God, whether it be money, time, or talent, we must remember the significance of why we do what we do. It should be to worship Him in truth, not in obligation. Our sacrifices will mean nothing if done for the wrong reasons. So Asaph tells us what to sacrifice before we do anything else, give God a sacrifice of thanksgiving (Psalm 50:14-15). Our situation may need dire help or even a miracle. But asking God for the cattle before offering thanksgiving is not going to reach His ears effectively. Instead, thank Him first for who He is and for what He has already done for us. I have been guilty of not effectively using the resources God has already given me. So I now have a gratitude journal. This journal helps me remain intentional at thanking Him for the cattle, or resources, already in my stable. It helps me to stay focused on thanking Him, instead of listing the needs for Him to supply. The process of writing in it reminds me to ask God to help me use my current cattle to its full potential. Sometimes what we need is already in our stable.

Today's Challenge To Dig Deeper:
Do you have a gratitude journal? If not, buy one today and start writing. Every day, write a few sentences in it thanking God for the cattle, or resources, you already have.

Evening Reflection:
What are your thoughts about the cattle you already have?

EMBRACE THE WOOD CHIPS
October 17

Morning Rinse: Psalms 51-54
Featured Verses: Psalm 51:10-12 *Create in me a clean heart, O God, and renew a steadfast spirit within me. Do not cast me away from Your presence and do not take Your Holy Spirit from me. Restore to me the joy of my salvation and sustain me with a willing spirit.*

Nearly each year as a child, my family would take our summer vacations at a youth camp or a fellowship camp meeting. From New Mexico to Kansas, to Michigan and Denver, we enjoyed our time reconnecting with old friends from past camps whose families would often do the same thing. I have so many memories from those childhood days. I remember swimming in the camp lake during free time. I remember some of the friends I made and even a few of my camp crushes. I remember the tire swing at one of the camps I was pushed on by one of those camp crushes. I remember the spiders in our cabins and a few occasional snakes slithering across a walking path. I remember the canoes and the baptismal services. Of course, I remember my dad preaching as well, and my mom teaching some of the classes. I also remember the wood chips digging into my knees when praying at the altar after the evening service. And I remember singing many psalms during worship. One camp especially comes to mind because I recall those psalms being led by a red headed guitar player named Derald Rhineberger. Today's Featured Verses include one of those psalms we sang. Childhood memories are what make us. They mold us. They shape us. But despite spending a lifetime going to church, or attending summer youth camps, and growing up as a preacher's kid, I still must fight my carnal tendency that tries to sin. David understood this. He, unfortunately, followed his natural leaning when he took another man's wife. His sin, though, is spoken and preached on as an example of God's forgiveness following our confession and repentance. David knew whether we are a king, a preacher's kid, a teacher, a mom, a youth director, or any one of God's children, having a clean heart is vital to maintaining a growing relationship with our Heavenly Father. When we sin, that relationship is bruised, and our joy can be squelched. But oh, when we repent and ask God to purify us, He is faithful to answer that prayer. Sometimes those altar prayers with the wood chips digging into my knees, included asking for forgiveness. May I always be willing to take the uncomfortable feeling of those wood chips, or the uncomfortable feeling of humility, over having a heart separated from God.

Today's Challenge To Dig Deeper:
Repeat the Featured Verses and take them to heart. Even if God brings to light some uncomfortable subjects, accept what He has to say. Let God dig a little deeper to create a clean heart. Embrace the wood chips.

Evening Reflection:
Write about anything your heart felt today regarding your wood chips.

A TEAR-FILLED BOTTLE
October 18

Morning Rinse: Psalms 55-58
Featured Verse: Psalm 56:8 *You have taken account of my wanderings; put my tears in Your bottle. Are they not in Your book?*

Sometimes while reading the book of Psalms, I will think to myself, "Goodness. David sure did mourn a lot." He did seem sad, with a consistent undertone of grief, fear, and anxiety. Can you imagine, though, living a life constantly being chased and hunted to be killed? I cannot. The awful part about his dilemma is he was hunted, not by his enemies, but by a former close friend (55:12-13). His honest feelings are raw, showing us that he shed many tears as he went through this. Just as God knows the number of hairs on our heads (Matthew 10:30), He also knows about every tear we cry. I was once on a leadership team for the Women's Ministry at a church I attended years ago. In preparation for our quarterly gathering, our guest speaker decided to speak on the topic of our tears. To give the ladies something tangible to remember the truth she spoke about, we used some of the ministry funds to purchase small glass bottles with a cute matching lid for each of the ladies as a keepsake. I still have my bottle, and it sits on my office bookshelf. I have often gazed at that bottle as a reminder that no matter what I am going through, He catches my tears in His heavenly bottle. I have even pictured Him in my mind's eye, holding that bottle close to His heart, letting me know He cares and understands my pain. He wants us to be honest with Him. But He does not want us to hold our pain. He wants us to take our burdens to Him and leave them there. In fact, David advised us to cast our burdens to Him (Psalm 55:22). When one is casting something, in essence, they are forcefully throwing it. This applies to examples like fishing, shot put, softball or baseball pitching, and even spear throwing. And yes, it even applies to casting our burdens. God wants us to throw them forcefully, or intentionally, to Him. And in the casting, we must fully let go, cutting anything that ties us to the burden. We must fully release them and hand Him our bottle.

Today's Challenge To Dig Deeper:
Buy a little bottle today. You can look through most online stores, your local discount store or even swing by a thrift store and find one you like. Put it in a place where you will occasionally see it so you are reminded God sees your tears.

Evening Reflection:
Did you know God puts your tears in a bottle? Write down how this makes you feel.

LONG TO BE LED
October 19

Morning Rinse: Psalms 59-62
Featured Verses: Psalm 61:1-2 *Hear my cry, O God; give heed to my prayer. From the end of the earth I call to You when my heart is faint; lead me to the rock that is higher than I.*

Do you ever ask the question, "What is happening in my life?" Or "Why am I in this situation?" Sometimes we are in predicaments we could have avoided if we had made wiser choices. And then, surprisingly, other situations are a direct result of our obedience to God and being His child. The psalms continue to capture the heart cry of David, as he continues to reach out to God in his specific circumstances. In this season of David's life, the challenges he has seem to be his normal state of condition. Despite his situation, we know David does not want to rely on his own strength. He puts his continual trust in the one true God, asking for his cries to be heard. David declares that no matter what he is going through, he will call on God, and we know God hears his cries. Just like David, our cries are heard as well. God is present when our heart is faint. And we know He will lead us to a place of security in Him. In today's Featured Verses, David mentions the higher rock, which is a symbol of that security. However, David mentions something often overlooked. It is the fact that he is asking to be led there. Are we leadable? Do we trust God's leading no matter what the circumstances are that we are led into? Even when people talk about us or try to do us harm, are we still leadable? Do we long for God to lead us, even if it is in a valley? And once we are there, are we comfortable staying there for as long as God would have us remain? Or are we constantly asking God to lead us out of the situation He just brought us to? The beautiful thing, though, is if we are teachable and leadable, God will use our challenges to teach us how to be led. During these moments, choose to praise Him in the challenge, and choose to continually long for His leading. In Him, we will have a place of security all the way to the other side of our situation.

Today's Challenge To Dig Deeper:
If you are struggling in an area, ask God to lead you to a place of security in your heart.

Evening Reflection:
It is hard to compare our struggles to David's, especially since most of us do not have people chasing us down to kill us. But whether our struggle is vast or small, we can go to the rock of God and be secure. Write down what you went to God about. Do you feel more secure in Him?

PASSION IN THE MESS
October 20

Morning Rinse: Psalms 63-66
Featured Verse: Psalm 63:1 *O God, You are my God; I shall seek You earnestly; My soul thirsts for You, my flesh yearns for You, in a dry and weary land where there is no water.*

Scholars believe David wrote this psalm during Absalom's rebellion (2 Samuel 15-18). During this time, David was in hiding. He was in the middle of a mess. Can you relate? I know I can. I have been in the middle of messes before where I had no idea how it was going to turn out. In fact, a few of my messes were so dirty and awful, I literally thought I would lose everything I owned. But in the middle of our messes, God wants to perform a miracle, and He wants us to be ready to receive that miracle. What does David do in his mess? He glorifies God. He seeks Him with passion. He looks to Him as his provider. Oh, how I want David's passion for God in my messes.

Today's Challenge To Dig Deeper:
If you are lacking passion, ask God for more. He sees you. He loves you. And He wants to help you increase your passion for Him.

Evening Reflection:
Write what you feel in your heart. And write what God spoke to you about in terms of your passion for Him.

JUST SAY IT
October 21

Morning Rinse: Psalms 67-69
Featured Verses: Psalm 69:30-32 *I will praise the name of God with song and magnify Him with thanksgiving. And it will please the Lord better than an ox or a young bull with horns and hoofs. The humble have seen it and are glad; you who seek God, let your heart revive.*

I grew up Pentecostal. So going to services where the shouting and praising gets a little loud does not intimidate me, nor does it seem unnatural. In fact, God desires for His people to clap and shout (Psalm 47:1 KJV). Our praise and thanksgiving please Him more than the highest quality sacrifice we could ever offer Him. When we praise Him, when we seek Him, when we offer thanksgiving, when we magnify Him over everything in our lives, then our hearts will revive. This is something that is learned. What does it look like in our every day lives?

1. First, it is praising Him for who He is. It is as simple as saying, "I praise you for who You are. You are God. You are my Creator. You are the Prince of Peace." So try it. Say it out loud. Even if it feels uncomfortable. If you need to start with a whisper, start with a whisper. But say it out loud.
2. Then thank Him for what He is doing in your life. It is also simply saying something like, "God, I thank you for the little victories you bless me with. I thank you for moving in my life, even when I do not see it. I thank you for (name the specific things you are hoping for)."
3. And, finally, make Him larger than anything going on. "God, I magnify you. You are bigger than my problems at work. You are bigger than the problems in my family. You are bigger than any situation and I will never idolize my circumstances over you." Just say it.

Even if you do not feel your spirit reviving immediately, just begin to say these things out loud. The words do not need to be exactly set in stone. But when you begin, your words will grow. Just begin. Just say it.

Today's Challenge To Dig Deeper:
Speak out loud today and focus on God above anything going on in your life. If you already have this practice as a habit, increase your praise. Magnify him more. And as uncomfortable as it is, get alone today, whether that is in your car, on a hike, or in your basement. Shout to God with a shout of praise. Try it.

Evening Reflection:
Can you make today's challenge a lifestyle? Can you be more vocal in your day-to-day activities to say the praises out loud? Write your thoughts.

I DECLARE THAT I WILL DECLARE
October 22

Morning Rinse: Psalms 70-72
Featured Verses: Psalm 72:8-11 *May he also rule from sea to sea and from the River to the ends of the earth. Let the nomads of the desert bow before him, and his enemies lick the dust. Let the kings of Tarshish and of the islands bring presents; the kings of Sheba and Seba offer gifts. And let all kings bow down before him, all nations serve him.*

One of my closest friends, Dawn Long, made a Declarations Notebook. This 3-ring binder holds a working document filled with verses divided into topical sections that she is constantly referencing and adding to. During the day, and before falling asleep, she pulls out her notebook and declares the verses applicable for the situations she is going through. I decided to start my own Declarations Notebook and I started my working document with today's Featured Verses. Psalm 72 was written by David's dad, Solomon, and is a prayer over his son to rule with wisdom and righteousness. How wonderful to be able to read the words of a dad praying over his son. I decided to use these same verses as the foundation for my notebook to not only pray over myself, but to also pray over my husband, my children, their spouses, and other loved ones. Of course, today's Featured Verses can be spoken over any leader for blessings on what they put their hands on, including blessings over everyone they lead. And they can be used to ask God to help rise above enemies, as well as bring blessings from needed resources for our lives. God is moved by our prayers. He is moved by our words. He is moved by our faith. I believe many times we think we are waiting on God, but the reality is, He is waiting on us to declare His Word with faith. So I am making the commitment to myself. "I declare that I will declare" His Word over my life more often. It is one thing to memorize a few verses and pull them out in times of need, or when we are in emergency situations. I have been guilty of this many times. I have also been guilty of not declaring in faith, what I see in the spirit realm, but instead complaining about what I see in the natural world. I do not want to be a Christ follower that God must wait on before He can manifest things in my life. I want to be a declarer of His Word NOW. So I declare that I will declare. Will you join me?

Today's Challenge To Dig Deeper:
Begin making your Declaration Notebook with verses and promises from God's Word on a working document. Print it out and put it in your notebook. I put today's Featured Verses under the subject 'Leadership.' Continue to add verses to this document that speak to you, updating it as God speaks to you, and reprinting it as needed. Make the commitment to yourself that you will declare the promises of God through His Word. I have pulled out my Declarations Notebook many times to pray over those in need. God will use it more than you can even imagine.

Evening Reflection:
Did you start your Declaration Notebook? Did you speak out loud and declare any verses today? What were they?

CONTINUE TO DECLARE: FOREVER
October 23

Morning Rinse: Psalms 73-75
Featured Verses: Psalm 75:8-9 *For a cup is in the hand of the Lord, and the wine foams; It is well mixed, and He pours out of this; surely all the wicked of the earth must drain and drink down its dregs. But as for me, I will declare it forever; I will sing praises to the God of Jacob.*

The cup of wine in today's Featured Verses symbolizes the judgement of God coming to the wicked. It is the same principle of sowing and reaping that we learn about as a Christ follower. Some people call it *Karma*. Others say the person is *getting a taste of their own medicine*. Regardless of how you describe it, the evil actions, thoughts or wishes a wicked person is guilty of will return to them on the day of judgement (Habakkuk 2:16). The wicked will reap what they sow. But oh, how sweet it is to reap God's blessings. It is a daily choice. Yesterday, we started a Declarations Notebook to begin a daily journey of vocalizing verses and promises from God that speak to us. It is ironic, timely, and divine that in today's Morning Rinse, Asaph states, too, that he will declare and sing praises to God forever. God sees our efforts to praise and live righteously. He sees our hunger and wants to meet that. So do not stop declaring. Do not stop praising. Do not stop adding to your notebook. Watch how you will reap your efforts as God lifts you up. I bought a special yellow binder with stickers to decorate mine in a special way. Yellow brings me joy, and since The Word gives me strength and brings me joy, what better color for my notebook? The stickers may seem a bit kiddish to some, but for me, they further the powerful message I want, making my Declarations Notebook that much more special. Stay focused. Commit to declare, forever.

Today's Challenge To Dig Deeper:
Work some more on your Declaration Notebook by adding more verses to your working document. Reprint the document and replace the old one. Declare all the verses out loud, and make a commitment to read some of the verses every day.

Evening Reflection:
Did you state the verses in your notebook yet? If not, declare them out loud now. Write your thoughts.

GENERATIONAL DECLARATION
October 24

Morning Rinse: Psalms 76-78
Featured Verse: Psalm 78:4 *We will not conceal them from their children, but tell to the generation to come the praises of the Lord, and His strength and His wondrous works that He has done.*

We know the importance of speaking over our own lives, declaring verses and promises God has given us. We also know the power in speaking those declarations over our loved ones' lives, inserting their names into scriptures from our Declaration Notebook we made a few days ago. Taking it a step further, there is such power in verbally communicating to the next generation the lessons from history, our own personal testimony, and all the wonderful works God has performed in other's lives as well. Asaph, the author of the psalms from today's Morning Rinse, understood what this meant. He declared that he would not conceal these stories from the next generation because he knew the power of building up faith through stories. He promised he would not be silent. We must also make this promise so the stories of our testimony, the stories from the Bible, and the stories of God's marvelous works will pass on.

Today's Challenge To Dig Deeper:
Tell at least one child or teen a lesson from the Bible, something great that God has done in your life, or a testimony you have heard from someone else.

Evening Reflection:
Who did you share with and what did you share? Did it grow your faith in sharing?

HEAVENLY SMILE
October 25

Morning Rinse: Psalms 79-82
Featured Verses: Psalm 80:7, 19 *O God of hosts, restore us and cause Your face to shine upon us, and we will be saved.*

Have you ever been in a service where the pastor or priest concluded the sermon with "May the Lord bless you and keep you and may His face shine upon you and be gracious to you"? This scripture, or something similar, has been repeated for centuries, either through the Bible or in church. It is a blessing of protection and favor over our lives. It is a prayer of guidance and grace, and is seen several times in the Bible, including two times in this chapter alone. If we are praying this and asking God to shine His face upon us, this shows He does not shine His face on everyone. In fact, there are times in scripture where the writer will give hopeful statements, hoping God does not hide His face from them (Psalm 69:17). Oh, what joy it is when we desire God, want to do His will, and feel His face shining on us. Even when we mess up, He restores us, delights in us, and shines His face on us by His approval. This is His love, grace, favor, and protection, and is one of the most encouraging things we can feel as a child of God. Do you feel God's face shining on you today? It is a heavenly smile.

Today's Challenge To Dig Deeper:
If you have messed up today, or feel a little distant from God, talk to Him. Ask Him to restore you and build you up. Ask Him to shine His face on you.

Evening Reflection:
Did you feel God smiling down on you today? Write about it.

EMPTY SHELVES
October 26

Morning Rinse: Psalms 83-85
Featured Verse: Psalm 84:11 *For the Lord God is a sun and shield; the Lord gives grace and glory. No good thing does He withhold from those who walk uprightly.*

I once heard a story told about a man getting a tour of heaven. During his tour, Jesus took him inside a huge building full of shelves lined with wrapped presents stacked to the ceiling. Out of curiosity, the man asked Jesus who the presents were for. Jesus turned and with loving eyes said, "These were your gifts that were never opened." The man, filled with sadness, asked, "Why did I never receive them?" Jesus said, "Two reasons. First, there were times you were not walking completely upright. But when you were, there were times you never asked for them." As a parent, I want the best for my children. I want them to have the desires of their heart and grow up happy and thriving. I want to provide for them and give them a safe environment to be the very best they can possibly be, living out their full God-given potential. And of course, I want them to follow the heart of God with passion. How much more does God want these same things, and more, for His children? We cannot even imagine what He wants for us. I do not want unopened gifts to be sitting on shelves that were meant to be mine while on this side of heaven. I want the building used to store my gifts to be full of empty shelves. I want every good thing from the Lord that He has for me.

Today's Challenge To Dig Deeper:
Be excited today about all that God has for you. Begin walking in expectation and hope for what He has for you. With that excitement, send a bold prayer to His throne, asking Him to show you the gifts you have yet to open. Prepare your heart to receive from Him today. And make sure you are ready to use the gifts He gives you once you open them.

Evening Reflection:
Did your faith grow today? Was there anything you felt God saying to you about your gifts from Him?

HALLELUJAH AND GOD BLESS YOU!
October 27

Morning Rinse: Psalms 86-89
Featured Verse: Psalm 89:1 *I will sing of the lovingkindness of the Lord forever; to all generations I will make known Your faithfulness with my mouth.*

When I first met Dawn Long, one of the ladies in my tribe group (read my acknowledgement section), I was not sure what to think about her. I do not think I have ever heard anyone vocally praise as much as she does during even the simplest of conversations. From the very beginning of our friendship, she literally almost always ends our exchanges by saying, "God bless you." Many times, she speaks blessings over things like tasks I am working on, or business endeavors, or even relationship decisions I am going through. For example, if I ask for prayer regarding something, or if I am watching my kid play in a sporting event and she is talking to me about it, she will state, "God bless you with that." I have witnessed her going through some grievous seasons where her heart is completely torn with pain, and yet she still praises God and offers blessings to others. She will also rejoice with me during exciting times in my life, always giving God the glory despite what she is going through. When something wonderful occurs in our tribe group, she will joyfully express with a passionate smile, "HALLELUJAH!" This simple word *Hallelujah* is an exclamation. It is a strong declaration that means "God be praised." There is something powerful about rejoicing with others, no matter what you are personally going through. And there is something mighty about speaking blessings over others, even when your own heart may be troubled. I also know she speaks these same blessings over her own life, which is spiritually fierce and powerful. No matter what you are facing, sing of His lovingkindness and faithfulness. Make it known with your mouth.

Today's Challenge To Dig Deeper:
Say "Hallelujah" at least 10 times today, finding moments to praise God. Also, when you are with others, find reasons to express, "God bless you" to them. Avoid only saying it in your *goodbyes*. But instead, speak it over their actions and efforts as well, blessing them as they share stories of things they are doing.

Evening Reflection:
How did it feel to say "Hallelujah" and "God bless you" throughout your day? Did it feel awkward at first? Did it begin to feel more natural as you kept saying it? Consider making these words more of your daily expressions in conversation.

PILLAR PRAYER OF PROTECTION
October 28

Morning Rinse: Psalms 90-92
Featured Verses: Psalm 91:1-4 *He who dwells in the shelter of the Most High will abide in the shadow of the Almighty. I will say to the Lord, "My refuge and my fortress, My God, in whom I trust." For it is He who delivers you from the snare of the trapper and from the deadly pestilence. He will cover you with His pinions, and under His wings you may seek refuge; His faithfulness is a shield and bulwark.*

To read today's Morning Rinse and not highlight Psalm 91 would be like showing up to a red carpet event barefoot. Psalm 91 is a pillar prayer of protection for our Christian walk. God does not promise we will be void of hardship and attacks from the enemy. But He does promise He will be with us through it all. Praying this prayer of protection can thwart the enemy's darts as they come our way. We must dwell in His shelter, though. His presence must be our living quarters, not just when we need help. If we dwell there, then while going through life's valleys, His shadow, His protection, and His presence will cover us. He will not force us to abide or rest in Him, though. It is a choice. I am not talking about choosing salvation. I am talking about seeking Him after salvation with every decision, every step, and every move made in this life, trusting Him to guide us along the journey. I am talking about daily choosing His shelter and protection instead of trying to do life on our own. When our enemy sets traps along the pathway of life, God will cover us with His wings. He is the shield for our lives. He is the supernatural bulwark. He is our pillar of protection. And so is this prayer.

Today's Challenge To Dig Deeper:
Write today's Featured Verses on an index card and put it somewhere for your family to see every day. Then also type out the entire chapter in your Declarations Notebook we made in the devotion titled 'I Declare That I Will Declare.' Let the entire chapter be part of what you state out loud every day from this day forward.

Evening Reflection:
Did Psalm 91 increase your faith? As you were typing it out for your notebook and reading it out loud, could you sense an inner strength rising inside of you? Write out any thoughts.

LINKING ARMS
October 29

Morning Rinse: Psalms 93-96
Featured Verse: Psalm 94:18 *If I should say, "My foot has slipped," Your lovingkindness, O Lord, will hold me up.*

A group of protesters gather in the street hoping their voices are heard for the cause they are standing for. They are not screaming out chants or pointing to passersby for attention or even holding up signs. Instead, they quietly stand together with their arms linked with each other, forming a line. This line is a picture of strength, determination, and focus, and while they are silent, their voice is still heard. Those passing can feel the unbreakable bond and the tangible picture of unity for what they believe in. Even though the protestors are quiet, they are shouting for their mission. They are shouting with linked arms. And if they would start walking down the street, all at the same time in that line, the force of that line would be exponentially stronger than walking alone. If they progress down the street, what do you think would happen if one of the protestors slipped and started to fall? This is the beauty of the linked arms. There would be a person on each side of them to hold them up. We will slip up at times in our walk with God. None of us are perfect. This is why it is so important to link arms with Him, and stay humble as He guides us. But if we are linked with Him, He is right there to hold us up and keep us from falling. This analogy of linking arms is a powerful message with several meanings, or examples, of how we can do that in our daily lives. First, we must stay close to God, with our arms linked to Him in every step we take, allowing Him to guide us as we walk out our journey. We also must stay linked to the body of Christ just like the protestors are linked together. I see too many times where someone in the body of Christ will break the link by gossiping or causing discord. Determine today that you will not be the one who breaks the line. Choose to link arms with not only Christ, but also with fellow believers, by living in peace and love for others, as well as serving in your local church.

Today's Challenge To Dig Deeper:
Do you feel a little unlinked today? Ask God to give you the passion you need to stay linked to Him as well as linked to others so you are not walking out your faith journey alone.

Evening Reflection:
Write out any thoughts you have about the power of linking arms.

THE BALL CALLED THANKFULNESS
October 30

Morning Rinse: Psalms 97-100
Featured Verses: Psalm 100:1-2 *Shout joyfully to the Lord, all the earth. Serve the Lord with gladness; come before Him with joyful singing.*

There are times when I ask God to meet my needs, but forget to thank Him for the answers. Admittedly, I realize that my thankful attitude is nowhere in sight. In fact, it is a little ball hidden in the grass on the other side of the fence behind left field. In other words, it is so far away from me that it is not even in my game called life. Today's Featured Verses, as well as the entire Psalm 100, show us how to pick up the ball of thankfulness again. In fact, the version of my Bible has titles for some of the psalms and the title for Psalm 100 is, "A Psalm for Thanksgiving." We can learn a lot from this little psalm, including several different things we can do to pick up the ball called thankfulness. We can shout joyfully, serve the Lord with gladness, sing joyfully and then acknowledge He is God. All these things help us have a thankful attitude. And did you notice David did not just instruct us to shout or serve or go before God, and then we would have a spirit of thankfulness? Instead, he instructs us to pick up joy and gladness and THEN shout and serve and approach God. If we want to have a thankful heart, we must make some attitude adjustments. Choosing to live our life with joy and gladness, despite what we are going through, is one of those adjustments. If we choose joy and gladness, it will be so much easier to walk through life with our ball of thankfulness, ready to throw it in every situation. Being thankful is a choice, and is an example of how we make the scriptures come to life. A former pastor of mine, Dr George Westlake, Jr, would often say in his sermons, "You do not feel your way into action. You act your way into feelings." There is a path to acting our way into a thankful attitude. If we want breakthroughs in thankfulness in our game of life, shout joyfully, serve with gladness, and sing joyfully to God. Choose to keep the ball called 'thanksgiving' on your ball field instead of tucked in your glove. Then throw it out into the world by your words and actions. Watch your heart transform.

Today's Challenge To Dig Deeper:
First, shout 'Hallelujah' ten times today with a joyful spirit. Next, choose to serve the Lord. If you are not serving Him in some capacity, ask Him to show you where He wants you to serve. Then sing a joyful song and tell Him you KNOW He is God. Choose to do your part.

Evening Reflection:
Did your thankful attitude grow? Write down how your heart feels.

THE LIST (PART 1)
October 31

Morning Rinse: Psalms 101-103
Featured Verse: Psalm 103:2 *Bless the Lord, O my soul, and forget none of His benefits.*

Do you know of anyone that exhibits offensive characteristics or has a lack of integrity, making it hard to trust them? The list of these offensive acts can easily grow each time there is a harmful interchange. We all have a choice to either keep lists about people, or to let the offenses go. The hard truth is, Jesus could have a list on us for the things we have said or done against Him and even against His children. It is a reality we oftentimes do not like to face, and yet we are quick to keep lists on others. But when we accept Jesus as our Savior, He erases the list of our offensive actions. Not only does He continually pardon our iniquities, He heals our diseases, redeems us from death, crowns us with lovingkindness and compassion, and He satisfies us with good things (Psalm 103:3-5). If these benefits were not enough to be joyful about, He also performs righteous deeds (103:6), is compassionate and gracious to us (103:8, 13), and is slow to anger (103:8). We do not deserve any of these benefits from Him. But He loves us so much that He erases our list and continues to bless us with favor, as we fear Him and live for Him. Even amid David going through hard times, he remembered the list of God's characteristics, and made that his focus instead of his challenges. If we truly want to be more Christ-like, we will strive to have the character of God. We will erase the list against others and instead, replace it with the list of who God is. When we focus on God's character, it is hard to focus on the list of offensive characteristics of others. What list will you choose to focus on?

Today's Challenge To Dig Deeper:
Underline all the characteristics of God throughout Psalm 103. Thank Him for each one of these benefits. Then ask Him to expose to you if you carry a list of offenses in your heart towards anyone, and repent. Begin focusing on the list of God's characteristics. If you need to, write them down for easy reference, when tempted to focus on the wrongdoings of others.

Evening Reflection:
How is your heart? Was it easy to let go of the lists you carried about the characteristics of others?

November Rinsing

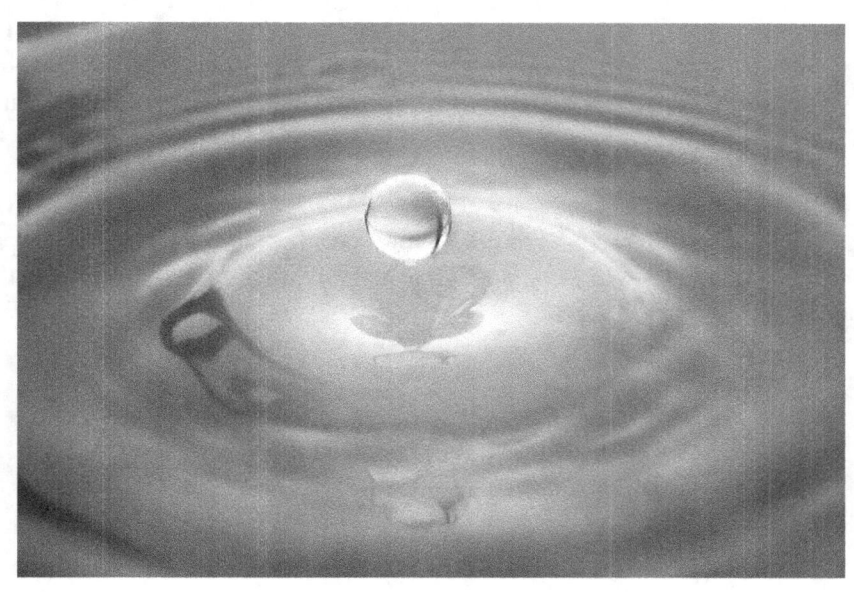

THE LIST (PART 2)
November 1

Morning Rinse: Psalms 104-105
Featured Verse: Psalm 105:1 *Oh give thanks to the LORD, call upon His name; Make known His deeds among the peoples.*

If you have never experienced a testimony service, it is something you will want to put on your bucket list. The church that my family attended for most of my childhood was a little church in Weston, Missouri. The Sunday night service consisted of about fifteen minutes of testimonies where those in attendance could stand in their pew and share with the rest of the attendees something good from that last week. It was testimony time. This was a miniature version of an entire service dedicated to testimonies, which I have experienced a few times as well. It is powerful when we, His children, remember His works and His wonders, and then share it with others for encouragement and building faith. When we seek Him, it is easy to see His handiwork all around us. In Part 1 of this two-part devotion, we focused on the list of God's characteristics versus keeping a list of the wrongdoings of others. Now, we are taking it one step further and making a second list. Today's Featured Verse encourages us to give thanks to God, and tell others the things He has done. This is our second list, which is also our personal testimony list. Sometimes we must remind ourselves of the blessings in our lives. When we seek His face, we see His works, and those works are what we must remember.

Today's Challenge To Dig Deeper:
Make a list of all the things God has done for you. Try and fill up several pages in a notebook or in a document. Once you make your list, tell at least one person something from the list today.

Evening Reflection:
Who did you tell what God has done for you? How did the conversation go? Did it feel good to talk about His wondrous works, and did it build your faith?

PRAISE PRAYER
November 2

Morning Rinse: Psalms 106-108
Featured Verse: Psalm 108:3 *I will give thanks to You, O Lord, among the peoples, and I will sing praises to You among the nations.*

Have you ever had a nudge to praise God in a situation, but instead complained about it? I am not talking about moments when God overtakes us with blessings and favor, but we focus on the imperfections of it. For instance, if we get blessed with a new car, but focus on the rusty bumper. Yes, this attitude still needs an adjustment. But I am talking about times when our circumstances seem dire. Maybe you get laid off from a company you hoped to build a long-term career with. Maybe a loved one makes some horrendous choices causing them to go down a path they were never meant to go down. What about when a contractor runs off with your deposit without finishing the job you hired him for or when your toilet floods, pouring water down the walls and into the floor below. What about when three vehicles get totaled in a short two-year time frame, or you experience the total loss of a new business. Or maybe one of your best friends stabs you in the back and steals a promised opportunity from you. Believe it or not, all these situations have happened to me. I wish I could tell you that I spoke out of praise when they occurred. But I must be honest, I complained in every one of these situations. In each one, I had the opportunity to praise God, but unfortunately I missed it. It was the perfect chance to switch my tendency of complaining to a new habit of praise. What if I had said a Praise Prayer instead? "God, I do not know what you have planned, but I am going to trust you. I am Your child, and I will not live in fear. I know all things work together for good, and I choose to praise You in this situation. I thank you for this opportunity to give You praise, and I will continue to shout of Your goodness to the nations. I look forward to seeing what You have planned for my future because You are God!" When we take this stance and sing of God's goodness, it is hard to complain about our challenging situations. When others see us responding with a Praise Prayer, this attitude will spread, causing them to grow in their faith as well.

Today's Challenge To Dig Deeper:
Choose to say a Praise Prayer like the one above, and speak it out even to those around you. Believe and vocalize that everything will be okay. Live in faith and commit to exchanging complaints for praise.

Evening Reflection:
Did you say a Praise Prayer today? How did it change your heart and mind?

GOD'S RIGHT HAND
November 3

Morning Rinse: Psalms 109-112
Featured Verse: Psalm 110:1 *The Lord says to my Lord, "Sit at My right hand until I make Your enemies a footstool for Your feet."*

It is obviously clear why Psalm 110 is one of the most quoted psalms in the New Testament. David wrote this psalm with references to Jesus and His majestic power, beginning with the mention of God's right hand. For as long as I can remember, scriptures noting God's right hand, or the right hand in general, have always intrigued me. Why are these two words, *right hand*, used together so much? What about God's left hand, or just merely both of His hands in general being referenced? The mention of the right hand symbolizes some powerful attributes worth noting. Of course, the left hand is important and has different meanings, but the right hand has some commanding representation. Not only does today's Featured Verse show being at the right hand is a place of honor and favor, but this reference is also shown in 1 Kings 2:19. Then in Ephesians 1:20-22, it states Jesus Himself sits at the right hand of God, sitting FAR above any other authority or power. Upon further research of the combination of these two words, *right hand*, I discovered it also communicates God's righteousness and holiness (Isaiah 41:10). It also shows His authority and power (1 Peter 3:21-22), His strength (Psalm 18:35), and even the transfer of blessings when someone lays their hands on others (Genesis 48:18). And finally, the right hand is used when handshaking or historically holding weapons or signing a decree. According to a blogger, the writer discovered the words *right hand* in the Bible are referenced together 132 times![25] WOW. Knowing God created us, He guides us, and He loves us, His right hand showing us His favor should give us an empowered confidence to stand taller, have more faith, and walk out this life with a clearer perspective that His will for our life is good. What better place to be than to have His right hand over our lives!

Today's Challenge to Dig Deeper:
Look up all the references listed in today's devotion about the words *right hand*. Then say this prayer, "God, I thank You for Your right hand over my life guiding me every day. Help me to understand and accept Your guidance, and help me trust You as I make decisions to serve and obey You. Help me walk in authority and the confidence that You have transferred power to me as Your child, and help me never forget this power You have given me through Your right hand."

Evening Reflection:
What are your thoughts about the meaning of the right hand of God, or these two words together in general? Did God speak to you today about His right hand over your life?

---

[25] https://www.heholdsmyrighthand.com/p/why-right-hand.html

PASS THE PAIN TO THE PROMISE
November 4

Morning Rinse: Psalms 113-115
Featured Verse: Psalm 115:14 *May the Lord give you increase, you and your children.*

Back in 1997, I made an entry into my three-ring binders, the foundation of this book. "God, I want to claim verses like this. But it is hard, especially after failure. It is also hard now that my ministry leader has put me on the shelf." I do not know what failure I was referencing, but I distinctly remember the situation regarding the ministry leader I wrote about. At the time, I was serving in my church youth group. One evening, the youth pastor approached me and said, "Anita, I have been praying about this and want to talk to you. As you know, I have a youth board. These are youth leaders that are loyal to this ministry and who live a life set apart. I see that in you, and want to offer you a place on the board." I remember the feeling I had after that interchange. I drove home feeling so alive, so believed in, and so honored. I could hardly sleep that night. It was like God saw me and wanted to bless me. The youth pastor told me he just had to get approval from the current board for my addition and would be in touch. Unfortunately, a week later I was blindsided. The increase I felt God had just given me was stripped away. He regretfully stated that he had to rescind his offer because one of the board members did not agree with him adding me. This person blocked my blessing, and while I never knew the full reason why, I was told it was because I was a woman. I knew who stated it and I also knew, it was no secret to me that this person was at odds with me, and was not a big cheerleader of mine. But I never thought it would get to this. And yes, sometimes rejection is protection. But we all have these instances in our lives where others will try to stop an increase from coming our way, just like this man stopped my acceptance into this place of honor. Sometimes we can feel like blessings of increase are stripped from us, and verses like these are hard to receive. However, God sees us, and His ultimate plan for our lives will not be stopped by a person who could potentially be operating out of flesh, and not spiritually. It was very hard for me to be rejected from this honored leadership position, but I had to choose to lay down my bitterness and pain and claim this verse. I had to pass the pain and claim the promise. Since then, I have seen more increase in my life than I can even keep track of. And for those who have no children, your increase can come through you to the next generation when you give back to those around you.

Today's Challenge To Dig Deeper:
Do you have any bitterness or unforgiveness towards someone who had a hand in thwarting your increase, or blessing? Forgive. Go past the pain and claim the promise.

Evening Reflection:
Did you forgive someone today? Who was it?

MOUNTAINS, FLATLANDS, EXITS AND VALLEYS
November 5

Morning Rinse: Psalms 116-118
Featured Verse: Psalm 118:24 *This is the day which the Lord has made; Let us rejoice and be glad in it.*

Our journey as a Christ follower is guaranteed to appear like a highway spanning the great country of America. Some days we will feel like everything is going perfect and beautiful like the views from a Montana mountain. There are other days when nothing seems too extravagant or out of the ordinary. Life seems steady, good, and uneventful, paralleled to the flatlands in Western Kansas enveloped with wheat fields as far as the eye can see. Then there are times in our lives where we take an exit off the road we are traveling. Maybe our exit is due to sin and we need to quickly repent, or maybe we need to pause and adjust our attitude on how we handle the bumps in the road. An exit is also great to rest and recoup from a valley we might have just endured. These exits can be used to help us refuel and refocus before getting back on the pathway God has us on. And finally, there are days when we face the valleys. These are the low points of life we usually do not like experiencing. They are the days blanketed with extreme grief, uncertainty, hardship or even pain from the actions of others. It may not always be easy to rejoice during these moments. But time and time again, the psalmists are honest with God through their valleys. What is so noteworthy is that during their honesty through hardship, they constantly end with praise. God knows what we are going through and the challenges we face. He will be with us amidst every stretch of our road, whether on the mountaintop, through the flatlands, off an exit, or deep in the valley. Rejoice no matter what your day looks like. For He is the one who made our day. While He does not control the actions of others, He still deserves our praise.

Today's Challenge To Dig Deeper:
Memorize today's Featured Verse. Write it on a 3x5 index card and tape it to your bathroom mirror as a reminder that God made each day. Go about your day and be intentional with rejoicing, no matter what you face.

Evening Reflection:
What thoughts went through your head regarding today's Featured Verse? Did anything occur that might have gotten you off track in your attitude, but you handled it differently knowing that God made your day? Did you intentionally rejoice during it?

THE SAFE OF OUR HEARTS
November 6

Morning Rinse: Psalm 119:1-88
Featured Verse: Psalm 119:11 *Your word I have treasured in my heart, that I may not sin against You.*

We have a safe in our home where we keep some of our valuables. These items are tucked inside to be protected from fire, theft, looting, or other forms of destruction. Some of the items include important paperwork that would be a hassle to replace. Other items are treasures we hold dear and want to preserve as keepsakes. Items of value do not have to be worth a lot monetarily. They can also be any item that you hold dear, as a treasure in your heart. Items that, if you lost everything, you would want to preserve because they are a symbol of the core of who you are. We hide what is important to us because it is of value. It is a treasure. It is of high worth in some way. So how do we hide His Word in our heart? We study it. We memorize it. We value it. We honor it. We protect it. We prize it. And ultimately, when we value His Word in this fashion, we will obey it. We will be guided to love more, forgive more, praise Him more, tithe more, sacrifice more, give more, and serve more. And at the end of the day, when all is said and done, we will ultimately sin less. May we get to a point that if we lost everything, we would still have the treasure of His Word tucked in the safe of our hearts.

Today's Challenge To Dig Deeper:
Memorize today's Featured Verse. Ask God to help you treasure His Word in a greater capacity than ever before. Ask Him to grow your hunger and love for His Word. Keep this prayer of hunger close to your heart and repeat it throughout your life as God brings it to your memory.

Evening Reflection:
Write down any thoughts you had throughout the day about the treasure of God's Word.

GORILLA TAPED BIBLE
November 7

Morning Rinse: Psalm 119:88-176
Featured Verse: Psalm 119:105 *Your word is a lamp to my feet and a light to my path.*

Ah! The power of duct tape. Have you ever had an experience where you were using duct tape for a project, and it got stuck to your clothes or skin? It is tough to remove, and once it folds over and attaches to itself, it is time to start all over with a new piece because there is no easy way to separate it again. Imagine using Gorilla tape. It is a reinforced form of duct tape that is claimed to be three times stronger than the standard duct tape. Several times when I have prayed over people, I have seen a picture in my mind's eye about this kind of tape. In the scene, there are two Bibles laying on the ground. The person walks up to the Bibles and stands on top of them, one under each foot. Then they grab a roll of this powerful tape and wrap it around their feet, securing the Bibles to them. I know it is a funny visualization. But what kind of influence would the church have if we all committed to spiritually Gorilla taping The Word to our every step, every decision, everything we speak, and every turn we take in our lives? What if we put The Word and its instructions as our guide, even in the small decisions we make, laying down our fleshly tendencies? If this became a lifestyle, then even if we are surrounded by darkness or are in places where our convictions are challenged, our life would be a light based on The Word. May we all spiritually Gorilla tape the Bible to our feet.

Today's Challenge To Dig Deeper:
Close your eyes and picture you are walking with a Bible Gorilla taped to the bottom of each of your feet. Then keep this picture in your mind as you walk throughout your day. Let it be a reminder to base every decision on the principles and commandments found in The Word. This includes conversations you are in. When we stand on The Word, we stand taller in Him.

Evening Reflection:
Write down any thoughts or revelations you gained today regarding Gorilla taping the Bible to your feet.

OUR TONGUE IS A WEAPON
November 8

Morning Rinse: Psalms 120-125
Featured Verse: Psalm 120:2 *Deliver my soul, O Lord, from lying lips, from a deceitful tongue.*

Our tongue is such a powerful weapon. I believe that if we really knew the impact it makes in the spiritual realm, we would reconsider most of what comes out of our mouth. How we use our words are points of reference in many verses throughout scripture, so we know this subject is important to our Heavenly Father. Our words impact His heart and cause Him to take notice. We can either use our words to cry out for help and to gain victory through praise, impacting His kingdom, or we can use that same tongue for the enemy's kingdom. Lying and a deceitful tongue are characteristics completely opposite of God's standards and help further the enemy's kingdom. God is a God of truth. A God of honesty. A God of authenticity. These are the characteristics to strive for. When we follow His standards and commit to do and say good things, we are choosing to live out good for His kingdom. The question we must ask ourselves daily can sting a little, but if we strive for goodness with our tongue, God's kingdom will be a stronger force. The question is, how do we use our tongue, the weapon? Do we use our tongue for God's kingdom, or do we use it to further the enemy's kingdom? The choice is yours.

Today's Challenge To Dig Deeper:
Ask yourself what kingdom you further with your tongue. Be honest when you answer. If there is anything that comes to mind that you need to change, then purpose in your heart to raise your standard. Use your words for God's kingdom, doing good for His glory and His house. Repent and start a new day today, being on guard with your words.

Evening Reflection:
Did you make any changes today in your heart regarding how you use your tongue, that will impact God's kingdom in a positive way? Will you praise more? Will you live in truth and authenticity? Will you cease gossip? Write out what changes you are making.

CHILDREN AS A REWARD
November 9

Morning Rinse: Psalms 126-130
Featured Verse: Psalm 127:3 *Behold, children are a gift from the Lord, the fruit of the womb is a reward.*

As I sit quietly in the early morning hours, writing today's Morning Rinse, I am writing from the home of my oldest daughter, Haley, who lives in Dallas, and her husband, my first son-in-love, Dre. Haley was about five years old when I first grasped the power of today's Featured Verse, and now she and Dre have a five-year-old. During that notable moment of soaking in the message of these verses years ago, I asked God to help me see her as a reward. And now I have the heart to see my grandchildren as a reward, too. Rewards come in various forms. They can be a gift, a medal, a bonus at work, a form of compensation or incentive, a trophy, or even some form of a prize. This is how God views children, and how we should view them as well. We all have children in our lives, whether from our own womb or from someone else's. Regardless of who the birth parents are, we all have access to the younger generation. If you do not have children of your own, you might be an aunt or uncle. You might be a teacher. Or, you might have friends with children. Whatever the case may be, claim the full assurance and guarantee that God sees children as extremely valuable, and therefore, so should we. Children are not inconvenient. They are not invaluable. They are not a nuisance. They are not insignificant. They are a high prize.

Today's Challenge To Dig Deeper:
Ask God to help you see children as valuable as He sees them. Ask Him to increase your love for children to an even greater capacity, even seeing them as a reward or a prize. In your efforts of loving children more today, do something special for either your child(ren), or someone else's child. Send a note. Take them for a special trip for ice cream. Buy a small gift. Do something tangible to let them know how special they are.

Evening Reflection:
What did you do for a child, or children, in your life today? How did it go? How did they receive your act of love?

UNIFIED FOR PURPOSE
November 10

Morning Rinse: Psalms 131-135
Featured Verse: Psalm 133:1 *Behold, how good and how pleasant is it for brothers to dwell together in unity.*

There is something magical when an audience experiences a dance performance where the dancers are flawlessly synced, or when a sports team plays so well together that seemingly every play has a purpose or strategy behind it. It is as if there is an underlying conversation amongst those involved that fuses them together where words are often not even needed. The silence is already understood due to each team member having the same end purpose. This is true unity. The experience is magical and beautiful. Yet, to be unified is not magic. It is not a mystery. It is not science. It is a matter of the heart. Unfortunately, unity is misunderstood and even disobeyed in the church. But if we all grasped the teachings of David deep in our hearts, we would understand being unified does not always mean we will agree on how things should be done in an organization or on a team. It is instead, being fused together to complete a final purpose. The church's purpose is to reach the lost and make disciples. The HOW is often what trips us up and causes disunification. We sometimes get so caught up in wanting things done our way, we bruise relationships, displaying a bad example to those in the world. The church should be the very best example of unity there is for the purpose of drawing people out of darkness. And yet, I have seen church members get stuck on the process of the purpose, instead of the end goal of the purpose. Dancers must unify for their final performance. Sports teams must be unified to win games. Believers must unify to effectively fulfill God's purpose. Church members having an underlying unified conversation of purpose causes the church to be pleasant for both those new to a congregation, as well as those already part of the community.

Today's Challenge To Dig Deeper:
I can venture to say we have all been guilty of contributing to disunification in our church community at one point or another, whether through a judgmental heart, a gossiping conversation, or selfish acts. Search your heart. If the Lord recalls any behavior that has been disunifying, ask for forgiveness and cease from those activities. Purpose in your heart to lay down selfish desires, and be a unified team member for the final purpose of God's kingdom.

Evening Reflection:
Did the Lord talk to you about any disunifying behaviors you have, whether present or in the past? What changes did you make to be more unified?

IMPRECATORY PSALMS
November 11

Morning Rinse: Psalms 136-138
Featured Verses: Psalm 137:8-9 *O daughter of Babylon, you devastated one, how blessed will be the one who repays you with the recompense with which you have repaid us. How blessed will be the one who seizes and dashes your little ones against the rock.*

Part of studying the Bible is trying to understand passages such as today's Featured Verses. In 1997, I wrote in my 3-ring binder the question, "What does this verse mean?" It was not until decades later that I made a concerted effort to answer this question. No, God does not advocate dashing kids against rocks. To understand these verses, we must understand the context of all of Psalm 137. I began reading what commentators and theologians wrote about these verses and learned many describe Psalm 137 as an 'imprecatory psalm.' "Imprecatory" means "to invoke evil or curses on an enemy."[26] A few other examples of imprecatory psalms are Psalms 69, 94, 109, and 143, just to name a few. Without understanding the context, the words in these psalms can raise ethical questions on exactly why they are even in the Bible. The inclusion of imprecatory psalms has some common theories, including the idea that when these specific psalms were spoken, they were allegorical and belonged to a specific time period. Psalm 137 was written during the time of the Jewish exile in Babylon, where they were taken as slaves after the city of Jerusalem was burned down. The Jews were then told to sing one of the songs of Zion (137:1). This command was almost a form of mockery. One commentator described this scenario as like the time of slavery when a slave owner beat a slave and then asked him to sing. The slave would begin singing in his own language for only the other slaves to understand. The words of that song could have gone like this, "You have caused us much pain. May your crops vanish like the dew. You have beaten our children. May the same thing happen to you." The slave owner never knew the wish of revenge the slaves were singing. But these songs are like the imprecatory psalms sung by the Israelites. They had sung for all the nations of their enemies to be destroyed. God sees our hurts. He is never blind to our tears nor silent to our pain. He hears our honest cries of revenge and heals the pain if we let Him.

Today's Challenge To Dig Deeper:
Run a search on an *imprecatory psalm* and read about the context of these types of passages. Many atheists use imprecatory psalms to discredit the Bible. As we study, understanding context is vital to our walk and having the confidence to stand up for The Word.

Evening Reflection:
What did you learn about the context of an imprecatory psalm?

---

[26] https://www.thefreedictionary.com/imprecatory

GOD'S BOOK
November 12

Morning Rinse: Psalms 139-141
Featured Verse: Psalm 139:16 *Your eyes have seen my unformed substance; and in Your book were all written the days that were ordained for me, when as yet there was not one of them.*

Have you ever looked at your life and accepted the fact that God has purposefully chosen you for important missions to further His kingdom? When we walk in Him, we are walking out that ordained purpose. When we are guided by His voice and walk in obedience, every appointment we have is divine and written in His book before we were even born. Think about that. God has a book with our name in it, and He wrote it before you were even born! He has already blessed our way, and it is not only written down, but the path is already prepared for us. Doors are in front of us to be opened. If we let Him, He will guide us when to walk, when to sit, when and what to speak, how to go about our life, and even where to live. He has even sent an angel to help keep us on the path He has prepared for us (Exodus 23:20). How do we walk out what God has written in His book? We simply obey His Word, and listen to the still, small voice that warns us when we are about ready to do or say something we should avoid. Our name is in His book with a plan for our lives, and He wants us to succeed in that plan.

Today's Challenge To Dig Deeper:
Read Psalm 139 again, and then look up a few more Bible translations of verses 16-18. One translation I particularly like for this passage is The Passion Translation (TPT). Soak in the fact that God values you and wants you to fulfill a great assignment. Stay true to your purpose and live out today knowing you are written in His book.

Evening Reflection:
Did you get a deeper revelation today of your purpose, or the fact that you are meant for an assignment? How did you respond or feel?

PLANTS AND PILLARS
November 13

Morning Rinse: Psalms 142-144
Featured Verse: Psalm 144:12 *Let our sons in their youth be as grown-up plants, and our daughters as corner pillars fashioned as for a palace.*

I usually do not like scrolling social media before my morning devotions. I tend to get lost in the world of Instagram, Facebook, and other platforms, only to realize an hour or maybe even two has passed by, and the intent to be productive with my time is wasted. This morning, though, as I was preparing to read today's Morning Rinse and write this devotion, I opened my Instagram and happened upon a post from Priscilla Shirer, an author and speaker. She was praying for all the youth out in the world who are preparing to leave their homes for their first or second year of college. How timely to come across her prayer, just moments before I began writing. In her prayer, she first repented for our society not prioritizing a relationship with God, and she asked God to reintroduce Himself to the younger generation. She then prayed for our daughters to be like walls, strong and solid, and that God would give our youth a spiritual backbone to be a loud voice of truth on their campuses. She prayed they would know who they are in Christ. Her prayer continued, modeling after David's prayer in today's Featured Verse, by asking God to grow and blossom our youth with integrity and character. I'm grateful I have a generation before me who has prayed. My mother-in-law, Marty Jones, is a prime example. She used to put verses on the soles of my husband's shoes as he went off to college. And she prays these types of prayers still to this day. Just as King David, Priscilla, my parents, and many leaders of faith have prayed, we too can pray effectively for our youth, and reach the heart of God with our voices. Prayers help move His hand to be a guide for our sons to grow in maturity and wisdom beyond their years, like plants growing to mature trees in a forest. God's hands help grow our daughters to become pillars of faith like the pillars holding up the foundation of a palace. David's prayers from the Bible can truly be used for our lives today. May God protect the next generation. May He keep them shielded from physical harm, and protect their souls and their minds.

Today's Challenge To Dig Deeper:
Make a list of every youth you know that is headed off to college for their first or second year. Pray over them today. If you feel inclined, send a note, call them, have flowers delivered, or even send a little special gift to them, just to let them know you are praying for them.

Evening Reflection:
Who did you pray for today? Did you reach out to them? Did you send them a card or gift?

PROMISE TO PRAISE
November 14

Morning Rinse: Psalms 145-147
Featured Verse: Psalm 145:2 *Every day I will bless You, and I will praise Your name forever and ever.*

We can at times have the belief if we do good, think good, have a good heart, and act on good intensions, our character will never be attacked. This is simply not true. An example of this is in the life of David. He is described several times as a man after God's own heart. First by Samuel (1 Samuel 13:14), and then again by the Apostle Paul (Acts 13:22). While David was not perfect, his peers witnessed his life of worship. In fact, his repentance written in Psalm 51 became a nationwide song proclaiming God's grace and mercy. He ended up writing seventy-three of the psalms, and potentially some of the forty-nine psalms with anonymous authors. His heart of praise led him to do plenty of good, like taking care of the ark, appointing people to worship around the clock, and leaving a legacy of a king who never turned to idolatry, unlike most of the forty-two kings who ruled Judah and Israel. Despite his goodness, though, his character was still attacked. He was also talked about, and even hunted for years by a former friend, after he became a national hero. Even though he experienced these things, he remained a warrior at heart. Not just on the battlefield, but in his daily life. What can we learn from David on how to respond when our own character gets attacked, even when we do good or make positive influences in our community? We see the answer in today's Featured Verse. No matter what David was going through, he made a positive declaration that he would praise God's name forever, and he would bless His name every day. When someone attacks your character, worship. When a friend turns their back on you, praise. If the character of David, a man after God's own heart, can be attacked, we must squelch the false belief that we are somehow shielded. Lay down this belief, and instead, promise to praise.

Today's Challenge To Dig Deeper:
Have you been underlining the positive affirmations as we have studied Psalms? (See the devotion for October 6.) Underline today's Featured Verse in your Bible. Then read the verses again as a promise to praise even when your character is attacked.

Evening Reflection:
Did you promise to praise, no matter what is going on in your life? Write about it.

ORCHESTRA OF PRAISE!
November 15

Morning Rinse: Psalms 148-150
Featured Verse: Psalm 150:6 *Let everything that has breath praise the Lord. Praise the Lord!*

There is no better way to end the book of Psalms than on a high, climactic note of praise directed right to our Heavenly Father. You can almost hear the melody of this book ending with a loud, beautiful note, like the ending of an orchestra concert, when the conductor unifies the instrumentalists to hold the last critical note by the raising of his baton. This last note resounds through the air, and moves the audience so powerfully they rise to their feet in a standing ovation. The applause from the crowd fills the air, making it difficult to leave the beautifully charged atmosphere the orchestra created. The last climactic note causes even the chairs and floor to respond in vibration. This is the picture of how the book of Psalms ends, and this is what happens when all of creation praises Him. Can you imagine what God sees from His throne, when He hears the praises given to Him? This is what He longs for from us. No matter what we go through, we must continue to praise Him. And this, my friend, is the main message of the entire book of Psalms. The amazing part about this message is, we have been given a seat in the orchestra of global praise. Our seat is next to all of the heights in heaven, His angels, His hosts, the sun and moon, all the stars, the highest heavens, the waters above, the earth, sea monsters and all deeps, fire, hail, snow, clouds, stormy winds, mountains, hills, fruit trees, cedars, beasts, cattle, creeping things, winged fowl, kings of the earth, all people, princes, judges, young men, virgins, old men, children, His godly ones, and the sons of Israel. We have a seat in the orchestra of climactic praise meant for Him. Will we accept our part of praising every day, no matter what we endure? Throughout the book of Psalms, we learned how to praise through positive declarations. Praise can also be given by singing, dancing, and playing musical instruments. May we all stay seated in the global orchestra that praises our Heavenly Father.

Today's Challenge To Dig Deeper:
Use a highlighter and highlight every time 'Praise the Lord' or 'Praise Him' is written throughout today's Morning Rinse. Take to heart the importance of your seat in the global orchestra of praise, and never stop praising Him, no matter what you go through. Commit to having a heart of worship like David.

Evening Reflection:
Did you gain any revelations about praise from today's Morning Rinse? What are any last thoughts, as we close out the study of Psalms?

READ, HEED, AND PROCEED
November 16

Morning Rinse: Revelation 1-3
Featured Verse: Revelation 1:3 *Blessed is he who reads and those who hear the words of the prophecy, and heed the things which are written in it; for the time is near.*

Let me first say how proud I am of you for your commitment to read the book of Revelation with me. As a preacher's kid, I cannot count the number of times I have heard people say they will not read this book because it is too hard to understand. While those statements usually come from a good heart, it is key to recognize that we will be blessed when we read the entire Bible, not just the parts that make us comfortable. To begin our understanding of this book, John wrote down three main messages from Jesus that we will explore. In Revelation 1:19, Jesus instructs him to "*Therefore write the things which you have seen, and the things which are, and the things which will take place after these things.*" John wrote what he saw in a vision. Some Bible scholars believe he was transported into the future by the spirit, just as a prophet sees into the future. These first few chapters set us up to not only heed what he saw, but to make it applicable to our lives today. First, God instructs John to write letters to the seven churches in Asia (1:4). These churches are Ephesus, Smyrna, Pergamum, Thyatira, Sardis, Philadelphia, and Laodicea. Out of these churches, two of them received no correction and are churches for us to use as role models as we live our own lives of faith even today. These two churches are Smyrna and Philadelphia. The other five may have good deeds within their common behaviors, but unfortunately have things that God held against them. We need to examine how their behaviors might apply to our own lives, as well as our church body as a whole. These letters may convict us and stir us to make a change in our own personal lives, or maybe even find a new church community to connect with. Or they may give us hope with confirmation that we are already in a Smyrna or Philadelphia-type church. Regardless of how these letters spoke to you, may we all read, heed, and proceed to live a life, so we are ready when Jesus returns.

Today's Challenge To Dig Deeper:
Highlight in your Bible the entire letters to Smyrna and Philadelphia as a reminder that these are the two churches to model after. While we ultimately need to model after Christ, it is important to have role models on this earth. If there are behaviors in any of the letters that convict you, repent and ask God to help you become more like these two churches.

Evening Reflection:
Write down any revelation the Lord gave you about the seven letters and how they may apply to your life or your church. Do you have any action steps to take in becoming more like Smyrna and Philadelphia?

GUARDING WITH CHARACTER
November 17

Morning Rinse: Revelation 4-5
Featured Verses: Revelation 4:6-7 *And before the throne there was something like a sea of glass, like crystal; and in the center and around the throne, four living creatures full of eyes in front and behind. The first creature was like a lion, and the second creature like a calf, and the third creature had a face like that of a man, and the fourth creature was like a flying eagle.*

Today's Morning Rinse makes it incredibly exciting to read about the futuristic scene John was invited to watch. My mind's eye can only vaguely imagine the breathtaking setting as he was caught up in this vision that revealed heaven's stage. His eyes probably spanned the atmosphere, and then landed on Jesus sitting on the throne. Oh, that would be enough, right? But his eyes capture more. They reveal the beauty and vastness of all of heaven's environment, and it had to be nearly indescribable. He illustrates colors, some probably too hard to define. He also tells of a rainbow around the throne illuminated with thunder and lightning above it, and a crystal-like floor paving a way right up to it. Oh, the beauty. The awestruck wonder. The glory. This scene culminates an atmosphere of praise, with all of creation giving glory and honor to the one true King. Some of what John writes about is very similar to the writings of Daniel and Ezekiel, including the four living creatures. I wonder if John had an 'ah-ha' moment where he enthusiastically thought, "This is what they saw, too!" Scholars agree these creatures are not true animals, but are a symbol of the characteristics of God, and give a picture of who He is. The lion represents His majesty and power. The calf, or some Bible translations call it an ox, show His faithfulness and servanthood. The man represents His intelligence, and His human form coming to us sinless. And the eagle represents His sovereignty and divinity. These creatures embody God's character, which is what guards his throne. Heaven embodies God's character. Do you guard the beauty of your world by your character?

Today's Challenge To Dig Deeper:
Underline in your Bible all the adjectives describing heaven in today's Morning Rinse. Just like heaven is guarded by God's character, we can also guard our homes and testimonies by our character. Our world on this earth is a small picture of all of God's beauty. Be thankful for what you have, and remind yourself we will see His throne too, someday.

Evening Reflection:
Do you have a heart of awe and wonder, not just of heaven, but of the picture of heaven in your own world? Do everything you can to protect your world with your character.

OPENING THE SEALS (PART 1)
November 18

Morning Rinse: Revelation 6-7
Featured Verses: Revelation 6:1-2 *Then I saw when the Lamb broke one of the seven seals, and I heard one of the four living creatures saying as with a voice of thunder, "Come." I looked, and behold, a white horse, and he who sat on it had a bow; and a crown was given to him, and he went out conquering and to conquer.*

Today's Morning Rinse begins to describe the event most Christians define as The Great Tribulation. This event will last for seven years and commence at the opening of the first seal. Depending on your denomination and belief, you may interpret events in Revelation a little differently than other believers. The first interpretation to examine is whether the church, or believers, will experience any part of this event. Some believe the church will be taken before the Tribulation Period begins, while others believe some of the church will endure some, or even all of it. What you believe regarding this topic may determine your interpretation of who is sitting on the white horse. Most people who believe the church will not go through the Tribulation, believe this rider is the Antichrist. This is my belief, and here are my reasons. First, Jesus is the one opening all the seals. It would be inconsistent for the one opening the seals to also be the actual contents of the first seal. Second, throughout scripture the Antichrist is the one who comes to begin the Tribulation period. The rider is bringing on this event, making it my interpretation that it is the Antichrist. Third, Jesus already has a crown on His head, so it must be someone else who is receiving one. And lastly, Jesus only needs the Word as His weapon, not a bow, which usually represents military power. The first six seals describe what is going to happen in the first three and a half years of the Tribulation Period. Another interpretation to research is to determine what events happen during the middle of the Tribulation Period. Many believe chapter seven of Revelation is describing what happens during this time, and there seems to be a moment when heaven pauses. This pause reveals four angels holding back the last judgement (7:1), seal number seven. During this moment, all of heaven takes note of all the people who died in the first half of the Tribulation Period, while applauding the one hundred forty-four thousand evangelists from out of Israel.

Today's Challenge To Dig Deeper:
If you do not know what your pastor believes regarding ideas mentioned in today's devotion, ask him. Ask for scriptural references he uses to come to his conclusion. Try to form an individual interpretation of what you believe.

Evening Reflection:
What is your interpretation of who the rider is in the first seal? Do you believe the church will go through part or all of the Tribulation Period?

OPENING THE SEALS (PART 2)
November 19

Morning Rinse: Revelation 8-10
Featured Verses: Revelation 10:9-10 *So I went to the angel, telling him to give me the little book. And he said to me, "Take it and eat it; it will make your stomach bitter, but in your mouth it will be sweet as honey." I took the little book out of the angel's hands and ate it, and in my mouth it was sweet as honey; and when I had eaten it, my stomach was made bitter.*

Today's Morning Rinse continues with the opening of the last of the seven seals. Many believe this last seal launches the last half of the Tribulation Period, and includes the greatest destruction and manifestation of evil ever known to man. Within the seventh seal are seven angels, each with a trumpet. When they each blow their trumpet, God's judgement is released. Sadly, nature and creation will not be safeguarded, which will cause grave devastation. For instance, when a third of the trees and all the green grass is burned up (8:7), the process of photosynthesis and production of oxygen will be disrupted. Then one third of the animals in the sea will be destroyed, some believe by an earthquake, which also destroys all ships out to sea (8:9). One third of all the streams and rivers are made bitter, killing those who drink from these waters (8:11). The fourth trumpet of judgement will withhold one third of the light from the sun, moon, and stars (8:12). This judgement reaches far beyond earth, and clearly shows that our sins affect so much more than we could ever imagine. The fifth angel will sound his trumpet, releasing what many believe is Satan himself, the fallen angel. He is then given authority to release the demons confined in the Abyss (Luke 8:30-31, Jude 6). The sixth angel releases four more angels believed to be leaders of the great army mentioned in 9:16. While the angels are blowing their trumpets, one more angel comes down from heaven who has a rainbow over his head, and his face shines like the sun (10:1). In today's Featured Verses, a book is referenced and given to John to eat by this angel. This book is both bitter and joyful, and represents God's final plan for this world. The sweetness represents how believers view the Word of God as sweet, but the bitterness comes from the fact that those who deny Christ will suffer eternal damnation. This knowledge is hard to digest, and should give us a greater desire to pray for those who are lost.

Today's Challenge To Dig Deeper:
Do you know anyone who is not saved? Make a list of those names and pray that God will make Himself known to them in a powerful way, and the Holy Spirit will draw them to salvation.

Evening Reflection:
After reading about the seven seals, how do you feel about the Tribulation Period?

JOHN'S FLASHBACK
November 20

Morning Rinse: Revelation 11-12
Featured Verse: Revelation 12:10 *Then I heard a loud voice in heaven, saying, "Now the salvation, and the power, and the kingdom of our God and the authority of His Christ have come, for the accuser of our brethren has been thrown down, he who accuses them before our God day and night."*

Have you ever read a book where the writer gave so much description to one event, it took several chapters to portray all the details? This is like what is happening in today's Morning Rinse. John is still describing events occurring near the middle of the Tribulation Period. This includes the death and resurrection of the two witnesses. It also includes the blowing of the seventh trumpet in the seventh seal (11:15), which instigates the bowl judgments that we will read about in the coming chapters. Imagine the utter chaos across the globe where no one is spared from the pandemics, food shortages, wars, environmental issues, water impurities, riots, deaths, and the vast suffering. There will be no rest from God's judgement during this time. After the seventh trumpet is blown in John's vision, he then sees a flashback. Starting with chapter 12, this flashback displays where sin indeed came from, and the war between God and Satan during that time. My former pastor, Dr. George Westlake, Jr, and author of a book called *Daniel and Revelation*, describes several events in the book of Revelation as a Parenthetical Enlargement (PE). These specific events referenced as a PE are throughout portions of chapters 7, 10-14 and then in 17-18. A PE is merely a deeper description of an event that has already been mentioned in the Bible. John writes one PE of the woman, representing Israel, the son, representing Jesus, and the dragon, representing Satan. Also in the flashback, he sees Satan and one third of the angels waging war against God, all being thrown from heaven. Then he hears a loud voice declaring salvation, power and the kingdom of God delivered by the death of Jesus on the cross. This flashback should remind us Jesus came to save us, and God will ultimately destroy evil once and for all so we can live free from the chains of bondage, forever in His presence. Evil must be destroyed, and Revelation is just a description of how the destruction will occur. Do not be afraid. Be thankful we are God's children and have eternal life through Jesus Christ.

Today's Challenge To Dig Deeper:
Take one portion of today's Morning Rinse and do a little research on how various commentators explain it. For example, research the two witnesses, or the seventh seal, or about Satan being thrown from heaven.

Evening Reflection:
What portion did you research? What did you learn?

GOD'S MESSAGE WILL NOT BE SILENCED
November 21

Morning Rinse: Revelation 13-14
Featured Verses: Revelation 14:6-7 *And I saw another angel flying in midheaven, having an eternal gospel to preach to those who live on the earth, and to every nation and tribe and tongue and people; and he said with a loud voice, "Fear God, and give Him glory, because the hour of His judgement has come; worship Him who made the heaven and the earth and sea and springs of waters."*

The third act in a movie is when the climax of all nail-biting moments occurs. It is when the audience is often brought to tears or scoot to the edge of their theater seats. Today's Morning Rinse describes events that make it like a third act. Emotions are high and fear is rampant, which is the engine driving evil to appear successful on the earth. The chaos continues to climb as Satan gains power, passing this power on to those under his authority. He even spiritually possesses the Antichrist and brings him back to life after a fatal wound (13:12). Other leaders under Satan's power rise across the globe, and all blaspheme God, joining with the Antichrist to make war on all believers (13:7). Also, the false prophet enters the scene, deceiving people on the earth with his signs and wonders, including making a demonic statue speak (13:13-15). Regardless of the evil across the earth, each person still has a choice and opportunity to accept God's truth. Knowing time is running short and the Tribulation Period is nearing the end, God makes a way for all to hear one final warning. This warning is preached to everyone across the globe. I have heard commentators voice an opinion that this last message will probably come by way of the internet. Regardless of how it will be delivered, all will hear it. This message of truth will not be silenced, and no one will be able to say they never heard of Jesus. We know global leaders have already put systems into place to try to muzzle those spreading the gospel by way of censorship and even detainment. But we can also know these temporary, seemingly large victories of evil are just that – temporary. God's voice will not be silenced. Victory is ultimately His, and Satan does not want this message told. Just wait. The final chapters are coming.

Today's Challenge To Dig Deeper:
Ask your sphere of influence, whether that be your pastor, members of your church, friends, or through social media, for the name of a missionary in a country that forbids the preaching of the gospel. Pray for him/her today, and then send a note of encouragement.

Evening Reflection:
What is the missionary's name? What did you learn about him/her?

WHERE IS GOD'S ARMY?
November 22

Morning Rinse: Revelation 15-17
Featured Verse: Revelation 16:21 *And huge hailstones, about one hundred pounds each, came down from heaven upon men, and men blasphemed God because of the plague of the hail, because its plague was extremely severe.*

Can you feel the intensity in today's Morning Rinse? John is literally watching a movie unfold. I can imagine how fast his heartbeat must have been, as he beheld the seven angels making their appearance and then releasing God's wrath on the earth. I can imagine the chain of emotions in his heart, as he watches his mind's eye take in the first six bowls of judgement. Despite these judgements transpiring across the globe, a mass awakening will not occur. Instead, people will continue to blaspheme God due to the evil and hatred overtaking their hearts. As if evil could not get any thicker, or the climax of this vision any stronger, John sees a global army forming with the sole purpose to battle against Jesus. I wonder how he felt watching the ultimate battle of good versus evil materialize before his very eyes. In fact, in 16:13, John watches how Satan's global army is enlisted. Three frog-like demons come out of the mouth of the dragon, the beast, and the false prophet, and go into the world to gather the soldiers. Some scholars believe the beast is not actually a being or a person, but rather a global system of control. Whoever takes its mark will be easily found and probably demon-possessed by now. All will follow these demons to war, which is called the Battle of Armageddon. When this global army is positioned for war, the seventh bowl is released, and a voice from heaven says, "It is done" (16:17). Up to this point in today's Morning Rinse, John has been observing a high-level view of the events leading up to this final battle. Then in chapter 17, the angels take him in for his close-up, to give him more detail about what led up to this battle. Unfortunately, the corruption includes the harlot, symbolizing what many scholars believe is a picture of the false church. The world government and the false church have a great relationship, helping to surmount the evil in the world. However, the false church becomes so fake, even those ruling with the Antichrist will turn on them (17:16). But where is God's army? Just wait.

Today's Challenge To Dig Deeper:
Do you know of anyone who blasphemes God? Pray for them today. Remember, we do not fight against flesh and blood. Pray for their salvation.

Evening Reflection:
How are you feeling about this high-level study of Revelation?

BE READY, BE READY, BE READY!
November 23

Morning Rinse: Revelation 18-19
Featured Verses: Revelation 19:11-14 *And I saw heaven opened, and behold, a white horse, and He who sat on it is called Faithful and True, and in righteousness He judges and wages war. His eyes are a flame of fire, and on His head are many diadems; and He has a name written on Him which no one knows except Himself. He is clothed with a robe dipped in blood, and His name is called The Word of God. And the armies which are in heaven, clothed in fine linen, white and clean, were following Him on white horses.*

Behold, He comes. And with Him are His armies. That includes all who are redeemed by the blood of the Lamb. Are you excited yet? Can you envision how this story ends? Jesus will come back and, in His righteousness, will judge and wage war against evil. And He wins! That means WE WIN TOO! His entry onto the scene is what many describe as the Second Coming of Christ. Many believe this event is separate from the rapture, which is when the church is taken up. When He comes back, He seizes the beast and the false prophet and throws them both into the lake of fire forever and ever. The person governing the world system, or the beast, is the Antichrist. I believe the reference of throwing the beast in, means throwing the Antichrist into the lake of fire, which also includes his power over the world system and Babylon. His power over this system, and even the false church, will be destroyed. At this time, the false church has become so corrupt, even the demons have made themselves right at home. How can this be? These so-called Christians opened the door to every evil spirit, allowing strongholds to take over their lives. It starts with allowing the little things to overtake, like worry and selfishness. It also includes complaining, gossiping, and being offended. These sins can then grow into sexual promiscuity, drugs, and even demonic worship. We do not like to admit this, but unfortunately, there are people who attend church even today who practice these things. However, during the Tribulation Period, those who practice these behaviors will become the norm. Jesus tells us that before the Tribulation Period even begins, half of the church will not be the true church (Matthew 24:40-42, Luke 17:34). Be ready, be ready, be ready! Behold, He is coming, and He wins.

Today's Challenge To Dig Deeper:
Look up the song called "The Days of Elijah." There are several artists who have recorded it, so you will find various versions, but the lyrics are the same. I personally enjoy Judy Jacobs. Let the message sink in.

Evening Reflection:
How do you feel about winning in the end?

OUR FOREVER HOME
November 24

Morning Rinse: Revelation 20-22
Featured Verses: Revelation 21:1-2 *Then I saw a new heaven and a new earth; for the first heaven and the first earth passed away, and there is no longer any sea. And I saw the holy city, new Jerusalem, coming down out of heaven from God, made ready as a bride adorned for her husband.*

These last three chapters of the book of Revelation cover many years and a lot of information. After the Antichrist and the false prophet are thrown into the lake of fire, Satan is bound for a thousand years in the abyss (20:3). This is like a holding cell in a prison. Those in Christ will rule and reign with Him on earth during this time (20:6). After the thousand years are over, which some call The Millennium, Satan is released. He once again deceives the nations and gathers all the forces of evil to attack the saints (20:9-10), but this time he is thrown into the lake of fire forever. John then sees the great white throne of God appear. This throne is the throne of judgement, where every person from history will stand to be judged by their deeds. No one will escape this throne. This is also where verification of each person's salvation will occur. If a name is not written in the book of life, it is evidence of that person not accepting salvation, and he cannot be in God's presence. He made his choice of how he wanted to live eternally and will be thrown into the lake of fire forever with Satan, his chosen god. John begins to describe the new heaven and the new earth. For all eternity, there will no longer be death, tears or evil, but instead those saved will be in the presence of the one true God. John describes this perfect city made of jasper, pure gold, and every precious stone including pearls. Not only is it beautiful beyond anything we have ever seen, but God's glory will illuminate the atmosphere, no longer requiring the sun or the moon. John saw the end of the story where we will live with Christ here forever. May we all stay on the path that leads to this city, our forever home.

Today's Challenge To Dig Deeper:
Pray again for those not saved. Ask the Holy Spirit to bring them to salvation so they may live in this great city with Jesus. Give thanks to God that you have seen the light.

Evening Reflection:
Write any last reflections you have from reading Revelation. Write how you feel and any last thoughts, including how proud you are to have completed this book.

CIRCUMCISION OF THE HEART
November 25

Morning Rinse: Romans 1-2
Featured Verse: Romans 1:16 *For I am not ashamed of the gospel, for it is the power of God for salvation to everyone who believes, to the Jew first and also to the Greek.*

If you are reading this devotional the way I designed it, then you just finished the book of Revelation. The ending of that book gives us a dynamic portrayal and picture of heaven, where Christ followers will spend eternity with Him. The book of Romans is a fantastic continuation of Revelation because it gets back to the heart of man, which is what leads us to our salvation journey and having a lifestyle of passionately living for God on this earth. Today's Featured Verse is one of the main themes of the book of Romans. When Paul says, "Jews first," he does not mean that Jews are more important. The Jews just received the gospel first. And when he says "Greek," this encompasses anyone not a Jew. Paul shows us we all have the chance to receive Christ and become equal brothers and sisters of faith. In this letter, Paul shares how we all sin, and he explains the practice of outward circumcision is not what brings salvation, but it is the circumcision of the heart. In Bible times, circumcision was an outward ritual signifying God's covenant with His people. But Jesus came to show us that rituals mean nothing if our heart is not right. Circumcising our heart is when we allow God to remove anything that keeps us from being fully devoted to Him, fully obedient to His Word, and completely unashamed of the gospel of truth. Paul is bold about sin in his letter to the Roman church, and encourages them to focus on their hearts, removing anything that goes against what Jesus taught.

Today's Challenge To Dig Deeper:
Allow God to cut anything away that is keeping you from growing stronger in your faith.

Evening Reflection:
What did God speak to you today regarding circumcising your heart? Is there anything He wants to cut away that is holding you back from a deeper relationship with Him?

CALLING IT FORTH
November 26

Morning Rinse: Romans 3-5
Featured Verse: Romans 4:17 *(as it is written, "A Father of many nations have I made you") in the presence of Him whom he believed, even God, who gives life to the dead and calls into being that which does not exist.*

I believe as we grow in faith, the desires in our hearts will continually mold and shape to become more like what God wants for our lives. These desires and directions are what some people call the 'vision for our life.' As we continue growing and living out our faith walk, we will naturally and organically get closer to our Heavenly Father. His perfect plan will continue to embed itself into our hearts, until our desires for our lives align perfectly with His desires. It is a beautiful thing when the vision we have in our hearts matches God's vision. Consistently seeing these desires with faith, will help us believe they will truly come to fruition. But not only do we need to see it finished, we need to guard it with our mouth. What comes out of our mouth is so important. Guarding God's vision for our life can be as simple as being careful who we tell. Unfortunately, some people do not always have our best interest at heart and can act selfishly, so we must have discernment in what we say and who we speak to about what God has put in our heart. Also, what we speak and what we see should govern how we pray. Today's Featured Verse is full of faith. It shows us it is okay to claim our vision before we see it fully manifested. If God calls something into being before it has been manifested, then we can too. So I ask you, what is in your heart that you know is from God, but has not yet been manifested on this earth? Do you pray for it to manifest, or do you just wait for it to happen without calling it forth? Maybe it is time to use your mouth to manifest your faith.

Today's Challenge To Dig Deeper:
Pray about the vision you have for your life. Ask God to help it align perfectly with His will. Ask Him to teach you how to pray and how to call forth the desires of your heart so your faith will increase.

Evening Reflection:
Did you grow in faith today as you began calling forth some of the things in your life?

ORDER IN THE COURT
November 27

Morning Rinse: Romans 6-8
Featured Verses: Romans 8:1-2 *Therefore there is now no condemnation for those who are in Christ Jesus. For the law of the Spirit of life in Christ Jesus has set you free from the law of sin and of death.*

The courtroom is full as you sit on trial while Satan seeks to convince the jurors to convict you. He recites everything you have ever done wrong, and in fact, brings witnesses to join him in the critique. Some of these witnesses are former friends, and some are even a few relatives. Their talking points have some validity, but Satan's lies of exaggeration compound their arguments. Their disruptive anger fills the courtroom. God hits a gavel on His desk and with authority declares, "Order in the court!" The shouting subsides and Satan finishes his closing argument, saying why you should be sentenced to death. All hope of redemption appears to be gone as you silently listen with tears of pain, remorse and repentance streaming down your face. Satan mercilessly finishes his report, and a guilty sentence appears inevitable. But suddenly the door to the courtroom opens and Jesus enters the room. He sovereignly walks to the empty space next to you and Satan sits down, knowingly defeated and humiliated at what he knows is coming next. The courtroom is silent as God focuses on Jesus and asks, "Do you have something to say in defense of this case?" Jesus glances at you with loving eyes and a smile. Hope surfaces again in your heart as you await Jesus' response. Jesus looks back at God and answers with a commanding voice, "I have freed him from this sentence by the cross. He has asked for forgiveness and his sins are never to be remembered again." This disturbs Satan and his witnesses, causing disorder once again. God hits the gavel on His desk again and firmly repeats, "Order in the court!" When silence returns, God turns to you and says, "Therefore, I have no condemnation for you. Jesus took your place. You are free. Go and sin no more." With an overwhelming sense of gratitude and relief, you rest in Jesus' loving embrace. After He releases you from this beautiful hug, He looks at you with a smile, grabs your hand, and together the two of you walk out of the courtroom, much to the dismay of all the condemners. This is the heart of the gospel.

Today's Challenge To Dig Deeper:
Memorize today's Featured Verses. We have all been given the chance to be free from a death sentence. Let this embed deep in your heart.

Evening Reflection:
Write down any thoughts you have about the courtroom scenario. Have you been judged, or have you been guilty of judging others?

TRUST THE MOLDER
November 28

Morning Rinse: Romans 9-11
Featured Verse: Romans 9:21 *Or does not the potter have a right over the clay, to make from the same lump one vessel for honorable use and another for common use?*

Sometimes I need to be reminded that God does not need me to counsel Him regarding things happening in my life. Can anyone else relate to this, or am I the only one who requires this reminder? As ridiculous as this sounds, I think it can be easy to remember that He is our creator, but difficult to trust that He knows more than we do regarding our daily endeavors. I am convinced in our moments of distrust, God finds humor in the conversations we have with Him. "God, do You see what just happened? What are you going to do about it?" Or what about those moments of self-pity when we ask, "God, but what about me?" I can envision Him smiling at us as He shakes His head with a fatherly gentleness and tries to impart His words of faith and wisdom into our hearts. We must remember we do not know more than He does. He created us, and He created us for a specific purpose. This may shock many, but He also does not owe any of us an answer or an explanation as to how He chooses to mold our lives. He is the potter, and we are His clay. He has the right to mold us and use us how He wants, and we have no right to criticize how He chooses to accomplish it. God knows our future and we do not. This can be tough to accept when we want things to go our way and in our own timing. We have no right to demand anything from Him. Instead, we must learn to trust and believe Him, letting go of our lives so He can mold them as He wishes. When we not only let go, trust, and become completely moldable, we ultimately resist our flesh, and rely on the Spirit to guide us in all things. Some may view this as a bit stifling. But instead, this is true freedom.

Today's Challenge To Dig Deeper:
Do you have moments of resisting the molding? Ask God to purge this from you. Ask Him to help you let go, while remaining moldable and trusting Him, the ultimate Molder.

Evening Reflection:
Write down any thoughts you have about letting go and being completely moldable.

PAUL'S DAILY LIVING INSTRUCTIONS
November 29

Morning Rinse: Romans 12-14
Featured Verses: Romans 12:9-10 *Let love be without hypocrisy. Abhor what is evil; cling to what is good. Be devoted to one another in brotherly love; give preference to one another in honor;*

Paul, in his letter to the Roman church, devotes an entire section to how to behave as a Christ follower. He writes about the importance of sacrificing our bodies to holiness, obeying authority, and operating in our spiritual gifts. He also includes how to act in practical, everyday living. Beginning with today's Featured Verses and continuing through verse 12:21, he makes a list of how to do this. What do you think his first item on his list is? He begins with love. He is not talking about simple love manifested by actions such as showing respect or surface compassion. He is talking about deep, heartfelt care and kindness that is authentic and true. This includes having brotherly devotion towards fellow Christ followers, honoring them, and putting their requests above our own desires. Loving others in this way takes a true investment of intentionality, united with purity. This does not mean we allow others to walk over us like a doormat. Instead, it is seeing the best in people and choosing to bless them even when we disagree with them. It is also choosing to hold close those who are in our inner circle, being continually strengthened by their love as we walk out this life here on earth. When we live in this kind of pure love, the rest of Paul's *daily living instructions* will be easier to follow. Rejoicing in hope, persevering in trials, and staying devoted to prayer (12:12), will become like second nature. When walking in this kind of love, it is easier to contribute to the needs of others and practice hospitality (12:13). Of course, Paul does not ask that we invite our enemies, or those who persecute us, into our homes. In fact, Paul instructs us to have humility, filling our inner circle with like-minded individuals who also live a life of humility (12:16). And finally, Paul wants us to live in peace whenever possible. The friends I mention in my acknowledgement section of this devotional are friends who live out this kind of love. Do you know anyone with these traits? Cherish them. Keep them. Hold them tight.

Today's Challenge To Dig Deeper:
Write a thank you note to all those you know who practice the traits Paul writes about.

Evening Reflection:
Who did you send a note to? Write down why you sent it to the individual(s) you chose.

ON THE FIELD OR ON THE SIDELINE
November 30

Morning Rinse: Romans 15-16
Featured Verses: Romans 15:15-16 *But I have written very boldly to you on some points so as to remind you again, because of the grace that was given me from God, to be a minister of Christ Jesus to the Gentiles, ministering as a priest the gospel of God, so that my offering of the Gentiles may become acceptable, sanctified by the Holy Spirit.*

Paul admits some of the things he wrote throughout his letter to the Romans are very bold. He may have even offended people regarding subjects he touched on. For example, some of the Jews at this time did not fully accept that the salvation gospel was for the Gentiles as well. But he makes it clear to the Roman church that it is for everyone, and encourages the church to unite with him so the Gentiles will accept his ministry. Did you know we, too, can play a role in how effective a ministry can be, even if we are not even involved in that ministry? Paul is not encouraging the church body to support ministries, or even preachers who do not align with the gospel. But he is encouraging saints to unify as a lifestyle, accepting and encouraging those who do preach the gospel, so all of our ministries can be a light to the world. If someone unsaved is getting ministered to, and then another Christ follower makes judgmental comments regarding how that ministry operates, the unsaved person may get turned off at the disunification of the church body and reject the gospel altogether. Paul is wanting a unified message felt and seen so as to not confuse those that are unsaved. So how do we unify as a body? By humbly living our lives for Christ, fleeing from sin, gossip, judgement, disunification, and offense. Also, the desire to be used for the glory of God must continue to grow in our hearts. It is easy to be thankful when God uses us for His kingdom, and we are in the spotlight of accolades, or when we see our fruit manifested. But are we equally as happy and joyful when God uses others? We, as Christ followers, should be a team. When we surrender to God as the coach, the unified spirit will ooze from our soul, out to the world. Sometimes we will be on the field, and other times we will be on the sidelines cheering for our teammates, as God uses them for the next play. Are we okay with both positions?

Today's Challenge To Dig Deeper:
Repent for any judgment calls you have made, and commit to unifying.

Evening Reflection:
As we end Romans, review your reflections about how to live. Make any last thoughts on what God did in your heart with this book.

December Rinsing

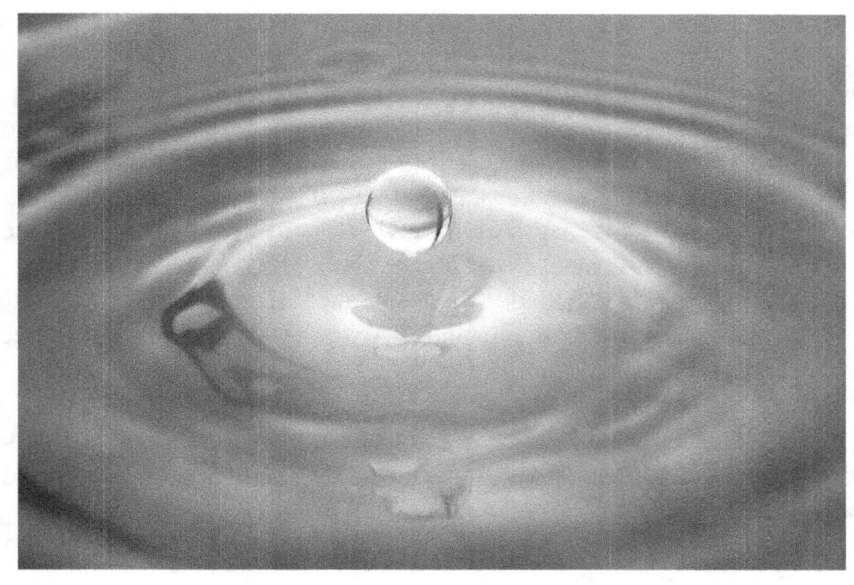

HOLY STUBBORNNESS
December 1

Morning Rinse: Ruth 1-2
Featured Verses: Ruth 1:16-17 *But Ruth said, "Do not urge me to leave you or turn back from following you; for where you go, I will go, and where you lodge, I will lodge. Your people shall be my people, and your God, my God. Where you die, I will die, and there I will be buried. Thus may the Lord do to me, and worse, if anything but death parts you and me."*

AH! Ruth! One of my favorite books of the Bible. Ruth's story opens by letting us know of a famine in the land. This famine had to have lasted for many years and must have been very serious. In fact, so serious, Elimelech moved Naomi and their two sons to Moab, despite it being a nation known for resentment towards Israel. After moving, both their sons marry Moabite women, one named Ruth and the other named Orpah. Tragically, not only did Elimelech die, but both sons died as well, leaving all three women as widows. This scenario can easily lead anyone to a season of depression, especially for Naomi. She lost not only her husband, but both her sons. To top off this difficult time, she was living in a foreign land. According to Judges 2 and 3, a war was occurring around this time between Moab and Israel. Could these men have died in this war? Possibly so. Despite these two nations at odds, Ruth and Naomi's relationship was very special. During this trying time, Naomi decides to return to her home in Israel. I can only imagine what she was going through. She believed moving back was best for herself, but out of love for her daughters-in-law, she persisted three times that they should stay with their Moabite families. Having to say goodbye to the three men closest to her through the tragedy of death, and now saying goodbye to Ruth and Orpah because of her planned move, had to be extremely grievous for her. Through her tears, she bade the ladies farewell, and Orpah returned to her family. Ruth, on the other hand, disagreed with Naomi, and insisted she stay with her. Ruth's decision was a direct result of her sensitivity to the Holy Spirit and what I call *holy stubbornness*. This bold trait surfaced and pushed the situation past Naomi's determination, and probably her depression as well. If Ruth had not displayed this tenacity with Naomi insisting NOTHING would come between them, there may not have been the book of Ruth, nor would she have been in God's perfect plan.

Today's Challenge To Dig Deeper:
Is there a decision you need to make that requires holy stubbornness? Could God be wanting you to have a holy boldness like Ruth? Be brave like Ruth. Obey like Ruth. Listen to God like Ruth.

Evening Reflection:
What does your holy stubbornness look like in your situation?

CARPE MOMENTS
December 2

Morning Rinse: Ruth 3-4
Featured Verses: Ruth 4:13-15 *So Boaz took Ruth, and she became his wife, and he went in to her. And the Lord enabled her to conceive, and she gave birth to a son. Then the women said to Naomi, "Blessed is the Lord who has not left you without a redeemer today, and may his name become famous in Israel. May he also be to you a restorer of life and a sustainer of your old age; for your daughter-in-law, who loves you and is better to you than seven sons, has given birth to him."*

A widely known Latin phrase, *carpe diem*, is most translated as *seize the day*. The Roman poet, Horace, was the first one known to have used this phrase in his poem called "Carpe Diem." He launched this phrase to encourage his readers to grab their day, making it purposeful in every action.[27] Unfortunately, if our days are filled with complaints and excuses, we will miss opportunities to be intentional and purposeful in every action and miss what this phrase intends. But when we do experience the pleasantry of *carpe diem*, we will say things like "I had the best day ever." How can we begin to experience *carpe diem* every day? One way is to do what I have adopted as *carpe moments*. When we seize *carpe moments*, the compound effect will give us our *carpe diem*. This is what Ruth and Boaz did. Ruth seized daily opportunities like working hard in the fields and living with integrity by not chasing men. Her intentional *carpe moments* ultimately led to a life of excellence known throughout the city (3:11), Boaz seized his *carpe moments* when he took notice of Ruth and protected her in his field (2:9-10). He also showed integrity and purity with her when he could have easily taken advantage of her (3:9-11). And he was also a man of his word, wasting no time in doing the right thing by giving his brother, the rightful heir of Elimelech's possessions, the opportunity to buy it all and honor their deceased relative. Since his brother was not able to make this purchase, Boaz seized the moment and purchased it all for himself and married Ruth. This power couple knew the importance of capturing these pure and holy *carpe moments*. His godly *carpe moments* ultimately set him and Ruth up to become the great-grandparents of David. You know what that means, right? They were in the lineage of Jesus!

Today's Challenge To Dig Deeper:
Each day is filled with *carpe moments* to help us seize our day for purpose, making an impact in the lives around us for God's kingdom. Look for them today and commit to building your days with *carpe moments* so your year can be full of *carpe diems*.

Evening Reflection:
Did you have any godly *carpe moments* today? What were they?

---

[27] https://homework.study.com/explanation/who-first-said-carpe-diem.html#:~:text=The%20first%20known%20use%20of,'

TINGLING EARS
December 3

Morning Rinse: 1 Samuel 1-3
Featured Verse: 1 Samuel 3:11 *The Lord said to Samuel, "Behold, I am about to do a thing in Israel at which both ears of everyone who hears it will tingle."*

Many historians agree that Samuel is around eleven years old when God wakes him up in the middle of the night by calling his name. At this young age, it is understandable that any child would assume their caretaker or parent is the one calling their name, especially if they are elderly and poor in eyesight like Eli (3:2). After being awakened a third time (3:8), Eli realizes the voice Samuel hears is the voice of God. So he sends him back to bed to wait on what was obviously God wanting to deliver a message to this youngster. Can you imagine Samuel lying in bed waiting for his name to be called by God Himself? I am sure sleep was far from his mind, and in fact, I can imagine him lying with wide eyes, blinking into the night, anxiously anticipating what would happen next. Waiting was also something his mother, Hannah, experienced. She waited for years to be blessed with a son (1:7). Her waiting included weeping, praying, and finally even making a promise of exchange to God by declaring if He gave her a son, she would give him back to Him to be consecrated for a life of service in the church. Like mother, like son, they connect in their waiting. Unlike Hannah, though, Samuel only had to wait moments. But I am sure for an eleven-year-old boy lying in the dark, the time felt like hours. Hannah's waiting ended in an answer to prayer with the conception of her baby boy, Samuel. And Samuel's waiting ended in God birthing an intimate relationship with him, calling him in the night, and starting him on a journey to become one of Israel's greatest prophets. God was getting Samuel ready to share news that would tingle, or shock, the world. God will use our waiting as well, to bring forth His message which will also tingle the ears of those listening. Your message may be exactly what others need, and may tingle their ears towards change. Stay waiting.

Today's Challenge To Dig Deeper:
Are you praying for an answer to prayer or a message from God? Don't give up. Stay waiting. Your answered prayer may be what is needed to shock those around you towards heart change.

Evening Reflection:
What were you about ready to give up on? Write your thoughts about waiting.

WITNESSING THE MESSAGE
December 4

Morning Rinse: 1 Samuel 4-6
Featured Verses: 1 Samuel 4:1-2 *Thus the word of Samuel came to all Israel. Now Israel went out to meet the Philistines in battle and camped beside Ebenezer while the Philistines camped in Aphek. The Philistines drew up in battle array to meet Israel. When the battle spread, Israel was defeated before the Philistines who killed about four thousand men on the battlefield.*

The message God gave Samuel from yesterday's Morning Rinse spread throughout the entire nation of Israel. This message was that God was going to destroy Eli's household because he did not properly handle the sins of his two sons (3:12-14). When this destruction came about, it caused many to die, beginning with four thousand men in a battle against the Philistines (6:2). After the Israelites were defeated, the rest of the people took matters into their own hands by removing the ark from the holy of holies, thinking it would protect them from any further destruction. I am sure Eli tried to convince them otherwise, knowing even more destruction would come if they took the ark. But his leadership voice was not adhered to. This can be a dangerous position as a leader. If your family or those you lead do not heed your direction, others may not either. Due to the people not listening to him, I am convinced he and Samuel were helpless in trying to retain the ark in Shiloh, and therefore, the people grabbed it. It boils down to selfishness. Eli was selfish about how he handled his family affairs, and the Israelites were selfish and disobedient about how they handled the ark. The removal of the ark from its safe place allowed the Philistines to steal it from the Israelites, resulting in more deaths throughout their cities. Even the statue of the Philistine god, Dagon, could not stand in the presence of the one true God (5:2-4). By the time the ark was returned to Israel, the total recorded deaths were fifty-four thousand and seventy Israelites, not including the unrecorded deaths throughout the Philistine cities. Sin and destruction go hand in hand, and it starts with leadership. Samuel's eyes, those same eyes blinking in the middle of the night waiting for God's voice, witnessed the consequences of the message he was given. His front row seat to the events probably helped strengthen the foundation of how he lived his life through the years as one of the greatest prophets of Israel.

Today's Challenge To Dig Deeper:
Is there a word from the Lord you have witnessed that has changed your life? These moments can be pivotal in our faith, and are part of our story. Think of what that occurrence was and begin writing it down.

Evening Reflection:
Did you finish writing down your pivotal moment? If not, finish writing it before you go to sleep. Make a note of where you wrote it down if it was not on these pages.

INSTANT ELEVATION
December 5

Morning Rinse: 1 Samuel 7-10
Featured Verse: 1 Samuel 9:17 *When Samuel saw Saul, the Lord said to him, "Behold, the man of whom I spoke to you! This one shall rule over My people."*

I wonder if the elders were recollecting the impact of the sins of Eli's son to justify their desired change for the nation. Against God's perfect plan, they requested Samuel anoint a king over Israel, instead of one of his sons as the next judge. It is hard to fully understand why they asked this of Samuel, especially since God's hand was against the Philistines all throughout Samuel's time as a judge (7:13). One would think keeping Samuel's blessings close through his lineage would be a no brainer. Maybe after reminiscing about the events under Eli's leadership, they were afraid of the nation's destiny upon Samuel's death, though. Nonetheless, they do not listen to Samuel, but instead pressure him to fabricate Israel like other nations, with a king over the military instead of a judge over the nation. Despite being displeased with their request, God tells Samuel to go ahead and appoint a king. Hence, the introduction of Saul. Saul was a man whose family was not only Benjaminites, the smallest tribe of Israel, but his family was also the lowest in the tribe, making it a shock to even be considered for this high position to guide the nation. However, God worked it out for him to become that king. Saul was just as surprised as everyone else, and in his insecurity, even questioned Samuel (9:20-21). But the moment Samuel laid eyes on him, Samuel knew God had called him for this purpose. In an instant, Saul went from a man searching for lost donkeys, to being elevated at the head of Samuel's dinner table (9:22). I am convinced God's hands led those wandering donkeys right into Samuel's path. Saul's elevation was sealed when Samuel anointed him as Israel's first king. Even though this was an imperfect plan, God began to use Saul to further the journey of a nation. In Saul's instant elevation, God changed his heart to not only the heart of a king, but the heart of a prophet (10:6), fully prepared for his purpose. We may not expect an instant elevation, or even think we are ready for one, but God can change our hearts as part of the preparation. And even after Saul knew what was ahead for his life, it took some time to let it soak in. In fact, he was selective in sharing about this instant elevation and even tried to hide on the day the public announcement was made (10:22). But there is no stopping God's instant elevation. Are you ready for yours?

Today's Challenge To Dig Deeper:
Sit quietly for thirty minutes and listen for God's voice. Ask Him to change your heart in preparation for your instant elevation. Be mindful of who you share this conversation with.

Evening Reflection:
What did God speak to you about today?

QUIT? MAY IT NEVER BE
December 6

Morning Rinse: 1 Samuel 11-13
Featured Verses: 1 Samuel 12:23-24 *"Moreover, as for me, far be it from me that I should sin against the Lord by ceasing to pray for you; but I will instruct you in the good and right way." Only fear the Lord and serve Him in truth with all your heart; for consider what great things He has done for you. But if you still do wickedly, both you and your king will be swept away.*

In today's Morning Rinse, the transition from Samuel's leadership to Saul's is now complete. The length of this transition is unclear, but it did not happen immediately, like Saul's instant elevation. Transition of power can take time. Samuel may have even drug it out by repeatedly expressing his disagreement with the Israelites' request to have a king (12:12). Maybe he did not want them to forget, with the passing of time, it was not God's perfect plan. To prove he was accurate in this opposition, he even asked God to send thunder and rain, a miracle during the dry harvesting season. The people knew they had committed this evil act against God, requesting a king, and yet He showed mercy and grace to them. It is wonderful the Israelites had Samuel to encourage them to get back on track, though. Quitting on them was not an option for him. In fact, he told them it would be a sin for him to quit praying for them. Not only does God want us constantly praying for the body of Christ, but He wants us to be examples of good and right ways. If we do not pray and live right, we are not maintaining our responsibilities as Christ followers. On top of this, when we do not pray for others, especially when they sin or misbehave, we, in essence, have quit on them. And equally so, when we choose to not live a life pointing others to a good and right way, we give up not only on them, but on ourselves. Quit? May it never be.

Today's Challenge To Dig Deeper:
Is there someone close to you who has made a mistake or made some sinful choices? Pray for them today. Then pray for yourself, asking God to help you live a life that shows others the good and right way to live. Are there any behaviors you need to change to fulfill this?

Evening Reflection:
Who did you pray for today? Did you find your heart feeling more compassion for them as you prayed? Are there any behaviors you need to change to be an example of good and right ways for them and others?

OBEDIENCE IS BETTER THAN SACRIFICE
December 7

Morning Rinse: 1 Samuel 14-16
Featured Verses: 1 Samuel 15:22-23 *Samuel said, "Has the Lord as much delight in burnt offerings and sacrifices as in obeying the voice of the Lord? Behold, to obey is better than sacrifice, and to heed than the fat of rams. For rebellion is as the sin of divination, and insubordination is as iniquity and idolatry. Because you have rejected the word of the Lord, He has also rejected you from being king."*

I must admit, I have wondered about the meaning of the popular adage, *obedience is better than sacrifice*. But the context of today's Morning Rinse brings clarification. Are we not obeying, when we make sacrifices to God? And are our sacrifices not an act of worship to Him? The answer is yes. Unless, of course, God leads us otherwise. If He instructs us to not do something, but we continually rebel, then it is clearly disobedience and ultimately what He calls 'witchcraft.' God wants full obedience, despite our logical justifications to act otherwise. Saul had been king now for several years, and repeatedly had difficulty putting God first. For instance, instead of building an altar to God immediately upon being appointed king, he waited to finally build one as a last resort in hopes to receive answers regarding his next battle (14:35). Did he allow pride to take hold of his heart after his elevation to power? Did this pride transform him from being that lowly and humble man? Possibly. Whatever caused his heart to change also reinforced his selective obedience, making God regret ever putting him in a position of power (15:11, 35). Yes, Samuel went to war out of obedience. But his obedience was selective. He then disobeyed by allowing the people to take the oxen and sheep for sacrifices, which was against God's instructions. God did not want these sacrifices. He wants our full obedience versus excuses for our selective obedience. If He cannot trust us, He may have to choose someone else whom He can.

Today's Challenge To Dig Deeper:
Are you making any excuses that help you justify not being in full obedience to God? Are you blaming someone else for your choices? Stop it. Cease from the excuses, and enter full obedience today with the Lord.

Evening Reflection:
What decisions did you make to enter full obedience with what God is asking you to do?

CHAMPIONS ARE MADE IN THE PASTURE
December 8

Morning Rinse: 1 Samuel 17-19
Featured Verse: 1 Samuel 17:45 *Then David said to the Philistine, "You come to me with a sword, a spear, and a javelin, but I come to you in the name of the Lord of hosts, the God of the armies of Israel, whom you have taunted."*

How did David obtain the kind of faith to believe he would win against Goliath? This Philistine champion was over nine feet tall, carried nearly one hundred thirty pounds of armor, and the head of his spear alone weighed fifteen pounds.[28] He was incredibly intimidating, and yet David, with faith filled boldness, made his way through the panicked Israelite army basically asking, "Who does he think he is?" (17:27). I can almost hear his sarcasm. And then there is Saul. He was the tallest man of the Israelites, and probably expected to be the one to fight against Goliath, and yet he was filled with fear (17:11). However, David was not intimidated. His bold faith did not come overnight, and he did not mature into a champion the moment he killed Goliath. He became a champion back in his pasture as he tended his father's flock. He first had to allow the creation of a champion heart. How? It was created on his harp, sitting under a shade tree while praising God. And with the champion heart was a champion character. This was formed while facing his battles against attackers, all in the name of the Lord. His daily life of consistent worship and faith molded him into a man after God's own heart (13:14). I doubt many people knew of his daily victories, like keeping the sheep together, or saving them by killing the lion and the bear. He may not have even been known across the land for his weaponry skill set, which is possibly why he had to convince Saul of his ability to conquer Goliath. Even though Saul knew David as a warrior harpist, he must not have known him as a warrior shepherd. I believe these kinds of extraordinary daily happenings in the pasture became normal to David, which is why opposition did not break his spirit. He worshiped in song while attacking with his sling. So despite facing Goliath, despite his own brother accusing him of a wicked heart, and despite Saul later trying to kill him, David retained his champion heart of humility. He remained steadfast in the faith that was formed in the quietness of the pasture. His champion heart then led the way to other champions. One being Jonathon, Saul's son.

Today's Challenge To Dig Deeper:
What can you do better in secret to continue becoming a champion for God in public? Is it gossiping less or thinking the best of others? Is it changing who is in your inner circle? Let God show you.

Evening Reflection:
What changes did you make to continue having a champion lifestyle?

---

[28] www.Unitcoverters.net

CHAMPIONS DIE EMPTY
December 9

Morning Rinse: 1 Samuel 20-22
Featured Verses: 1 Samuel 20:41-42 *When the lad was gone, David rose from the south side and fell on his face to the ground, and bowed three times. And they kissed each other and wept together, but David wept the more. Jonathan said to David, "Go in safety, inasmuch as we have sworn to each other in the name of the Lord, saying 'The Lord will be between me and you, and between my descendants and your descendants forever,' " Then he rose and departed, while Jonathan went into the city.*

Just because champions are known for conquering opposition, this does not mean it is easy when they face it. Jonathan discovered his father, Saul, had intentions of killing David. In an angry reaction to the news that David would not be joining them for dinner, Saul even tried to kill Jonathan. With Saul's evil plans exposed, Jonathan had to privately send David away to save David's life and ultimately preserve his purpose. This intense moment of sadness was overwhelmingly heart wrenching. The deep well of tears flowed down their cheeks as they expressed their goodbyes towards one another. They had become best of friends, experiencing a soul-tie of companionship that began the moment they met. But it was inevitable for them to part ways, making these two champions weep with grief for the loss of each other. Jonathan and David were influencers. They were champions. They were marked with God's hands still full of purpose for their lives. Dying with unfulfilled purpose was not part of God's plan. Dying empty, with their purpose completed, was. So this separation was inescapable to dodge the hands of Saul's murderous heart. The weeping finally ceased, and David set out alone into an unknown future, with his enemy lurking to kill him. Sometimes hard decisions must be made to preserve and protect our destiny. We should all want to protect it in any way we can so we complete what God has asked us to do, and die empty. A portion of Jonathan's purpose was fulfilled that day when he helped preserve David's purpose by saving his life. This was very risky for him to do, but he chose to help, despite the danger it put him in. Champions do what it takes to die empty. And champions help other champions do the same.

Today's Challenge To Dig Deeper:
Do you or a friend have a decision that needs to be made to preserve and protect a purpose? Struggle no more. Do what it takes to protect it. That could be any number of things, even as simple as keeping information about the purpose confidential.

Evening Reflection:
While you may not be faced with daily life altering decisions, when they do come, how do you respond?

YOU ARE NEXT
December 10

Morning Rinse: 1 Samuel 23-26
Featured Verse: 1 Samuel 23:17 *Thus he said to him, "Do not be afraid, because the hand of Saul my father will not find you, and you will be king over Israel and I will be next to you, and Saul my father knows that also."*

I wrote today's Morning Rinse in 2021, the year after the worldwide pandemic called Covid. I was facing a big decision that was centered around the Covid issue and pertained to several events I was a part of, one right after the other. Attending both events caused concern, due to the risk of catching Covid. The first event was the International Christian Film and Music Festival (ICFF), the largest Christian film festival in the world, and what some call a family reunion for filmmakers of faith. This festival, like most events, was cancelled the year prior, so it had not only been several years since it had occurred, but it has been several years since my tribe, whom I mention in the acknowledgement section, had been together in person. On top of those anticipated special reunions at ICFF, there was a private screening of a movie I am in called *Don't Say My Name*. As an actress, I believe being present at special screenings is important because it is a 'now' moment, not only to showcase my work, but to meet new people for future opportunities. However, the shoot dates for my next film, *Running The Bases (RTB)*, began the week following my scheduled return from ICFF. The dates of these pivotal events did not conflict, but the producers of RTB encouraged all cast and crew who were going to be on set the first week of shooting, to avoid going to large events to safeguard against Covid. They made it clear that if we tested positive, we would have to be recast. I battled the inward struggle of what to do. I did not want to live in fear of not only this disease, but missing potential 'now' opportunities centered around the movie screening. On the flip side, if I chose to go, I had the high potential of disappointing the producers of RTB because of their request. I remember crying out to God, telling Him I did not want to be afraid of missing out on both my 'now' moment and my 'next' moment. (If I caught Covid at ICFF, I would be recast). David was also afraid of the unknown, and in fact, Jonathan went out searching for him in the wilderness to encourage him. Even David had to be reminded that God still had his 'next' coming, despite what his 'now' looked like. The truth is, David was destined to be the next king and Jonathon was destined to be with him. Instead of David taking matters into his own hands and killing Saul, David protected his character by sparing Saul's life and protecting his 'next.' God did not forget David, nor has He forgotten you. Trust Him and do not take your 'now' circumstances into your own hands. Instead, believe God will divinely arrange for your 'next.' As hard as it was, I canceled my trip to ICFF and let go of my 'now' moments in exchange for protecting my 'next.' Believe His Word that you are next instead of fearing you are not.

Today's Challenge To Dig Deeper:
Do you have any fear of being forgotten for your 'next'? What is your fear based on? Allow God to speak to you today and encourage you.

Evening Reflection:
Do you have a renewed faith that God still has His hand over your 'next' destiny? Write about it.

LIFT AND RALLY
December 11

Morning Rinse: 1 Samuel 27-31
Featured Verse: 1 Samuel 30:6 *Moreover David was greatly distressed because the people spoke of stoning him, for all the people were embittered; each one because of his sons and his daughters. But David strengthened himself in the Lord his God.*

David and his men wanted to join a Philistine friend, Achish, in the next Philistine battle against Israel. It is rather odd to join the forces of your nation's enemy, but with Saul chasing David, he and his men had to find a new home. So they began living in the Philistine land for a while. The Philistine commanders did not trust David and believed he would turn on them during the battle against Saul, which created a few challenges while preparing for war. But God knew if David's army joined the Philistine army, they would have to fight not only against Saul, but against Jonathan. So God spared David from this horrible situation. David was prepared to do what he was good at, being a warrior. I was also prepared to do what I do and attend the festival I spoke of yesterday. Naturally, we both got a little irritated at not being able to do what we wanted to do. But God always knows more than we do, and He knew Saul and Jonathan would be killed in this battle, and it may have crushed David to be a part of that scenario. Sometimes horrible things happen for a reason. Upon David's return to Ziklag to prepare for the next battle, he and his men discovered their families had all been captured, and their belongings had been stolen. During their time of grief, David's men turned on him. Disappointed from multiple hurts, this champion warrior was once again alone. With the fresh sting of being rejected as a warrior, the losses from their stolen possessions, and his entire army now wanting him dead, he had no one except God by his side. So he went to Him in this urgent situation and strengthened himself in the Lord. But just because he strengthened himself, that did not mean he quit hurting. He just pushed past the pain so he could hear from God. He wasted no time in his inquiry for help, and did not sulk with a *woe is me* attitude. Instead, he lifted himself up in the Lord, and then rallied his men again to rejoin him in a rescue plan for what was stolen from them. The men not only retrieved all that was stolen, but they obtained even more by acquiring the enemy's spoils. It is time to lift our spirits and rally for the next mission.

Today's Challenge To Dig Deeper:
Do you have a *woe is me* attitude about anything? Is there something you have been complaining about? It is time to say 'goodbye' to yesterday, lift yourself up and rally strength for your increase.

Evening Reflection:
Did you have a breakthrough of a *lift and rally* today? Write about it. And always remember, others are watching how you respond in disappointing circumstances.

DAVID, A MAN OF PASSION AND HONOR
December 12

Morning Rinse: 2 Samuel 1-5
Featured Verse: 2 Samuel 3:36 *Now all the people took note of it, and it pleased them, just as everything the king did pleased all the people.*

Being a role model on this earth is a great responsibility, so studying other great role models is vital as we grow in our faith. David was not one who lived to follow the crowd and please the people. He was one who passionately wanted to please God, and so he usually made his decisions according to this desire. Not only was he passionate for God, but he radically pursued what he believed honored Him. One way he did this was by honoring His anointed, even in their death. Through the years, I have heard various people state their dislike in attending funerals because "the person has passed, so why do I need to attend?" However, I believe attending funerals gives honor not just to the loved ones left behind, but to the one who is gone. A crowd at a funeral can also give a beautiful picture of how God used their life to shine His light on this side of heaven. Surprising to us, David even publicly honored Saul, despite Saul's pursuit to kill him (1:11-12). As we walk through David's story through the book of 2 Samuel, make note of any godly characteristics you see in him. While he was still human and made some horrible mistakes, he was still a man after God's own heart and a man we can learn from. We can take his godly characteristics and model after them in our own personal walk with God. David was a man who honored those around him, especially those called by God, despite their behaviors and failures. We can certainly have this same passion and honor for others as well.

Today's Challenge To Dig Deeper:
Which character trait, passion for God or being a person of honor, speaks to you? Is there an opportunity in your life that is providing you a chance to grow in this area? Let God speak to you about it today.

Evening Reflection:
Reflect on any thoughts you had today about living passionately for God or living in honor of others.

DAVID, A MAN OF COURAGE AND KINDNESS
December 13

Morning Rinse: 2 Samuel 6-9
Featured Verses: 2 Samuel 7:27-28 *For You, O Lord of hosts, the God of Israel, have made a revelation to Your servant, saying, "I will build you a house"; therefore Your servant has found courage to pray this prayer to You. Now, O Lord God, You are God, and Your words are truth, and You have promised this good thing to Your servant.*

When I think of a champion, or warrior, I instantly think of someone who conquers against an enemy, whether on a tangible battlefield or in a prayer closet. It has been easy to establish King David as this type of individual for the nation of Israel. Champions must become experts at pushing past fear and fighting their battles. David had courage to protect his father's sheep. He had courage to fight Goliath. And he had courage when thousands of Philistine troops sounded their war cry. But what about having courage to fight for his own heart? He yearned to construct a monumental house of worship for the ark, a much needed place for God's presence to dwell. But God said no. David learned it would not be his calling to build it, but instead it would be his son's mission to complete. It can be hard when we are told no, and yet David did not fight for this desire. Instead, he fought for a courageous heart to trust God's answer. He had to fight to believe God was doing something bigger with his legacy by saying no to him. Another of David's character traits from today's Morning Rinse was his kindness. David discovered Saul's grandson, Jonathan's son Mephibosheth, was still alive. Mephibosheth was not able to fight on the battlefield like what most men were expected to do, and it was because of his inability to walk. This kept him home during the war that killed his father, uncles, grandfather, and probably all the men in his family line. These deaths resulted in Saul's lineage losing their property and many of their belongings. Mephibosheth's inability to walk may have been a hard thing to live with, but it saved his life and was also used to restore their family-owned land. David brought him into the palace and granted him a lifetime seat at his table, instituting provision for his family and servants, including restoring all of Saul's property back into his family line. This act of kindness confirmed the covenant of Jonathan and David's seed being established forever. David showed Mephibosheth kindness, not because of an obligation to Saul, but out of love for Saul's lineage and God's plan. He did not allow bitterness towards Saul to take root in his heart, but instead let kindness reign.

Today's Challenge To Dig Deeper:
Which of these two character traits, courage or kindness, speaks to you today? Is there an opportunity in your life that provides you with a chance to grow in either of these areas? Let God speak to you about it.

Evening Reflection:
Did God show you anything about having courage or kindness?

DAVID, A MAN OF REPENTANCE AND WORSHIP
December 14

Morning Rinse: 2 Samuel 10-12
Featured Verse: 2 Samuel 12:20 *So David arose from the ground, washed, anointed himself, and changed his clothes; and he came into the house of the Lord and worshiped. Then he came to his own house, and when he requested, they set food before him and he ate.*

I remember as a kid peering out the window of our blue station wagon on the drive home from our regular Sunday services. The trip was about a thirty-minute ride from that old country church, with significant landmarks along the way, showing us how much farther we had to go. A few of the landmarks included a huge sign pointing to a nearby apple orchard, a small overpass, and a fork in the road with an auction house off to the left. I knew our trip was nearing the end when we came to one of the last landmarks, which was crossing over the Missouri River on a huge steel bridge. There are also events, or landmarks, in our personal lives. We all have them. They are significant moments that include some of our greatest highs and unfortunately some of our most sorrowful lows. These events mark a fork in the road of choice, make memories that change us, or are moments that deepen our faith. Today's Morning Rinse captured several of David's most noteworthy ones. The story of his adulterous act with Bathsheba while her husband, Uriah, was off to war, marked one of his lowest landmarks of his life. After she got pregnant, David tried to cover up his sin by encouraging Uriah to go home to her. This would have made the child appear to be his. But after Uriah refused several times, David had him killed, hoping this adulterous sin would then remain hidden. David was at an all-time low when God used Nathan to rebuke him. Getting out of a cycle of sin can be extremely difficult. The best way for God to get us to end this cycle is to reveal the truth. How we respond to rebuke will determine the growth of our character. This landmark of David's repentance marks a story that has been repeated many times to remind us of God's grace. But there are still consequences to our actions. Due to David's sin, his son died. But he accepted the responsibility of his actions and did not place blame nor become bitter towards God. Instead, he chose to worship. What came next was redemption. God used Bathsheba to not only mark David's lowest landmark, but also one of his highest, the birth of Solomon.

Today's Challenge To Dig Deeper:
Which of the two character traits, repentance or worship, speaks to you today? Is there an opportunity in your life that provides you with a chance to grow in either of these areas? Let God speak to you about it.

Evening Reflection:
Write out a landmark of either repentance or worship to remind you of your journey.

DAVID, A MAN OF FAITHFULNESS AND PRAYER
December 15

Morning Rinse: 2 Samuel 13-16
Featured Verse: 2 Samuel 15:31 *Now someone told David, saying, "Ahitophel is among the conspirators with Absalom." And David said, "O Lord, I pray, make the counsel of Ahitophel foolishness."*

Today's Morning Rinse was a little hard for me to read, honestly. For days, we have been cheering for King David and studying what makes him a champion so we can model these traits too. We have been standing on the sidelines watching him win. Then shaking our heads while witnessing his sinful act with Bathsheba, and then once again cheering him on through his repentance. But today was a continuation of watching this fallen champion suffer, due to his sin with her. Yes, he repented. But sin affects our lives, including the lives of our friends and families, and sometimes those consequences can be felt for months if not years. And since David held a position of authority, his choices also affected the entire nation of Israel. The cliffhangers in the storyline of his life are now full of deception, lies, rape, murder, and finally the nation turning against him and crowning his deceptive son, Absalom, in his place. David, in deep sorrow and tears, had to flee Jerusalem with his loyal followers, and head out to the wilderness. But God still works in the wilderness of consequences. He still loves us and wants us to remain faithful. And this is exactly what David did. He remained faithful to God despite what he was going through, continually praying in his time of need. Absalom, the new reigning king, was receiving counsel from a conspirator named Ahitophel. So David prayed that his counsel would be foolish. God heard his prayer, unfolding the story of Ahitophel advising Absalom to set up a tent and bring in David's concubines, one by one, to take them sexually. This was a symbol of power revealed in an evil manner, dishonoring David. Although David was living in the wilderness of consequences, he believed God was still working in his life. No matter what our consequences may be, let us always remain faithful and in a state of prayer. God still hears. And he still answers, just like he answered David's prayer.

Today's Challenge To Dig Deeper:
Which of these two character traits, faithfulness or prayer, speaks to you today? Is there an opportunity in your life that provides you with a chance to grow in either of these areas? Let God speak to you about it.

Evening Reflection:
Reflect on your life today and what God spoke to you about faithfulness or your life of prayer. Did He encourage you to stay faithful? Did He ignite some prayer in you? Write it down.

DAVID, A MAN OF LEADERSHIP AND HUMILITY
December 16

Morning Rinse: 2 Samuel 17-20
Featured Verse: 2 Samuel 18:3 *But the people said, "You should not go out; for if we indeed flee, they will not care about us; even if half of us die, they will not care about us. But you are worth ten thousand of us; therefore now it is better that you be ready to help us from the city."*

Pause and search within. I wonder if this is what David did at this moment. I wonder how he felt when his people verbalized to him how they felt about him, as their leader. I wonder if he already knew how powerful his impact was, or if this was a defining moment for him. His people believed in him. They were willing to die for him. And they were willing to do what it took to protect him and his leadership. Great leaders do not view their voices as all-knowing, but are willing to listen to the voices God has placed in their lives. So he listened to their request and stayed off the battlefield. In this battle, his evil son Absalom was killed. I believe God once again spared David from the horrible situation of killing someone who he may not have had the ability to kill. God had spared David from this same situation in the battle that killed Saul. And now, God kept him from the battle that killed his son Absalom. Both were making evil choices, but both men had strong roots in David's heart, and David loved his son. Grieving would be normal for any father. However, he grieved so deeply, it caused his people to question his loyalty to them. The way David responded to Absalom's death hurt the very people who saved his life from him. So Joab went to David and reprimanded his actions, explaining how it was causing confusion. Once again, David listened. And in the listening, he was humble, making corrections in his behavior for the sake of the nation of Israel. His humility brought unity to the people, setting the stage for the transition and restoration of him as king once again. Leaders listen. Leaders are humble. Leaders pause and search within.

Today's Challenge To Dig Deeper:
Which character trait, leadership or humility, speaks to you today? Is there an opportunity in your life that provides you with a chance to grow in either of these areas? Let God speak to you about it.

Evening Reflection:
Growing in the godly characteristics that King David showed, is how we become a person after God's own heart. Write about moments of leadership or humility that God has worked in your life today.

DAVID, A MAN OF LEGACY AND INFLUENCE
December 17

Morning Rinse: 2 Samuel 21-24
Featured Verses: 2 Samuel 22:36-37 *You have also given me the shield of Your salvation, and Your help makes me great. You enlarge my steps under me, and my feet have not slipped.*

What made King David a man of such influence, leaving one of the greatest legacies in history? His character. Was he perfect? No. In fact, another example of a flaw was found in today's Morning Rinse, when he forced Joab to take a census of the people. God never asked him to do this. Once again, his error caused many people to die. However, he was quick to repent and accept his responsibility. Our mistakes do not define us. But our responses do. This is what forms our character. King David was a man of repentance and growth, and his character displayed this. As David learned for himself, he then taught by example, leaving a legacy founded on his passion and pursuit for God. Even when he messed up, his heart never turned dark, which we can clearly witness in today's Featured Verses. He still gave God praise, solidifying his legacy and influence. So many times I hear of stories where someone makes a mistake, and instead of quickly repenting, they allow the sin to keep growing and manifesting until they slip and completely fall. David messed up, but turned right back to God, hungry for a relationship with Him. He was teachable, and despite his failures, wanted to please God. David's heart towards God opened the door for God to position him for the continual expansion of his influence. Other writers even mention him centuries later, proving this influence, including Paul (Acts 13:22). What will people say about you? David knew he was not perfect, and he admits it repeatedly in the psalms. But he shows us how to run after the one who is perfect, leaving a legacy of influence. We, too, can be like King David, who is after God's heart.

Today's Challenge To Dig Deeper:
Which character trait, legacy or influence, speaks to you today? Is there an opportunity in your life that provides you with a chance to grow in either of these areas? Let God speak to you about it. Pray about writing out a family mission statement.

Evening Reflection:
Write out any thoughts you have about a mission statement for yourself and your family.

THE TRUE LOVE STORY
December 18

Morning Rinse: Song of Solomon 1-4
Featured Verses: Song of Solomon 1:14-16 *My beloved is to me a cluster of henna blossoms in the vineyards of Engedi. How beautiful you are, my darling, how beautiful you are! Your eyes are like doves. How handsome you are, my beloved, and so pleasant! Indeed, our couch is luxuriant!*

According to 1 Kings 4:32, King Solomon wrote three thousand proverbs and one thousand and five songs. Out of all the one thousand songs he wrote, this is THE song, and the one that received its very own book. I was married at the age of thirty, and while I have studied the Bible since high school, I put off reading this book until my mid-twenties. First, I did not think it applied to me as a single person. But on top of this erroneous mindset, I remember shying away from reading things that I thought would potentially make me sad or bitter that I was not married yet. I mean, this song is all about a love story between a husband and a wife, correct? Yes, it is undoubtedly full of beautiful words and deep descriptions. It is a picturesque conversation between them. Back and forth they speak, continually sharing their love through captivating words. One will utter phrases of love and then the other will convey compliments in return. It is almost as if they are trying to outdo the other with their adoration. So while it is true that this book allows us to read about a holy marital love, it is so much more. It is also a beautiful picture of the heavenly love between Jesus and His bride. What if we grew so in love with Christ that we experienced this level of relationship with Him? Nothing could stop us. Our trust in Him would be so deep, so mighty, so strong, and so guided by Him, as we walk out our purpose by His side. What if we carried that love with us to the world? Yes, this book is about a holy marital love that anyone can desire to have with a spouse. But it is also a holy, heavenly love towards the one who died for us. This is the true love story. Not just a one-sided love from God to us, but a shared love reciprocated back to Him, and then taken to the world.

Today's Challenge To Dig Deeper:
Do you have this kind of love towards Jesus? Ask Him to help you grow, learning to love Him and passionately pursue Him like He does us. Ask Him to help you portray this love towards your spouse, whether now or in your future, and then to the world around you.

Evening Reflection:
What are your thoughts about the book of Song of Solomon? Did you have a mind shift about this book, or did anything stand out to you today?

WORDS OF LOVE
December 19

Morning Rinse: Song of Solomon 5-8
Featured Verse: Song of Solomon 6:3 *I am my beloved's and my beloved is mine, he who pastures his flock among the lilies.*

Pleasure. Joy. Delight. Savor. Happiness. Relish. Treasure. Value. Enjoy. Appreciate. Adore. Cherish. Esteem. Attraction. Regard. Devotion. Elation. Passion. Tenderness. Satisfaction. Glee. Ecstasy. Bliss. Wonder. Worth. Revere. Satisfaction. Gratitude. Merriment. Prize. Honor. Belong. Esteem. Respect. Admire. Thrill. Like. Love.

When you read these words, what kind of a relationship comes to mind? If you are married, is this how you describe the feelings you have for your spouse? They certainly describe the love that King Solomon and his bride, the Shulammite woman, have for each other. This love story gives us a picture of the purity of marital love and what it can look like for all of us. They highly regard one another and are dedicated to fostering these feelings, instead of letting their love die. They belong to each other, and it is evident in their display of affection towards one another. But look at the words again. These words can also be used to describe the feelings Jesus has for us, His bride. We belong to Him and He to us as well. What better earthly relationship to mirror, than the one shown in the Song of Solomon, to help us understand the heavenly bond we can have with Christ. While our human brains are limited in fully understanding the vast depth of God's love for us, this little book gives us a glimpse of the beauty of how heavenly love can truly be. And while I understand that some earthly marriages may be broken or have failed, our relationship with God will stand the test of time. He will never leave us nor forsake us. The depth of a perfect love will never reach its full beauty until we gain perfection in our glorified bodies. But we can devote ourselves to the pursuit of it. It is the act of desiring Him daily. It is longing for His presence daily. It is running after Him daily. It is accepting these words of love He has for us daily.

Today's Challenge To Dig Deeper:
Read the words of love again. Look up the meanings of some of the words and ask God to deepen that word of love in you as you gain understanding of it through your research.

Evening Reflection:
What word, or words of love did you focus on today? Write down any thoughts you had about the meaning and how you can apply it to your relationships, whether in your marriage or with God.

SOUND FORTH
December 20

Morning Rinse: 1 Thessalonians 1-3
Featured Verse: 1 Thessalonians 1:8 *For the word of the Lord has sounded forth from you, not only in Macedonia and Achaia, but also in every place your faith toward God has gone forth, so that we have no need to say anything.*

I recently heard a pastor speak on one of the last chapters in the book of Revelation, describing the new heaven and the new earth. He spoke about our impact on this world, and encouraged us to keep spreading the good news of Christ's return so others could be saved and see this new heaven and new earth. How we live and what we say can very well bring others to know Christ, pointing others to a way of eternal salvation. While this pastor was closing out his sermon in prayer, I literally saw a picture unfold in my mind's eye of what it might look like being caught up in the sky to meet Christ. As I watched myself heading to heaven, I saw several people behind me who were there because of my witness. In this vision, God gave me a picture of what my influence could look like. I then asked Him to help me change more lives so I could lead a whole crowd into heaven, not just a few people. Paul, the writer of Thessalonians, knows the impact of a life change. He formerly hunted Christians to kill them. But when God changed him, he went from hating Christ followers, to recruiting them. His impact on both the Jews and the Gentiles was widespread and a threat to the standard teachings of that time. He was such a threat that authorities bound him with the hopes to keep him silent, and keep his followers at bay. But his chains could not contain the message he needed to bring. He ended up writing nearly half of the New Testament, including the book of Revelation. Today's Featured Verse shows how encouraged he was to hear that these new fellow believers were strong in their faith. In fact, the Word of God was *sounding forth* from their life and ministry so much that Paul, their leader, did not even have to say anything to help them stay on track. Everywhere they went, their faith was displayed for others to see. Does our life make this strong of an impact on others?

Today's Challenge To Dig Deeper:
Just like Paul sent letters of encouragement and thanks, write three thank you notes today to those who have encouraged you, or whose lives *sound forth* the gospel. Also, ask God to help you have a stronger impact on lives in your world as well. Ask Him to help you sound forth in all you do.

Evening Reflection:
Who did you write notes to today? Why did you choose them?

NEVER THE LAST PERFORMANCE
December 21

Morning Rinse: 1 Thessalonians 4-5
Featured Verses: 1 Thessalonians 4:9-10 *Now as to the love of the brethren, you have no need for anyone to write to you, for you yourselves are taught by God to love one another; for indeed you do practice it toward all the brethren who are in all Macedonia. But we urge you, brethren to excel still more.*

The accolades ring loud and the applause lingers on. The best of the best complete their bow and glide off the stage where their director meets them behind the curtain. With a gleaming smile, he tells each of the performers how proud of them he is. He credits their flawless moves, perfect leaps, and graceful twirls. After he concludes his praises, he reminds them of their practice time the following day. He informs them of the specifics they will be working on and then pauses. They wait for his next comment. As he concludes his wonderful encouragement, he then imparts to them a phrase they knew was coming. "You can do better the next time you glide across the stage." Was this conversation a blow to some of these top performers? Absolutely not. In fact, it was a statement they were used to hearing. Any great instructor knows the full potential of a performer is never their last performance. So an instructor must see beyond their perfect moves and push them to the next show, the higher calling. Great instructors know they must pull the best out of the best. And elite performers know there is always something to improve on. This analogy is like what Paul was doing with the Thessalonian church. He was telling them how great they were doing in their walk with Christ, and yet urging them to do better. How can these great saints, these amazing leaders, do even better? In chapter five of today's Morning Rinse, Paul explains how. Keep encouraging one another, love more, keep rejoicing, pray always, give thanks in all things, live in peace, and avoid every kind of evil. As great as the Thessalonians were doing, there was still more areas to grow in. And this is the same for us. There is always the next day, the next interaction with someone, the next performance for God's kingdom in our lives. Never stop striving to do better. Our greatest ministry day will never be our last performance.

Today's Challenge To Dig Deeper:
Watch for an opportunity today to do better at situations in your life. Even if you have a habit of handling something with love, do better. Pray more, rejoice more, praise more, seek more.

Evening Reflection:
Was there an opportunity to do better today? To excel? Write about it.

OH, BE CAREFUL LITTLE EARS WHAT YOU HEAR
December 22

Morning Rinse: 2 Thessalonians 1-3
Featured Verses: 2 Thessalonians 2:1-2 *Now we request you, brethren, with regard to the coming of our Lord Jesus Christ and our gathering together to Him, that you not be quickly shaken from your composure or be disturbed either by a spirit or a message or a letter as if from us, to the effect that the day of the Lord has come.*

The title of today's devotion is the title of a song with lyrics that encourage us to be careful what we touch, what we hear, what we see, and where we go. While this song is mainly for children, the message still rings true for adults. In fact, this message is a common theme throughout the Bible for the life of a Christ follower. The book of 2 Thessalonians is a great example of how we all, even the most faith-filled Christians, must be vigilant, watchful, and careful. The Thessalonians were a great group of people whom Paul boasts of in his first letter to them, telling them how proud he is of them. However, not long after his first letter is received, he hears of confusion in the Thessalonian church body. This confusion came from multiple sources, including a message from someone falsely teaching them, and even from someone who wrote the church letters claiming to be Paul. These messages had a similar theme, stating Jesus had already returned for his people. Unfortunately, some of the members of the Thessalonian church believed these letters, causing discouragement and even some slacked in their faith due to hopelessness. Paul reassures them of the error, encourages them to quit listening to false teachers, and to keep living for Christ. We all must be careful what we listen to because the wrong teachings can sway us away from the message of the Bible. And we all must guard ourselves against opinions that could derail us from living a holy life.

Today's Challenge To Dig Deeper:
Several times I have had to question the truth of certain voices speaking into my life. These voices were in error, and therefore, I had to turn the TV off, lay a book down, or even remove a friend from my inner circle. Is it time for you to do the same?

Evening Reflection:
Turning off voices does not mean we are better than someone. But it does mean we are protecting our hearts from confusion and hurt. Write down how you have turned off voices from your life.

CONTEXT IS KEY
December 23

Morning Rinse: 1 Timothy 1-3
Featured Verses: 1 Timothy 3:2-3 *An overseer, then, must be above reproach, the husband of one wife, temperate, prudent, respectable, hospitable, able to teach, not addicted to wine or pugnacious, but gentle, peaceable, free from the love of money.*

Timothy was a young man mentored by Paul. Paul even referred to him as a true child of faith (1:2). So when the Ephesus church started adopting false teachings, Paul knew he could send Timothy to help eradicate any beliefs that did not line up with the gospel. Based on a few verses from today's Morning Rinse, some people believe that women are not allowed in leadership positions, such as pastors, elders, and teachers. Paul was not against this at all. In fact, Paul advocated for both men and women as leaders, including Priscilla (Acts 18:24-26). Understanding the context of scripture is key. Back in the first century of Jewish culture, women were not given permission to study, so they had to learn from their husbands or friends. Oftentimes, the women in the Ephesus church would ask questions during synagogue, causing a distraction. Therefore, Paul requested they be quiet and wait until after service. When a false teacher would surface, these women were extremely susceptible to believing them. So Paul conveyed the importance of putting people in leadership who were seasoned and could discern the false teachers.[29] Today's Featured Verses hit home with me. I have had men use this verse to keep me from positions of authority merely because a man felt women should not be in certain key positions based upon the words 'the husband of one wife.' Moments like this have helped form my strong belief in the importance of understanding the context of scripture. May we all do better at this.

Today's Challenge To Dig Deeper:
Take any part of today's Morning Rinse that seemed a little confusing and do some research on what it could possibly have meant during the time of Paul.

Evening Reflection:
What did you learn today in your research?

---

[29] NASB Life Application Bible notes

CONDUCT CONTROL
December 24

Morning Rinse: 1 Timothy 4-6
Featured Verse: 1 Timothy 4:12 *Let no one look down on your youthfulness, but rather in speech, conduct, love, faith and purity, show yourself an example of those who believe.*

Being a pastor's kid, I can vouch for the criticism a pastor receives. No matter the age or how long one has been in ministry, criticism is inevitable. A leader in the church will never please everyone who attends. I have heard pastors critiqued because their church was too small. I have heard others critiqued because the church was too big. I have also heard complaints that the choir was too loud, the message on tithing was too long, or the music was not upbeat enough. You name it, a pastor has probably heard every complaint there is. But regardless of the murmurings, a pastor should always do what God is guiding them to do, and live with godly conduct. This is the main message Paul was saying to Timothy, as a young pastor. It was natural for Paul to address the complaints about his lack of experience and youthfulness. This same advice is great for any of us, and can apply to any part of a person's life when we enter a new season. Even though the context of today's Featured Verse applies to Timothy's age, it does not have to only apply to how old someone is. We can be *young* in other areas. What about a newlywed couple? What about a new parent? Even with today being Christmas Eve, I think of Mother Mary. The reference of young can even be when someone is inexperienced. I am sure as she was about to give birth to baby Jesus, she felt a lack of confidence in her mothering skills. Just because there may be a lack of experience in a new season of life, though, does not mean the person's advice and leadership in that area should be discounted or looked down on. When any of us enter a new phase, it is common to lack the confidence needed initially to flourish in that area. Therefore, we need to have confidence in God as He guides us. Keep obeying Him. Do not focus on your lack of knowledge in that area, but instead, conduct yourself in a manner that no matter your age or experience, your life is an example. We will never lack criticism, no matter what we do. This is uncontrollable. But what we CAN control is our conduct.

Today's Challenge To Dig Deeper:
Are you wanting to do something new, but are worried about the criticism you might receive? Do not let anyone look down on you because of your age or experience, but fully rely on God leading you. Keep your conduct pure, your stance tall in Christ, and go for it.

Evening Reflection:
What are you starting new?

CHRISTMAS GIFT RETURNED
December 25

Morning Rinse: 2 Timothy 1-4
Featured Verse: 2 Timothy 1:6 *For this reason I remind you to kindle afresh the gift of God which is in you through the laying on of my hands.*

If you are following this devotional based on the dates, then you know today is Christmas. The spirit of giving is at its strongest during this season, as we celebrate the birth of our Savior. Children narrate the birth in Christmas plays, lights outline rooftops, a thick atmosphere of joy fills the local department stores, families gather around dinner tables, and yes, even the gifts placed under the Christmas tree all help bring to life the heavenly message of hope. It is so tangible it can be felt in the air. There is something so special about this time of year, especially in the gift giving. I am sure we can all relate to the feeling of joy when delivering that special present to a loved one, that perfect gift that tangibly shows our love towards them. Our greatest wish regarding the gift is that they love it as much as we do, and put it to good use. But our greatest disappointment is felt when it is put on a shelf, only to collect dust. I wonder if this disappointment we feel is also how God feels when we do not use what He has given us. The gift is still there, but the receiver must choose to use it. Paul's message in today's Featured Verse certainly captures the spirit of Christmas giving. He was writing this last letter to Timothy, knowing his time was ending on this side of heaven. This last message to the world reminds us that God has given us many gifts, but it is up to us to kindle them, to use them, to grow in them and surrender them for their intended kingdom purpose. Christmas day represents the birth of Jesus, God's gift of life and salvation to the world. Our lives can be a Christmas gift returned to Him when we use what He has given us. In essence, we are returning the Christmas gift of life by kindling and using our gifts, which will ultimately provide life to others for His kingdom!

Today's Challenge To Dig Deeper:
Are there any gifts God has given you that are collecting dust? What are they? Pull out your planner today and carve out 30 minutes each day from this point forward to kindle those gifts. Commit to the kindle. Wipe off the dust. And may next year be a birth to sharing your gift with the world.

Evening Reflection:
What are the gifts you are going to kindle?

HEAVENLY FRUIT
December 26

Morning Rinse: Titus 1-3
Featured Verse: Titus 3:14 *Our people must also learn to engage in good deeds to meet pressing needs, so that they will not be unfruitful.*

Over the last few days, we have read the letters from Paul to Timothy, and today we read his letter to Titus. The letters to these two men mark the end of Paul's life on this earth, and are his last writings.[30] They are full of rich advice on church leadership, including how to conduct oneself. As Paul closes out his letter to Titus, he ties his message with a bow called fruitfulness, which is also a powerful sowing and reaping principle. What a legacy. Whether you are reading this devotional based on the dates, which today would then be the day after Christmas, or you are reading it based on another standard, the message of giving remains strong. Yesterday, we were challenged to kindle the gifts God has given us. When we use our gifts, we are giving back to God. Today, Paul continues this message to Titus as well. We must look for ways to meet pressing needs in our community by using the resources we have. Meeting the needs of others is another way of using our gifts for God's kingdom. And Paul makes it very clear that if we do not help meet the needs around us, we are being unfruitful. There are many ways of helping our community. We can use our resources to help meet financial needs. We can help meet needs by giving away things like clothing and food to those lacking. We can use our time to meet emotional needs through mentoring. And we can also provide for spiritual needs, encouraging those going through life's challenges. When we sow into others, we will be fruitful. Planting in God's field by meeting needs around us will ultimately yield heavenly fruit. The question is, are we willing to sow?

Today's Challenge To Dig Deeper:
Ask God to show you a need in your community today. Commit to helping meet that need.

Evening Reflection:
What need did God show you today, and how did you choose to meet it?

---

[30] Notes in The Life Application Bible NASB

SATAN, THE ACCUSER, IS SILENCED
December 27

Morning Rinse: Zechariah 1-3
Featured Verses: Zechariah 3:1-4 *Then he showed me Joshua the high priest standing before the angel of the Lord, and Satan standing at his right hand to accuse him. The Lord said to Satan, "The Lord rebuke you, Satan! Indeed, the Lord who has chosen Jerusalem rebuke you! Is this not a brand plucked from the fire?" Now Joshua was clothed with filthy garments and standing before the angel. He spoke and said to those who were standing before him, saying "Remove the filthy garments from him." Again, he said to him, "See, I have taken your iniquity away from you and will clothe you with festal robes."*

Who is Zechariah? Most people rarely read this book or hear his name in sermons. I am guilty, through the years of studying the Bible, of defaulting to books such as Matthew, John, Psalms or Proverbs, and skipping entirely over this little gem. But out of all the minor prophets in the Old Testament, some claim the book of Zechariah is one of the most important of them all.[31] Why? Because he wrote more about the Messiah than any other minor prophet. This little book is filled with big messages of hope to God's people, and these messages can be read through eight visions that Zechariah had. These powerful revelations were enriched with vivid details of what was to come. Today's Morning Rinse captures four of the eight visions, each having clear and impactful significance. The vision portrayed in today's Featured Verses is about Joshua the high priest. To be clear, this is not Joshua who followed Moses. This is the high priest mentioned in Haggai 1:1. Zechariah's image of Joshua gives us a picture of what it looks like when Jesus redeems us from our sins. Joshua was not free of guilt, and Satan was ready to accuse him of his wrongdoings. But Zechariah records that Joshua's filthy garments were taken off and replaced with festal robes. This is our hope and what Jesus, our Messiah, does for us when we accept Him as our Savior. Satan will never stop accusing us of our sins. But there is no need to be discouraged. Jesus has come to give us life and change our filthy garments to festal robes, silencing Satan as our accuser. This is who Christ is.

Today's Challenge To Dig Deeper:
Pause and soak in the fact that Jesus has made you new and has silenced the accuser. If you know anyone who needs salvation, pray for them to accept Christ. And if you need a salvation prayer, there is one you can reference in the back of this book.

Evening Reflection:
Today, as you relished in Jesus silencing the accuser, did it give you hope, and did you walk in more confidence instead of focusing on your past sins?

---

[31] Preclude to Zechariah in The Life Application Bible NASB

SMALL BEGINNINGS
December 28

Morning Rinse: Zechariah 4-6
Featured Verses: Zechariah 4:9-10 *The hands of Zerubbabel have laid the foundation of this house, and his hands will finish it. Then, you will know that the Lord of hosts has sent me to you. For who has despised the day of small things? But these seven will be glad when they see the plumb line in the hand of Zerubbabel – these are the eyes of the Lord which range to and fro throughout the earth.*

I cannot tell you how many times I have heard the popular quote, *despise not small beginnings*, repeated in sermons throughout the years. But where does it come from? I have often wondered if there was a story it links to, or if it was just a great motivational phrase. But today's Featured Verses show us the scripture reference. Zechariah was one of the prophets who ministered to the Jews who returned to Judah to rebuild the temple. Zerubbabel was one of these men who returned (Ezra 1:1-2), and he quickly became governor of Judah (Haggai 1:1). As he was laying the foundation for the rebuilding job, some of the Jews realized the new temple was not going to be as brilliant and majestic as the first temple King Solomon built. Some of the Jews even become very discouraged. However, Zechariah was there to inspire them and teach them the eyes of the Lord. God is not looking for us to outperform those before us, or even equal a ministry or mission that others have built. He is not looking for us to compete in what we do for Him. We all know we should not compare our calling with the calling of others, just like this group of Jews were not called to construct a temple equivalent to King Solomon's. Zechariah was there to encourage them to not be disheartened, but to love their specific mission and what they were doing for God, even if it was smaller than they had hoped for. We must start with what we have, building on the right foundation. Our small beginnings do not mean they are less beautiful in God's eyes. In fact, the beauty is in the heart, not in the attention of what is built. As this year is coming to an end, and we are almost finished reading the Bible, be hopeful for the things you will launch in the coming seasons of life, and know that God sees your heart. Be excited for the inauguration of what is next in your small beginnings.

Today's Challenge To Dig Deeper:
Have you found yourself comparing what you are doing for the Lord to what others are doing, and believing it to be less valuable? Have you found yourself discouraged by what may seem like a smaller project or mission? Be encouraged. Realize your small beginnings are just as beautiful in God's eyes when your heart is pure.

Evening Reflection:
Did you have a heart change today? Are you encouraged now?

FLESH PARTIES CANCELED
December 29

Morning Rinse: Zechariah 7-10
Featured Verses: Zechariah 8:16-17 *"These are the things which you should do; speak the truth to one another; judge with truth and judgement for peace in your gates. Also let none of you devise evil in your heart against another, and do not love perjury; for all these are what I hate," declares the Lord.*

It is that time of year when friends and family are planning a New Year's Eve party. If you are following the dates in this devotional, New Year's Eve is just two days away. You may be planning on attending one yourself. Parties are usually a celebration of past accomplishments with an excitement of what is new on the horizon. There are all kinds of parties. Retirement parties, birthday parties, graduation parties, bridal parties, and going away parties are all just a few examples of celebrations in one's life. But have you heard of *flesh parties*? I am not proud of this, but I used to host quite a few *flesh parties* for myself. Unlike the standard bash, these parties celebrate the accomplishments of our flesh. Mine would commence by running my mouth about someone I was harboring bitterness towards, and regurgitating how I had been wronged. I would then expand the story by using phrases like, "And, *I think* they did this," or "Did you hear about *this*?" I would often exaggerate a situation without knowing the full truth, just to make myself look better than them. These actions were not encouraging peace, but instead were revealing the evil in my heart. I would then excuse my chatter by saying to my listener, "Oh, sorry. I was just having a flesh party." These kinds of parties need to be canceled. While today's Featured Verses pertain to guidelines and instructions under oath, they are guidelines for daily living as well. We should be under oath with God to adopt His standards of holiness, and flesh parties are the opposite of that. Why do people exaggerate stories or thrive on spreading gossip and rumors? Because unfortunately there is a fruit of bitterness somewhere in their heart. When I first started taking notes on the book of Zechariah back in 1998, I made the commitment to remove the words *flesh party* from my vocabulary. I realized when I was hosting these parties, I was looking for pity or attention. Zechariah was trying to get the people to grow up by pointing out things God hates, and these types of parties are on the list. Stay focused on the Lord. Stay focused on His Word. Stay truthful in your speech. Cancel your flesh party.

Today's Challenge To Dig Deeper:
Have you ever hosted a *flesh party*? Have you ever attended one? Commit to canceling any future parties like this, as well as leaving when you are found at one. Keep on the lookout today. One of these parties might present itself.

Evening Reflection:
What are your thoughts about *flesh parties* in your life?

WOUNDING A FRIEND
December 30

Morning Rinse: Zechariah 11-14
Featured Verse: Zechariah 13:6 *And one will say to him, "What are these wounds between your arms?" Then he will say, "Those with which I was wounded in the house of my friends."*

Yesterday, you learned about my former *flesh parties*. What I did not address in yesterday's devotion was all the damage done by having those parties. When we have been wronged by others, we can choose to forgive, or we can choose to harbor bitterness. Of course, anyone attending a flesh party knows what choice was selected. But with this choice comes great harm both to those spoken about and to those attending. It surmounts the confirmation of where one can go in their heart, and can cause extreme amounts of untrustworthiness in relationships. This is an example of wounding a friend. There are also times when we do not know we are wounding a friend. The unknowing hurts can still cut just as deep as the knowing hurts, and both can cause scarring in someone's heart. Jesus has scars, too. He took upon Himself the wounds we have caused, and He loves us despite our mistakes. Zechariah closes out his book by warning us of sinful behaviors, but gives us hope of a new heaven and a new earth, all because Christ died for our sins, taking on wounds beyond what we could ever imagine. Heal us all, Lord. Bring healing to those we have hurt, and help us all run the race to the end.

Today's Challenge To Dig Deeper:
If you know of anyone that you have hurt, ask God how you should handle it. Ask Him to help you live in peace, not only with yourself, but with the one you inflicted pain upon.

Evening Reflection:
Did God show you anything regarding pain you have caused to others?

GOD'S SMILE OVER YOU
December 31

Morning Rinse: Zephaniah 1-3
Featured Verses: Zephaniah 3:16-17 *In that day it will be said to Jerusalem; "Do not be afraid, O Zion; Do not let your hands fall limp. The Lord your God is in your midst, a victorious warrior, He will exult over you with joy, He will be quiet in His love, He will rejoice over you with shouts of joy."*

Have you ever imagined God delighting over you with shouts of joy? Today's Featured Verses describe this sense of hope and joy, but it is certainly not displayed in the front pages of the book of Zephaniah. He starts out by addressing God's judgment over those who will not obey His voice and who live a life of sin. Israel had turned their back on Him, choosing to remove themselves from His covering. It might be easy to feel like we are deserving of judgement at times because of mistakes we have made. But this little book does not leave us with a feeling of conviction. It ends with Zephaniah telling of God's mercy and grace towards a remnant of people who will obey His voice. His words climax with a resounding hope, telling of God's love for His people. Yes, He is sad when we do not follow Him, but our story is not defined by our mistakes. It is defined by God's grace and mercy through our repentance. May we never forget how He feels towards us. He rejoices over us with shouts of joy and gladness. He delights in our presence. He gathers in our midst. He gloats over us with pride, and He loudly sings over us for all of heaven to hear. What a message to end with in our alphabetical study of the Bible. Walk forward knowing the truth of how the King of Kings and Lord of Lords feels about you. This is the last page of this devotional, but it's the first day of the rest of your life. Go shout with Him, walking out your journey with the knowledge that He is shouting for joy, with a smile on His face because of you.

Today's Challenge To Dig Deeper:
Envision God walking hand in hand with you through your day. Look at Him and picture Him looking back with a big smile on His face. Smile back. Then turn and look ahead into your bright future, knowing He is by your side.

Evening Reflection:
As you write your last reflection, write down how you feel about God's love for you.

INDEX

C

D

H

I

Y

Salvation Prayer

If you are ready to give your life to Christ, or if you want to recommit your life to Him, say this simple prayer:

Dear God, I acknowledge that I have sinned and know that I need the gift of salvation. I repent of my sins, and confess that Jesus is Lord, and that He died on the cross for my sins. I ask for forgiveness. I commit my life to You and accept You as my Lord and Savior. Thank You for Your gift of salvation. Help me as I live for You every day. Amen.

www.ingramcontent.com/pod-product-compliance
Lightning Source LLC
Chambersburg PA
CBHW080755120626
46557CB00006B/1271